BEHAVIOR SCIENCE OUTLINES

VOLUME III

OUTLINE OF WORLD CULTURES

4TH EDITION, REVISED

GEORGE PETER MURDOCK

PUBLISHED BY

HUMAN RELATIONS AREA FILES, INC.
755 PROSPECT STREET
NEW HAVEN
1972

1st EDITION, 1954
2d EDITION (REVISED), 1958
3d EDITION (REVISED), 1963
4th EDITION (REVISED), 1972

ISBN 0-87536-656-2

LIBRARY OF CONGRESS CATALOG CARD NUMBER: 70-185817

© COPYRIGHT 1972
HUMAN RELATIONS AREA FILES, INC.
NEW HAVEN, CONNECTICUT

PREFACE

The success of the Human Relations Area Files (HRAF) in achieving broad inter-university support and in obtaining substantial outside funds for the expansion of its work has emphasized the need for supplementing the topical classification of the Outline of Cultural Materials with a new outline organizing and classifying the known cultures of the world. The present work is a preliminary attempt to fill this need. It is issued in the hope that it will stimulate criticism and correction so that a revised and definitive Outline of World Cultures can be prepared within a very few years.

The lack of a classification of the world's cultures has hampered the work of HRAF in several ways. In the first place, each decision to process the materials on a new region or culture has necessitated extensive preliminary research to define the precise geographical and temporal limits of each culture for which a new file is to be established. This has often resulted in considerable delay in the initiation of actual work on the new files. The present outline should largely obviate the need of preliminary research in the future and thus greatly expedite the beginning of actual processing.

A second defect of the work of HRAF to date has been its inability to excerpt materials in the sources processed that pertain to cultures other than those for which files have been definitely established. For example, data on the Austrians, the Jews, and the Sudeten Germans encountered in the sources covered for Czechoslovakia have been omitted and thus lost because no files had been established to receive them and because neither time nor funds were available for the research necessary to set them up definitively. The present outline provides a place for data on every society in the world, including extinct historical and prehistoric peoples. In the future, therefore, no item of cultural or background information will be overlooked or lost because contained in a source dealing primarily with another society.

A third difficulty has been that of assuring that the societies selected for processing approach the ideal of a representative sample of the world's cultures. The special requirements of the member universities and of contracting agencies will necessarily lead in many instances to the selection of societies which will not appear in a world sample or will find a place there only when the sample becomes very large. In general, however, the member institutions are primarily interested in HRAF for the comparative or cross-cultural research which it will facilitate, and sampling is of the utmost importance for such purposes. The financial contributions of the member institutions should in general, therefore, be used to add new files which will contribute toward and help round out a representative world sample of known cultures. The analysis of past and present cultures required to compile this outline has made it possible to draw up such a world sample and to arrange the cultures included in an order of priority such that at any point they will constitute a reasonably representative sample of all those known to history and ethnography. New cultures can hereafter be chosen for processing so as to extend progressively the size and range of the sample.

The societies and cultures of the world are classified in this outline according to a flexible system under which each society or group of culturally related societies is designated by a symbol consisting of one or two letters followed by a number and denoting an actual or potential file of classified information. Except for the letter W, which is reserved for a few potential files of worldwide information, each initial letter denotes a major geographical region of the world. Eight such great regions are distinguished, as follows:

A Asia, exclusive of Indonesia, the Middle East, and Asiatic Russia.

E Europe, exclusive of the portion ruled directly by the Soviet Union.

F Africa, exclusive of the northern and northeastern portions which belong culturally with the Middle East.

M Middle East, comprising southwestern Asia and northern and northeastern Africa.

N North America, including the northern portion of Central America.

O Oceania, comprising Australia, Indonesia, the Philippines, and the islands of the Pacific Ocean.

R Russia, including the portions of Europe and Asia ruled directly by the Soviet Union.

S South America, including the West Indies and the southern portion of Central America.

For each of the above eight major regions, a few potential files of very general information are distinguished merely by adding a number to the letter representing the region, e.g., A1, E2, F3. All other potential files are designated by a second letter which represents a regional subdivision, usually political, of the major region, e.g., AA for Korea, EA for Poland, FA for French West Africa. Within each such sub-region, each potential file of specific cultural information is designated by an added number, e.g., AM11 for the Vietnamese, EI9 for the Imperial Romans, FX13 for the Hottentot. Specific allowance is made for important linguistic groupings and culture areas as well as for geographical regions, and likewise for historical and archeological cultures as well as for contemporary tribes and nations.

The enumeration and classification of cultures is reasonably complete and definitive for five of the eight major regions--Europe, Africa, Russia, North America, and South America. For Asia, the Middle East, and Oceania it is incomplete for a few of the regional subdivisions, notably for India, New Guinea, and aboriginal Australia, where only a substantial number of the most fully described societies have been separately enumerated. The system of classification, however, is purposely flexible. As additional cultures are distinguished, they can be added to those of the appropriate regional sub-division by assigning them the next higher numbers. Similarly, as mistakes are discovered in the present classification they can be rectified by combining two or more potential files into one or dividing a single file into two or more separate ones.

The preparation of this outline incidentally provides an opportunity to indicate to scholars wishing to use the Files precisely what materials are available for research purposes. A letter H in parentheses after the name of a file indicates that each of the sixteen university members of HRAF already possesses a file of classified information on the particular region or culture which is sufficiently complete to be usable for research purposes. A letter P in parentheses indicates that such a file is currently in process of preparation and should be available at member institutions within a few months after the publication of this outline. A letter C in parentheses indicates that a substantial amount of information, not as yet reprocessed by HRAF, is assembled in organized form in the files of the Cross-Cultural Survey at Yale University (Room 241, Institute of Human Relations), where it is available for the use of scholars who can visit New Haven.

When the new system for the regional classification of cultures goes into effect with the publication of this outline, the member institutions of HRAF must be prepared for a modest number of procedural changes. They will shortly begin to receive small amounts of material on many cultures for which complete files are not projected, at least for the immediate future. They can readily absorb such materials if they will simply provide a set of single separator cards bearing the identifying symbols for the regions and cultures distinguished in this outline. When they then receive, for example, a few notes on the Sudeten Germans culled incidentally from the sources processed for Czechoslovakia, they can place these behind the card numbered EL9 (Sudeten Germans). Not until a complete file is undertaken on the Sudeten Germans will it be necessary to devote a full set of separator cards to this file. The new system will make it possible for HRAF to process a considerable amount of scattered information on many peoples, including cultural summaries and selective bibliographies, long in advance of systematic coverage of the sources, and such materials are likely to have utility for certain restricted research purposes. They will, of course, be arranged in the order of the category numbers of individual slips, as in the case of completed files.

The new system will also necessitate certain changes in referring to "Sources Processed" and "Texts"--numbered respectively 111 and 116 in the Outline of Cultural Materials. Hitherto HRAF has pursued two different procedures with respect to the location of full bibliographical references and of the complete text of the sources covered. Sometimes, e.g., for the Navaho, they have been deposited in the file for the particular culture, and sometimes, e.g., for Indochina, they have been deposited in the file for the region or political division rather than in that for the individual culture. Neither of these systems allows for ready reference to the appropriate bibliography slips or complete text in the case of notes on one culture culled from sources processed for another.

This difficulty will be overcome in the future by indicating, in the upper right-hand corner of every file slip, not only the name of the region, culture, and/or sub-culture primarily covered by the source but also, by the symbols of this outline, both the file or files under which the slip will be placed and that under which the bibliographical data and complete text will be found. For example, a few sheets with incidental data on the Thai of Siam excerpted from a source dealing primarily with the related Laotians of Indochina might bear the following notation on the upper right-hand corner:

AM1 Indochina
Laotians AM8
Thai A01

The postposited symbols would indicate that these particular sheets contained information on both the Laotians and the Thai and would be filed under both AM8 and A01 but not in the file on Indochina, whereas the preposited symbol would indicate that the bibliography slips and complete text would be found in File AM1 on Indochina and not in either the Laotian or Thai files. If a particular sheet contained only information on the Thai and none on the Laotians, the "AM8" would be omitted or crossed out. If it contained general data on Indochina, this would be indicated by a postposited as well as a preposited symbol, thus: AM1 Indochina AM1, and an additional copy would be placed in the general Indochina file. In short, postposited symbols indicate each file which is to receive a copy of the note, while a preposited symbol indicates the file where the reference materials are to be found.

Member institutions should be aware that it will by no means always be necessary to set up separate files corresponding to each potential file distinguished in this outline, even when substantial materials have been processed. It will save separator cards and often be only slightly inconvenient to the researcher if several related files are combined into one. This outline, for example, distinguishes five different potential files for Czechoslovakia, namely, EB1 (Czechoslovakia), EB2 (Historical Czechoslovakia), EB3 (Prehistoric Czechoslovakia), EB4 (Czechs), and EB5 (Slovaks). All five can quite satisfactorily form a single actual file. Here, historical and prehistoric materials will be naturally segregated to a large extent by topic. The same will be true to a lesser degree for the EB1 materials, which will be mainly geographic, demographic, economic, and political. On strictly cultural topics, Czech and Slovak materials can be readily distinguished by the notations on the upper right-hand corner of the individual slips. If this particular combination file were actually set up, it would be only necessary for the member institution to place a note behind the separator cards for EB2, EB3, EB4, and EB5 stating that the materials for these potential files are actually deposited under EB1.

The representative sample of the world's known cultures was arrived at in the following manner. The initial decision was to select 400 cultures as slightly better than a ten per cent sample of all those known to history and ethnography. These were allocated to the eight major regions in the following proportions: 60 each to Africa, North America, and Oceania, 50 each to Asia and South America, and 40 each to Europe (including its colonial off-shoots), the Middle East, and Russia. The regions with the greatest cultural diversity, the largest number of distinctive cultures, and the most adequate descriptive materials have received the larger numerical representation. On the other hand, the proportional representation is appreciably greater for the regions with the largest populations and the most complex civilizations. Thus nearly a third of the total sample are literate peoples from history and the modern world. The choice represents the best compromise of which the author is capable between the sociological point of view which would emphasize population and the anthropological point of view which would emphasize cultural diversity. In leaning somewhat in the former direction he is motivated by the theoretical consideration that the societies with the largest populations and most complex civilizations are presumably, by and large, those whose cultures have proved best adapted to the conditions of human existence and therefore deserve a slightly disproportionate representation in a sample which will be used primarily in the comparative study of man's cultural adaptations. Primitive cultures, though proportionately underrepresented, have been accepted in sufficient numbers so that probably no known major variation in patterned human behavior is actually unrepresented in the sample.

The sample for each of the eight major regions was selected independently in such a way as to be fairly representative of all the geographical sub-regions and culture areas and to include, as far as possible, only cultures on which sound and substantial descriptive information is available. The sample cultures for each region were then arranged in a numerical order of priority, starting with a culture already processed by HRAF and ordering the rest so that at any given point the selection up to that point would be as representative as possible of the entire region. This seemed preferable to any purely random or chance arrangement since it allowed for giving preference to the best described culture whenever there was an alternative among several equally representative ones.

The sample cultures for all eight regions were then interdigited in accordance with the numerical representation assigned to each, yielding a total sample of 400 arranged in numerical order. This is presented in full in Appendix A. In the text, each of the sample cultures is identified by a letter S in parentheses, followed by a numeral denoting whether it falls into the first, second, third, or fourth quartile of the total sample.

Future ethnographic and historical research will certainly result in many changes in the sample, making possible the inclusion of cultures now excluded for lack of data, the elimination of some discovered to be too similar to others, and the substitution of one for another representative of a particular sub-region on the basis of superiority of descriptive information. The author will welcome all suggestions for the improvement of the sample as well as for the expansion and correction of the classification of cultures itself.

Thanks are gratefully acknowledged to those who have given helpful advice on difficult points, among them Harold C. Conklin, John Honigmann, David G. Mandelbaum, Benjamin Paul, Verne F. Ray, and Karl A. Wittfogel, and particularly to Frank M. LeBar, whose research assistance has been especially valuable.

George Peter Murdock

NOTES ON FOURTH EDITION, REVISED

This edition of the <u>Outline of World Cultures</u> contains minor changes in all sections and major revisions in Southeast Asia (by Frank M. LeBar), Africa and Madagascar.

The Africa section has been substantially revised, primarily by Robert O. Lagacé, with respect to the regional and country-level units. The latter have been systematically expanded and sub-divided on a strictly temporal basis. It should be noted that the term "Colonial," used in the heading of some country-level units, is interpreted in a broad sense to mean any type of political dependency under the control or administration of a foreign power. Revisions have also been made in some of the ethnic group units, but lack of time prevented the completion of this task. A systematic and thorough review of all the ethnic unit categories is still required. Hopefully, this will be accomplished for a subsequent edition.

The Madagascar section has been revised by Peter J. Wilson.

TABLE OF CONTENTS

WORLD

W1. <u>World</u>. General descriptive, analytical, or classificatory data on the world as a whole or on several of its major divisions, e.g., Old World. Materials classified herewith will include, for example, data on geological processes, meteorology, and oceanography; general classifications of fauna, flora, human races, and physical environments; distribution of natural resources, population, diseases, and types of culture; statistics on international trade; general discussions of international relations, colonialism, underdeveloped areas, missionary enterprise, and world revolutionary movements. For general data on the New World as a whole see both N1 and S1.

W2. <u>World History</u>. General data on human origins, cultural evolution, intercontinental diffusion of culture traits or complexes, parallelisms in invention or development, and universal or widespread historical movements such as intercontinental migrations and empire building.

W3. <u>Behavior Theory</u>. General and specific data of a theoretical and scientific nature on basic human nature, the mechanisms of perception and learning, personality development, the nature of society and culture, and principles governing the economic, political, religious, artistic, and other aspects of human behavior, whether such data are derived from experimental research, from clinical experience, from cross-cultural or comparative studies, from the investigation of crucial instances, or from scientific hypotheses as yet incompletely validated. Theories explaining behavior in particular societies on the basis of local geographic, historical, economic, or other culture-limited factors will be included only under the society in question rather than here. For scientific theories not pertaining to human behavior, e.g., geological, botanical, or anatomical, see W1.

W4. <u>Primate Behavior</u>. General and specific data on the behavior of primates inferior to man, especially on the anthropoid apes and the monkeys.

W5. <u>Polar Regions</u>. General and specific data on the uninhabited polar regions of the world, i.e., the Antarctic continent and the Arctic region.

W6. <u>Cross-Cultural Research</u>. General and specific data drawn from a number of societies, expressing or interpreting quantitative and/or qualitative materials for comparative purposes, including theoretical or methodological contributions to cross-cultural studies.

W7. <u>United Nations</u>. General and specific data on the history, activities and organization of the United Nations.

A1. Asia. General data on modern Asia and its peoples, either exclusive or inclusive of Siberia and the Middle East, including data pertaining to any three or more of the political divisions distinguished below. For data on the Middle East see M1, on Soviet Russia see R1, on the Old World in general see W1.

A2. Historical Asia. General data of an historical nature, i.e., no longer directly relevant to the modern scene, on Asia, its peoples and cultures, and its political history. For data on world history in general see W2.

A3. Prehistoric Asia. General data on the prehistoric peoples and cultures of Asia. For data on the prehistory of the Middle East see M6-M8.

Korea

AA1. Korea. General and specific data on modern Korea, the Korean people, and their culture.

AA2. Historical Korea. General and specific data on the history of Korea prior to 1910 and on historically recorded past phases of Korean culture.

AA3. Prehistoric Korea. Specific data, particularly archeological, on the prehistoric peoples and cultures of Korea.

AA4. Cheju-do. Specific data on Cheju Island (Quelpart) and its inhabitants.

AA5. North Korea. General and specific data on North Korea and The People's Democratic Republic of Korea after 1945.

AA6. South Korea. General and specific data on the Republic of Korea after 1945.

Japan

AB1. Japan. General data on modern Japan, the Japanese people, and their culture. For data on the regional cultures of modern Japan see AB5.

AB2. Feudal Japan. Specific data on the history and culture of Japan during the Tokugawa period (c. 1600-1868).

AB3. Early Japan. Specific data on the history and historically recorded culture of Japan prior to 1600 A.D.

AB4. Prehistoric Japan. Specific data on the prehistoric peoples and cultures of Japan.

AB5. Japanese Regional Cultures. Specific data on particular local or regional cultures in modern Japan. For data on the regional cultures of certain island groups off the coast of Japan see AB7-AB10 and AC4. For data on the former prefecture of Okinawa-Ken (1879-1945) see AC5-AC9.

AB6. Ainu. Specific data on the Ainu people, including those of Sakhalin and the Kurile Islands as well as of Hokkaido. For other data on the Kuriles see RZ2, on Sakhalin see RX1.

AB7. Izu. Specific data on the Izu Islands and their inhabitants. For data on the Bonin Islands see AZ3.

AB8. Koshiki. Specific data on the Koshiki and Uji Islands and their inhabitants.

AB9. Osumi. Specific data on the Osumi and Tokara Islands and their inhabitants, including the islands of Kuchino, Kuchinoyerabu, Nakano, Suwanose, Tanega, Tokara, Yaku, and their lesser neighbors.

AB10. Tsushima. Specific data on the Tsushima Islands and their inhabitants.

Ryukyus

AC1. Ryukyus. General data on the modern Ryukyu Islands and their inhabitants.

AC2. Historical Ryukyus. Specific data on the history and recorded culture history of the Ryukyu Islands prior to 1871.

AC3. Prehistoric Ryukyus. Specific data on the prehistoric peoples and cultures of the Ryukyu Islands.

AC4. Amami. Specific data on the northern islands of the Ryukyu chain and their inhabitants, including the islands of Amami, Kakeroma, Kika, Okinoyerabu, Tokuno, Yoron, and their lesser neighbors.

AC5. Daito. Specific data on the Daito groups of islands, i.e., Kita, Minami, and Okino, and their inhabitants.

AC6. Miyako. Specific data on the Miyako group of islands and their inhabitants, including Erabu, Miyako, Tarama, and their lesser neighbors.

AC7. Okinawa. Specific data on Okinawa and its inhabitants, including Ie, Iheya, Izena, the Kerama group, and other lesser offshore islands.

AC8. Sento. Specific data on the Sento group of islands, i.e., Kitako, Minamiko, and Uotsuri, and their inhabitants.

AC9. Yaeyama. Specific data on the southwestern islands of the Ryukyu chain, including Haderuma, Iriomote, Ishigaki (the sample), Yonakuni, and their lesser neighbors.

AD1. <u>Formosa</u>. General and specific data on the island of Formosa (Taiwan) and
its non-aboriginal inhabitants.

AD2. <u>Historical Formosa</u>. Specific data on the history and recorded culture history
of Formosa prior to 1895.

AD3. <u>Prehistoric Formosa</u>. Specific data on the prehistoric peoples and cultures
of Formosa.

AD4. <u>Formosan Aborigines</u>. General data on the Formosan aborigines, including
the highly sinicized and acculturated groups on the western coastal plains,
e.g., Luilang, Pazeh, Kavalan, Ping-pu, etc.

AD5. <u>Taiwan Hokkien</u>. Specific data on the Hokkien (Min-nan)-speaking people of
Taiwan. For information on the Hokkien-speaking people of South China,
see AF17.

AD6. <u>Taiwan</u>. General and specific data on the island of Formosa (Taiwan) since
1945, including specific data on the Republic of China since 1949.

AD7. <u>Taiwan Hakka</u>. Specific data on the Hakka-speaking people of Taiwan. For
information on the Hakka people in general, see AE8.

AD8. <u>Atayal</u>. Specific data on the Atayal (Tayal), including the Sedeq.

AD9. <u>Saisiyat</u>. Specific data on the Saisiyat (Saisiat).

AD10. <u>Bunun</u>. Specific data on the Bunun (Vonum).

AD11. <u>Tsou</u>. Specific data on the Tsou (Tsono, Tsoo, Tsowu), including the
Kanakanabu and La'arua (Sa'aroa).

AD12. <u>Thao</u>. Specific data on the Thao.

AD13. <u>Paiwan</u>. Specific data on the Paiwan.

AD14. <u>Rukai</u>. Specific data on the Rukai (Tsalisen, Taroma).

AD15. <u>Puyuma</u>. Specific data on the Puyuma (Panapanayan, Puguma, Pyuma).

AD16. <u>Ami</u>. Specific data on the Ami.

AD17. <u>Yami</u>. Specific data on the Yami of Botel Tobago.

AE1. <u>Greater China</u>. General data on eastern Asia as a whole, on the Sinitic-speaking peoples in that area, and on the non-Han peoples in China's border regions. For data on China see AF1, on Formosa see AD1, on Hong Kong see AY3, on Macao see AY4, on Manchuria see AG1, on Mongolia see AH1, on Sinkiang see AI1, on Tibet see AJ1, on Hainan see AE2.

AE2. <u>Hainan</u>. General data on the island of Hainan and specific data on the Li people. For data on the Yao of Hainan see AE6, on the Chinese inhabitants see AF17.

AE3. <u>Sino-Tibetan Border</u>. General and specific data on the Ch'iang, Kutsung, Lutzu, Sifan (Hsifan), and other non-Han peoples near or across the borders with Tibet, Burma, and Indochina not listed elsewhere. For data on the Wa see AP12, on the Akha see AO4, on the Lahu see AP13, on the Lisu see AE10, on the Minchia see AE11, on the Nakhi see AE12.

AE4. <u>Lolo</u>. Specific data on the Lolo-speaking peoples, including those of Szechwan (Nosu), Yunnan and Kweichow (Yi), and Indochina (Houni, Ho, Penti).

AE5. <u>Miao</u>. Specific data on the Miao-speaking peoples, including those of Indochina and Thailand, where they are commonly called Meo.

AE6. <u>Yao</u>. Specific data on the Yao-speaking peoples, including those of Thailand and Indochina, where they are called Man.

AE7. <u>Pai-i</u>. General data on the Chinese Thai or Shan in southwestern China and specific data on the Pai-i people (including Lu and Nua) of the Sip Song Panna and Chinese Shan states in Yunnan. For data on the Thai people of Burma see AP11, on other tribal Thai groups see AL3. For data on the related Lüe of northern Thailand see AO6.

AE8. <u>Hakka</u>. Specific data on the Hakka people of southern China. For data on the Taiwan Hakka see AD7.

AE9. <u>Monguor</u>. Specific data on the Mongols of the Kansu region, including the Monguor (Tujen), Santa, and Sant'chuan. For data on the Mongols as a whole see AH1.

AE10. <u>Lisu</u>. Specific data on the Lisu-speaking peoples in Yunnan, Burma (where they are called Yawyin), and northern Thailand where they are known by the Chinese term Lisaw.

AE11. <u>Minchia</u>. Specific data on the Minchia (Ber Dser, Petsu, LaBhu) people in the Tali and adjacent areas of Yunnan.

AE12. <u>Nakhi</u>. Specific data on the Nakhi (Moso, Nahsi) people of northwestern Yunnan and adjacent Szechwan.

AE13. <u>Panthay</u>. Specific data on the Moslem Chinese people of the Burma-China border, where they are known as Panthay, Pang-hse, or Hwei.

AE14. <u>Haw</u>. Specific data on the Han Chinese hill farmers of southwestern Yunnan, northern Thailand and Laos, where they are known as Haw or Ho.

China

AF1. <u>China</u>. General data on China proper, the modern Chinese, and their culture. For data on Greater China as a whole see AE1.

AF2. <u>Ch'ing</u>. Specific data on the history and culture of China during the Ch'ing period (1644-1911 A.D.).

AF3. <u>Ming</u>. Specific data on the history and culture of China during the Ming period (1368-1644 A.D.).

AF4. <u>Liao-Chin-Yuan</u>. Specific data on the history and culture of the Liao (907-1125 A.D.), Chin (1115-1234 A.D.), and Yuan (1206-1368 A.D.) dynasties.

AF5. <u>Sui-Sung</u>. Specific data on the history and culture of China during the Sui (589-618 A.D.), T'ang (618-907 A.D.), Wu-tai (Five Dynasties, 907-960 A.D.), and Sung (960-1279 A.D.) periods.

AF6. <u>San-kuo to Nan-ch'ao</u>. Specific data on the history and culture of China during the San-kuo (Three Kingdoms, 220-265 A.D.), Tsin (265-420 A.D.), and Nan-ch'ao (Southern Dynasties, 420-589 A.D.) periods.

AF7. <u>Pei-ch'ao</u>. Specific data on the history and culture of North China during the Pei-ch'ao (Northern Dynasties, 386-581 A.D.) period.

AF8. <u>Ch'in-Han</u>. Specific data on the history and culture of China during the Ch'in (255-206 B.C.) and Han (206 B.C. - 220 A.D.) periods.

AF9. <u>Shang-Chou</u>. Specific data on the history and culture of China during the Shang (c.1766 - c. 1122 B.C.) and Chou (c. 1122 - 255 B.C.) periods.

AF10. <u>Prehistoric China</u>. Specific data on the prehistoric and protohistoric peoples and cultures of China.

AF11. <u>Chinese Regional Cultures</u>. General and specific data on Chinese regional cultures which do not accord with those distinguished below.

AF12. <u>North China</u>. Specific data on the regional culture of the northern Chinese provinces of Hopei, Shantung, Honan, and Shansi.

AF13. Northwest China. Specific data on the regional culture of the northwestern Chinese provinces of Shensi, Kansu, and Chinghai.

AF14. Central China. Specific data on the regional culture of the central Chinese provinces of Anhwei, Kiangsi, Hupeh, and Hunan.

AF15. East China. Specific data on the regional culture of the eastern Chinese provinces of Kiangsu and Chekiang.

AF16. Southwest China. Specific data on the regional culture of the southwestern Chinese provinces of Yunnan, Kweichow, Szechwan, and Sikang.

AF17. South China. Specific data on the regional culture of the southern Chinese provinces of Fukien, Kwangtung, Kwangsi and Hainan.

AF18. Peoples Republic. General and specific data on the Peoples Republic of China since 1949.

Manchuria

AG1. Manchuria. General and specific data on modern Manchuria and its inhabitants.

AG2. Historical Manchuria. Specific data on the history and recorded culture history of Manchuria prior to 1912.

AG3. Prehistoric Manchuria. Specific data on the prehistoric peoples and cultures of Manchuria.

AG4. Manchu. Specific data on the Manchu people and their culture. For data on the related Tungusic peoples see RU5 and RX3.

AG5. Dagur. Specific data on the Dagur (Dahur, Daur) Mongols of northern Manchuria.

Mongolia

AH1. Mongolia. General data on Mongolia and its inhabitants and on the Mongol peoples as a whole. For specific data on the Buryat see RW1, on the Dagur see AG5, on the European Kalmyk see RF4, on the Hazara see AU5, on the Mogol see AU1, on the Monguor see AE9.

AH2. Historical Mongolia. Specific data on the history and recorded culture history of Mongolia and the Mongols from around the third century B.C. to 1911.

AH3. Prehistoric Mongolia. Specific data on the prehistoric peoples and cultures of Mongolia.

AH4. <u>Khalkha</u>. Specific data on the Mongols of central and eastern Outer Mongolia, including the Khalkha (the sample) and the Darkhat and Dariganga Mongols. For data on the Khalkha Mongols after 1910 see AH7.

AH5. <u>Kalmyk</u>. Specific data on the Mongols known collectively as Kalmyk (Kalmuck) (the sample), or Oirat of western Outer Mongolia and northern Sinkiang, including the Bayit (Bait), Dörbet, Dzakhachin, Khoit (Hoit), Khoshut (Hoshut), Mingat, Ölöt, Uriankhai, and kindred groups of the Alashan, Edsin Gol, Kuku Nor, and Tsaidam regions. For data on the European Kalmyk see RF4, on the Turkic Oirot and Kalmyk see RS2, on the Turkic Uriankhai see RS3.

AH6. <u>Inner Mongolia</u>. General data on Inner Mongolia and specific data on its Mongol inhabitants, including the Jerim, Josotu, Jouda (Chao-uda), Silingol (Shilongol), and Ulanjab Leagues, the Tumet comprising Bayan Tala League, the Ordos (Urdus) comprising Yeke Ju (Ikhe Chao) League, and the Chahar Mongols; specific data on the Inner Mongolian Autonomous Region.

AH7. <u>Outer Mongolia</u>. General data on modern Outer Mongolia (since 1911) and specific data on the Mongolian People's Republic. For specific data on the Khalkha before 1910 see AH4, on the Kalmyk see AH5.

Sinkiang

AI1. <u>Sinkiang</u>. General and specific data on modern Sinkiang or Chinese Turkestan and its inhabitants. For data on China in general see AE1.

AI2. <u>Historical Sinkiang</u>. Specific data on the history and recorded culture history of Sinkiang prior to 1912.

AI3. <u>Prehistoric Sinkiang</u>. Specific data on the prehistoric peoples and cultures of Sinkiang.

AI4. <u>Uigur</u>. Specific data on the Uigur people and their culture.

Tibet

AJ1. <u>Tibet</u>. General data on modern Tibet and its inhabitants.

AJ2. <u>Historical Tibet</u>. General and specific data on the history and recorded culture of Tibet prior to 1790.

AJ3. <u>Prehistoric Tibet</u>. Specific data on the prehistoric peoples and cultures of Tibet.

AJ4. <u>West Tibetans</u>. Specific data on the Tibetan speaking peoples of India especially those of the former Kingdom of Ladak (in Kashmir) and those of Lahul and Spiti (in Panjab). For data on the Balti see AV2. For specific data on the Tibetans of Chinese Tibet and on the Tibetan peoples in general see AJl, on the Bhutanese see AK2, on the Sikkimese see AK3, on the tribes of the Chinese-Tibetan borderland see AE3.

AJ5. Tangut. Specific data on the Tangut people of eastern Tibet.

Himalayan States

AK1. Nepal. General data on Nepal and its inhabitants and specific data on Nepalese groups not distinguished below.

AK2. Bhutan. General and specific data on Bhutan and its inhabitants.

AK3. Sikkim. General data on Sikkim and its inhabitants and specific data on Sikkimese groups not distinguished below.

AK4. Gurkha. Specific data on the Gurkha people.

AK5. Lepcha. Specific data on the Lepcha people.

Southeast Asia

AL1. Southeast Asia. General data on the countries, peoples, languages and cultures of mainland southeastern Asia or of greater Southeast Asia. For data on the Malayo-Polynesian peoples in general see O4. For general data on Indonesia and the Philippines see Ol. For data on the Formosan aborigines see AD4 and AD8 through AD17.

AL2. Mon-Khmer. General data on the languages and cultures of the Mon-Khmer peoples, and specific data on Mon-Khmer groups not listed elsewhere. For specific data on the Cambodians see AM4, on the Garo see AR5, on the Khasi see AR7, on the Mon see AP9, on the Moi-Kha tribes of Indochina see AN14 through AN39, on the Nicobarese see AZ7.

AL3. Shan-Thai. General data on the Shan-Thai peoples of Indochina, Burma, Thailand, and southern China, and specific data on the Black Thai, Chuang, Dioi (Chung-chia), Nhang, Nung, Puthai, Red Thai, Tho, Tung, White Thai, and other Thai and Kadai groups not separately listed elsewhere. For specific data on the Western Lao see AO6, on the Laotian Thai see AM8, on the Shan see AP11, on the Lu see AE7, on the·Li see AE2, on the Central Thai (Siamese) see AO7, on the Southern Thai (Thai Islam) see AO8, on Ahom see AR3.

Indochina

AM1. Indochina. General data on former regional Indochina and its inhabitants, and specific data on its non-aboriginal inhabitants; e.g., Chinese and French. For specific data on the Black, Red and White Thai and on the

Nhang, Puthai and Tho see AL3, on the Man or Yao see AE6, on the Meo or Miao see AE5.

AM2. <u>Historical Indochina</u>. Specific data on the history and recorded culture history of Indochina prior to 1887.

AM3. <u>Prehistoric Indochina</u>. Specific data on the prehistoric peoples and cultures of Indochina.

AM4. <u>Cambodia</u>. Specific data on modern Cambodia and on the Cambodian or Khmer people. For general data on the Mon-Khmer peoples see AL2.

AM5. <u>Cham</u>. Specific data on the Chams of South Vietnam and Cambodia.

AM6. <u>Jarai</u>. Specific data on the Jarai (Djarai), a complex of Malayo-Polynesian-speaking tribes in southern Vietnam and neighboring Cambodia, including Arap, Habau, Hodrung and Sesan.

AM7. <u>Phnong</u>. General and specific data on the Mon-Khmer-speaking hill-tribes of Cambodia and southeastern Thailand, referred to collectively as Phnong or Pnong, and including Chong, Kui (Kuoy, Soai), Pear (Porr), Saoch (Samre) and Chaobon.

AM8. <u>Laos</u>. Specific data on Laos, the Laotian Thai (Eastern Lao), and their culture. For data on the tribal Thai of Indochina see AL3. For data on the Western Lao of Thailand see AO6.

AM9. <u>Moi-Kha</u>. General data on the Mon-Khmer and Malayo-Polynesian-speaking hilltribes of Vietnam and Laos, and specific data on those not listed elsewhere. For data on the Lawa and Yumbri of northern Thailand see AO5 and AO9, on the Palaung and Wa of Burma see AP10 and AP12, on the Chaobon and Kui of southeastern Thailand see AM7.

AM10. <u>Muong</u>. Specific data on the Muong people of former Tonkin.

AM11. <u>Vietnam</u>. Specific data on modern Vietnam (former Annam, Cochinchina, and Tonkin), the Vietnamese people, and their culture.

AM12. <u>North Vietnam</u>. Specific data on the Democratic Republic of Vietnam following the 1954 partition.

AM13. <u>South Vietnam</u>. Specific data on the Republic of Vietnam following the 1954 partition.

AM14. <u>Alak</u>. Specific data on the Mon-Khmer hilltribes of the Alak cluster in southern Laos, including Brao, Loven, Nha Heun, Kasseng, Katang, Ngeh and Oy.

AM15. Bahnar. Specific data on the Mon-Khmer-speaking Bahnar tribes near Kontum in South Vietnam, including Alakong, Bonam, Golar, Ho Drong, Jo Long, Roh, Tolo and To Sung.

AM16. Bru. Specific data on the Bru (Baru), a Mon-Khmer hill people of central Vietnam, including Kalo and Tau-Oi.

AM17. Chrau. Specific data on the Mon-Khmer-speaking Chrau tribes of the southern Vietnam highlands, including the related Mru, Jre and Bla.

AM18. Churu. Specific data on the Malayo-Polynesian-speaking Churu (Chru) of the Darlac Plateau in South Vietnam.

AM19. Cua. Specific data on the Cua (Khua), a Mon-Khmer-speaking upland people of central Vietnam.

AM20. Halang. Specific data on the Mon-Khmer-speaking Halang tribes of southern Laos and neighboring Kontum Province, Vietnam.

AM21. Hre. Specific data on the Hre, a Mon-Khmer upland people of central Vietnam.

AM22. Hroy. Specific data on the Malayo-Polynesian-speaking Hroy (Bahnar Chams) of South Vietnam.

AM23. Jeh. Specific data on the Mon-Khmer-speaking upland Jeh (Die) tribes of southern Laos and neighboring Kontum Province, Vietnam, including Halang Doan, Menam, Noar, and Sayan.

AM24. Katu. Specific data on the Katu, a Mon-Khmer-speaking tribal complex of central Vietnam.

AM25. Kayong. Specific data on the Kayong (Ca-Rong), a Mon-Khmer hill people near Kontum, South Vietnam.

AM26. Khmu. Specific data on the Khmu (Kha Mou, Mou), scattered groups of Mon-Khmer speakers in the uplands of northern Laos and adjacent Thailand.

AM27. Koho. Specific data on speakers of the Koho cluster of Mon-Khmer languages in highland South Vietnam, including Lat, Laya, Nop, Pru, Rien, Sre, and Tring.

AM28. Lamet. Specific data on the Lamet, a Mon-Khmer upland people of northwestern Laos.

AM29. Ma. Specific data on the Mon-Khmer-speaking Ma (Cau Ma) tribes of highland South Vietnam, including Bosre, Da Dong, Sop and Tou.

AM30. Monom. Specific data on the Monom (Bonom), a Mon-Khmer upland people of Kontum Province, South Vietnam.

AM31. Mnong. Specific data on the Mon-Khmer-speaking Mnong tribal complex of the Darlac Plateau, South Vietnam, including Cil (Kil), Gar, Kuen, Nong, Preh, Prong, and Rlam.

AM32. Pacoh. Specific data on the Pacoh (Pakho), upland Mon-Khmer speakers of central Vietnam.

AM33. Raglai. Specific data on the Malayo-Polynesian Raglai (Glai, Roglai) tribes of highland South Vietnam.

AM34. Rengao. Specific data on the Rengao (Reungao), Mon-Khmer highlanders of South Vietnam near Kontum.

AM35. Rhade. Specific data on the Malayo-Polynesian Rhade (E-de) tribes of the Darlac Plateau, South Vietnam, including A'dham, Blo, Epan, H'wing, K'drao, Kpa, and M'dur.

AM36. Sedang. Specific data on the Sedang, a Mon-Khmer people of the South Vietnamese highlands.

AM37. So. Specific data on the So, scattered groups of Mon-Khmer speakers along the southern Laos-Thailand border.

AM38. T'in. Specific data on the T'in (Thin), scattered groups of Mon-Khmer speakers along the border of northwestern Laos and adjacent Thailand.

AM39. Stieng. Specific data on the Mon-Khmer-speaking Stieng tribal complex of the South Vietnam-Cambodia border, including the linguistically related Budip, Budeh, Bulach, and Bulo.

Malaya

AN1. Malaya. General data on Singapore and the Federation of Malaya and their inhabitants, and specific data on their non-aboriginal inhabitants, e.g., Arabs, British, Chinese, and Indians. For data on the Federation of Malaysia see AN8.

AN2. Historical Malaya. Specific data on the history and recorded culture history of Malaya prior to the twentieth century.

AN3. Prehistoric Malaya. Specific data on the prehistoric peoples and cultures of Malaya.

AN4. Jakun. Specific data on the Jakun people.

AN5. Malays. Specific data on the peninsular Malays and on their kinsmen across the Strait of Malacca in Sumatra. For data on the Orang Laut or Sea Gypsies see OB4, on the Malayo-Polynesian peoples in general see O4. For data on the Minangkabau of Sumatra see OD10.

AN6. Sakai. Specific data on the Sakai or Senoi tribes of Malaya. For data on the Sakai of Sumatra see OD8.

AN7. Semang. Specific data on the Semang or Negrito tribes of Malaya and adjacent Thailand. For data on the Andamanese Negritos see AZ2, on the Negritos of the Philippines see OA31.

AN8. Malaysia. Specific data on the modern Federation of Malaysia, formed of the Federation of Malaya, Sabah and Sarawak in 1963. For information on Sabah and Sarawak prior to 1963 see OC4.

AN9. Singapore. Specific data on the Republic of Singapore since 1965.

Thailand

AO1. Thailand. General data on the geography, history, politics, economics, etc., of modern Siam or Thailand and its inhabitants; general data on the Thai (Siamese) and their culture; and specific data on the Chinese and other non-aboriginal inhabitants of Thailand. For data on the Chaonam (Sea Gypsies) see AP8, on the Kui and Chaobon see AM7, on the Yumbri see AO9, on the Lawa see AO5, on the T'in see AM38, on the Khmu see AM26, on the Akha see AO4, on the Haw see AE14, on the Karen see AP7, on the Lahu see AP13, on the Lisu see AE10, on the Miao (Meo) see AE5, on the Yao see AE6, on the Pattani Malays see AN5, on the Mon see AP9.

AO2. Historical Thailand. Specific data on the history and recorded culture history of Thailand prior to about 1850.

AO3. Prehistoric Thailand. Specific data on the prehistoric peoples and cultures of Thailand.

AO4. Akha. Specific data on the Akha or Kaw people of eastern Burma, northern Thailand, northwestern Laos, and southwestern Yunnan. For data on other peoples of the Sino-Tibetan borderland see AE3.

AO5. Lawa. Specific data on the Lawa (Lwa) of northern Thailand. For data on the Chaobon (Lawa) see AM7.

AO6. Western Lao. Specific data on the Thai-speaking Lao of northern Thailand, where they are known as Khon Muang, Yuan or Lannathai, and of northeastern Thailand, where they are known as Thai Isan or Phuthai, and including the Lu (Lüe) of the North Thailand-Laos border

area. For data on the related Lao of Laos (Eastern Lao) see AM8.
For data on the related Lu of southwestern Yunnan see AE7.

AO7. <u>Central Thai</u>. Specific data on the Central Thai people, particularly on
the community of Bang Chan (the sample).

AO8. <u>Southern Thai</u>. Specific data on the lowland inhabitants of extreme
southern Thailand, referred to variously as Thai Islam or Thai Malay.
For data on Semang Negritos see AN7.

AO9. <u>Yumbri</u>. Specific data on scattered groups of Mon-Khmer speakers in
northern Thailand and adjacent Burma and Laos, referred to variously
as Yumbri, Mrabri, Phi Tong Luang, or Ma Ku.

Burma

AP1. <u>Burma</u>. General data on modern Burma and its inhabitants and
specific data on its non-aboriginal inhabitants and on Burmese
tribes not specifically distinguished below.

AP2. <u>Historical Burma</u>. Specific data on the history and recorded culture
history of Burma prior to the first Anglo-Burman War in 1824.

AP3. <u>Prehistoric Burma</u>. Specific data on the prehistoric peoples and cultures of Burma.

AP4. <u>Burmese</u>. Specific data on the Burmans or Burmese people and their
culture.

AP5. <u>Chin</u>. Specific data on the Chin (Khyen) tribes of the Chin Hills.

AP6. <u>Kachin</u>. Specific data on the Kachin or Chingpaw (Singpho) people,
including the related Achang, Atsi, Lashi, Maru, and Nung.

AP7. <u>Karen</u>. Specific data on the Karen people including the Kayah, P'wo,
Sgaw, and also including those Karen in Thailand.

AP8. <u>Mergui</u>. Specific data on the Mergui Archipelago and its inhabitants,
including the Salon (Selong), Mawken (Sea Gypsies), and Chaonam. For
data on the Orang Laut or Sea Gypsies of Malaya and Indonesia see OB4.

AP9. <u>Mon</u>. Specific data on the Mon or Talaing, including those in Thailand.
For general data on the Mon-Khmer people see AL2.

AP10. <u>Palaung</u>. Specific data on the Palaungs (Ta-ang, Rumai) and their culture.

AP11. Shan. Specific data on the Thai-speaking Shans of Burma and Thailand. For data on the Shan-Thai peoples in general see AL3, for Chinese Shans see AE7.

AP12. Wa. Specific data on the Wa tribes, including those in the adjacent Yunnan province of China where they are called Kawa. For data on other peoples of the Sino-Tibetan borderland see AE3.

AP13. Lahu. Specific data on the Lahu or Musso people of eastern Burma, northern Thailand, northwestern Laos, and southwestern Yunnan. For data on other peoples of the Sino-Tibetan borderland see AE3.

AP14. Union of Burma. Specific data on the modern Union of Burma since 1948.

Greater India

AQ1. Greater India. General data on the Indian subcontinent and its peoples, on southern Asia as a whole, or on major linguistic groupings in the area, e.g., Dravidian. For general data on the Mon-Khmer peoples see AL2, on the Indo-European peoples see E9.

AQ2. British India. Specific data on the history of India and Greater India from the beginnings of European penetration in the eighteenth century to the independence of India and Pakistan in the mid-twentieth century.

AQ3. Mogul India. Specific data on the history and culture history of Greater India from the time of Tamerlane (c. 1400) to the end of Mogul rule (c. 1707).

AQ4. Early India. Specific data on the history and culture history of Greater India from the rise of Buddhism (c. 500 B.C.) to the time of Tamerlane (c. 1400 A.D.).

AQ5. Indo-Aryans. Specific data on the history of India during the period of the Aryan invasion and expansion and on the culture of the ancient Indo-Aryans.

AQ6. Prehistoric India. Specific data on the prehistoric peoples and cultures of India, including the Harappa civilization of the Indus River valley.

Assam

AR1. Assam. General data on modern Assam and its inhabitants and specific data on Assamese tribes not specifically distinguished below. For data on the history, culture history, and archeology of Assam see AQ2-AQ6.

AR2. Abor. Specific data on the Abor tribe.

AR3. Ahom. Specific data on the Ahom or Assamese people and their culture.

AR4. Chittagong. Specific data on the tribes of the Chittagong Hills, including the Banjogi, Chakma, Kyoungtha, Khumi, Marma (Mogh), Mru, Pankho, Shindu, and Tippera.

AR5. Garo. Specific data on the Garo tribe.

AR6. Kachari. Specific data on the Kachari or Bodo people, including the related Dhimal and Koch.

AR7. Khasi. Specific data on the Khasi people, including the Lynngam and Synteng.

AR8. Kuki-Lushai. Specific data on the Kuki-Lushai peoples, including the Aimol, Kom, Kuki, Lakher (the sample), Lushai, and Thado. For data on the Chin see AP5.

AR9. Meithei. Specific data on the Meithei or Manipuri people and their culture.

AR10. Mikir. Specific data on the Mikir tribe.

AR11. Miri. Specific data on the Miri tribe, including the kindred Dafla and the Apa Tani.

AR12. Mishmi. Specific data on the Mishmi people.

AR13. Naga. Specific data on the Naga tribes, including the Angami (the sample), Ao, Chang, Kabui, Kacha (Zemi), Kalyo-Kengyu, Konyak, Lhota, Mao (with the Maram), Naked Rengma, Rengma, Sangtam, Sema, Tangkhul, and Yachumi.

East Pakistan

AS1. East Pakistan. General data on the eastern section of modern Pakistan or East Bengal and specific data on its inhabitants. For data on Pakistan in general see AT1, for data on Bengal in general before partition see AW20, for data on the Chittagong tribes see AR4.

Pakistan

AT1. Pakistan. General data on modern Pakistan and its inhabitants and on the western section of Pakistan, and specific data on West Pakistan peoples not separately listed below. For historical data see AQ2, AQ6, for data on the Dard see AV3, on East Pakistan see AS1, on the Kafir tribes see AU6.

AT2. Baluchi. Specific data on the Baluchi or Baloch people, including the Brahui and the people of both groups resident in adjacent Iran.

AT3. West Panjabi. Specific data on the Panjabi and Lahnda speaking people of West Pakistan. For data on the Panjab in general before partition see AW6.

AT4. Pathan. Specific data on the Pathan people. For data on the kindred Pashtun of Afghanistan, see AU4.

AT5. Sindhi. Specific data on the Sindhi people.

Afghanistan

AU1. Afghanistan. General data on modern Afghanistan and its inhabitants, and specific data on peoples not separately listed below. For data on the Kirgiz see RP2, on the Tadzhik see RO2, on the Turcoman see RM2, on the Uzbek see RN5.

AU2. Historical Afghanistan. Specific data on the history and recorded culture history of Afghanistan before 1900, or the beginning of the modern period.

AU3. Prehistoric Afghanistan. Specific data on the prehistoric peoples and cultures of Afghanistan.

AU4. Pashtun. Specific data on the Pashtun (Pakhtun) or Afghan proper of central and southern Afghanistan. For data on the kindred Pathan of Pakistan see AT4.

AU5. Hazara. Specific data on the Hazara people. For data on the Mongol peoples in general see AH1.

AU6. Nuri. Specific data on the Nuri (Kafir) tribes of northeastern Afghanistan and adjacent Pakistan.

Jammu and Kashmir

AV1. Kashmir. General data on the disputed state of Jammu and Kashmir, and specific data on peoples not separately listed below. For historical data, see AQ2-AQ6. For data on the Ladaki see AJ4.

AV2. Balti. Specific data on the Balti people. For data on the Ladaki, see AJ4.

AV3. Dard. Specific data on the Dard people, including those of adjacent Pakistan.

AV4. Kashmiri. Specific data on the people of the Valley of Kashmir.

AV5. (Deleted).

AV6. <u>Dogra</u>. Specific data on the Dogra people of Jammu and neighboring areas.

AV7. <u>Burusho</u>. Specific data on the Burushaski-speaking people of Hunza and Nagar.

India

AW1. <u>India</u>. General data on modern India and its inhabitants and on Hindu religion and culture. For historical data see AQ2-AQ6, for data on the Indian subcontinent as a whole see AQ1, on Assam see AR1, on former French India see AY2, on the Indians of Natal see FX15, on Kashmir see AV1, on former Portuguese India see AY5, on Sikkim see AK3.

AW2. <u>Bihar</u>. Specific data on the state of Bihar and its inhabitants, other than the tribal groups separately listed below.

AW3. <u>Bombay</u>. General data on the state of Bombay. For specific data on the Gujarati see AW7, on the Kanada see AW10, on the Marathi see AW12.

AW4. <u>Madhya Pradesh</u>. General data on the Hindu-speaking region of Madhya Pradesh and on the former states of Bhopal, Madhya Bharat, and Vindhya Pradesh, and specific data on their inhabitants other than the tribal groups separately listed below. For the Marathi see AW12.

AW5. <u>Coorg</u>. Specific data on the former state of Coorg and its inhabitants.

AW6. <u>East Panjab</u>. Specific data on the state of Delhi and on the former states of East Panjab, Patiala and East Panjab States Union and their inhabitants. General data on Panjab before partition.

AW7. <u>Gujarati</u>. General data on the state of Gujarat and specific data on the Gujarati-speaking peoples.

AW8. <u>Hyderabad</u>. General data on the former state of Hyderabad. For specific data on the Kanada see AW10, on the Marathi see AW12, on the Telugu see AW17.

AW9. <u>Kutch</u>. Specific data on the former state of Kutch and its inhabitants.

AW10. <u>Kanada</u>. General data on the state of Mysore, excluding Coorg, and specific data on the Kanada-speaking people of the former states of Bombay, Hyderabad, and Mysore, including the Okkalinga.

AW11. Kerala. Specific data on the former state of Tranvancore-Cochin and the Malabar district of the former state of Madras and their inhabitants, e.g., the Nayar caste and the Syrian Christians.

AW12. Marathi. General data on the state of Maharashtra and specific data on the Marathi-speaking people of the state of Maharashtra (a part of the former state of Bombay).

AW13. Orissa. Specific data on the state of Orissa and the Oriya-speaking peoples, other than the tribal groups separately listed below.

AW14. Pahari. Specific information on the state of Himachal Pradesh and its inhabitants and on the Pahari-speaking people of Uttar Pradesh.

AW15. Rajasthan. Specific information on the state of Rajasthan and the former state of Ajmer and their inhabitants, including the Rajput.

AW16. Tamil. General data on the former state of Madras and specific data on the Tamil-speaking peoples.

AW17. Telugu. General data on the state of Andhra Pradesh and specific data on the Telugu-speaking people.

AW18. Tulu. Specific information on the Tulu-speaking people of the South Kanara district of Mysore.

AW19. Uttar Pradesh. General data on the state of Uttar Pradesh (United Provinces) and specific data on its plains inhabitants, including the Chamar. For data on the hill districts see AW14.

AW20. West Bengal. Specific information on the state of West Bengal and its inhabitants and general information on Bengal before partition. For data on East Bengal see AS1.

AW21. Parsi. Specific data on the Parsi sect and their culture. For data on the modern Zoroastrians of Iran see MA8.

AW22. Tribal India. General data on the tribal groups of India.

AW23. Agaria. Specific data on the Agaria or Agariya people.

AW24. Baiga. Specific data on the Baiga people.

AW25. Bhil. Specific data on the Bhil or Bhilala people.

AW26. Birhor. Specific data on the Birhor people.

AW27. Bhuinar. Specific data on the Bhuinar or Bhuinhar people.

AW28. Bhuiya. Specific data on the Bhuiya or Bhuia people.

AW29. Bhumij. Specific data on the Bhumij people.

AW30. Bondo. Specific data on the Bondo Poroja people.

AW31. Gadaba. Specific data on the Gadaba people.

AW32. Gond. Specific data on the Gond peoples including Bhatra, Dhruva, Gotta, Koi (Koya), Maria (including Bison Horn or Doria), Muria (Koitur), Pardha (Gond Bards), and Parja.

AW33. Ho. Specific data on the Ho people.

AW34. Kamar. Specific data on the Kamar people.

AW35. Kandh. Specific data on the Kandh (Kandha, Kondh).

AW36. Kharia. Specific data on the Kharia people including the Juang.

AW37. Kol. Specific data on the Kol people.

AW38. Korku. Specific data on the Korku or Korwa people.

AW39. Oraon. Specific data on the Oraon or Kurukh people.

AW40. Maler. Specific data on the Maler or Malto people.

AW41. Munda. Specific data on the Munda people.

AW42. Santal. Specific data on the Santal people.

AW43. Savara. Specific data on the Savara or Saora people including the Saharia.

AW44. Warli. Specific data on the Warli (Varli) people.

AW45. Northern Tribes. Specific data on Gangetic and Subhimalayan tribes not mentioned above, such as Aheria, Bahelia, Ban Manus, Bhar, Bhoksa (Bhuksha), Bora, Dhartu, Dusadh, Gidhia, Kangharia, Kanjar, Kolta, Pawaria, Raji, Rawalta, and Tharu.

AW46. Central Tribes. Specific data on tribes of Chota Nagpur, Mirzapur, and Chattisgarh not mentioned above such as Andh, Asur, Bedia, Bharia, Bhumia, Bhogta, Binjhwar, Birjia, Chero, Dhanwar, Dombo, Ghasi,

Kawar, Kherwar, Kolam, Konda-Dora, Mahli, Mal Paharia, Parhaiya (Paraiya), and Turi.

AW47. <u>Bombay Tribes</u>. Specific data on tribes of Bombay not mentioned above such as Chodhara, Daga, Dhodia, Dubla, Gamta (Gamit, Gamti), Katkari, Koli, Naika (Naikda, Nayak), Vasawa, etc.

AW48. <u>Rajasthan Tribes</u>. Specific data on tribes of Rajasthan and Madhya Bharat not mentioned above such as Bharaiya, Grassia (Garasia), Meo, Mer, Merat, Mina, Rawat, etc.

AW49. <u>Bengal Tribes</u>. Specific data on tribes not mentioned above or in the Assam files.

AW50. <u>Badaga</u>. Specific data on the Badaga people.

AW51. <u>Chenchu</u>. Specific data on the Chenchu people.

AW52. <u>Eruka</u>. Specific data on the Eruka or Erukala people.

AW53. <u>Irula</u>. Specific data on the Irula people.

AW54. <u>Kadar</u>. Specific data on the Kadar people.

AW55. <u>Kota</u>. Specific data on the Kota people.

AW56. <u>Kurumba</u>. Specific data on the Kurumba and Kadu Kurumba people.

AW57. <u>Malser</u>. Specific data on the Malser people.

AW58. <u>Nayadi</u>. Specific data on the Nayadi people.

AW59. <u>Reddi</u>. Specific data on the Konta or Hill Reddi (Konda-Reddi) people.

AW60. <u>Toda</u>. Specific data on the Toda people.

AW61. <u>Yenadi</u>. Specific data on the Yenadi or Yanadi people.

AW62. <u>Yerava</u>. Specific data on the Yerava (Yeruva) people.

AW63. <u>Madras Tribes</u>. Specific data on tribes of Madras not mentioned above such as Aranadan, Ernadu, Kasuba, Kudubi, Kunnuvan, Malasar, Paniyan, Porja, etc.

AW64. <u>Travancore Tribes</u>. Specific data on tribes of Travancore-Cochin (Kerala) not mentioned above such as Eravalan, Kadan, Kanikkaren, Kuravan, Mala-Arayan (Malayarayan), Malamkiravan, Mala Pantaram (Panturani), Malapulayan, Malavettan, Mannan, Muthuvan (Mattuvan, Muduvan), Paliyan, Thanta Pulayan, Ullatan, Urala (Urali), etc.

Ceylon

AX1. Ceylon. General data on modern Ceylon and its inhabitants.

AX2. Historical Ceylon. Specific data on the history and recorded culture history of Ceylon prior to the twentieth century.

AX3. Prehistoric Ceylon. Specific data on the prehistoric peoples and cultures of Ceylon.

AX4. Sinhalese. Specific data on the Sinhalese people and their culture.

AX5. Vedda. Specific data on the Vedda tribes.

Minor Asiatic Colonies

AY1. Minor Asiatic Colonies. General data on the surviving petty European colonial possessions in Asia and specific data on similar possessions given up during the twentieth century.

AY2. Former French India. Specific data on the former French possessions in India, i.e., Karakal, Pondichery, and Yanaon.

AY3. Hong Kong. Specific data on the British colony of Hong Kong. For data on China and the Chinese see AF1.

AY4. Macao. Specific data on the Portuguese colony of Macao.

AY5. Former Portuguese India. Specific data on the former Portuguese possessions in India, i.e., Damao, Diu, and Goa.

Asiatic Islands

AZ1. Asiatic Islands. Specific data on the Chagos and other lesser islands off the coast of Asia not individually listed below. For data on Ceylon see AX1, on Formosa see AD1, on Hainan see AE2, on Hong Kong see AY3, on Japan see AB1, on the Mergui Archipelago see AP8, on Quelpart Island see AA4, on the Ryukyu Islands see AC1.

AZ2. Andamans. Specific data on the Andaman Islands and their inhabitants, especially on the aboriginal Andamanese Negritos and their culture.

AZ3. Bonins. Specific data on the Bonin and Volcano Islands and their inhabitants.

AZ4. Laccadives. Specific data on the Laccadive Islands and their inhabitants.

AZ5. Maldives. Specific data on the Maldive Islands and their inhabitants.

AZ6. <u>Marcus</u>. Specific data on Marcus Island and its utilization.

AZ7. <u>Nicobars</u>. Specific data on the Nicobar Islands and the Nicobarese people.

AZ8. <u>Cocos Islands</u>. Specific data on the Cocos or Keeling Islands and their inhabitants.

EUROPE

E1. Europe. General data on Europe and its peoples, either exclusive or inclusive of Russia, and data pertaining to any three or more of the political divisions distinguished below. For general data on Soviet Russia see R1, on the Finno-Ugrian peoples see RG1.

E2. Late Modern Europe. General data, primarily historical, on modern Europe since the beginning of the French Revolution (1789).

E3. Early Modern Europe. General data on the history and civilization of Europe from the discovery of America to the French Revolution (1492-1789).

E4. Medieval Europe. General data on the history and civilization of Europe from the fall of Rome (476 A.D.) to the discovery of America.

E5. Roman Europe. General data on the history and civilization of Europe from the rise of Rome to political domination after the Second Punic War (201 B.C.) to the fall of Rome. For data on Roman Italy see E14.

E6. Protohistoric Europe. General data on the history and civilization of Europe from the beginning of the Bronze Age to the rise of Rome. For specific data on the ancient Greeks see EH4-EH6, on the Etruscans see E15, on Minoan civilization see EH10, on the protohistoric period in the Middle East see M6, on the Scyths see RA4.

E7. Neolithic Europe. General data on the culture and culture history of Europe during the Neolithic period.

E8. Paleolithic Europe. General data on the cultures and culture history of Europe during the Paleolithic and Mesolithic periods.

E9. Indo-Europeans. General data on the languages and culture of the Indo-European peoples. For data on the Slavs see RA5, on the Baltic Slavs see RB3, on the Armenians see RJ3, on the Iranians see MA9, on the Indo-Aryans see AQ5.

E10. Celtic Peoples. General data on the languages and culture of the Celtic peoples. For specific data on the Bretons see EW8, on the Cornish see ES9, on the Gauls see EW5, on the Irish see ER4, on the Scots see ES10, on the Welsh see ES11.

E11. Germanic Peoples. General data on the languages and culture of the Germanic peoples, or of the High Germans, the Low Germans, or the

Scandinavians. For specific data on the Austrians see EK1, on the Danes see EM1, on the Dutch see ET4, on the English see ES1, on the Flemings see EV2, on the Frisians see ET5, on the Germans see EL1, on the German Swiss see EJ5, on the Goths see EL4, on the Icelanders see EQ2, on the Norwegians see EP1, on the Swedes see EN1.

E12. <u>Latin Peoples</u>. General data on the languages and culture of the Latin or Romance peoples. For specific data on the French see EW1, on the French Swiss see EJ4, on the Italians see EI1, on the Italian Swiss see EJ6, on Latin Americans see S1, on the Portuguese see EY1, on the Rumanians see ED1, on the Spaniards see EX1, on the Walloons see EV3.

E13. <u>Balkan Peoples</u>. General data on the peoples and cultures of the Balkan Peninsula.

E14. <u>European Jews</u>. General and specific data on the Jews of Europe and their culture. For specific data on the Polish Jews see EA4, on Israel see MF1, on the Jews of the Middle East see MF4.

E15. <u>Gypsies</u>   General and specific data on the Gypsies and their culture, including those of Asia and America as well as of Europe.

E16. <u>Slavic Peoples</u>. General data on the Slavic peoples, languages, and cultures. For specific data on the Balto-Slavs see RB3, on the Belorussians see RC1, on the Bulgarians see EE1, on the Croats see EF4, on the Czechs see EB1, on the Great Russians see RF2, on the Indo-Europeans in general see E9, on the Poles see EA1, on the Serbs see EF6, on the Slovaks see EB1, on the Slovenes see EF7, on the Ukrainians see RD4.

Poland

EA1. <u>Poland</u>   Specific data on Poland since 1918 and on the modern Poles and their culture. For general data on Slavic culture see E16.

EA2. <u>Historical Poland</u>. Specific data on the history and recorded culture history of Poland prior to 1918.

EA3. <u>Prehistoric Poland</u>. Specific data on the prehistoric peoples and cultures of Poland.

EA4. <u>Polish Jews</u>   Specific data on the Jews of Poland and their culture. For general data on the Jews of Europe see E14, on the Jews of Israel see MF1.

Czechoslovakia

EB1.   Czechoslovakia   Specific data on Czechoslovakia since 1918 and on the modern Czechs and Slovaks and their culture. For data on the Jews of Czechoslovakia see E14, on the Ruthenians or Carpathian Ukrainians see RD3, on the Sudeten Germans see EL9.

EB2.   Historical Czechoslovakia. Specific data on the history and recorded culture history of Bohemia, Moravia, and Slovakia prior to 1918.

EB3.   Prehistoric Czechoslovakia. Specific data on the prehistoric peoples and cultures in the territory of modern Czechoslovakia.

Hungary

EC1.   Hungary   Specific data on Hungary since 1918 and specific data on the modern Hungarians (Magyars) and their culture. For data on the Finno-Ugrian peoples in general see RG1, on the Hungarian Jews see E14.

EC2.   Historical Hungary. Specific data on the history and recorded culture history of Hungary and the Magyar people prior to 1918.

EC3.   Prehistoric Hungary. Specific data on the prehistoric peoples and cultures of Hungary.

Rumania

ED1.   Rumania   Specific data on Rumania in the twentieth century and specific data on the modern Rumanians and their culture. For data on Moldavia or Bessarabia see RE1, on the Rumanian Jews see E14, on the Balkan peoples in general see E13, on the Hungarians of Transylvania see EC1.

ED2.   Historical Rumania. Specific data on the history and recorded culture history of Rumania prior to the twentieth century.

ED3.   Prehistoric Rumania. Specific data on the prehistoric peoples and cultures of Rumania.

Bulgaria

EE1.   Bulgaria. General and specific data on modern Bulgaria, the Bulgarian people, and their culture. For data on the Balkan peoples in general see E13.

EE2. Historical Bulgaria. Specific data on the history and recorded culture history of Bulgaria and the Bulgarians prior to the twentieth century, including data on the original Turkic Proto-Bulgars.

EE3. Prehistoric Bulgaria. Specific data on the prehistoric peoples and cultures in the territory of modern Bulgaria.

Yugoslavia

EF1. Yugoslavia   General data on Yugoslavia and its peoples subsequent to 1918 and on the South Slavs in general. For general data on the Balkan peoples see El3, on the Slavic peoples see El6.

EF2. Historical Yugoslavia. Specific data on the history and recorded culture history of the Serbs, Croats, Slovenes, and Montenegrins prior to 1918.

EF3. Prehistoric Yugoslavia. Specific data on the protohistoric and prehistoric peoples and cultures in the territory of modern Yugoslavia.

EF4. Croats. Specific data on modern Croatia and the Croat people.

EF5. Montenegrins. Specific data on the modern Montenegrins and their culture.

EF6. Serbs   Specific data on modern Serbia and the Serb people.

EF7. Slovenes   Specific data on modern Slovenia and the Slovene people.

EF8. Contemporary Macedonians. Specific data on modern Macedonia and the Macedonians.

Albania

EG1. Albania. Specific data on modern Albania, the Albanian people, and their culture, including the Gheg and the Tosc.

EG2. Historical Albania. Specific data on the history and recorded culture history of Albania and the Albanians prior to the twentieth century.

EG3. Prehistoric Albania. Specific data on the protohistoric and prehistoric peoples and cultures in the territory of modern Albania.

Greece

EH1. Greece. General and specific data on modern Greece and the Greek people, including those of Asia Minor and the Aegean islands. For specific data on Greek regional cultures see EH12, on modern Crete and the Cretans see EZ5.

EH2. Turkish Greece. Specific data on the history and culture history of Greece and the Greeks from the Turkish capture of Constantinople in 1453 to the beginning of the twentieth century. For general data on the Turkish period in the Middle East see M2.

EH3. Byzantine Civilization   Specific data on the history and culture of the Greek world under the Byzantine Empire, from its separation from the Roman Empire of the West in 395 A.D. to the fall of Constantinople. For general data on the Slavic peoples see E16.

EH4. Hellenistic Greece. Specific data on the history and culture of the Greek world from 335 B.C. to 395 A.D. For data on the Graeco-Roman period in the Middle East in general see M4, on ancient Macedonia see EH8.

EH5. Hellenic Greece. Specific data on the history and culture of Greece and the Greeks, including those of Asia Minor, from about 700 to 335 B.C. For specific data on Periclean Athens see EH11, on ancient Sparta see EH9, on the Greek colonies of Sicily and southern Italy see E15.

EH6. Homeric Greece   Specific data on the Greeks and their culture during the Homeric age (c. 900-700 B.C.).

EH7. Prehistoric Greece. Specific data on the prehistoric peoples and cultures of Greece from the early Paleolithic to the end of the Mycenaean period.

EH8. Ancient Macedonians. Specific data on the Macedonians and their culture under Philip and Alexander (359-323 B.C.).

EH9. Ancient Spartans   Specific data on ancient Sparta and its culture.

EH10. Minoan Civilization. Specific data on the Minoan civilization of ancient Crete (c. 3000-1400 B.C.).

EH11. Periclean Athens   Specific data on the civilization of Athens in the age of Pericles (c. 495-429 B.C.).

EH12. Greek Regional Cultures. Specific data on the local and regional cultures of modern Greece.

EH13. Mt. Athos. Specific data on the history and culture of the semi-autonomous monastic community of Mt. Athos.

EH14. Sarakatsani. Specific data on the culture of the Sarakatsani nomadic pastoralists of northern Greece.

EH15. Vlachs. Specific data on the nomadic Vlachs.

Italy

EI 1. Italy. General data on modern Italy, including Sicily, and its inhabitants, and specific data on its history since political unification in 1861. For data on Sardinia see EZ8, on the Italian Swiss see EJ6, on the regional cultures of Italy see EI 7.

EI 2. Early Modern Italy. Specific data on the history and culture history of Italy from the beginning of the Italian Renaissance (c. 1300) to Italy's political unification. For specific data on Renaissance Florence see EI 8.

EI 3. Medieval Italy. Specific data on the history and culture history of Italy from the fall of the Roman Empire of the West (476 A.D.) to the beginning of the Italian Renaissance. For general data on medieval Europe see E4.

EI 4. Roman Italy. Specific data on the history of Italy and the civilization of Rome from the rise of Rome as a political power in Italy (dated from the conquest of southern Etruria in 396 B.C.) to the fall of the Roman Empire of the West. For specific data on Roman civilization at the height of the imperial period see EI 9.

EI 5. Protohistoric Italy. Specific data on the history and culture history of Italy from the beginning of the Bronze Age to the rise of Rome, including data on the Etruscans and the Greek colonies in Sicily and southern Italy.

EI 6. Prehistoric Italy. Specific data on the peoples and cultures of Italy during the Paleolithic, Mesolithic, and Neolithic periods.

EI 7. Italian Regional Cultures. Specific data on the local and regional cultures of modern Italy. For specific data on Sicilian culture see EI 10.

EI 8. Florentines   Specific data on the culture of Florence at the height of the Italian Renaissance.

EI 9. Imperial Romans   Specific data on the civilization of ancient Rome at the height of the imperial period.

EI 10. Sicilians   Specific data on the culture of the modern Sicilian people.

EI 11. Vatican City. Specific data on the culture and history of the Vatican City.

Switzerland

EJ1. Switzerland. General data on modern Switzerland and its inhabitants and specific data on its history during the twentieth century.

EJ2. Historical Switzerland. Specific data on the history and recorded culture history of Switzerland prior to the twentieth century.

EJ3. Prehistoric Switzerland. Specific data on the prehistoric peoples and cultures of Switzerland.

EJ4. French Swiss. Specific data on the French-speaking population of modern Switzerland and their culture.

EJ5. German Swiss. Specific data on the German-speaking population of modern Switzerland and their culture.

EJ6. Italian Swiss. Specific data on the Italian-speaking population of modern Switzerland and their culture, including also the speakers of Rhaeto-Romanic or Ladin.

EJ7. Liechtenstein. Specific data on the petty state of Liechtenstein and its inhabitants.

Austria

EK1. Austria. Specific data on modern Austria, its people and culture, and its history since 1918. For specific data on the Tyrolese see EK4.

EK2. Historical Austria. Specific data on the history and recorded culture history of Austria in particular and of Austria-Hungary in general prior to 1918.

EK3. Prehistoric Austria. Specific data on the prehistoric peoples and cultures of Austria.

EK4. Tyrolese Specific data on the modern inhabitants of the Austrian Tyrol and their culture.

Germany

EL1. Germany. General data on modern Germany and its inhabitants, and specific data on its history since 1871. For data on East Germany or the so-called German Democratic Peoples Republic see EL11, on the German Jews see E14, on the Germanic peoples in general see E11, on West Germany or the so-called Bonn Republic see EL10.

EL2. Early Modern Germany. Specific data on the history and culture history of Germany and the Germans from 1500 to 1871.

EL3. Medieval Germany. Specific data on the history and culture history of the Germans from the accession of Otto I as Holy Roman Emperor in 962 to the beginning of the German Renaissance (c. 1500). For general data on medieval Europe see E4.

EL4. Early Germans. Specific data on the history and culture history of the German tribes from the time of Tacitus (c. 100 A. D.) to 962, including the Teutonic tribes of Tacitus and the later Goths, Lombards, and Vandals. For specific data on the Franks see EW4, on Visigothic Spain see EX4, on the Vandals in North Africa see MU2.

EL5. Prehistoric Germany. Specific data on the prehistoric peoples and cultures of Germany.

EL6. German Regional Cultures. Specific data on the regional cultures of Germany. For data on the Austrians see EK1, on the German Swiss see EJ5, on the Prussians see EL8.

EL7. East European Germans. Specific data on the German colonies and cultural enclaves in Russia and the Balkan countries.

EL8. Prussians   Specific data on the modern Prussians and their culture.

EL9. Sudeten Germans. Specific data on the Sudeten Germans of Czechoslovakia prior to World War II.

EL10. West Germany. Specific information on the so-called Bonn Republic and its inhabitants as well as on the Western sectors of the city of Berlin and its inhabitants since 1945.

EL11. East Germany. Specific information on the so-called German Democratic Peoples Republic and its inhabitants and the Soviet Zone of Occupation since 1945.

EL12. Wends. Specific data on the culture of the Slavic-speaking Wends of the Spreewald District of Brandenburg.

Denmark

EM1. Denmark   Specific data on modern Denmark, the Danish people, and their culture. For data on the Danes of Greenland see NB1, on the Faeroe Islands see EZ1.

EM2. Historical Denmark. Specific data on the history and recorded culture history of Denmark prior to the twentieth century.

EM3. Prehistoric Denmark. Specific data on the prehistoric peoples and cultures of Denmark.

Sweden

EN1. Sweden   Specific data on modern Sweden, the Swedish people, and
their culture. For data on the Lapps of Sweden see EP4.

EN2. Historical Sweden. Specific data on the history and recorded culture
history of Sweden prior to the twentieth century.

EN3. Prehistoric Sweden. Specific data on the prehistoric peoples and cultures of Sweden.

Finland

EO1. Finland   Specific data on modern Finland, the Finnish people, and
their culture. For data on the Karelian Finns see RG5, on the Lapps
see EP4, on the Finno-Ugrian peoples in general see RG1.

EO2. Historical Finland. Specific data on the history and recorded culture
history of Finland and the Finns prior to 1918.

EO3. Prehistoric Finland. Specific data on the prehistoric peoples and cultures of Finland.

Norway

EP1. Norway. Specific data on modern Norway, the Norwegian people, and
their culture. For data on Spitzbergen see EZ10.

EP2. Historical Norway. Specific data on the history and recorded culture
history of Norway prior to the twentieth century. For specific data
on the Vikings see EP5, on the early Icelanders see EQ2.

EP3. Prehistoric Norway. Specific data on the prehistoric peoples and cultures of Norway.

EP4. Lapps   Specific data on the Lapp people and their culture, including those of Finland, Russia, and Sweden as well as of Norway.
For data on the Finno-Ugrian peoples in general see RG1.

EP5. Vikings. Specific data on the Norse sea rovers of the eighth to the tenth
century, A. D.

Iceland

EQ1. <u>Iceland.</u> Specific data on Iceland, its history, its modern inhabitants, and their culture.

EQ2. <u>Early Icelanders</u>   Specific data on the Icelanders of the period of the <u>Eddas and Sagas</u>, i. e., the tenth to the thirteenth century, A. D.

Ireland

ER1. <u>Ireland.</u> General data on Ireland and its inhabitants, and specific data on Eire and its history since the achievement of political independence. For specific data on Northern Ireland see ER5.

ER2. <u>Historical Ireland.</u> Specific data on the recorded history of Ireland.

ER3. <u>Prehistoric Ireland.</u> Specific data on the prehistoric peoples and cultures of Ireland.

ER4. <u>Celtic Irish.</u> Specific data on the early Celtic Irish and their culture. For data on the Celtic peoples in general see E10.

ER5. <u>Northern Ireland.</u> Specific data on modern Northern Ireland and its inhabitants, and general data on the so-called Scotch-Irish.

ER6. <u>Rural Irish</u>   Specific data on the Irish of rural Eire and their culture.

Great Britain

ES1. <u>Great Britain.</u> General data on Great Britain, or on the British Isles as a whole, and their inhabitants, and on the British Empire as a whole. For data on the Orkney Islands see EZ7, on the Shetland Islands see EZ9.

ES2. <u>Industrial Britain.</u> Specific data on Great Britain, its people, and its history since the beginning of the Industrial Revolution (c. 1830).

ES3. <u>Georgian Britain.</u> Specific data on Great Britain, its history, and its culture during the Georgian period (1714-1830).

ES4. <u>Early Modern Britain</u>   Specific data on the history and culture of Great Britain as a whole during the Stuart period (1603-1714) and of England and Wales also during the Elizabethan period (1558-1603), the latter serving as the sample. For data on Scotland prior to 1603 see ES6.

ES5. Medieval England. Specific data on the history and culture of England from 1066 to 1558. For general data on medieval Europe see E4.

ES6. Early Scotland. Specific data on the history and recorded culture history of Scotland and the Scots prior to 1603. For data on the modern Highland Scots see ES10, on the Scotch-Irish see ER5, on the Celtic peoples see E10.

ES7. Early England. Specific data on the history of England and Wales from the Roman to the Norman Conquest (84 to 1066 A.D.) and on Briton and Anglo-Saxon culture.

ES8. Prehistoric Britain. Specific data on the prehistoric peoples and cultures of Great Britain.

ES9. Cornish. Specific data on the language and traditional culture of the Cornish people. For data on the Celtic peoples in general see E10.

ES10. Highland Scots   Specific data on the language and traditional culture of the people of the Scottish highlands and the Hebrides. For data on the Celtic peoples in general see E10.

ES11. Welsh. Specific data on the language and traditional culture of the people of Wales. For data on the Celtic peoples in general see E10.

ES12. Manx. Specific data on the culture of the Celtic-speaking population of the Isle of Man.

Netherlands

ET1. Netherlands. General data on Holland and its inhabitants and on the Low Countries as a whole. For data on Dutch culture see ET4, on the Low German peoples in general see E11.

ET2. Historical Netherlands. Specific data on the history and recorded culture history of Holland in particular and the Low Countries in general.

ET3. Prehistoric Netherlands. Specific data on the prehistoric peoples and cultures of the present territory of Belgium, Luxembourg, and the Netherlands.

ET4. Dutch   General and specific data on the Dutch people of modern times and their culture. For data on the Afrikanders see FX7, on the Flemings see EV2.

ET5. Frisians. Specific data on the language and culture of the Frisian people of northeastern Netherlands and adjacent Germany.

Luxembourg

EU1. Luxembourg. Specific data on Luxembourg and its inhabitants. For prehistoric and all except recent historical data see ET2-ET3.

Belgium

EV1. Belgium. General data on Belgium and its inhabitants and specific data on modern Belgian history. For most historical and all prehistoric data see ET2-ET3.

EV2. Flemings. Specific data on the Dutch-speaking Flemish people of Belgium and their culture. For general and specific data on the Dutch people see ET4.

EV3. Walloons. Specific data on the French-speaking Walloon people of Belgium and their culture. For data on French regional cultures see EW7.

France

EW1. France. General data on modern France and its inhabitants, and specific data on the history of France since 1789. For specific data on the regional cultures of modern France see EW7.

EW2. Early Modern France. Specific data on the history and culture of France from the beginning of the French Renaissance (c. 1500) to the outbreak of the French Revolution (1789).

EW3. Medieval France. Specific data on the history and culture history of France from 987 to 1500 A.D. For general data on medieval Europe see E4.

EW4. Franks   Specific data on France during the rule of the Merovingian and Carolingian Franks (471-997 A.D.) and on Frankish culture.

EW5. Gauls. Specific data on the Gauls and their culture and on the history of Gaul from the Roman to the Frankish conquest. For data on the Celtic peoples in general see E10.

EW6. Prehistoric France. Specific data on the prehistoric peoples and cultures of France. For European prehistory in general see E6-E8.

EW7. French Regional Cultures. Specific data on the regional cultures of modern France. For specific data on the Basques see EX8, on the Bretons see EW8, on the Corsicans see EZ4.

EW8.   Bretons   Specific data on the language and traditional culture of
the Breton people. For data on the Celtic peoples in general see E10.

EW9.   Parisians   Specific data on metropolitan Paris and its inhabitants.

EW10. Alsatians.   Specific data on the German-speaking population of Alsace
and their culture.

Spain

EX1.   Spain. General data on modern Spain and its inhabitants and specific
data on Spanish history since the beginning of the eighteenth century.
For data on the regional cultures of modern Spain see EX6, on
the Balearic Islands see EZ3, on Spanish America see S1.

EX2.   Climactic Spain. Specific data on the history and culture of Spain at the
height of its power and influence, i. e., from the accession of
Ferdinand V in 1474 to the end of the seventeenth century.

EX3.   Moorish Spain   Specific data on the history of Spain during the
Moorish period, i. e., from the eighth to the fifteenth century, and
on the culture of Moorish Spain. For data on Moorish Morocco see
MW2.

EX4.   Early Iberia. Specific data on the history and recorded culture history of
the Iberian Peninsula prior to the Moorish period, i. e., during the
Carthaginian, Roman, Visigothic, and early medieval periods.

EX5.   Prehistoric Iberia. Specific data on the prehistoric peoples and cultures
of the Iberian Peninsula.

EX6.   Spanish Regional Cultures. Specific data on the regional cultures of
modern Spain. For data on the Basques see EX8, on the Catalans
see EX9.

EX7.   Andorra. Specific data on the petty state of Andorra and its inhabitants.

EX8.   Basques   Specific data on the Basque people of Spain and adjacent
France and on their language and traditional culture.

EX9.   Catalans   Specific data on modern Catalonia, its people, and their
culture.

EX10. Gibraltar. Specific data on modern Gibraltar and its inhabitants.

Portugal

EY1.   Portugal   General and specific data on modern Portugal, the

Portuguese people, and their culture.

EY2. **Historical Portugal.** Specific data on the history and recorded culture history of Portugal. For data on early and prehistoric Portugal see EX4-EX5.

European Islands

EZ1. **European Islands.** General and specific data on the Faeroe and other smaller islands off the coast of Europe not individually listed below. For data on the Aegean islands see EH1, on Great Britain see ES1, on Iceland see EQ1, on Ireland see ER1, on Madeira see MZ6, on Sicily see EI1 and EI10.

EZ2. **Azores.** Specific data on the Azores archipelago and its inhabitants.

EZ3. **Balearics.** Specific data on the Balearic Islands and their inhabitants.

EZ4. **Corsica.** Specific data on Corsica, the Corsican people, and their culture.

EZ5. **Crete.** Specific data on modern Crete and its inhabitants. For historical data see EH2-EH6, for data on the ancient Minoan civilization see EH10.

EZ6. **Malta.** Specific data on modern Malta and the Maltese people.

EZ7. **Orkneys.** Specific data on the Orkney Islands and their inhabitants.

EZ8. **Sardinia.** Specific data on modern Sardinia and its inhabitants.

EZ9. **Shetlands.** Specific data on the Shetland Islands and their inhabitants.

EZ10. **Spitzbergen.** Specific data on Spitzbergen and its utilization.

AFRICA

F1. Africa. General data on Africa south of the Sahara (or on the continent as a whole), on its geography, natural resources, and demography, and on the history of European exploration, economic penetration, including the slave trade, and colonial expansion. For general data on northern or Islamic Africa see M1.

F2. Black Africa. General data on the indigenous peoples, languages, and cultures of Africa south of the Sahara from the beginning of recorded or oral history, including ethnological and archeological generalizations, linguistic classifications, human biology, ethnic and culture history, and changes related to Arab, European, or other contacts. For general data on Blacks of African descent in the New World see N5.

F3. Prehistoric Africa. General data on Africa south of the Sahara, its peoples and cultures, from the earliest evidences of man to the beginning of recorded or oral history. For general data on the prehistoric periods in North Africa see M6-M8.

F4. Deleted.

West Africa

FA1. French-speaking West Africa. General data on the history, geography, demography, non-indigenous inhabitants, economy, and politics of French-speaking West Africa (or of West Africa as a whole), either exclusive or inclusive of its Islamic northern section, and specific data on the government of the former Federation of French West Africa. For general data on the history of the Sahara and Muslim Sudan see MS2. For data on the specific countries of Dahomey, Guinea, Ivory Coast, Togo, and Upper Volta see FA38-FA57. For data on the specific countries of Mali, Mauritania, Niger, and Senegal see MS34-MS37.

FA2. West African Peoples. General data on the indigenous peoples and cultures of West Africa, either exclusive or inclusive of its Islamic northern section, from the beginning of recorded or oral history, including their ethnic and culture history, and changes related to North African, European, or other contacts, and general and specific data on the history, polity, and economy of the "medieval" West African empires of Ghana, Mali, and Gao or Songhay. For specific data on the dominant ethnic group of each of these empires respectively see MS21 Soninke, FA27 Malinke, and MS20 Songhai. For general data on the peoples of the Sahara and the Muslim Sudan see MS1.

FA3. Prehistoric West Africa. General data on the prehistoric peoples and cultures of West Africa, either exclusive or inclusive of the northern Sudan. For general data on the prehistoric Sahara and northern Sudan see MS3.

FA4.   Guinea Coast Peoples. General data on the indigenous peoples and
        cultures of the West African coastal zone from Cameroon to Gambia.

FA5.   Anyi-Baule. Specific data on the Abure (Akapless, Assini, Issinese),
        Afema, Ahanta, Anno (with the Gan), Anyi (Ndenie), Attie (Kuroba),
        Baule, Betie, Mekyibo (Vyetre), Safwi, and Sanwi tribes of the Ivory
        Coast. For data on the related Twi see FE12.

FA6.   Atakpame. Specific data on the Atakpame or Ana tribe of Togo, includ-
        ing the related Tsha of Dahomey. For data on the Yoruba peoples in
        general see FF62.

FA7.   Baga. Specific data on the Baga tribe of Guinea.

FA8.   Bambara. Specific data on the Bambara or Banmana tribe of Mali,
        including the kindred Kagoro.

FA9.   Bargu. Specific data on the Bargu (Bariba) nation of northern Dahomey,
        plus the related Besorube, Dompago, Kilinga, Namba, Pilapila,
        Somba, and Tamberma.

FA10. Basari. Specific data on the Basari tribe of Togo, including the related
        Chamba or Akasele.

FA11. Bobo. Specific data on the Bobo people of Mali and Upper Volta, com-
        prised of the Bua (Black Bobo, Bobofing, Boua), Kian (Bobo-zbe,
        Tian, White Bobo), Nienige (Nieniegue), and Tara (Bobo-oule, Red
        Bobo).

FA12. Busansi. Specific data on the Busansi (Busanse) tribe of Upper Volta,
        including the Bisa.

FA13. Chakossi. Specific data on the Chakossi tribe of Togo. For data on the
        kindred Twi see FE12.

FA14. Diola. Specific data on the Diola (Jola) peoples of the Casamance region
        of Senegal, comprised of a number of subgroups including the Bayot,
        Bliss-Karone, Diamat, Dyiwat, Felup, Fogny, and Her.

FA15. Diula Tribes. Specific data on a group of dispersed mercantile tribes of
        presumable Soninke origin scattered throughout West Africa and
        variously known as Dafi, Diula, Huela, Ligbi, Marka, Mau, Sia, and
        Yarse. For data on the Vai see FD9.

FA16. Dogon. Specific data on the Dogon (Dogom, Habe, Kado, Tombo)
        nation of Mali, including the related Deforo.

FA17. Ewe. Specific data on the Ewe nation of Togo, including the Anglo,
        Glidyi, Ho, and other component tribes.

FA18. Fon. Specific data on the Fon or Dahomean nation, including the related Adja, Agonglin, Aizo (Whydah), Djedj, Gun (Goum), Mahi, Popo, and Watyi tribes. For data on the kindred Ewe see FA17.

FA19. Futajalonke. Specific data on the Futajalonke nation, including the related Fulakunda and Hubu tribes, who are a branch of the Fulani (see MS11) residing in Fouta Djalon, Guinea.

FA20. Gurma. Specific data on the Gurma nation of Upper Volta.

FA21. Guro. Specific data on the Guro tribe of the Ivory Coast, including the kindred Gagu.

FA22. Kabure. Specific data on the Kabure (Cabrai, Kabre) people of Dahomey, plus the related Difale, Logba, and Lossa.

FA23. Kissi. Specific data on the Kissi tribe of Guinea.

FA24. Konkomba. Specific data on the Konkomba or Kpankpam tribe of Togo, including the related Moba.

FA25. Lagoon Tribes. Specific data on the small tribes of the Ivory Coast lagoon, namely, the Abe, Ajukru, Alagya (Jackjack), Ari (Abiji), Avikam (Brinya, Kwakwa), Ebrie (Kyama), and Mbato (Gwa).

FA26. Lobi. Specific data on the Dian (Dyan), Dorosie, Gan, Kulango, Lobi (LoWilisi), Loron, and Tegessie peoples of the Ivory Coast.

FA27. Malinke. Specific data on the Malinke or Mandingo (Mandinka, Mandino, Soce, Sosse) people of Mali, Guinea, Ivory Coast, the Gambia, and Senegal, plus the related Kassonke.

FA28. Mossi. Specific data on the Mossi nation of Upper Volta, especially the kingdoms of Ouagadougou (Wagadugu) and Yatenga, plus the related Lilse (Fulse, Kurumba, Nioniosse).

FA29. Ngere. Specific data on the Ngere or Guere people of the Ivory Coast, plus the related Dan (Gio), Lo, Tura, and Wobe.

FA30. Samo. Specific data on the Samo tribe of Upper Volta.

FA31. Senufo. Specific data on the Senufo or Siena nation of Upper Volta, Mali, and northern Ivory Coast, including the kindred Komono, Mbuin (Gwin), Minianka, Nafana, Natioro, Turuka, and Wara (Guala).

FA32. Serer. Specific data on the Serer nation of Senegal. For data on the related but Islamized Wolof see MS30.

FA33. Susu. Specific data on the Susu (Soso, Soussou) people of Guinea, plus the related Dialonke (Djallonke, Dyalonke) or Yalunka (Yalonke) of Guinea and Sierra Leone.

FA34. Tem. Specific data on the Kotokoli and Temba peoples of Togo, plus the related but detached Ntribu mainly in Ghana.

FA35. Adele. Specific data on the Adele and other "splinter tribes" of central Togo, including the Akposo, Avatime, Basila, Buem, and Kebu.

FA36. Tenda. Specific data on the Badyaranke (Akhous or Khous, Badiaranke, Bigola or Agola), Bassari (Aliyan or Aliane, Ayan or Biyan, Ayaon, Ouo, Tenda Boeni, Tenda-Dounka, Tenda Mayo, Tenda-Niokolo), Bedik or Tendanke, and Koniagui (Awoen, Awouhen, Azen, Coniagui, Tenda-Dounka, Wonyadiji) of Guinea and Senegal.

FA37. Diander. Specific data on the remnant Ndut (N'Doute), Non (None), and Safen of northwestern Senegal.

FA38. Dahomey. General data on the geography, demography, and indigenous peoples and cultures, and specific data on the national institutions, multi-ethnic urban areas, non-indigenous inhabitants, and broad sociocultural trends of the Republic of Dahomey.

FA39. Colonial Dahomey. General data on the geography, demography, and indigenous peoples and cultures, and specific data on the colonial rule, non-indigenous inhabitants, Eurafrican urbanization, and broad sociocultural trends of Dahomey during the colonial period.

FA40. Traditional Dahomey. General data on the geography, demography, and African peoples and cultures, and specific data on European or other contacts, non-African inhabitants, and broad sociocultural trends of Dahomey from the beginning of recorded or oral history up to the onset of colonial rule.

FA41. Prehistoric Dahomey. Specific data on the prehistoric peoples and cultures of Dahomey.

FA42. Guinea. General data on the geography, demography, and indigenous peoples and cultures, and specific data on the national institutions, multi-ethnic urban areas, non-indigenous inhabitants, and broad sociocultural trends of the Republic of Guinea (formerly French Guinea).

FA43. Colonial Guinea. General data on the geography, demography, and indigenous peoples and cultures, and specific data on the colonial rule, non-indigenous inhabitants, Eurafrican urbanization, and broad sociocultural trends of Guinea during the colonial period.

FA44. Traditional Guinea. General data on the geography, demography, and African peoples and cultures, and specific data on European or other contacts, non-African inhabitants, and broad sociocultural trends of Guinea from the beginning of recorded or oral history up to the onset of colonial rule.

FA45. <u>Prehistoric Guinea</u>. Specific data on the prehistoric peoples and cultures of Guinea.

FA46. <u>Ivory Coast</u>. General data on the geography, demography, and indigenous peoples and cultures, and specific data on the national institutions, multi-ethnic urban areas, non-indigenous inhabitants, and broad socio-cultural trends of the Republic of the Ivory Coast (Cote d'Ivoire).

FA47. <u>Colonial Ivory Coast</u>. General data on the geography, demography, and indigenous peoples and cultures, and specific data on the colonial rule, non-indigenous inhabitants, Eurafrican urbanization, and broad sociocultural trends of the Ivory Coast, excluding the region which subsequently became Upper Volta, during the colonial period.

FA48. <u>Traditional Ivory Coast</u>. General data on the geography, demography, and African peoples and cultures, and specific data on European or other contacts, non-African inhabitants, and broad sociocultural trends of the Ivory Coast from the beginning of recorded or oral history up to the onset of colonial rule.

FA49. <u>Prehistoric Ivory Coast</u>. Specific data on the prehistoric peoples and cultures of the Ivory Coast.

FA50. <u>Togo</u>. General data on the geography, demography, and indigenous peoples and cultures, and specific data on the national institutions, multi-ethnic urban areas, non-indigenous inhabitants, and broad sociocultural trends of the Republic of Togo.

FA51. <u>Colonial Togo</u>. General data on the geography, demography, and indigenous peoples and cultures, and specific data on the colonial rule under both the Germans and French, non-indigenous inhabitants, Eurafrican urbanization, and broad sociocultural trends of Togo during the colonial period.

FA52. <u>Traditional Togo</u>. General data on the geography, demography, and African peoples and cultures, and specific data on European or other contacts, non-African inhabitants, and broad sociocultural trends of Togo from the beginning of recorded or oral history up to the onset of German colonial rule.

FA53. <u>Prehistoric Togo</u>. Specific data on the prehistoric peoples and cultures of Togo.

FA54. <u>Upper Volta</u>. General data on the geography, demography, and indigenous peoples and cultures, and specific data on the national institutions, multi-ethnic urban areas, non-indigenous inhabitants, and broad socio-cultural trends of the Republic of Upper Volta (Haute-Volta).

FA55. Colonial Upper Volta. General data on the geography, demography, and indigenous peoples and cultures, and specific data on the colonial rule, non-indigenous inhabitants, Eurafrican urbanization, and broad sociocultural trends of Upper Volta during the colonial period, both as a separate colony and during periods when this area was partitioned among other colonies, mainly the Ivory Coast.

FA56. Traditional Upper Volta. General data on the geography, demography, and African peoples and cultures, and specific data on European or other contacts, non-African inhabitants, and broad sociocultural trends of Upper Volta from the beginning of recorded or oral history up to the onset of colonial rule.

FA57. Prehistoric Upper Volta. Specific data on the prehistoric peoples and cultures of Upper Volta.

Portuguese Guinea

FB1. Deleted.

FB2. Portuguese Guinea. General data on the geography, demography, and indigenous peoples and cultures, and specific data on the colonial rule, non-indigenous inhabitants, Eurafrican urbanization, modern economy and local government, and broad sociocultural trends of Portuguese Guinea since the onset of Portuguese control.

FB3. Traditional Portuguese Guinea. General data on the geography, demography, and African peoples and cultures, and specific data on European or other contacts, non-African inhabitants, and broad sociocultural trends of Portuguese Guinea from the beginning of recorded or oral history up to the onset of colonial rule. For data on Prehistoric Portuguese Guinea see FB7.

FB4. Bijogo. Specific data on the Bissagos Islands and the indigenous Bijogo people.

FB5. Landuma. Specific data on the Landuma tribe, including the related Tiapi.

FB6. Pepel. Specific data on the Balante, Banyun (Bainuk), Biafada (Biafar, Bifra), Bram (Bola, Burama), Kassanga, Kobiana, Kunante, Mandyak (Mandjak, Mandyako), Mankanya (Mankagne), Nalu, and Pepel peoples.

FB7. Prehistoric Portuguese Guinea. Specific data on the prehistoric peoples and cultures of Portuguese Guinea.

Sierra Leone and The Gambia

FC1. Sierra Leone. General data on the geography, demography, and indigenous peoples and cultures, and specific data on the national institutions, multi-ethnic urban areas, non-indigenous inhabitants, especially the descendants of Black immigrants from Nova Scotia and of other freed slaves, and broad sociocultural trends of contemporary Sierra Leone.

FC2. Colonial Sierra Leone. General data on the geography, demography, and indigenous peoples and cultures, and specific data on the colonial rule, non-indigenous inhabitants, especially the Black immigrants from Nova Scotia and other freed slaves, plus their descendants, Eurafrican urbanization, and broad sociocultural trends of Sierra Leone during the colonial period.

FC3. Traditional Sierra Leone. General data on the geography, demography, and indigenous peoples and cultures, and specific data on European or other contacts, non-indigenous inhabitants, and broad sociocultural trends of Sierra Leone from the beginning of recorded or oral history up to the onset of colonial rule. For data on Prehistoric Sierra Leone see FC10.

FC4. Kono. Specific data on the Kono tribe.

FC5. Koranko. Specific data on the Koranko tribe. For data on the related Malinke see FA27.

FC6. Loko. Specific data on the Loko tribe.

FC7. Mende. Specific data on the Mende nation.

FC8. Sherbro. Specific data on the Sherbro tribe, including the related Bulom and Krim.

FC9. Temne. Specific data on the Temne nation, including the related Limba.

FC10. Prehistoric Sierra Leone. Specific data on the prehistoric peoples and cultures of Sierra Leone.

FC11. Gambia. General data on the geography, demography, and indigenous peoples and cultures, and specific data on the national institutions, multi-ethnic urban areas, non-indigenous inhabitants, and broad sociocultural trends of The Gambia.

FC12. Colonial Gambia. General data on the geography, demography, and indigenous peoples and cultures, and specific data on the colonial rule, non-indigenous inhabitants, Eurafrican urbanization, and broad sociocultural trends of Gambia during the colonial period.

FC13. Traditional Gambia. General data on the geography, demography, and African peoples and cultures, and specific data on European or other contacts, non-African inhabitants, and broad sociocultural trends of Gambia from the beginning of recorded or oral history up to the onset of colonial rule.

FC14. Prehistoric Gambia. Specific data on the prehistoric peoples and cultures of Gambia.

Liberia

FD1. Liberia. General data on the geography, demography, and indigenous peoples and cultures, and specific data on the national institutions, multi-ethnic urban areas, non-indigenous inhabitants, especially the descendants of Black immigrants from the United States and of other freed slaves, and broad sociocultural trends of the Republic of Liberia since 1944.

FD2. Historical Liberia. General data on the geography, demography, and indigenous peoples and cultures, and specific data on the development and functioning of national institutions, non-indigenous inhabitants, especially Black immigrants from the United States and other freed slaves, plus their descendants, immigrant-based urbanization, national relations with indigenous peoples, and broad sociocultural trends of Liberia from the establishment of the Commonwealth of Liberia in 1838 up to 1944.

FD3. Traditional Liberia. General data on the geography, demography, and indigenous peoples and cultures, and specific data on European or other contacts, non-indigenous inhabitants, and broad sociocultural trends of Liberia from the beginning of recorded or oral history up to the establishment of the Commonwealth of Liberia in 1838. For data on Prehistoric Liberia see FD10.

FD4. Gbande. Specific data on the Gbande (Gbandi, Bandi) people.

FD5. Gola. Specific data on the Gola tribe.

FD6. Kpelle. Specific data on the Kpelle (Guerze) people.

FD7. Kru. Specific data on the Kru-speaking peoples, including the Bakwe, Bassa, Belle, Bete, Dei (De, Dey), Grebo (Glebo, Gweabo), Krahn (Kran), Kru proper (Krao), Padebu, Putu (Pudu), Sapo, Sikon, and other component groups.

FD8. Toma. Specific data on the Toma (Buzi, Loma) people.

FD9. Vai. Specific data on the Vai people.

FD10. Prehistoric Liberia. Specific data on the prehistoric peoples and cultures of Liberia.

FE1. <u>Ghana</u>. General data on the geography, demography, and indigenous peoples and cultures, and specific data on the national institutions, multi-ethnic urban areas, non-indigenous inhabitants, and broad sociocultural trends of the Republic of Ghana (formerly the Gold Coast and British Togoland).

FE2. <u>Colonial Ghana</u>. General data on the geography, demography, and indigenous peoples and cultures, and specific data on the colonial rule, non-indigenous inhabitants, Eurafrican urbanization, and broad sociocultural trends of Ghana during the colonial period.

FE3. <u>Traditional Ghana</u>. General data on the geography, demography, and African peoples and cultures, and specific data on European or other contacts, non-African inhabitants, and broad sociocultural trends of Ghana from the beginning of recorded or oral history up to the onset of colonial rule. For data on Prehistoric Ghana see FE14.

FE4. <u>Dagari</u>. Specific data on the Dagari-speaking Birifor (Lober), Dagaa-Wiili, Dagaba, and LoDagaa, the last comprised of the LoDagaba and the LoWiili.

FE5. <u>Dagomba</u>. Specific data on the Dagomba or Dagbamba tribe, including the related Nanumba.

FE6. <u>Ga</u>. Specific data on the Ga tribe, including the related Adangme.

FE7. <u>Grusi</u>. Specific data on the Grusi (Grunshi)-speaking Awuna (Aculo), Builsa (Kanjaga), Chakalle, Degha (Dyamu, Mo), Isala (Sisala), Kasena, Nunuma, Siti, Tampolense, and Vagala.

FE8. <u>Guang</u>. Specific data on the Gonja (Ngbanya) nation, including the related Atyuti, Bazanche, Brong (Abron), Chimbaro, Chumbuli, Krachi, Kunya, Nawuru, and Nchumuru (Nchumbulung) peoples.

FE9. <u>Mamprusi</u>. Specific data on the Mamprusi tribe.

FE10. <u>Nankanse</u>. Specific data on the Nankanse or Gurensi (Gorensi), plus the kindred Kusasi and Namnam.

FE11. <u>Tallensi</u>. Specific data on the Tallensi people.

FE12. <u>Twi</u>. Specific data on the Twi-speaking peoples, including the Akwapim, Akyem, Asen-Twifo, Ashanti, Fanti, Kwahu, and Wasa. For data on the related Anyi-Baule see FA5, on the Chakossi see FA13.

FE13. Wamole. Specific data on the Mole-speaking Mara, Nome, Safaliba, and Wala.

FE14. Prehistoric Ghana. Specific data on the prehistoric peoples and cultures of Ghana.

Nigeria

FF1. Nigeria. General data on the geography, demography, and indigenous peoples and cultures, and specific data on the national institutions, multi-ethnic urban areas, non-indigenous inhabitants, and broad sociocultural trends of the Federation of Nigeria. For data on the Fulani see MS11, on the Hausa see MS12, and on the Kanuri see MS14.

FF2. Colonial Nigeria. General data on the geography, demography, and indigenous peoples and cultures, and specific data on the colonial rule, non-indigenous inhabitants, Eurafrican urbanization, and broad sociocultural trends of Nigeria during the colonial period.

FF3. Traditional Nigeria. General data on the geography, demography, and African peoples and cultures, and specific data on Arab, European, or other contacts, non-African inhabitants, and broad sociocultural trends of Nigeria from the beginning of recorded or oral history up to the onset of colonial rule. For data on Prehistoric Nigeria see FF66.

FF4. Ada. Specific data on the Ada, including the Abam and Aro, who are a culturally distinctive branch of the Ibo (FF26).

FF5. Afo. Specific data on the Afo tribe.

FF6. Angas. Specific data on the Angas tribe, including the related Ankwe, Bwol, Dimuk, Goram, Gurkha, Kwolla, Miriam, Montoil, Ron (Baron, Boram), and Sura.

FF7. Bachama. Specific data on the Bachama tribe.

FF8. Bassa. Specific data on the Bassa (Basa) tribe, plus the detached Bassa-Komo (Basakomo).

FF9. Birom. Specific data on the Birom (Berom, Borom, Burum, Kibo, Kibyen), included the related Aten (Ganawuri, Jal, Ngell), and Pyem (Paiema).

FF10. Bolewa. Specific data on the Bolewa tribe.

FF11. Bula. Specific data on the Bula (Mbula), including the Bare.

FF12. Bura. Specific data on the Bura nation, including the related Bata (with the Bolki, Bulai, Gudo, Kofa, Malabu, Muleng, Njei, and Zumu), Cheke (with the Jilbu and Mubi), Gabin, Hiji (with the Baza, Kapsiki, and Nkafa), Holma, Hona, Margi (with the Chibak, Kilba, Sukur, Tur, Woga, and Wuba), and Pabir (Babur).

FF13. Busa. Specific data on the Busa people, including the related Boko, Shanga (Shangawa), and Tienga (Kenga, Kengawa).

FF14. Buta. Specific data on the Buta or Butawa, including the Bamberawa.

FF15. Chamba. Specific data on the Chamba tribe, including the Donga, Lekon, Mumbake, and Wom.

FF16. Chawai. Specific data on the Chawai tribe, including the neighboring Irigwe or Aregwa.

FF17. Cross River Tribes. Specific data on the Bete, Boki (Nki), Mbenbe (with the Adun, Igbo, and Oshopong), Ododop (with the Korop and Okoiyong), Orri, Uge, Ukelle, Uyanga, Yache, Yakori, and Yale (Iyala). For data on the Yako see FF60.

FF18. Daka. Specific data on the Daka tribe, including the neighboring Jen, Kam, and Munga.

FF19. Dera. Specific data on the Dera or Kanakura tribe.

FF20. Dumbo. Specific data on the Dumbo or Mbembe tribe, including the Mfumte (Kaka) and Misaje (Metcho).

FF21. Edo. Specific data on the Edo-speaking peoples, including the Edo proper or Bini of the Benin Kingdom, the Ishan, the Northern Edo comprised of the Ivbiosakon, Etsako, Northwest Edo, and Ineme, the Urhobo and Isoko, and on the Yoruba-speaking Itsekiri or Jekri.

FF22. Ekoi. Specific data on the Ekoi nation, embracing the Akaju, Assumbo-Ambele, Ejagham or Ekoi proper, Keaka, Manta, Nde, Nkumm, Obang, and Olulumo.

FF23. Gbari. Specific data on the Gbari or Gwari nation.

FF24. Gwandara. Specific data on the Gwandara tribe, including the Gade.

FF25. Ibibio. Specific data on the Ibibio-speaking people comprised of six main sub-divisions: Eastern or Ibibio Proper, Western or Anang, Northern or Enyong, Southern or Eket, Delta or Andoni-Ibeno, and Riverain or Efik.

FF26. <u>Ibo</u>. Specific data on the Ibo (Igbo) people comprised of five main regional divisions: Northern or Onitsha Ibo, Southern or Owerri Ibo, Western Ibo, Eastern or Cross River Ibo, and Northeastern Ibo (Ogu Uku). For data on the kindred Ada see FF4.

FF27. <u>Idoma</u>. Specific data on the Idoma tribe, including the neighboring Agatu, Aike, and Arago.

FF28. <u>Igala</u>. Specific data on the Igala or Igara tribe.

FF29. <u>Igbira</u>. Specific data on the Igbira tribe, including the related Kakanda (Okanda), Nge (Bassa-Nge), and Okpoto (Kwotto).

FF30. <u>Ijaw</u>. Specific data on the Ijaw or Ijo nation, including the Brass and Kalabari.

FF31. <u>Jarawa</u>. Specific data on the Jarawa group, including the Afusara or Hill Jarawa (with the Anaguta) and the Plains Jarawa (with the Bankalawa and Barawa).

FF32. <u>Jerawa</u>. Specific data on the Jerawa people, including the Amap, Bujawa (Buji), Chara, Chokobo, Jenji, Jengre, Piti, Ribam, Ribanawa, Rukuba, Sangawa, and Taurawa.

FF33. <u>Jukun</u>. Specific data on the Jukun or Korofawa nation, including the related Jibu, Kentu (Kyatu, Nidu), and Kona.

FF34. <u>Kadara</u>. Specific data on the Kadara tribe, including the Ajure, Koro, and Yeskwa (Jesko).

FF35. <u>Kahugu</u>. Specific data on the Kahugu tribe, including the Gure and Sangawa.

FF36. <u>Kamberi</u>. Specific data on the Kamberi nation, including the Baushi, Dakakari, Dukawa, Kamuku, Ngwoi, Pongo, Reshe (Gungawa), and Uru.

FF37. <u>Karekare</u>. Specific data on the Karekare tribe, including the Ngamo (Ganawa).

FF38. <u>Katab</u>. Specific data on the Katab tribe, including the related Araka, Ikulu, Jaba, Kachichere, Kagoma, Kagoro, Kaje, Kamantan and Morwa.

FF39. <u>Kom</u>. Specific data on the Kom (Bekom, Hom), including the adjacent Wum (Aghem).

FF40. <u>Kossi</u>. Specific data on the Kossi (Bakosi, Nkossi), including the related Bo (Abo), Elong, Fo (Bafo), Long (Balung), Mbo, and Sossi (Basossi).

FF41. Kundu. Specific data on the Kundu (Bakundu), including the related Baji, Efu, Issangili, Kogo, Kole, Kombe, Lue (Balue), Lundu (Barondo), Mbonge (Barombi), Ngolo, and northern Tanga (Batanga).

FF42. Kurama. Specific data on the Kurama tribe, including the Jangi.

FF43. Kwiri. Specific data on the Kwiri (Bakwele, Bakwili), plus the Mboke (Bamboko) and the Kpe.

FF44. Longuda. Specific data on the Longuda or Nungula tribe.

FF45. Mada. Specific data on the Mada tribe, including the adjacent Ayu, Kaleri, Mama, Ninzam, Numana, and Nungu (Lungu).

FF46. Maguza. Specific data on the ill-described group of pagan or incompletely Islamized Chad-Hamite tribes of the Bauchi region, notably the Afawa, Denawa, Galambawa, Gerawa, Gerumawa, Kudawa, Maguzawa, Ningawa, Rumada, and Warjawa.

FF47. Mandara. Specific data on the Mandara or Wandala nation, including the kindred Gamergu.

FF48. Mumuye. Specific data on the Mumuye tribe, including the related Gengle, Gola, Kugama, Kumba, Teme, Vere, Waka, Yendang, and Yofo.

FF49. Ndoro. Specific data on the Ndoro tribe.

FF50. Ngizim. Specific data on the Ngizim nation, including the related Bede and Shirawa.

FF51. Nsaw. Specific data on the Nsaw (Banso) people, plus the related or neighboring Bum, Fumbum (Bafumbum, Fungom), Fut (Bafut), Gam (Bagam, Eghap), Li (Bali, Bani), Mum (Bamum), Ndob (Mburikem), Ntem, and Nsungli (Dzungle, Njungene), including the Tang, War, and Wiya.

FF52. Nupe. Specific data on the Nupe nation, including the related Dibo (Ganagana).

FF53. Nyangi. Specific data on the Nyangi or Banyangi, plus the adjacent Anyang (Banyang).

FF54. Tangale. Specific data on the Tangale tribe, including the related Tula and Waja.

FF55. Tera. Specific data on the Tera tribe, including the related Hina and Jera.

FF56. <u>Tigong</u>. Specific data on the Tigong (Tigon, Tukum), plus the Ashaku and Nama.

FF57. <u>Tiv</u>. Specific data on the Tiv or Munshi nation.

FF58. <u>Widekum</u>. Specific data on the Widekum, including the Beba, Befang, Esimbi, Menka, Meta, Mogamaw, Ngemba, Ngie, and Ngwo.

FF59. <u>Wurkum</u>. Specific data on the Wurkum or Urku tribe, including the Bandawa, Kulu, and Walo.

FF60. <u>Yako</u>. Specific data on the Yako (Akunakuna, Ekuri) tribe. For data on other Cross River tribes see FF17.

FF61. <u>Yergum</u>. Specific data on the Yergum tribe, including the Dollong, Sayir, and Tarok and tentatively also the Bashera, Burrum (Boghorom, Borrom), and Seiyawa.

FF62. <u>Yoruba</u>. Specific data on the Yoruba people divided into over fifty king doms, but comprising seven principal groups: the Egba, Ekiti, Ife, Ijebu, Kabba, Ondo, and Oyo. For data on the Atakpame see FA6, on the Igala see FF28, on the Itsekiri or Jekri see FF21.

FF63. <u>Yukutare</u>. Specific data on the Yukutare (Bitare, Zuande) people, plus the Batu.

FF64. <u>Yungur</u>. Specific data on the Yungur or Binna tribe, including the Banga, Handa, Lala, Libo, and Mboi.

FF65. <u>Zumper</u>. Specific data on the Zumper (Djompra, Mbarike) tribe.

FF66. <u>Prehistoric Nigeria</u>. Specific data on the prehistoric peoples and cultures of Nigeria.

Equatorial Guinea

FG1. <u>Equatorial Guinea</u>. General data on the geography, demography, and indigenous peoples and cultures, and specific data on the national institutions, multi-ethnic urban areas, non-indigenous inhabitants, and broad sociocultural trends of the Republic of Equatorial Guinea (formerly the Spanish colonies of Fernando Po and Rio Muni).

FG2. <u>Colonial Equatorial Guinea</u>. General data on the geography, demography, and indigenous peoples and cultures, and specific data on the colonial rule, non-indigenous inhabitants, Eurafrican urbanization, and broad sociocultural trends of Equatorial Guinea during the colonial period.

FG3. <u>Bubi</u>. Specific data on the indigenous Bubi or Ediye people of the island of Fernando Po. For specific data on the indigenous peoples of the Rio Muni area see FH5, FH9, and FI26.

FG4. <u>Traditional Equatorial Guinea</u>. General data on the geography, demography, and African peoples and cultures, and specific data on European or other contacts, non-African inhabitants, and broad sociocultural trends of Equatorial Guinea from the beginning of recorded or oral history up to the onset of colonial rule.

FG5. <u>Prehistoric Fernando Po</u>. Specific data on the prehistoric peoples and cultures of the island of Fernando Po. For data on the prehistoric period of the Rio Muni area see FH25.

Cameroon

FH1. <u>Cameroon</u>. General data on the geography, demography, and indigenous peoples and cultures, and specific data on the national institutions, multi-ethnic urban areas, non-indigenous inhabitants, and broad sociocultural trends of the Federal Republic of Cameroon (formerly French Cameroun and British Southern Cameroons). For data on the Baya see FI9, on the Fulani see MS11, on the Gam and Mum see FF51, on the Puku see FI26, on the Shuwa see MS9.

FH2. <u>Colonial Cameroon</u>. General data on the geography, demography, and indigenous peoples and cultures, and specific data on the colonial rule under the Germans, French, and British, non-indigenous inhabitants, Eurafrican urbanization, and broad sociocultural trends of Cameroon during the colonial period.

FH3. <u>Traditional Cameroon</u>. General data on the geography, demography, and African peoples and cultures, and specific data on European or other contacts, non-African inhabitants, and broad sociocultural trends of Cameroon from the beginning of recorded or oral history up to the onset of German colonial rule. For data on Prehistoric Cameroon see FH25.

FH4. <u>Cameroon Pygmies</u>. General and specific data on the Babinga, Bakielle (Bagielle), and other Pygmies of Cameroon. For data on the Pygmies of central Africa in general see FO4.

FH5. <u>Bea</u>. Specific data on the Bea (Bujeba, Ibea, Mabea), including the kindred Ngumba (Mvumba).

FH6. <u>Dari</u>. Specific data on the Dari tribe, including the neighboring Dama, Kali, Lame, and Mono.

FH7. <u>Duala</u>. Specific data on the Duala (Diwala) nation, including the Bodiman, Bonangando, Bonkeng, Dibombari, Kumbe (Ewuni), Lemba (Malimba), Marais, Mungo, Pongo, Subu (Bimbia, Isuwu), and Wuri (Buli, Eyarra, Oli).

FH8. <u>Fali</u>. Specific data on the true Fali tribes, i.e., the Broi, Kangu, Peske, and Tinguelin.

FH9. <u>Fang</u>. Specific data on the Fang (Fan, Mpangwe, Pahuin) nation, embracing the Bene, Betsi, Boale, Bulu, Eton (Toni), Mekei, Mokuk, Mwei, Mwelle, Ntum, Okak, Syeba (Osieba), and Yaunde tribes.

FH10. <u>Fia</u>. Specific data on the Fia (Bafia, Bapea, Begbak) tribe, including the neighboring Balom, Banen (Banend, Banyin, Ndiki, Penin), Bati, Njabeta, Njanti, Omand (Omeng), Ponend (Ponek), and Yambassa.

FH11. <u>Kaka</u>. Specific data on the Kaka (Kadei) tribe, including the Bakum and Besimbo.

FH12. <u>Koko</u>. Specific data on the Koko (Bakoko, Betjek, Mwelle) tribe, including the neighboring Bassa, Bimbi (Babimbi), and Ndogobessol.

FH13. <u>Kotoko</u>. Specific data on the Kotoko (Logon, Makari) nation, including the kindred Ngala.

FH14. <u>Mambila</u>. Specific data on the Mambila nation, including the Abo, Galim, Kamkam, Magu, Ndoren, Suga, and Wawa tribes.

FH15. <u>Matakam</u>. Specific data on the Matakam tribe, including the related Balda, Daba, Gauar, Gidder, Gisiga, Muffo, Musugoi, and Podokwo (Podogo, Mukulehe).

FH16. <u>Mbum</u>. Specific data on the Mbum (Bum) tribe, including the kindred Kare (Tali), Kepere (Byrre, Pere, Ripere), and Mbere.

FH17. <u>Musgu</u>. Specific data on the Musgu or Musuk tribe.

FH18. <u>Namshi</u>. Specific data on the Namshi tribe, including the related Duru, Kolbila, Kotopo (Kotofo), Kutin, Pape, Sari, Sewe, and Woko.

FH19. <u>Bamileke</u>. Specific data on the Bamileke, including the Ngangte (Bangangte, Ngoteng) tribe, and the adjacent Balung, Bamendzo, Bana, Bandem, Bangu, Banju, Bangwa, Basu, Batcham, Batongtu, Dibum, Fondang (Jang), Mbang, and Njokon.

FH20. <u>Njem</u>. Specific data on the Njem (Dzem) tribe, including the kindred Kwele (Bakwele, Bakwili), Maka (Makie), and Ndsime (Mendsime).

FH21. Nzimu. Specific data on the Nzimu tribe, including the related Badjue, Besom (Jerma, Jasua, Minyombo), Biakum (Bjakuk), Bidjuk, Bomam (Bomome), Bumbon (Mbumbung), Gundi (Bagunda), Kunabemba, Lissel (Essel), and Mbimu. For data on the kindred Sanga see FI27.

FH22. Tikar. Specific data on the Tikar or Ndomme tribe.

FH23. Tuburi. Specific data on the Tuburi nation, including the Gane (Banana) and Walia tribes.

FH24. Wute. Specific data on the Wute (Bafute, Bute, Mfute) nations.

FH25. Prehistoric Cameroon. Specific data on the prehistoric peoples and cultures of Cameroon and the Rio Muni area.

French-speaking Equatorial Africa

FI1. French-speaking Equatorial Africa. General data on the history, geography, demography, non-indigenous inhabitants, economy, and politics of French-speaking Equatorial Africa, either exclusive or inclusive of the Muslim zone in the north, and specific data on the government of the former Federation of French Equatorial Africa. For data on the specific countries of the Central African Republic, Congo-Brazzaville, and Gabon see FI35-FI46. For data on the specific country of Chad see MS33.

FI2. Equatorial African Peoples. General data on the indigenous peoples and cultures of French-speaking Equatorial Africa, either exclusive or inclusive of the Muslim zone in the north, from the beginning of recorded or oral history, including their ethnic and culture history, and changes related to Arab, European, or other contacts. For data specifically on the peoples of the Sahara and the adjacent Muslim fringe of the Sudan see MS1, for data on the Azande see FO7, on the Bagirmi see MS4, on the Fang see FH9, on the Shuwa see MS9, on the Sundi see FO21, on the Yombe see FO50.

FI3. Prehistoric Equatorial Africa. General data on the prehistoric peoples and cultures of French-speaking Equatorial Africa.

FI4. Equatorial African Pygmies. General and specific data on the Babi, Babinga, and other Pygmies of French-speaking Equatorial Africa. For data on the Pygmies of central Africa in general see FO4.

FI5. Bana. Specific data on the Bana tribe, including the related Kim, Marba, and Mussoi.

FI6. Banda. Specific data on the Banda nation, including the isolated Banza (Mbandja), Gobu, and Yangere (Yangeli) tribes.

FI7.   Bangi. Specific data on the Bangi (Abango, Babangi, Bobangi, Bubangi) tribe, including the related Boshi (Babochi, Mboshi), Furu (Apfuru, Bafuru), Irebu, Kuyu, Likuba, Loi (Baloi, Balui), Makua, Mboko (Mampoko), and Ngiri (Bangili).

FI8.   Banziri. Specific data on the Banziri or Gbanziri tribe, including the related Buraka, Dendi, Sango (Sahanga), and Yakoma.

FI9.   Baya. Specific data on the Baya or Gbaya nation, including the isolated Bofi, Bogoto, Ikasa, and Ngandu (Bumbe) tribes.

FI10.   Bua. Specific data on the Bua tribe, including the neighboring Fanyan (Fagnia), Koke, Nielim (Nyilem), and Tunia.

FI11.   Bwaka. Specific data on the Bwaka or Mbaka tribe, including the related Bondjo (Bandjo, Mbondjo) and Mondjembo.

FI12.   Duma. Specific data on the Duma (Aduma, Baduma, Maduma, Ndumu) tribe, including the related Bamba (Ambamba, Bambamba, Obamba), Changi (Batchangui), Kanike (Bakinike), Mbete (Ambete, Bambete, Umbete), Ndumbo (Andumbo, Bandumbo, Mindumbo), and Njawi (Banjabi).

FI13.   Gula. Specific data on the Gula tribe, including the related Homr (Mamun, Mogum), Kudia, Mali, Mufa, and Mulfa.

FI14.   Kalai. Specific data on the Kalai (Akalai, Akelle, Bakale, Bakelle, Bangomo, Bembance, Ingwesse, Kalay, Kele, Mbwe) tribe, including the detached Bangwe, Basisiu (Mochebo), and Ongom (Ongono).

FI15.   Kara. Specific data on the Kara tribe, including the Binga and Yulu.

FI16.   Kenga. Specific data on the Kenga or Kenya tribe, including the Babalia, Diongor, Masmadje, and Saba.

FI17.   Kota. Specific data on the Kota or Bakota nation, including the Buchamai, Chake (Bachake), Damboma, Hungwe (Mahoungoue), Kiba (Bokiba), Mbao (Bambao), Ndasa (Bandassa, Mindassa), Ndomo (Bandomo), Nghie (Banguie), Njambi (Bandjambi), and Pu (Bapou) tribes.

FI18.   Lakka. Specific data on the Lakka (Laka, Tolakka) tribe.

FI19.   Lumbo. Specific data on the Lumbo (Balumbo) tribe, including the related Bwisi (Babouisse), Ngove (Bangove), Rama (Barama, Varama), Shango (Ashango, Machango), Shira (Echira), Vungo (Bavungo), and Yaka (Bayaka).

FI20.   Mandjia. Specific data on the Mandjia (Mandja) people.

FI21. <u>Masa</u>. Specific data on the Masa tribe, including the adjacent Busso and Kung (Kuang).

FI22. <u>Mitaba</u>. Specific data on the Mitaba or Bomitaba tribe, with whom are tentatively grouped the Bangandu (Lobaje), Boka (Bokaka), Bonga, Bongili (Bongiri), Bota, Buno, Issungo, Ngundi, and Yakinga.

FI23. <u>Mpongwe</u>. Specific data on the Mpongwe (Bayugu, Pongo) tribe, including the related Galoa (Igulua, Ngaloi), Ininga (Enenga), Jumba (Adjumba), Nkomi (Camma), and Rungu (Orungu). The Mpongwe are not to be confused with the Mpangwe or Fang (FH9).

FI24. <u>Mundang</u>. Specific data on the Mundang or Moundan tribe, including the related Kiziere, Mangbei, and Yassing (Imbana, Zazing).

FI25. <u>Nzakara</u>. Specific data on the Nzakara tribe. For data on the kindred Azande see F07.

FI26. <u>Puku</u>. Specific data on the Puku (Bapuko, Buku) tribe, including the related Benga (Mabenga), Kumbe (Ewumi, Kombe, Ngumbi), Lengi (Balenge, Molingi), Noko (Banaka, Banoho), Nyong, and southern Tanga (Batanga).

FI27. <u>Sanga</u>. Specific data on the Sanga (Basanga, Bosanga, Missanga) nation, including the Bumali (Bomali), Lino, and Pomo. For data on the kindred Nzimu see FH21.

FI28. <u>Sara</u>. Specific data on the Sara nation, including the Dakpa, Daya, Dindje, Gulai, Joko, Kaba, Leto (Luto, Ruton), Mbai (Bai), Ndara, Ndemi, Nduka (Tane), Ngama, Tele, Tie, and Udio tribes.

FI29. <u>Seke</u>. Specific data on the Seke (Basheke, Museki, Sekiani, Shake) tribe.

FI30. <u>Shogo</u>. Specific data on the Shogo (Ashogo, Ishogo, Mitsogo) tribe, including the related Kanda (Okanda), Pubi (Bapubi, Pove), Puno (Apingi, Apono, Bapindji, Bapuni) and Simba (Asimba).

FI31. <u>Sokoro</u>. Specific data on the Sokoro or Bedanga tribe, including the Barein and Yalna.

FI32. <u>Somrai</u>. Specific data on the Somrai tribe, including the Chiri (Shere), Deressia, Dormo, Gaberi (Ngabre), Kabalai, Lele, Mesme, Miltu, Modgel, Nangire, Ndam, Sarwa, and Tumak.

FI33. <u>Teke</u>. Specific data on the Teke or Bateke nation, including the Mfumungu (Bamfumu, Bamfunuka, Banbunu, Banfungunu, Fumu, Mbunu, Wamfumu), Shikuya (Achikuya), Tegwe (Bategue), Tsaya (Mutsaya), Ngangulu (Bangangulu), Nunu (Banunu), and Wumbu.

FI34. Vili. Specific data on the Vili (Bafiote, Bavili, Fjort, Loango, Mfioti) nation.

FI35. Central African Republic. General data on the geography, demography, and indigenous peoples and cultures, and specific data on the national institutions, multi-ethnic urban areas, non-indigenous inhabitants, and broad sociocultural trends of the Central African Republic (Republique Centrafricaine, formerly Ubangi-Shari).

FI36. Colonial Central African Republic. General data on the geography, demography, and indigenous peoples and cultures, and specific data on the colonial rule, non-indigenous inhabitants, Eurafrican urbanization, and broad sociocultural trends of the Central African Republic during the colonial period.

FI37. Traditional Central African Republic. General data on the geography, demography, and African peoples and cultures, and specific data on European or other contacts, non-African inhabitants, and broad sociocultural trends of the Central African Republic from the beginning of recorded or oral history up to the onset of colonial rule.

FI38. Prehistoric Central African Republic. Specific data on the prehistoric peoples and cultures of the Central African Republic.

FI39. Congo-Brazzaville. General data on the geography, demography, and indigenous peoples and cultures, and specific data on the national institutions, multi-ethnic urban areas, non-indigenous inhabitants, and broad sociocultural trends of the People's Republic of the Congo (formerly Middle Congo or Moyen Congo).

FI40. Colonial Congo-Brazzaville. General data on the geography, demography, and indigenous peoples and cultures, and specific data on the colonial rule, non-indigenous inhabitants, Eurafrican urbanization, and broad sociocultural trends of Congo-Brazzaville during the colonial period.

FI41. Traditional Congo-Brazzaville. General data on the geography, demography, and African peoples and cultures, and specific data on European or other contacts, non-African inhabitants, and broad sociocultural trends of Congo-Brazzaville from the beginning of recorded or oral history up to the onset of colonial rule.

FI42. Prehistoric Congo-Brazzaville. Specific data on the prehistoric peoples and cultures of Congo-Brazzaville.

FI43. Gabon. General data on the geography, demography, and indigenous peoples and cultures, and specific data on the national institutions, multi-ethnic urban areas, non-indigenous inhabitants, and broad sociocultural trends of the Gabon Republic.

FI44. Colonial Gabon. General data on the geography, demography, and indi-
       genous peoples and cultures, and specific data on the colonial rule,
       non-indigenous inhabitants, Eurafrican urbanization, and broad
       sociocultural trends of Gabon during the colonial period.

FI45. Traditional Gabon. General data on the geography, demography, and
       African peoples and cultures, and specific data on European or
       other contacts, non-African inhabitants, and broad sociocultural
       trends of Gabon from the beginning of recorded or oral history up
       to the onset of colonial rule.

FI46. Prehistoric Gabon. Specific data on the prehistoric peoples and cultures
       of Gabon.

Nilotic Sudan

FJ1.   Nilotic Sudan. General data on the geography, demography, and indi-
       genous peoples and cultures, and specific data on the non-indigenous
       inhabitants, multi-ethnic urban areas, modern economy and local
       government, relations between the indigenous population and the
       national government, and broad sociocultural trends of the southern
       or non-Muslim portion of the Republic of Sudan (formerly Anglo-
       Eyptian Sudan) since 1956. For data on the northern portion or on
       the country as a whole see MQ1.

FJ2.   Nilotes. General data on the Nilotic peoples as a whole, including the
       effects of Arab, European, or other contacts. For data on the
       Azande see FO7, on the Babukur see FO33.

FJ3.   Historical Nilotic Sudan. General data on the geography, demography,
       and African peoples and cultures, and specific data on Arab, Euro-
       pean, or other contacts, colonial rule, non-indigenous inhabitants,
       and broad sociocultural trends of the Nilotic Sudan from the be-
       ginning of recorded or oral history up to 1956. For data on Prehis-
       toric Nilotic Sudan see FJ26.

FJ4.   Anuak. Specific data on the Anuak or Yambo nation, including the
       detached Beri (Bori, Fori, Pari).

FJ5.   Bari. Specific data on the Bari nation, including the related Fajulu
       (Fagdelu, Pojulu), Kakwa (Kakuak), Kuku, Ligi, Mondari (Mundar),
       and Nyangbara.

FJ6.   Beir. Specific data on the Beir (Ajiba, Marule, Murle) nation, including
       the Boma (Ekeita, Kapeta) and Pibor.

FJ7. Berta. Specific data on the Berta (Shangalla), including the related Fazoglo, Fung, Gamilla, Kele, Malkan, Sillok, and Tornasi, constituting the independent Bertan linguistic stock.

FJ8. Bongo. Specific data on the Bongo or Dor tribe.

FJ9. Burun. Specific data on the Burun nation, embracing the northern Burun, Jumjum, Meban (Gura, Maban), and Ulu tribes.

FJ10. Didinga. Specific data on the Didinga (Birra, Karoko, Toi) tribe, including the kindred Boya, Longarim, Nikoroma, and Terna.

FJ11. Dilling. Specific data on the northern Nuba tribes, speaking Nubian East Sudanic languages, i.e., the Nyima or Nyamang group (with the Afitti) and the Dilling group consisting of the Abu Garein, Abu Gunuk, Abu Seida, Bobai, Boska, Dair (except Afitti), Debri, Dulman, Fanda, Gulfan, Kabila, Kadero (Kodoro), Kasha, Kubja, Moron, Nyetto, Serva, Shanshan, Shifr, Shilma, Tabak, Turon, and Wali. For data on the Kordofanian-speaking Nuba see FJ21.

FJ12. Dinka. Specific data on the Dinka (Denkawi, Jang) nation, embracing the Agar, Aliab, Atwot, Bor, Cic, Mong, Padang, Thang, and Tur sub-tribes.

FJ13. Ingassana. Specific data on the Ingassana or Tabi tribe.

FJ14. Jur. Specific data on the Jur (Dyur, Gur, Jo-Luo, Lwo) tribe, including the kindred Bor (Baer, Behr, Mberidi, Mverodi), Dembo (Bodho), Fujiga, Kamum, Manageir, Shatt (Cat, Thuri), and Shilluk-Luo.

FJ15. Koma. Specific data on the Koma (Komo) tribe, including the related but not contiguous Aman, Ganza, Gule, Gumus (with Naga), Gwana, Kogo, and Udok, constituting the independent Koman linguistic stock.

FJ16. Krech. Specific data on the Krech (Kreish, Kredi) tribe, including the Ada, Baia (Gbaya), Mere, Woro, and Yomamgba.

FJ17. Lotuko. Specific data on the Lotuko (Latuka) tribe, including the related Koriuk, Lafit (Lopit), Lango (with the Dongotono, Logir, and Bira), and Lokoiya (Leria, Oghoriok).

FJ18. Mittu. Specific data on the Mittu tribe, including the related Baka (Abaka), Beli, Biti, Lori (with the Nyamusa), Moru Kodo, Moru Wadi, Sofi, and Wira.

FJ19. Moru. Specific data on the Moru nation, embracing the Avukaya (with the Yei), Kederu, Moru Misa (Moru proper), Ondri (with the Boliba), and Uggi (Ogi). For data on the Moru Kodo and Moru Wadi see FJ18.

FJ20. Ndogo. Specific data on the Ndogo (Ndugo) tribe, including the related Bai (Bari), Balembo, Biri (Bviri, Gamba, Mbegumba), Golo, Kare (Akale), Pambia, and Sere (Abire, Basiri, Chere, Sheri).

FJ21. Nuba. Specific data on the tribes of the Nuba Hills which speak languages of the Kordofanian stock, namely, the Katla (with the Gulud and Tima), Koalib (Kawalib), Korongo (with the Kadugli, Miri, and Tumtum), Moro, Nyaro (with the Fungor, Kao, and Werni), Otoro (with the Abol, Heiban, and Laro), Tagali (with the Kajaja, Moreb, Rashad, Tagoy, Tumeli, and Tumuk), Talodi (with the El Amira, Lafofa, Lumun, and Mesakin), Tira (with the Lumon and Tiramandi), and Tulishi (Tullishi). For data on Nuba tribes of other languages see FJ11 and FJ24.

FJ22. Nuer. Specific data on the Nuer nation.

FJ23. Shilluk. Specific data on the Shilluk nation.

FJ24. Temein. Specific data on the Temein, including the inhabitants of Keiga Girru and Teis-um-Danab, constituting the apparently independent Temainian linguistic stock.

FJ25. Topotha. Specific data on the Topotha or Dabosa tribe, plus the related Donyiro (Buni, Indongiro, Ignahatom, Nyangatom, Orogniro), Jiye, and Magoth (Magois), as well as the as yet linguistically unclassified Napore, Nyakwai, Nyangeya, Tepeth (Tepes), and Teuso (Teuth, Wanderobo).

FJ26. Prehistoric Nilotic Sudan. Specific data on the prehistoric peoples and cultures of the Nilotic Sudan.

Uganda

FK1. Uganda. General data on the geography, demography, and indigenous peoples and cultures, including data on the Interlacustrine Bantu as a group, and specific data on the national institutions, multi-ethnic urban areas, non-indigenous inhabitants, and broad sociocultural trends of the Republic of Uganda.

FK2. Colonial Uganda. General data on the geography, demography, and indigenous peoples and cultures, and specific data on the colonial rule, non-indigenous inhabitants, Eurafrican urbanization, and broad sociocultural trends of Uganda during the colonial period.

FK3. Traditional Uganda. General data on the geography, demography, and African peoples and cultures, and specific data on Arab, European, or other contacts, non-African inhabitants, and broad sociocultural trends of Uganda from the beginning of recorded or oral history up to the onset of colonial rule. For data on Prehistoric Uganda see FK14.

FK4. Acholi. Specific data on the Acholi (Gan, Shuli), including the related
    Labwor.

FK5. Alur. Specific data on the Alur or Luri tribe.

FK6. Chiga. Specific data on the Chiga (Bakyiga, Kiga) tribe.

FK7. Ganda. Specific data on the Ganda (Baganda, Waganda) nation, in-
    cluding the related Soga (with the Gwere, Kenyi, Nyuli, and Tama).

FK8. Karamojong. Specific data on the peoples of the Karamojong Cluster,
    including the Dodoth (Dodoso), Jie (Ajie, Egye, Gye, Jibbeh, Jiwe,
    Jiye, Kum, Negye, Ngiye, Njie), and Karimojong (Karamojong).
    For data on the component Turkana see FL17.

FK9. Lango. Specific data on the Lango or Umiro nation, who should not
    be confused with the Lango tribe of the Lotuko (FJ17).

FK10. Madi. Specific data on the Madi tribe, including the related Lokoi,
    Luluba, and Pandikeri.

FK11. Nyoro. Specific data on the Nyoro (Banyoro) nation, embracing the
    Horohoro (Waporoporo), Kitara (Nyoro proper), Nyankole
    (Banyankole), and Toro (Batoro) tribes.

FK12. Teso. Specific data on the Teso (Bateso, Iteso, Kedi) people, plus the
    kindred Itesyo (Elgumi, Wamia) and Kumam (Akum, Ikokolemu).

FK13. Gisu. Specific data on the Gisu (Bagesu, Bagishu, Bagisu, Geshu,
    Gesu, Gishu, Masaba, Sokwia) people.

FK14. Lugbara. Specific data on the Lugbara (Logbwari, Lubare, Lugbara,
    Lugbwara, Lugori, Lugwari) people of Uganda and the Congo.
    For data on the linguistically related Kaliko, Logo, and Madi see
    FO26, FK12. For data on the culturally similar Kakwa and Kuku
    see FJ5.

FK15. Prehistoric Uganda. Specific data on the prehistoric peoples and cul-
    tures of Uganda.

Kenya

FL1. Kenya. General data on the geography, demography, and indigenous
    peoples and cultures, and specific data on the national institutions,
    multi-ethnic urban areas, non-indigenous inhabitants, and broad
    sociocultural trends of the Republic of Kenya.

FL2. <u>Colonial Kenya</u>. General data on the geography, demography, and indigenous peoples and cultures, and specific data on the colonial rule, non-indigenous inhabitants, Eurafrican urbanization, and broad sociocultural trends of Kenya during the colonial period.

FL3. <u>Traditional Kenya</u>. General data on the geography, demography, and African peoples and cultures, and specific data on Arab, European, or other contacts, non-African inhabitants, and broad sociocultural trends of Kenya from the beginning of recorded or oral history up to the onset of colonial rule. For data on Prehistoric Kenya see FL18.

FL4. <u>Luhya</u>. Specific data on the Luhya (Abaluhya, Bantu Kavirondo) tribes, including the Bakusu, Gwe, Kabras (Nyala), Kakalelelwa, Kakamega (Isukha, Idakho), Khayo (Hayo, Khavi, Xayo), Kisa, Marachi (Mrashi), Maragoli (Logoli, Lokoli, Walako), Marama (Malama), Nyala, Nyole, Samia, Tachoni (Tadjoni, Tasoni), Tiriki, Tsotso, Vugusu (Kitosh), and Wanga (Bahanga, Hanga, Wawanga).

FL5. <u>Chuka</u>. Specific data on the Chuka (Suka) tribe, including the neighboring Emberre, Embu, Igoshi, Mweru (Meru), Mwimbe (Amwimbe), and Tharaka (Atharaka).

FL6. <u>Dorobo</u>. Specific data on the scattered hunting tribes of the Dorobo (Andorobo, Asa, Ndorobo, Okiek, Wandorobbo).

FL7. <u>Galla</u>. Specific data on the pagan lowland tribes of the Galla nation, comprising the Bararetta (Baole, Kobaba, Wajote, Wardai), Boran or Borana (with the Arusha), Rendile, Reshiat (Dathanaich, Galab, Geleba, Marille, Marle Rusia), and Sanye (Sania, Wassania). The Arbore and Aro are tentatively classed with the Reshiat. For data on the Galla tribes of Ethiopia see MN10, MP13, MP15, MP17, MP18, MP23, and MP25.

FL8. <u>Gusii</u>. Specific data on the Gusii (Gizii, Kisii, Kosova) tribe, including the related Kulya (Bakulia, Bulia, Kuria, Tende) and Suba or Soba (with the Simbiti and Sweta).

FL9. <u>Kamba</u>. Specific data on the Kamba (Akamba, Wakamba) nation.

FL10. <u>Kikuyu</u>. Specific data on the Kikuyu (Akikuyu, Gikuyu, Wakikuyu) people.

FL11. <u>Luo</u>. Specific data on the Luo (Jaluo, Nilotic Kavirondo, Nyifwa), including the related but detached Gaya (Girange, Wageia) and Jopadhola (Dama).

FL12. <u>Masai</u>. Specific data on the Masai nation, including the related Kwafi (with the Arusha and Humba) and Samburu or Burkeneji (with the Elburgu, Elmolo, Laikipiak, Mogogodo, and Njamus).

FL13. <u>Nandi</u>. Specific data on the Nandi people, plus the related Endo (Chebleng, Ndo), Kamasya (Kamasia, Tugen, Tuken), Keyu (Elgeyu), Kipsigis (Lumbwa, Sikisi), Kony (Elgonyi), Marakwet, Pok (Lako, Walako), Sabei (Sapei, Sebei, with the Bambe), Suk (Bawgott, Pokot), and Terik (Nyangori).

FL14. <u>Nika</u>. Specific data on the Nika (Mijikenda, Nyika, Wanyika) nation, embracing the Digo (Wadigo), Duruma (Durumba, Waduruma), Giryama (Giriama, Wagiliama), and Rabai (with the Chonyi, Jibana, Kambe, Kauma, and Ribe).

FL15. <u>Pokomo</u>. Specific data on the Pokomo (Wapokomo) tribe.

FL16. <u>Teita</u>. Specific data on the Teita (Taita, Wataita) people, and the Taveta (Wataveta).

FL17. <u>Turkana</u>. Specific data on the Turkana or Elgume people. For data on the other peoples of the Karamojong Cluster see FK8.

Zanzibar

FM1. <u>Zanzibar</u>. General data on the geography, demography, and indigenous peoples and cultures, and specific data on the non-indigenous inhabitants, multi-ethnic urban areas, modern economy and local government, and broad sociocultural trends of the islands of Zanzibar and Pemba since independence from British colonial rule in 1963. For data on the national aspects of Zanzibar as part of the Republic of Tanzania see FN30.

FM2. <u>Swahili</u>. General data on the Swahili or Shirazi, the Arabized inhabitants of Zanzibar and certain coastal sections of the adjacent mainland, and specific data on their component tribes, e.g., the Hadimu, Rufiji, and Segeju.

FM3. <u>Historical Zanzibar</u>. General data on the geography, demography, and African peoples and cultures, and specific data on Arab, European, or other contacts, non-African inhabitants, Portuguese, Arab, and British rule, and broad sociocultural trends of the islands of Zanzibar and Pemba from the beginning of recorded or oral history up to 1963.

FM4. <u>Prehistoric Zanzibar</u>. Specific data on the prehistoric peoples and cultures of the islands of Zanzibar and Pemba.

FN1. Tanganyika. General data on the geography, demography, and indi-
        genous peoples and cultures, and specific data on the non-indigenous
        inhabitants, multi-ethnic urban areas, modern economy and local
        government, and broad sociocultural trends of Tanganyika since
        independence from British colonial rule in 1961. For data on the
        national aspects of Tanganyika as part of the Republic of Tanzania
        see FN30. For data on the Ha and Vinza see FO42, on the Mambwe
        see FQ5, on the Masai see FL12, on the Swahili see FM2.

FN2. Colonial Tanganyika. General data on the geography, demography, and
        indigenous peoples and cultures, and specific data on the colonial
        rule under the Germans and British, non-indigenous inhabitants,
        Eurafrican urbanization, and broad sociocultural trends of Tanganyika
        during the colonial period.

FN3. Traditional Tanganyika. General data on the geography, demography,
        and African peoples and cultures, and specific data on Arab, Euro-
        pean, or other contacts, non-African inhabitants, and broad socio-
        cultural trends of Tanganyika from the beginning of recorded or
        oral history up to the onset of German colonial rule. For data on
        Prehistoric Tanganyika see FN29.

FN4. Chagga. Specific data on the Chagga (Wadschagga) nation, including
        the related Meru and Pare (Asu, Wapare).

FN5. Fiome. Specific data on the Fiome group, embracing the Burunge
        (Burungi, Mbulunge), Goroa (Gorowa, Fiome proper), Iraqw
        (Erokh, Iraku, Mbulu, Wambulu), Ngomwia (Wangomwia), and
        Wasi (Alawa) tribes.

FN6. Fipa. Specific data on the Fipa (Wafipa) tribe, including the kindred
        Pimbwe and Rungwa.

FN7. Gogo. Specific data on the Gogo or Wagogo nation.

FN8. Haya. Specific data on the Haya (Basiba, Heia, Kiziba, Wahaya,
        Wassiba, Ziba) nation, including the kindred Zinza (Sinja,
        Wassindja).

FN9. Hehe. Specific data on the Hehe (Wahehe) tribe, including the kindred
        Bena (Wabena), Sangu (Rori), Sowe (Wasove), and Zungwa (Chungwe).

FN10. Kerewe. Specific data on the Kerewe (Bakerewe, Wakerewe) tribe,
        including the Kara (Wakarra) of the adjacent island of Ukara.

FN11. Kindiga. Specific data on the Kindiga (Hadzapi, Hatsa, Kangeju, Tindiga,
        Watindega) tribe.

FN12. Kinga. Specific data on the Kinga tribe, including the adjacent Kisi, Mahasi, Mwelya, Pangwa, Sandia, and Wanji.

FN13. Makonde. Specific data on the Makonde (Wamakonde) nation, including the related Chobo, Kiturika, Matambwe, Matumbi (the Kilwa tribe of this name), Mwera (Wamuera), Ndonde (Wandonde), and Ngindo (Wangindo).

FN14. Matengo. Specific data on the Matengo tribe, including the related Nindi (Manundi, Ndendehule, Gutu) and the acculturated remnants of the Ngoni invaders of the nineteenth century, who are variously called Machonde, Mafiti, Magwangara, Mazitu, and Watutu. For data on the Ngoni of Malawi see FR5.

FN15. Mbugu. Specific data on the Mbugu (Wambugu), an isolated Cushitic tribe resident among the Pare (FN4).

FN16. Mbugwe. Specific data on the Mbugwe (Wambugwe), including the related Rangi (Irangi, Langi, Warangi).

FN17. Ngonde. Specific data on the Ngondė (Konde, Wangonde) nation, including the related Kukwe, Lugulu, Mwariba, Nyakyusa (Sokile), Saku, and Selya (Seria).

FN18. Nyamwezi. Specific data on the Nyamwezi (Banyamwezi, Wanyamwezi) nation, embracing the Bende (Vende, Wabende), Gala, Galaganza, Irwana (Bilwana), Kimbu, Konongo, Nankwila, Sukuma (Basukuma, Wassukuma), Sumbwa, and Tongwe tribes.

FN19. Nyaturu. Specific data on the Nyaturu (Lima, Toro, Turu, Walimi, Waniaturu) tribe, including the Iramba (Ramba), Iyambi, and Izanzu.

FN20. Pogoro. Specific data on the Pogoro (Wapogoro) tribe, including the neighboring Matumbi (Wamatumbi), Mbunga (Bunga, Wambunga), and Ndamba (Gangi, Wandamba).

FN21. Safwa. Specific data on the Safwa (Wassafwa) tribe, including the Iwa (Awiwa, Wawiwa), Lambya (Rambia, Warambia), Malila (Penya), Ndali, Nyamwanga (Ainamwanga, Winamwanga), Nyiha (Banyika, Wanjika), Poroto, Tambo, Wamba, Wandya, and Wungu (Bungu, Ungu, Vungu).

FN22. Sagara. Specific data on the Sagara (Sagala, Wasagara) tribe, including the kindred Kaguru (Wakaguru).

FN23. Sandawe. Specific data on the Sandawe or Wassandaui tribe.

FN24. <u>Shambala</u>. Specific data on the Shambala (Sambara, Washambala) tribe.

FN25. <u>Shashi</u>. Specific data on the Shashi (Washashi) nation, including the Ikizu, Ikoma, Jita (Wajita), Kenye, Kwaya, Nata, Nguruimi (Wangoroine), Ruri (Waruri), Sonjo, and Zanaki tribes.

FN26. <u>Tatoga</u>. Specific data on the Tatoga (Datoga, Mangati, Tatog, Taturu) tribe, including the Barabaig (Brariga) sub-tribe.

FN27. <u>Zaramo</u>. Specific data on the Zaramo (Saramo, Wasaramo) tribe, including the neighboring Doe (Wadoe), Kami (Wakami), Khutu (Wakutu), Kwere (Wakwere), Luguru (Waluguru), and Ndengereko.

FN28. <u>Zigula</u>. Specific data on the Zigula (Wasegua, Zigua) tribe, including the neighboring Bondei (Wabondei, Washensi), Nguru (Wanguru), and Ruvu.

FN29. <u>Prehistoric Tanganyika</u>. Specific data on the prehistoric peoples and cultures of Tanganyika.

FN30. <u>Tanzania</u>. Specific data on the national institutions, including national development programs, of the Republic of Tanzania created through the union of the Republics of Tanganyika and Zanzibar in 1964. For data limited to modern areas of Tanganyika or Zanzibar see FN1, FM1.

Zaire

F01. <u>Zaire</u>. General data on the geography, demography, and indigenous peoples and cultures, including data on the Congo basin as a whole, and specific data on the national institutions, multi-ethnic urban areas, non-indigenous inhabitants, and broad sociocultural trends of the Republic of Zaire (formerly the Belgian Congo, then Congo-Kinshasa). For data on the modern nations of Rwanda and Burundi see F051, F052. For data on the Alur see FK5, on the Banda and Gobu see FI6, on the Banziri and Yakoma see FI8, on the Bwaka see FI11, on the Bwile see FQ5, on the Lamba see FQ8, on the Mfumungu and Wumbu see FI33, on the Ndembu see FP14, on the Pygmies see F04, on the Shila see FQ5.

F02. <u>Colonial Zaire</u>. General data on the geography, demography, and indigenous peoples and cultures, and specific data on the colonial rule, non-indigenous inhabitants, Eurafrican urbanization, and broad sociocultural trends of Zaire during the colonial period.

F03.   Traditional Zaire. General data on the geography, demography, and
       African peoples and cultures, and specific data on Arab, European,
       or other contacts, non-African inhabitants, and broad sociocultural
       trends of Zaire from the beginning of recorded or oral history up
       to the onset of colonial rule. For data on Prehistoric Zaire see
       F056.

F04.   Pygmies. General data on the Pygmies of central Africa as a whole,
       and general and specific data on the Pygmy tribes of Zaire, in-
       cluding the Bambuti (Mbuti) of the Ituri Forest. For data on the
       Pygmies of Cameroon see FH4, of Equatorial Africa see FI4, of
       Zambia see FQ4.

F05.   Abarambo. Specific data on the Abarambo (Barambo) tribe, including
       the neighboring Amadi and Duga.

F06.   Amba. Specific data on the Amba (Awamba, Bahamba, Baamba,
       Buamba, Wawamba) tribe.

F07.   Azande. Specific data on the Azande (Niam-Niam, Sande, Zande)
       nation, including the detached Makaraka (Idio). For data on the
       kindred Nzakara see FI25.

F08.   Babwa. Specific data on the Babwa (Ababua, Bobwa) nation, including
       the Bati (Babati, Mobati, Mombati), Binza (Babinja, Mabinza,
       Wavinza), Mobenge (Amubenge, Bange, Bobenge, Mobanghi),
       Ngelima (Babeo, Bangelima, Mongelima), and the adjacent riverine
       Bakango.

F09.   Bali. Specific data on the Bali (Babai, Babali, Mabale, Mubali,
       Wabali) tribe, including the Lika (Balika, Malika, Walika) and
       Ndaka (Bandaka, Wandaka).

F010. Bashi. Specific data on the Bashi (Baniabungu, Wanyabungu) tribe,
       including the neighboring Fulero (Bafuleri, Wafulero) and Havu
       (Bahavu).

F011. Bira. Specific data on the Bira (Babira, Babeyru, Wawira) tribe,
       including the Kumu (Bakumbu, Wakumu), Lengola (Balengora,
       Walengola), Pere (Bapere), and the detached Plains Bira.

F012. Boloki. Specific data on the Boloki or Bangala (Bamangala, Mangara,
       Mongalla, Ngala, Wangala) nation, including the Lobala and
       Ngombe (Gombe).

F013. Budja. Specific data on the Budja (Mbudja) tribe, including the Maginza,
       the Mobale (Bale, Mabali), and the detached Bango (Babangi,
       Mobango) and Mbesa (Bombesa, Mombesa).

F014. Budu. Specific data on the Budu (Babudu, Banabuddu, Mabodo, Wabuddu) tribe.

F015. Buye. Specific data on the Buye (Babudjue, Babui, Babuya, Luba-Hemba, Wabuyu, Waruwa) nation, including the Goma (Wagoma), Kalanga (Bakalanga), Kunda (Bakunda), and Lumbu (Balumba).

F016. Dengese. Specific data on the Dengese (Bonkesse, Ndengese) nation, including the Songomeno (Basongo-Meno).

F017. Dinga. Specific data on the Dinga (Badinga, Badzing, Dzing) tribe, including the related Bunda (Ambunu, Babundu, Bambunda, Mbunu), Huana (Baguana, Bahungana, Wengana), Loli (Alwer, Balori), Mputu (Amput, Bamputu), Ngoli (Angul, Bangodi, Banguli), Nzari (Banjadi, Banzari), and Yanzi (Bayansi, Wachanzi).

F018. Holoholo. Specific data on the Holoholo (Baholoholo, Wahorohoro) tribe, also called Guha (Bagua, Vuahuha, Waguha) and Tumbwe (Batumbwe, Watombwa).

F019. Kela. Specific data on the Kela (Akela, Bakela, Ekela, Ikela) tribe, including the Balanga (with the Bakuti), Bambuli (Bambole), and Boyela.

F020. Kete. Specific data on the Kete (Bakete, Tukete) tribe, including the neighboring Mbagani (Bambagani) or Bindi (Babindi, Tubindi).

F021. Kongo. Specific data on the Kongo (Bakongo) nation, embracing the Bashikongo (Besikongo, Eshikongo, Mushikongo), Bembe (Babembe), Bwende (Babuende), Hungu (Mahungo), Kakongo (Cabinda, Makuango), Mbamba (Bamba), Mbata (Bambata, Batta), Mpangu (Pango), Nzombo (Bazombo, Zombo), Solongo (Asolongo, Bashilongo, Basolongo, Misorongo, Mossilongi, Musurongo), and Sundi (Basundi, Manyanga) tribes.

F022. Konjo. Specific data on the Konjo (Bakondjo, Wakondjo) or Nande (Banande, Wanande) tribe, including the related Hunde (Bahonde) and Nyanga (Banianga, Wanyanga).

F023. Kuba. Specific data on the Kuba (Bakuba, Bushongo, Tukubba) nation, including the Binji (Babinji, Tubishe).

F024. Lele. Specific data on the Lele (Bashilele) tribe, including the Wongo (Bawongo).

F025. Lendu. Specific data on the Lendu (Alendu, Bale, Balendu, Walendu) tribe, sometimes miscalled Lega or Balega.

F026. Logo. Specific data on the Logo tribe, plus the related Do (Ndo) and Kaliko (Keliko). For data on the linguistically related Lugbara see FK14.

F027. Luba. Specific data on the Luba (Baluba, Turruba, Waluba) nation, including the related Bena Kanioka to the west, Bena Kalundwe to the east, Hombo or Bangobango to the northeast, Lulua (Bena Lulua) to the northwest, Lunda (Alunda, Arund, Balunda, Kalunda, Valunda) to the extreme west, Songe (Bassonge, Wasonga) to the north, and Yeke (Bayeke) to the southeast. For data on the Buye or eastern Luba see F015, on the Kaonde or southern Luba see FQ7, on the Ndembu or southern Lunda see FP14.

F028. Luwa. Specific data on the Luwa or Balua tribe, including the adjacent Kwese (Bakwese), Nzofo, and Sonde (Basonde).

F029. Mangbetu. Specific data on the Mangbetu (Monbutto) tribe, including the kindred Maberu, Mabisanga, Makere, Malele, Mbae (Bamanga, Mambanga, Manga, Wambanga), Medje, Niapu, Popoi (Bagunda, Bapopoie, Mopoi), and Rumbi (Walumbi, Warumbi), as well as several subjugated and largely absorbed tribes of alien stock, notably the Badyo (Madjo), Bangba (Abangba, Mangba), Mayogu (Bayugu), and Ngbele (Bangbele, Mambere).

F030. Mbala. Specific data on the Mbala (Ambala, Bambala) tribe, including the adjacent Humbu (Bahumbu, Bavumbu), Ngongo (Bangongo), and Songo (Basongo).

F031. Momvu. Specific data on the Momvu (Mamvu) tribe, including the kindred Lese (Balese, Walese), Mbuba (Bambuba), and Mombutu.

F032. Mongo. Specific data on the Mongo nation, embracing the Bokete, Bosaka (with the Ekota), Ekonda, Linga (Balinga, Baninga, Elinga, Waninga), Lolo (Balolo or Mongo proper), Lomela Ntomba (with the Kutu or Bakutu), Mbole (Bole, Imoma), Ngata (Wangata), Ngombe (Bangombe), Nkundu (Bankundu, Elanga, Kundu, Nkundo), and Ntomba (Tumba) people, plus the kindred Bolia, Kuti (Bakuti, Bakutu), and Sengele (Basengere, Mosengele). The Yaelima tribe, including the related Batitu, Bokala, Bolendu, Bolongo, Booli (Bori), and Ipanga who are sometimes collectively called the Kutshu (Bakutshu) are also included here.

F033. Mundu. Specific data on the Mundu tribe, including the kindred Babukur.

F034. Ndoko. Specific data on the Ndoko or Doko tribe.

F035. Ngandu. Specific data on the Ngandu (Bangandu, Mongandu) nation, embracing the Bambole, Bolo (Ngandu proper), Lalia (Dzalia, Lolia), and Yasayama.

F036. Ngbandi. Specific data on the Ngbandi (Angbandi, Gbandi, Mogwandi, Wangandi) nation.

F037. Deleted.

F038. Nyari. Specific data on the Nyari (Babvanuma, Bahuku, Banyali, Banyoro-Wassongora) tribe.

F039. Pende. Specific data on the Pende (Bapende, Tupende) tribe.

F040. Poto. Specific data on the Poto (Bapoto, Mafoto) tribe.

F041. Rega. Specific data on the Rega (Balegga, Barega, Kalega, Valega, Warega) nation, including the Bembe (Balembe, Vabembe, Wabembe), Bwari (Wabwari), eastern Zimba (Bazimba, Wasimba), and the detached Mituku.

F042. Rundi. Specific data on the Rundi (Barundi, Warundi) and Ruanda (Banyaruanda) nations, each comprised of three ethnically distinct caste groupings, the Bahutu (Hutu), Batutsi (Tutsi), and Batwa (Twa), plus data on the kindred Ha (Abaha, Waha), and Vinza. For data on the national states of Rwanda and Burundi see F051, F052.

F043. Sakata. Specific data on the Sakata (Basakata) tribe, including the kindred Baye (Babaie, Bai, Bobai, Tollo), Boma (Baboma, Wabuma), Dia (Bajia, Wadia), and Tete (Batete).

F044. Soko. Specific data on the Soko (Basoko) tribe, including the adjacent Lokele (Likile), Topoke (Eso, Geso, Tofoke), and Turumba (Bolombo).

F045. Songola. Specific data on the Songola (Basongola, Goa, Watchongoa) tribe, including the adjacent Gengele (Bagengele), Genya (Baenya, Waenya, Wagenia, Wenya), Kwange (Bakwange), and western Zimba (Bazimba, Wasimba).

F046. Suku. Specific data on the Suku (Basuku) or Pindi (Bapindi, Pindji) tribe.

F047. Tetela. Specific data on the Tetela (Batetela) nation, including the related Hamba (Bahamba), Kusu (Bakusu, Wakusu), Nkutshu (Ankutshu, Bankutshu), Olemba, and Sungu tribes.

F048. Deleted.

F049. Yaka. Specific data on the Yaka (Bayaka, Djakka, Giaka, Jaca, Mayaka, Ngiaka, Yagga) nation.

F050. Yombe. Specific data on the Bayombe (Mayombe) nation, including the related Kunyi (Bakougni) and Yangela (Banyangela).

F051. Rwanda. General data on the geography and demography, and specific
       data on the national institutions, Eurafrican urban areas, non-
       indigenous inhabitants, and broad sociocultural trends of the Rwanda
       Republic (formerly part of the colony of Ruanda-Urundi). For data
       on the indigenous cultures of Rwanda see F042.

F052. Burundi. General data on the geography and demography, and specific
       data on the national institutions, Eurafrican urban areas, non-
       indigenous inhabitants, and broad sociocultural trends of the modern
       country of Burundi (formerly part of the colony of Ruanda-Urundi).
       For data on the indigenous cultures of Burundi see F042.

F053. Colonial Ruanda-Urundi. General data on the geography and demography,
       and specific data on the colonial rule under the Germans and Belgians,
       non-indigenous inhabitants, Eurafrican urbanization, and broad socio-
       cultural trends of Ruanda-Urundi during the colonial period.

F054. Traditional Ruanda-Urundi. General data on the geography and demo-
       graphy, and specific data on Arab, European, or other contacts, non-
       indigenous inhabitants, and broad sociocultural trends of Ruanda-
       Urundi from the beginning of recorded or oral history up to the onset
       of German colonial rule.

F055. Prehistoric Ruanda-Urundi. Specific data on the prehistoric peoples and
       cultures of Ruanda-Urundi.

F056. Prehistoric Zaire. Specific data on the prehistoric peoples and cul-
       tures of Zaire.

Angola

FP1.   Deleted.

FP2.   Angola. General data on the geography, demography, and indigenous
       peoples and cultures, and specific data on the colonial rule, non-
       indigenous inhabitants, Eurafrican urbanization and multi-ethnic
       urban areas, modern economy and local government, and broad
       sociocultural trends of Angola (Portuguese West Africa), including
       Cabinda, since the onset of Portuguese control in 1575. For speci-
       fic data on the indigenous population of Cabinda see FI34 and F021,
       on the Ambo see FX8, on the Bushmen see FX10, on the Pygmies
       see F04.

FP3.   Traditional Angola. General data on the geography, demography, and
       African peoples and cultures, and specific data on European or
       other contacts, non-African inhabitants, and broad sociocultural
       trends of Angola from the beginning of recorded or oral history up
       to the onset of colonial rule in 1575. For data on Prehistoric
       Angola see FP19.

FP4. Chokwe. Specific data on the Chokwe (Ahioko, Atsokwe, Bachoko, Badjok, Bakioko, Batchokwe, Chiboque, Kashioko, Kioko, Matchioko, Quioco, Shioko, Tsivokwe, Tsokwe, Vachioko, Watshokwe) nation, including the Minungu (Tuminungu).

FP5. Holo. Specific data on the Holo or Baholo tribe.

FP6. Kimbundu. Specific data on the Kimbundu (Ambundu, Mbundu) nation, embracing the Esela, Haku (Oako), Kipala (Cipala, Kibala), Kisama (Cisama, Quissama), Kisanji (Cisanje, Quissanje), Lemba (Malemba), Luanda (Loanda), Lupolo (Libolo), Mbaka (Ambaca, Ambaquista), Mbondo (Bongo), Mbui (Amboim, Mbuiyi, Ombe), Ndembu (Andembu, Atembu, Bandempo, Dembo, Jindembu), Pinda (Mupinda), Sele (Basele, Esele, Selle), Songo, Sumbe (Basumbe), and Tamba (Matamba) tribes. The Kimbundu should not be confused with the Mbundu (FP13).

FP7. Koroca. Specific data on the Koroca (Bakoroka, Coroca, Makoroko) people, including the Kwise (Bacuisso, Bakuise, Kwisso, Vakuise, Moquisse), Luheka (Valuheke), and Sorotua (Vasorontu). The Koroca are variously reported to be Bergdama or Bushman in affiliation.

FP8. Luchazi. Specific data on the Luchazi (Balochasi, Kaluchazi, Luxage, Malochazi, Valuchazi) tribe.

FP9. Luimbe. Specific data on the Luimbe (Loimbe, Baluimbe, Valuimbe) tribe, including the Mbande (Kimbande, Quimbande).

FP10. Mbangala. Specific data on the Mbangala (Bangala, Bengela, Imbangala) tribe, including the neighboring Shinje (Bashinshe, Chinge, Kasinji, Moshinji).

FP11. Mbukushu. Specific data on the Mbukushu (Hambukushu, Mambukushu, Mucusso) tribe, including the neighboring Kwangare (Makwangare, Ovakuangari).

FP12. Mbunda. Specific data on the Mbunda (Ambunda, Mambunda) tribe, including the kindred Mbwela (Ambuella).

FP13. Mbundu. Specific data on the Mbundu (Bimbundu, Ovimbundu) nation, also called Mbali (Mambari, Ovimbali) and Nano (Banano, Munano, Vakuanano), including the Bailundo (Mbailundu), Viye (Bihe), Wambu (Huambo), and other sub-tribes.

FP14. Ndembu. Specific data on the Ndembu (Andembu, Bandempo) or Southern Lunda nation, including the related Luena (Aluena, Kaluena, Muluena, Tulwena, Valwena) or Lovale (Balovale, Lobare, Luvale, Malobale). For data on the northern Lunda or Lunda proper see F027.

FP15. Ndombe. Specific data on the Ndombe (Andombe, Bandombe, Dombe, Mundombe) tribe, including the neighboring Hanya (Muhanha), Kilenge (Cilenge, Quilengue), Kwando (Bakuando), and Nganda (Ganda).

FP16. Ngonyelu. Specific data on the Ngonyelu (Ngonzellu) tribe, including the Nhemba (Nyamba). The name Ngangela (Ganguella, Vangangela) applies to the Ngonyelu but is often extended to include the Mbunda (FP12) and even the Luimbe (FP9) and Luchazi (FP8).

FP17. Ngumbi. Specific data on the Ngumbi (Bangumbi, Humbe, Khumbi, Muhumbe, Nkumbe, Ovakumbi, Vankumbe) tribe, including the neighboring Hinga (Ehinga, Ovahinga) and Kipungu (Cipungu, Pungu, Quipungu, Vatyipungu).

FP18. Nyaneka. Specific data on the Nyaneka (Banianeka, Munhaneca, Ovanyaneka, Vanyaneka) tribe, including the neighboring Chikuyu (Tyikuyu), Jau (Kwanyime, Ndyau), Mbuila (Huilla, Mohilla, Vamuila), Ngambue (Bangambue, Nevia), and Ngombe (Gombo).

FP19. Prehistoric Angola. Specific data on the prehistoric peoples and cultures of Angola.

Zambia

FQ1. Zambia. General data on the geography, demography, and indigenous peoples and cultures, and specific data on the national institutions, multi-ethnic urban areas, non-indigenous inhabitants, and broad sociocultural trends of the Republic of Zambia (formerly Northern Rhodesia). For data on the Iwa and Nyamwanga see FN21, on the Ndembu and Luena see FP14, on the Nsenga see FR4, on the Mpezeni Ngoni see FR5.

FQ2. Colonial Zambia. General data on the geography, demography, and indigenous peoples and cultures, and specific data on the colonial rule, non-indigenous inhabitants, Eurafrican urbanization, and broad socio-cultural trends of Zambia during the colonial period.

FQ3. Traditional Zambia. General data on the geography, demography, and African peoples and cultures, and specific data on European or other contacts, non-African inhabitants, and broad sociocultural trends of Zambia from the beginning of recorded or oral history up to the onset of colonial rule. For data on Prehistoric Zambia see FQ13.

FQ4. Zambian Pygmies. Specific data on the Pygmies or Twa of Zambia. For data on the African Pygmies in general see F04.

FQ5.   Bemba. Specific data on the Bemba (Awemba, Babemba, Wawemba) tribe, including the related Aushi (Avausi, Bahushi, Ushi, Waushi), Bisa (Abisa, Awisa, Babisa, Muiza, Wisa), Bwile (Babwile, Wawire), Chisenga (Wenachishinga), Kawendi (Kabende), Luapula (Alonda, Alunda, Bena Kazembe, Balonda), Lungu (Alungu, Marungu, Walungu, Warungu), Mambwe (Amambwe), Ngumbu (Wenangumbu), Senga (Asenga), Shila (Awasira, Bachila, Messira, Wasira), Tabwa (Batabwa, Batambwa, Itawa, Waitabwa), and Unga (Bahonga, Baunga, Honja, Waunga).

FQ6.   Ila. Specific data on the Ila (Baila, Bashukulompo, Mashukolumbwe) tribe, including the related Bizhi, Lenje (Balenje, Benimukuni), Lumbu (Nanzela), Lundwe, Mbala, and Sala (Basala).

FQ7.   Kaonde. Specific data on the Kaonde (Bakahonde, Bakaunde) tribe, including the Sanga (Basanga).

FQ8.   Lamba. Specific data on the Lamba (Balamba, Walamba) tribe, including the Ambo (Kambonsenga) and Lala (Balala, Bukanda).

FQ9.   Lozi. Specific data on the Barotse (Barutse, Marotse) kingdom, particularly on the dominant Lozi (Barozi, Rozi) ethnic group, called Luyi (Alui, Luyana) prior to 1838, and including the Kololo (Makololo) conquerors who ruled from 1838 to 1864, plus all the subject or assimilated tribes, including the Kwanda, Makoma (Bamakoma), Mbowe (Mamboe), Mishulundu, Muenyi (Mwenyi), Mwanga, Ndundulu, Nyengo, Shanjo, and Simaa.

FQ10. Lukolwe. Specific data on the Lukolwe (Balukolwe) or Mbwela (Bambwela, Mambwela, Mbwera) tribe, including the neighboring Lushange (Baushanga), Mashasha (Bamasasa), and Nkoya (Mankoya).

FQ11. Subia. Specific data on the Subia (Massubia, Masupia, Subiya, Subya) tribe, including the Leya.

FQ12. Tonga. Specific data on the Tonga (Batonga, Batonka) peoples, including the Gwembe Tonga (Valley Tonga, We) and the Plateau Tonga (Tonga proper), plus the kindred Gowa, Namainga, Toka (Batoka, Matoka), and Totela (Batotela, Matotela).

FQ13. Prehistoric Zambia. Specific data on the prehistoric peoples and cultures of Zambia.

Malawi

FR1.   Malawi. General data on the geography, demography, and indigenous peoples and cultures, and specific data on the national institutions, multi-ethnic urban areas, non-indigenous inhabitants, and broad sociocultural trends of Republic of Malawi (formerly Nyasaland). For data on the Ngonde see FN17, on the Yao see FT7.

FR2. <u>Colonial Malawi</u>. General data on the geography, demography, and indigenous peoples and cultures, and specific data on the colonial rule, non-indigenous inhabitants, Eurafrican urbanization, and broad sociocultural trends of Malawi during the colonial period.

FR3. <u>Traditional Malawi</u>. General data on the geography, demography, and African peoples and cultures, and specific data on Arab, European, or other contacts, non-African inhabitants, and broad sociocultural trends of Malawi from the beginning of recorded or oral history up to the onset of colonial rule. For data on Prehistoric Malawi see FR8.

FR4. <u>Maravi</u>. Specific data on the Maravi nation, embracing the Chewa (Achewa, Cewa, Cheva, Masheba), Chikunda (Achikunda), Chipeta (Achipeta, Cipeta), Nsenga (Senga), Nyanja (Anyanja, Wanyanja), Nyasa (Anyassa, Wanyassa), Sena (Asena, Wasena), and Zimba (Azimba, Bazimba, Wasimba) tribes. The Nyanja and Nyasa together are called Manganja (Wanganga).

FR5. <u>Ngoni</u>. General and specific data on the Ngoni (Angoni, Mangoni, Wangoni) or Gaza (Abagaza) peoples, most of whom are organized into centralized states or kingdoms generally named after the chiefs who led them on their invasions from Zululand in the mid-nineteenth century, the principal states being Ciwere, Gomani (central Ngoni kingdom), Mbelwa (Mombera, northern Ngoni kingdom), and Mpezeni, the last partly in Zambia. For data on the Ngoni of Tanganyika see FN14.

FR6. <u>Tumbuka</u>. Specific data on the Tumbuka (Batumbuka, Matumbuka, Watumbuka) nation, embracing the Fulilwa (Fulirwa), Fungwe (Wafungwe), Henga (Bahenga, Wahenga), Hewe (Hewa), Kamanga (Wakamanga), Kandawire, Nthali, Phoka (Poka), Sisya (Siska), Tonga (Batonga), Tumbuka proper, and Wenya tribes.

FR7. <u>Lakeside Tonga</u>. Specific data on the Lakeside Tonga. These Tonga seem to be completely unrelated to the Tonga of Zambia (FQ12).

FR8. <u>Prehistoric Malawi</u>. Specific data on the prehistoric peoples and cultures of Malawi.

Rhodesia

FS1. Deleted.

FS2. <u>Rhodesia</u>. General data on the geography, demography, and indigenous peoples and cultures, and specific data on the colonial rule, non-indigenous inhabitants, Eurafrican urbanization and multi-ethnic urban centers, modern economy and government, including changes related to the white-dominated unilateral declaration of independence in 1965, and broad sociocultural trends of Rhodesia (formerly Southern Rhodesia) since the onset of British control in the nineteenth century. For data on the Bushmen see FX10.

FS3.   Traditional Rhodesia. General data on the geography, demography, and
        African peoples and cultures, and specific data on Arab, European,
        or other contacts, non-African inhabitants, and broad sociocultural
        trends of Rhodesia from the beginning of recorded or oral history up
        to the onset of colonial rule. For data on Prehistoric Rhodesia see
        FS6.

FS4.   Ndebele. Specific data on the Ndebele (Amandebele, Matabele) of
        Rhodesia, who are to be distinguished from the Transvaal Ndebele
        (FX18).

FS5.   Shona. Specific data on the Shona or Mashona nation, embracing the
        Barwe (Bargwe, Wabargwe), Budja (Babudja, Wambudjga), Duma
        (Abaduma, Baduma, Maduma, Vaduma, Waduma), Fungwe (Bafungwi,
        Basungwe, Washungwe), Gova, Hera (Abahela, Wahera), Kalanga
        (Karanga, Makalaka, Vakaranga, Wakalanga), Manyika (Wanyika),
        Ndau (Njao, Vandau), Njanja (Banjanja, Sinjanja), Nyai (Abanyai,
        Banyai), Rozwi (Amalozwi, Barozwi, Warizwi), Shanga, Shankwe
        (Abashankwe, Bashankwe, Washangwe), Tawara (Matawara,
        Watawara), Teve, Tomboji, Tonga (Abatonga, Atonga, Batonka,
        Watonga), and Zezuru (Bazezuru, Mazizuru, Vazezuru, Wazezuru)
        tribes.

FS6.   Prehistoric Rhodesia. Specific data on the prehistoric peoples and cul-
        tures of Rhodesia, including the Zimbabwe people.

                                    Mozambique

FT1.   Deleted.

FT2.   Mozambique. General data on the geography, demography, and indi-
        genous peoples and cultures, and specific data on the colonial rule,
        non-indigenous inhabitants, Eurafrican urbanization and multi-
        ethnic urban areas, modern economy and local government, and
        broad sociocultural trends of Mozambique (Portuguese East Africa)
        since the onset of Portuguese control in the sixteenth century. For
        data on the Maravi see FR4, on the Shona see FS5.

FT3.   Traditional Mozambique. General data on the geography, demography,
        and African peoples and cultures, and specific data on Arab, Euro-
        pean, or other contacts, non-African inhabitants, and broad socio-
        cultural trends of Mozambique since the beginning of recorded or
        oral history up to the onset of colonial rule in the sixteenth century.
        For data on Prehistoric Mozambique see FT8.

FT4.   Chopi. Specific data on the Chopi (Batchopi, Tshopi, Vachopi) tribe,
        including the related Lenge (Valenge) and Tonga (Vatoka, Vatonga).

FT5. <u>Makua</u>. Specific data on the Makua (Wakua, Wamakua) nation, embrac-
ing the Chuabo (Achwabo, Chwampo), Lomwe (Acilowe, Alomwe,
Nguru, Walomwe), Makua proper, Mavia (Mabiha, Maviha, Mawia),
Mihavani, and Podzo (Wapodzo) tribes.

FT6. <u>Thonga</u>. Specific data on the Thonga (Bathonga, Shangana-Tonga) nation,
embracing the Hlengwe (with the Batswa and Nwanati), Ronga
(Baronga), and Thonga proper.

FT7. <u>Yao</u>. Specific data on the Yao (Achawa, Adjao, Adsoa, Ajawa, Ayo,
Hiao, Mudsau, Mujano, Mujua, Myao, Veiao, Wahaiao, Waiyao,
Wayao) nation.

FT8. <u>Prehistoric Mozambique</u>. Specific data on the prehistoric peoples and
cultures of Mozambique.

Swaziland

FU1. <u>Swaziland</u>. General data on the geography and demography, and specific
data on the national institutions, non-indigenous inhabitants, and
broad sociocultural trends of the Kingdom of Swaziland. For data
on the indigenous population see FU2.

FU2. <u>Swazi</u>. Specific data on the Swazi (Amaswazi) nation.

FU3. <u>Historical Swaziland</u>. General data on the geography and demography,
and specific data on European or other contacts, colonial rule, non-
indigenous inhabitants, and broad economic and political trends of
Swaziland from the beginning of recorded or oral history up to
national independence in 1968. For data on prehistoric Swaziland
see FX4.

Botswana

FV1. <u>Botswana</u>. General data on the geography, demography, and indigenous
peoples and cultures, and specific data on national institutions, non-
indigenous inhabitants, multi-ethnic urban areas, and broad sociocultural trends of the Republic of Botswana (formerly Bechuanaland).
For data on the Bushmen see FX10.

FV2. <u>Historical Botswana</u>. General data on the geography, demography, and
indigenous peoples and cultures, and specific data on European or
other contacts, colonial rule, non-indigenous inhabitants, and broad
sociocultural trends of Botswana from the beginning of recorded or
oral history up to national independence in 1966.

FV3.   <u>Prehistoric Botswana</u>. Specific data on the prehistoric peoples and cultures of Botswana.

FV4.   <u>Kgalagadi.</u>   Specific data on the Kgalagadi (Bakalahari) tribe.

FV5.   <u>Koba</u>. Specific data on the Koba (Bakoba, Bayei, Kuba, Maiye, Yeye) tribe.

FV6.   <u>Tswana</u>. Specific data on the Tswana (Bechuana) nation, embracing the Hurutshe (Bakuruthse, Khurutshe), Kgatla (Bakgotlha, Bakxatla), Kwena (Bakwena), Ngwaketse (Bangwaketse), Ngwato (Bamangwato), Rolong (Barolong), Tawana (Batwana), Tlhaping (Bachapin, Batlaping), Tlharu (Batlaro), and Tlokwa (Batlokwa, Dokwa, Tokwa) tribes.

Lesotho

FW1.   <u>Lesotho</u>. General data on the geography and demography, and specific data on the national institutions, non-indigenous inhabitants, and broad sociocultural trends of the modern country of Lesotho (formerly Basutoland). For data on the indigenous population see FW2.

FW2.   <u>Sotho.</u>   Specific data on the Sotho (Basotho, Basuto) nation.

FW3.   <u>Historical Lesotho</u>. General data on the geography and demography, and specific data on European or other contacts, colonial rule, non-indigenous inhabitants, and broad economic and political trends of Lesotho from the beginning of recorded or oral history up to national independence in 1966. For data on prehistoric Lesotho see FX4.

South Africa and Namibia

FX1.   <u>South Africa</u>. General data on the geography, demography, and non-White peoples and cultures, and specific data on the White-dominated national institutions, modern inhabitants of European extraction, migrant African laborers, mainly White or multi-ethnic urban areas, and broad sociocultural trends of the Republic of South Africa (formerly the Union of South Africa) since the formation of the Union in 1910. For specific data on the Cape Colored see FX11, on the Asian minority see FX15. For data on Namibia or South West Africa see FX22.

FX2.   <u>Historical South Africa</u>. General data on the geography, demography, and non-White peoples and cultures, and specific data on European colonization, urbanization, economy, and government, the Boer-African and Anglo-Boer wars, and broad sociocultural trends of South Africa during the eighteenth and nineteenth centuries (up to 1910). For specific data on nineteenth century Afrikanders culture see FX7, on the Zulu nation see FX20.

FX3. Traditional South Africa. General data on the geography, demography, and African peoples and cultures, and specific data on European or other contacts, non-African inhabitants, and broad sociocultural trends of South Africa from the beginning of recorded or oral history up to the eighteenth century.

FX4. Prehistoric Southern Africa. Specific data on the prehistoric peoples and cultures of South Africa, Namibia (South West Africa), Swaziland, and Lesotho.

FX5. Deleted.

FX6. Khoisan Peoples. General data on the speakers of the Khoisan or "click" languages. For specific data on the Bergdama see FX9, on the Bushmen see FX10, on the Hottentot see FX13, on the Kindiga see FN11, on the Koroca see FP7, on the Sandawe see FN23.

FX7. Afrikanders. Specific data on the culture of the Afrikanders or Boers during the nineteenth century.

FX8. Ambo. Specific data on the Ambo (Ovambo) nation, embracing the Eunda, Evale, Kafima (Okafima), Kualuthi (Ovanguuruze, Ukualuthi), Kuambi (Ovamguambi, Ukuambi), Kuanyama (Ovakuanyama, Vakuanyama), Mbalantu (Ombalantu, Ombarandu), Mbandja (Bandya, Cuamato, Ombandya), Ndonga (Ondonga, Ovandonga), Ngandjera (Ongandjera, Ovangandyera), and Nguangua (Onguangua) tribes.

FX9. Bergdama. Specific data on the Bergdama (Haukoin, Mountain Damara) tribe.

FX10. Bushmen. General and specific data on the Bushman tribes, who fall into three groups: (1) the Central Bushmen (Hiechware, Hukwe, Naron, Tannekwe, Tserekwe, etc.); (2) the Northern Bushmen (Auen, Heikum, Kung, etc.); and (3) the Southern Bushmen (Nusan, Xam, etc.). For data on the Khoisan peoples in general see FX6.

FX11. Cape Colored. Specific data on the modern "Cape Coloured" population of South Africa, a group of completely detribalized and acculturated people of mixed blood, basically a Hottentot-European cross with some Bantu, Bushman, and Malay admixture.

FX12. Herero. Specific data on the Herero (Damara, Ovaherero) nation, including the Mbandyeru and Himba (Shimba) tribes.

FX13. Hottentot. Specific data on the Hottentot nation, embracing the Cape Hottentot (the Attaqua, Chainoqua, Chariguriqua, Goringhaiqua, Grigriqua, Hancumqua, Hessequa, Kochoqua, Kora, and Outeniqua tribes), the East Hottentot (the Damaqua, Gonaqua, and Inqua tribes), the Korana (a seventeenth century offshoot of the Kora), and the Nama or Namaqua.

FX14. <u>Lovedu</u>. Specific data on the Lovedu (Balobedu) tribe, including the kindred Khaha, Mamidja, Narene, Phalaborwa, and Thabina.

FX15. <u>Natal Indians</u>. Specific data on the Indian population of modern South Africa, concentrated mainly in Natal.

FX16. <u>Pedi</u>. Specific data on the Pedi (Bapedi, Transvaal Sotho) nation.

FX17. <u>South Nguni</u>. Specific data on the South or Cape Nguni nation, embracing the Bomvana, Pondo (Mpondo), Tembu (Thembu), Xosa (Amaxosa, Kaffir, Xhosa), and other lesser tribes.

FX18. <u>Transvaal Ndebele</u>. Specific data on the Laka (Langa, Black Ndebele), Manala, Maune (Letwaba), and Ndzundza (Mapoch) tribes, known collectively as the "Transvaal Ndebele" to distinguish them from the Ndebele proper or "Rhodesian Ndebele" (FS4).

FX19. <u>Venda</u>. Specific data on the Venda (Bavenda) tribe, including the Lemba (Balemba, Malepa).

FX20. <u>Zulu</u>. Specific data on the Zulu (Amazulu, Natal Nguni) nation, including the kindred Bhaca, Fingo, and Hlubi. For data on other North Nguni tribes see FR5, FS4, FU2, and FX18.

FX21. Deleted.

FX22. <u>Namibia</u>. General data on the geography, demography, and indigenous peoples and cultures, and specific data on German and South African rule, non-indigenous inhabitants, Eurafrican urbanization and multi-ethnic urban areas, modern economy and local government, and broad sociocultural trends of Namibia (South West Africa) since 1884. For data on the Ambo see FX8, on the Bushmen see FX10, on the Herero see FX12, and on the Hottentot see FX13.

FX23. <u>Traditional Namibia</u>. General data on the geography, demography, and African peoples and cultures, and specific data on European or other contacts, non-African inhabitants, and broad sociocultural trends of Namibia from the beginning of recorded or oral history up to the onset of German colonial rule in 1884. For data on prehistoric Namibia see FX4.

Madagascar

FY1. <u>Malagasy Republic</u>. General data on the geography, demography, and indigenous peoples and cultures, and specific data on the national institutions, non-indigenous inhabitants, multi-ethnic urban areas, and broad sociocultural trends of the Malagasy Republic (Madagascar).

FY2. Colonial Madagascar. General data on the geography, demography, and indigenous peoples and cultures, and specific data on the colonial rule, non-indigenous inhabitants, Eurafrican urbanization, and broad sociocultural trends of Madagascar during the French colonial period.

FY3. Traditional Madagascar. General data on the geography, demography, and indigenous peoples and cultures, and specific data on Arab, European, or other contacts, non-indigenous inhabitants, and broad sociocultural trends of Madagascar from the beginning of recorded or oral history up to the onset of colonial rule in 1885. For data on Prehistoric Madagascar see FY22.

FY4. Betsimisaraka. Specific data on the Betsimisaraka tribe.

FY5. Merina. Specific data on the Merina (Antimerina, Imerina) tribe, including the Hova (Ovah) caste.

FY6. Sakalava. Specific data on the Sakalava tribe, including the Vezo sub-tribe, and the Masikoro tribe.

FY7. Anteimoro. Specific data on the Anteimoro (Antaimoro, Antaimorona, Antaimuro, Taimoro, Temoro, Temuru) tribe.

FY8. Tanala. Specific data on the Tanala (Antanala) tribe.

FY9. Antankarana. Specific data on the Antankarana (Tankara, Tankarana) tribe.

FY10. Tsimihety. Specific data on the Tsimihety tribe.

FY11. Betsileo. Specific data on the Betsileo tribe.

FY12. Sihanaka. Specific data on the Sihanaka (Antisianaka) tribe.

FY13. Bara. Specific data on the Bara (Ibara) tribe, including the neighboring Mahafaly and Antandroy (Tandruy).

FY14. Antanosy. Specific data on the Antanosy (Tanosy, Tanusi) tribe.

FY15. Antambahoaka. Specific data on the Antambahoaka tribe.

FY16. Anteifasy. Specific data on the Anteifasy (Antaifasy, Antaifasina, Taifasy, Tefasi) tribe.

FY17. Antaisaka. Specific data on the Antaisaka (Taisaka, Tesaka) tribe.

FY18. Mikea. Specific data on the Mikea and Makoa tribes.

FY19. Bezanozano. Specific data on the Bezanozano (Antaiva, Tankay) tribe.

FY20. Sainte Marien. Specific data on the Creole inhabitants of the island of Sainte Marien.

FY21. Vazimba. Specific data on the probably extinct aboriginal Vazimba peoples.

FY22. Prehistoric Madagascar. Specific data on the prehistoric peoples and cultures of Madagascar.

African Islands

FZ1. African Islands. General and specific data on the smaller islands off the coast of Africa, e.g., Aldabra (with Farquhar and Providence), Amsterdam (with St. Paul), Annobon, Bouvet, Crozet, Heard, Kerguelen, and Prince Edward (with Marion). For data on the Bissagos Islands see FB4, on Fernando Po see FG1, on Madagascar see FY1, on Zanzibar see FM1.

FZ2. Ascension. Specific data on the island of Ascension and its inhabitants.

FZ3. Comoros. Specific data on the Comoro Islands and their inhabitants.

FZ4. Mauritius. Specific data on the island of Mauritius (with the Coroados, Garavos, and Rodriguez Islands) and their inhabitants.

FZ5. Reunion. Specific data on the island of Reunion and its inhabitants.

FZ6. Saint Helena. Specific data on the island of Saint Helena and its inhabitants.

FZ7. Sao Thome. Specific data on the island of Sao Thome (with Principe) and their inhabitants.

FZ8. Seychelles. Specific data on the Seychelles Islands and their inhabitants.

FZ9. Tristan da Cunha. Specific data on the island of Tristan da Cunha (with Gough Island) and its inhabitants.

M1.   Middle East   General data on the modern Middle East, on the Islamic
      world, on the Near East or North Africa, or on any three or more of
      the political divisions distinguished below.   The Middle East is here
      considered as including southwestern Asia from Iran west, northern
      and northeastern Africa, the Sahara, and the adjacent Moslem fringe
      of the Sudan.   For data on the Hamito-Semitic peoples in general see
      M9, on the Gypsies see E15, on the Jews of the Middle East see MF4.

M2.   Middle East--Turkish Period.   General data on the Middle East during
      the period of Turkish domination (c. 1300-1900 A. D.), and specific
      data on the Ottoman Turks.   For data on the Turkic peoples in
      general see RL4, on modern Turkey see MB1.

M3.   Middle East--Arabic Period.   General data on the Middle East during the
      period of Arab domination (c. 650-1300 A. D.) and specific data on the
      Seljuk Turks.   For data on the Arabs in general see M10, on the Arabs
      of Baghdad under the Caliphate see MH3, on Moorish Spain see EX3.

M4.   Middle East--Graeco-Roman Period.   General data on the Middle East
      from Alexander the Great (c. 330 B. C.) to the Arab conquest (c. 650 A. D.).
      For data on the Byzantine Empire see EH3, on Hellenistic Greece see EH4,
      on the Jews of the Graeco-Roman period see MF6, on Roman Italy see EI4.

M5.   Early Historic Middle East.   General data on the Middle East from the
      dawn of history (c. 4000 B. C.) to Alexander the Great (c. 330 B. C.).

M6.   Protohistoric Middle East.   General data on the Middle East and its cul-
      ture from the so-called "Urban Revolution" to the beginning of record-
      ed history.

M7.   Neolithic Middle East.   General data on the Middle East and its culture from
      the so-called "Neolithic Revolution", through the Chalcolithic period, to
      the "Urban Revolution".   For data on the Neolithic period in Europe see E7.

M8.   Paleolithic Middle East.   General data on the Middle East and its culture
      from the earliest evidences of man, through the Paleolithic and
      Mesolithic periods, to the beginning of the "Neolithic Revolution".   For
      data on the Paleolithic period in Europe see E8.

M9.   Hamito-Semites.   General data on the Hamito-Semitic peoples.   For data
      on Arabian history see MJ2, on the Arabs see M10, on the Bedouin
      see MJ4, on the Berbers see M11, on the Cushites see M12, on the
      Maritime Arabs see MK2.

M10. Arabs. General data on the Arabic-speaking peoples of the Middle East and specific data on undefined Arab groups. For specific data on the Bedouin see MJ4.

M11. Berbers. General data on the Berber-speaking peoples of North Africa.

M12. Cushites. General data on the Cushitic-speaking peoples of Ethiopia and the Horn (Somaliland).

Iran

MA1. Iran. General data on modern Iran, its geography and inhabitants, its economy and government, and specific data on the Iranians and their culture. For data on the Arabs of Iranian Mesopotamia see MH8, on the Arabs of the Persian Gulf littoral see MK2, on the Armenians of Iran see RJ3, on the Azerbaijani see RK3, on the Baluchi and Brahui see AT2, on the Gypsies see E15, on the Hazara see AU5, on the Jews of Iran see MF4, on the Kazvin and adjacent settled Turkic tribes see RK3, on the Tadzhik see R02, on the Talysh see RK4, on the Turcoman see RM2.

MA2. Medieval Persia. Specific data on Iran or Persia, its peoples and their history from the acceptance of Islam (c. 650 A.D.) to the beginning of the modern period (c. 1900).

MA3. Graeco-Roman Persia. Specific data on Persia, its peoples, and their history from Alexander the Great (c. 330 B.C.) to the acceptance of Islam. For data on the Graeco-Roman period in general see M4.

MA4. Ancient Persia   Specific data on ancient Persia, its history, and its civilization from the beginning of recorded history to the conquest by Alexander.

MA5. Prehistoric Iran. Specific data on the prehistoric peoples and cultures of Iran.

MA6. Aissor. Specific data on the Aissor or modern "Assyrians", a Nestorian Christian sect, including those found in the Caucasus region and elsewhere.

MA7. Caspian Iranians. Specific data on the Caspian provinces of modern Iran and their inhabitants, particularly the Gilaki and Mazanderani peoples.

MA8. Gabr. Specific data on the Gabr (Gabar) or Zoroastrian sect of Iran. For data on the Zoroastrian Parsi of India see AW21.

MA9. [Deleted]

MA10. Khamseh. Specific data on the Khamseh tribes of Iran.

MA11. Kurd   Specific data on the Kurd people and their culture, including those living in Caucasia, Iraq, and Turkey.

MA12. Lur   Specific data on the Lur peoples, including the Bakhtiari (the sample), Kahgalu, and Mamassani.

MA13. Qashgai. Specific data on the Qashgai (Kashgai) people, including the Basseri.

Turkey

MB1. Turkey   General data on modern Turkey and its inhabitants, and specific data on the Turkish people and their culture. For data on the historical Ottoman Turks (c. 1300-1900 A.D.) see M2, on Byzantine Asia Minor see EH3, on the Hellenistic, Hellenic, and Homeric Greeks see EH4-EH6, on the modern Armenians see RJ3, on the Greeks of modern Turkey see EH1, on the Kurd see MA11, on the·Laz or Chan (Dhan) see RI10.

MB2. Ancient Asia Minor. General and specific data on the non-Greek peoples of ancient Asia Minor. For specific data on the Hittites see MB4.

MB3. Prehistoric Turkey. Specific data on the prehistoric peoples and cultures in the territory of modern Turkey.

MB4. Hittites. Specific data on the ancient Hittites and their civilization.

MB5. Yuruk   Specific data on the Yuruk and kindred "heterodox" peoples of modern Turkey.

MB6. Anatolian Greeks. Specific data on the Greeks of Eastern Anatolia and the Trebizond up to 1923.

Cyprus

MC1. Cyprus. Specific data on modern Cyprus and the Cypriote people. For historical data see EH2-EH5 and M2-M5.

MC2. Prehistoric Cyprus. Specific data on the prehistoric peoples and cultures of the island of Cyprus.

Syria

MD1. Syria   General data on modern Syria and its inhabitants, and specific data on the Syrian people and their culture.

MD2. Historical Syria. General and specific data on the history and recorded culture history of Syria. For data on the Syrian Christians of India see AW11

MD3. Prehistoric Syria. Specific data on the prehistoric peoples and cultures of Syria.

MD4. Rwala   Specific data on the Rwala tribes of Syria and Iraq. For data on the Bedouin in general see MJ4.

MD5. Syrian Bedouin. Specific data on Bedouin tribes of Syria other than the Rwala and groups closely akin to them.

MD6. Druze. Specific data on the Druze of Syria and Lebanon.

MD7. Alawites. Specific data on the Alawites.

Lebanon

ME1. Lebanon   General and specific data on modern Lebanon, the Lebanese people, and their culture.

ME2. Historical Lebanon. Specific data on the history and recorded culture history of Lebanon.

ME3. Prehistoric Lebanon. Specific data on the prehistoric peoples and cultures of Lebanon.

ME4. Phoenicians. Specific data on the ancient Phoenicians and their culture. For data on the Carthaginians see MU3.

Israel

MF1. Israel   Specific data on modern Palestine and its Jewish or Israeli inhabitants. For data on the Arabs of Israel see MG1-MG2.

MF2. Historical Palestine. Specific data on the history and recorded culture history of Palestine, including Jordan, and of its past inhabitants other than Jews.

MF3. Prehistoric Palestine. Specific data on the prehistoric peoples and cultures of Palestine, including Jordan.

MF4. Levantine Jews. General and specific data on Jews and Jewish culture throughout the Middle East in modern times. For data on European Jews see E14, on Yemenite Jews see ML4.

MF5. Jews of the Diaspora. General and specific data on the history and culture history of the Jews from their dispersion to the beginning of the
modern era.

MF6. Graeco-Roman Jews. Specific data on the Jews of the Graeco-Roman
world, including those of Judea at the time of Christ. For data on the
Graeco-Roman period in general see M4.

MF7. Ancient Hebrews   Specific data on the Hebrews and their culture
in the period covered by the Old Testament.

Jordan

MG1. Jordan   General data on modern Jordan and specific data on
its sedentary population, including the Palestinian Arabs. For
historical and prehistoric data see MF2 - MF3.

MG2. Jordanian Bedouin. Specific data on the Bedouin tribes of Jordan and
Palestine. For data on the nomadic Arabs see MJ4.

MG3. Samaritans. Specific data on the history and culture of the Samaritans of
Jordan and Palestine.

Iraq

MH1. Iraq   General data on modern Iraq and specific data on its sedentary
inhabitants. For data on the Azerbaijani of Iraq see RK3, on the Bedouin
see MJ4, on the Jews see MF4, on the Kurds see MA11.

MH2. Turkish Iraq. Specific data on Iraq and its inhabitants during the period of
Turkish domination. For the Turkish period in the Middle East in general see M2.

MH3. Bagdad Arabs   Specific data on Iraq and its inhabitants between 650
and 1300 A.D., and particularly on the culture of the Bagdad Arabs at
the height of the Caliphate (the sample). For data on the Arabic period
in the Middle East in general see M3.

MH4. Graeco-Roman Iraq. Specific data on Iraq or Mesopotamia during the
Graeco-Roman period (c. 330 B.C. to 650 A.D.). For data on the
Graeco-Roman period in general see M4, on Mesopotamia under the
ancient Persians see MA4.

MH5. Ancient Mesopotamia. General and specific data on the history, peoples,
and cultures of Mesopotamia from the dawn of history to the Persian
conquest (539 B.C.). For specific data on Babylonian civilization at the
time of Hammurabi see MH7, on Sumerian civilization see MH9.

MH6. Prehistoric Mesopotamia. Specific data on the prehistoric peoples and cultures of Mesopotamia. For data on Middle Eastern prehistory in general
see M6 - M8.

MH7.   Babylonians   Specific data on ancient Babylonian civilization at approximately the time of Hammurabi (2123 to 2080 B.C.).

MH8.   Iraq Bedouin.   Specific data on the culture of the Bedouin tribes of modern Iraq, including the Arabs of the adjacent lowland region of Iran.

MH9.   Sumerians   Specific data on the ancient Sumerian people (prior to 2900 B.C.) and their civilization.

MH10.   Yazidis.   Specific data on the Yazidi (Yezidi) of Iraq and Syria.

MH11.   Mandaeans.   Specific data on the culture of the Mandaeans or Sabaeans of Iraq and Iran.

MH12.   Surai.   Specific data on the culture and history of the Surai or so-called "Modern Assyrians" or Nestorians of Iraq and Syria.

MH13.   Madan.   Specific data on the Madan or Marsh Arabs of southern Iraq.

Kuwait

MI1.   Kuwait   Specific data on modern Kuwait and its inhabitants.   For historical and prehistoric data see MH2 - MH6.

Saudi Arabia

MJ1.   Saudi Arabia   General data on modern Saudi Arabia and its inhabitants and specific data on its agricultural and urban population.   Data on the Arabian Peninsula will be included here if not readily allocable to specific political or other divisions.   For data on its nomadic inhabitants see MJ4, on its maritime inhabitants see MK2.

MJ2.   Historical Arabia.   Specific data on the history and recorded culture history of Arabia.   For data on the Arabs in general see M10.

MJ3.   Prehistoric Arabia.   Specific data on the prehistoric peoples and cultures of Arabia.

MJ4.   Bedouin.   Specific data on the nomadic Arabs or Bedouin, particularly of Saudi Arabia, especially Mutair.   For data on the Arab peoples in general see M10.   For specific data on Rwala Bedouin see MD4, on the Bedouin of Egypt see MR11, of Iraq see MH8, of Jordan see MG2, of Libya see MT9, of Syria see MD5.

Oman

MK1.   Oman.   Specific data on modern Muscat and Oman and their inhabitants, including otherwise unallocable material on Eastern Arabia in general. For data on their nomadic inhabitants see MJ4, on their history and prehistory see ML2 - ML3, on Bahrain Islands see MZ2.

MK2. Maritime Arabs. Specific data on the maritime Arabs of Oman, Aden, and the shores of the Red Sea and the Persian Gulf, and general data on Arab trade and maritime activities in the past and present.

MK3. Qatar. Specific data on modern Qatar and its inhabitants. For data on its history and prehistory see MJ2-MJ3.

MK4. Trucial Oman. Specific data on Trucial Oman and its inhabitants. For data on its history and prehistory see MJ2-MJ3.

Yemen

ML1. Yemen. General data on modern Yemen and specific data on its inhabitants. For data on its maritime population see MK2, on its nomadic population see MJ4.

ML2. Historical South Arabia. Specific data on the history and recorded culture history of the peoples of southern Arabia. For data on the history of Arabia as a whole see MJ2.

ML3. Prehistoric South Arabia. Specific data on the prehistoric peoples and cultures of southern Arabia.

ML4. Yemenite Jews. Specific data on the Jews of Yemen and their culture. For data on Levantine Jews in general see MF4.

Aden

MM1. Aden. Specific data on colonial Aden. For historical and prehistoric data see ML2-ML3, for Maritime Arabs see MK2.

MM2. Hadhramaut. Specific data on Hadhramaut and Aden Protectorate and their inhabitants. For historical and prehistoric data see ML2-ML3, for data on the Maritime Arabs see MK2.

MM3. Southern Yemen. Specific data on the People's Republic of Southern Yemen, including Socotra.

Eritrea

MN1. Eritrea. General data on modern Eritrea and its inhabitants.

MN2. Historical Eritrea. Specific data on the history and recorded culture history of Eritrea.

MN3. Prehistoric Eritrea. Specific data on the prehistoric peoples and cultures in the territory of modern Eritrea.

MN4.   Afar.   Specific data on the Afar or Danakil nation, including the related
Saho (Shiho).

MN5.   Barea.   Specific data on the Barea tribe.

MN6.   Bogo.   Specific data on the Bogo or Belen (Bilin) tribe.

MN7.   Khamta.   Specific data on the Khamta tribe, including the kindred Khamir.

MN8.   Kunama.   Specific data on the Kunama people, apparently the sole
representatives of an independent linguistic stock.

MN9.   Tigre.   Specific data on the Tigre or Tigritian nation, including the Ad
Sheikh, Beit Asgede, Habab, Maria, Mensa, and Sabderat.   For data
on the Tigrinya see MP24.

MN10. Wollo.   Specific data on the Wollo, a detached Galla tribe.

Somaliland

M01.   Somali Republic.   General data on the Somali Republic and specific data
on their modern inhabitants other than the Somali.

M02.   Historical Somaliland.   Specific data on the history and recorded culture
history of Somaliland.

M03.   Prehistoric Somaliland.   Specific data on the prehistoric peoples and
cultures of Somaliland.

M04.   Somali.   Specific data on the Somali nation, including the Somali
proper (Samaale - the sample) comprised of the Dir, Isaaq, Hawiye
and Daarood and the Sab comprised of the Digil and Rahanwin.

M05.   Negroid Somaliland Peoples.   Specific data on the Negroid populations of
Somaliland, including the Bajun (Bagiuni), Wa Gosha, Wa Boni, Gobawein, Eile, Helai, Tunni Torre, Wa Ribi, the Webi Shebelle groups
and various other non-Somali groups.

M06.   Afars-Issis Territory.   Specific data on the peoples and cultures of the
territory formerly known as French Somaliland.

Ethiopia

MP1.   Ethiopia.   General data on modern Ethiopia or Abyssinia and its inhabitants.   For data on the Anuak see FJ4, on the Berta see FJ7, on the
Gumus and Koma see FJ15, on the Wollo see MN10.

MP2.   Medieval Ethiopia.   Specific data on Ethiopia and its peoples from
650 A.D. to the beginning of the modern period.

MP3. Ancient Ethiopia. Specific data on Ethiopia and its inhabitants from the beginning of recorded history to 650 A.D.

MP4. Prehistoric Ethiopia. Specific data on the prehistoric peoples and cultures of Ethiopia.

MP5. Amhara   Specific data on the Amhara nation, including the Argobba.

MP6. Awiya. Specific data on the Awiya people, including the Damot. For data on other speakers of Agau or Eastern Cushitic languages see MN7, MP9, and MP16.

MP7. Baditu. Specific data on the Baditu (Amarro) tribe, including the Keura (Koyra) and Zaysse.

MP8. Bako. Specific data on the Bako tribe, including the neighboring Amar, Biya(Biye), Boda, Burle (Bura), Dime (Dima, Dume), and Gayi.

MP9. Falasha   Specific data on Falasha (Agua Jews, Black Jews, Kayla).

MP10 Gimira. Specific data on the Gimira (Gemira) tribe, including the Bienesho, Kaba, Nao (Najo), Shako, She, and isolated Maji (Madshe, Mage, Mancho, Mazi).

MP11. Gurage. Specific data on the Gurage (Guraghe) people.

MP12. Harari. Specific data on the Harari, the Semitic-speaking people of the city of Harar.

MP13. Ittu. Specific data on the Ittu tribe, including the Ala, Arussi, Annia, Jarsso (Djarso), and Nole. For data on the kindred Galla of Kenya see FL7, on other Galla tribes of Ethiopia see MN10, MP15, MP17, MP18, MP23, and MP25.

MP14. Kafficho   Specific data on the Kafficho (Gomaro, Gonga, Kaffa) nation, including the Amaro, Gongicho, Gurabo, Hinnaro, Mocha (Sheka), and Tedshiwo.

MP15. Kambata. Specific data on the Kambata tribe, including the Alaba, Hadia(Gudiela), and Tambaro.

MP16. Kemant. Specific data on the Kemant (Qemant), including the Qara (Kwara). For data on the linguistically related Falasha see MP9.

MP17. Konso   Specific data on the Konso tribe, including the neighboring Burji, Bussa, Gardulla, Gidole, and Gowaze.

MP18. Macha. Specific data on the Macha (Metsha) nation, including the related Jimma (Gimma), Lieka, and Walega (Lega).

MP19. Mao. Specific data on the Mao (Anfillo, Mau) tribe.

MP20. Ojang. Specific data on the Ojang (Mageno, Masango, Mashongo, Ujang)
tribe, including the Bula (Buna) and Olam (Nyilam).

MP21. Shinasha. Specific data on the Shinasha or Bworo tribe.

MP22. Shuri. Specific data on the Shuri (Churi, Dhuri, Suri, Thuri) nation,
also called Kichepo (Kachipa, Kachuba, Ngachopo), Korma (Corma,
Surma), and Zuak (Thuak), including the kindred Kerre (Karo, Kira),
Mekan (Mien, Suro), Murzu (Maritu, Merdu, Merzu, Murse,
Murutu), Nyikoromo (Karoma, Makurma, Mursia, Musha, Nikaroma),
Tid (Dolot, Tod), and Tirma (Dirma, Terema, Terna, Tilma,
Tirmaga).

MP23. Sidamo. Specific data on the Sidamo tribe, including the Darassa.

MP24. Tigrinya. Specific data on the Tigrinya nation, embracing the Guzai,
Hamasien, and Serae (Sarae).

MP25. Tulama. Specific data on the Tulama or Shoa Galla, including the Jidda.

MP26. Walamo. Specific data on the Walamo (Walaitza, Wolomo) tribe, including the kindred Basketo, Chara, Doko, Dorsse (Dorze), Gofa,
Haruro, Konta, Kullo, Malo, and Zala.

MP27. Yangaro. Specific data on the Yangaro (Janjero, Yamna, Yemma) tribe,
including the neighboring Garo (Bosha).

Arab Sudan

MQ1. Sudan. General data on the Republic of Sudan and the former Anglo-
Egyptian Sudan and on its economy and government, particularly
on its northern or Moslem portion and its inhabitants. For data
on the southern or Nilotic Sudan see FJ1, on the Beja see MR9,
on the Berti, Bideyat, and Zaghawa see MS5.

MQ2. Historical Eastern Sudan. General and specific data on the history and
recorded culture history of the Arab Sudan prior to the twentieth
century, including the adjacent Chad district of northern former
French Equatorial Africa.

MQ3. Prehistoric Eastern Sudan. Specific data on the prehistoric peoples and cultures of the Arab Sudan, including the adjacent Chad district of former French Equatorial Africa.

MQ4. Anag. Specific data on the shattered remnants of northern Nuba tribes in the hills of Abu Hadid, Abu Tubr, El Haraza, Kaga, Katul, and Um Durrag in northern Kordofan. For data on the kindred Dilling farther south see FJ11.

MQ5. Baggara. Specific data on the Negroid cattle-herding Arabs along the southern frontier of the Arab Sudan, in particular the Habbania (with the Beni Helba), Hemat (Heimad), Kirdi (including the Abu Ghussun, Digguel, Kibet, and Murro), Messiria (with the Humr), Rizaykat (Riseighat), Selim (Beni Selim), and Taaisha (with the Taelba) tribes.

MQ6. Birked. Specific data on the Birked tribe.

MQ7. Dagu. Specific data on the Dagu (Dadio, Dadzo, Daju, Tagu) tribe, including the kindred Bego (Baygo). For data on the related Sila see MQ16.

MQ8. Fur Specific data on the Fur (For, Forawa), the dominant nation of Darfur.

MQ9. Kababish Specific data on the Kababish, Arab camel nomads west of the Nile, including the kindred Hawawir and Kerriat.

MQ10. Kordofan Arabs. Specific data on the semi-nomadic Arab tribes of central Kordofan, in particular the Aulad Hamayd, Bazaa, Bedayria, Beni Gerar, Beni Omran, Dar Hamid, Dubab, Fezara, Ghodiat, Gwamaa, Hamar, Hawazma, Kawahla, Maakle, Maalia, Shenable, Shuwaywat, Terayfia, Tomam, Tumbab, and Zayadia.

MQ11. Mandala. Specific data on the Mandala (Bandala), a tribe of escaped slaves, and on other Fertit (the collective name for such tribes).

MQ12. Masalit. Specific data on the Masalit tribe of Darfur.

MQ13. Midobi. Specific data on the Midobi or Meidob tribe.

MQ14. Nile Arabs. Specific data on the sedentary or semi-sedentary Arab tribes along the Nile River, in particular on the Gaaliin, Gamuia (with the Gemaab and Gimlab), Gimma (Gimaa), Hasania, Husaynat (Husseinat), Manasir, Mesallania, Mirafab, Shaikia (Cheykye), and Rubatab.

MQ15. Shukria. Specific data on the Shukria (Shukuriye) and other pastoral Arabs east of the Nile, including the Abdullab, Ahamda, Amarna, Batahin, Dubasiin, Fadnia, Guhayna, Hamran, Kawasma, Kenana, Khawalla, Lahawiin, and Rufaa.

MQ16. Sila. Specific data on the Sila of Dar Sila, including the related Kimr (Ermbeli, Guimr) of Dar Guimr, Erenga (Djebel), Sungor, Tama of Dar Tama, and the detached Dagu or Shat of the Nuba Hills.

Egypt

MR1. Egypt. General data on modern Egypt and its inhabitants, and specific information on its urban population. For data on the agricultural population see MR13, on the pastoral population see MR11.

MR2. Turkish Egypt. Specific data on the history and culture of Egypt during the Turkish period (c. 1300 to 1900 A.D.). For general data on the Middle East during this period see M2.

MR3. Arabic Egypt. Specific data on the history and culture of Egypt during the Arabic period (c. 650 to 1300 A.D.). For general data on the Middle East during this period see M3.

MR4. Graeco-Roman Egypt. Specific data on the history and culture of Egypt from Alexander the Great to the Arab conquest (c. 330 B.C. to 650 A.D.). For general data on the Middle East during this period see M4.

MR5. Ancient Egypt. Specific data on the history and culture of Egypt from the dawn of history (c. 4000 B.C.) to the time of Alexander the Great. For specific data on Egyptian civilization under the New Kingdom see MR6.

MR6. Eighteenth Dynasty Egypt Specific data on the civilization of ancient Egypt at the height of the New Kingdom, i.e., during the XVIII Dynasty or shortly before and after 1400 B.C.

MR7. Prehistoric Egypt. Specific data on the prehistoric peoples and cultures of Egypt. For general data on the prehistory of the Middle East see M6-M8.

MR8. Barabra. Specific data on the Barabra or Nubians, including the Danagla, Feyadicha, Kenuzi, Kerrarish, and Mahass.

MR9. Beja Specific data on the Beja nation, embracing the Ababda, Amarar, Beni Amer (with the Maria), Bisharin (Bichari), Haddendowa, and Halenga tribes.

MR10. Copts. Specific data on the Copts and Coptic culture, including historical materials.

MR11. Egyptian Bedouin. Specific data on the nomadic Arab tribes east of the Nile, including those of the Sinai Peninsula. For data on the Egyptian Bedouin west of the Nile see MT9.

MR12. Egyptian Oases. Specific data on the oases of western Egypt and their inhabitants, in particular on Bahariya (Little Oasis), Dakhla, Farafra, and Kharga. For data on the Siwa oasis see MR14.

MR13. Fellahin   Specific data on the agricultural Egyptians or Fellahin along the Nile River.

MR14. Siwans   Specific data on the oasis of Siwa or Jupiter Ammon and its inhabitants.

MR15. Suez Canal. Specific data on the history, operation, and defense of the Suez Canal and on the life and activities of the personnel who contribute directly or indirectly to its administration, maintenance, and use.

Sahara and Sudan

MS1. Sahara and Sudan. General data on the Sahara region of North Africa and the adjacent Moslem fringe of Sudan, their geography, modern inhabitants, trade routes and commerce, etc. Since the Sahara is not a political unit, pertinent information is likely to be found in other files, particularly those on Algeria (MV1), Arab Sudan (MQ1), former French Equatorial Africa (FI 1), and former French West Africa (FA1). For data on North Africa in general see M1, on the Arabs in general see M10, on the Berbers in general see M11, on the Kenga tribe see FI16, on the Kotoko see FH13, on the Sila see MQ16, on the Sokoro see FI31, on the Tienga see FF13. For data on the modern nations of Chad, Niger, Mali, Mauritania, and Senegal see MS33 - MS37.

MS2. Historical Sahara and Sudan. General and specific data on the history and recorded culture history of Sahara and adjacent Sudan. For historical data on eastern Sudan see MQ2.

MS3. Prehistoric Sahara and Sudan. Specific data on the prehistoric peoples and cultures of the Sahara and adjacent Sudan. For data on African prehistory in general see F3.

MS4. Bagirmi. Specific data on the Bagirmi, the dominant people of the state of Bagirmi in the Republic of Chad.

MS5. Bideyat. Specific data on the Bideyat (Anna, Baele, Terawia) nation, including the Berti, Gaida, Morea, Murdia, Nakaza (Anakatza), Unia, and Zaghawa (Soghaua, Zorhawa), of the Ennedi region of the Republic of Chad and the northwestern part of the Arab Sudan.

MS6. Bozo. Specific data on the Bozo tribe of the Mali Republic.

MS7. Buduma. Specific data on the Buduma (Yedina) tribe of the islands in Lake Chad.

MS8. Bulala. Specific data on the Bulala (Lisi, Maga), including the Abu Semen, Kuka, and Midogo, of the Republic of Chad.

MS9. Chad Arabs. Specific data on the Mahamid (with the Atayfat, Eraykat, Mahria, and Nawaiba), Shuwa (with the Assale, Aulad Hamid, Dagana, Dekakire, Khozzam, and Salamat), and Soliman or Aulad Sliman (with the Mgharba), of which the Mahamid and Soliman are camel nomads and the Shuwa semi-sedentary cattle Arabs akin to the Baggara (MQ5).

MS10. Djenne. Specific data on the mercantile city of Djenne in the Mali Republic and particularly on its two principal indigenous inhabitants, the Songhai-speaking Djennenke and the Mande-speaking Nono (Nunu).

MS11. Fulani   Specific data on the widespread Fulani (Felata, Fulah, Fulbe, Peul), including the Bororo, who are scattered throughout the western Sudan from Senegal to northern Cameroun with especially heavy concentrations in the Fouta district of Senegal (their original center), the Fouta Djalon district of Guinea (see FA19), the Masina district of the Sudan, the Liptako district of Upper Volta, the Sokoto and Bauchi districts of northern Nigeria, and the Adamawa district of Cameroun. For data on the kindred Tukulor see MS27.

MS12. Hausa. Specific data on the Hausa nation of northern Nigeria and the Republic of Niger, including the Azna (Arna), Daurawa, Gobir, Kanawa, Katsenawa, Kebbawa, Mauri, Tazarawa, and Zazzau (Zazzagawa, Zaria) tribes.

MS13. Kanembu. Specific data on the Kanembu nation, the principal ethnic group of Kanem in the Lake Chad region, including the Magumi (Magomi) of northern Nigeria and the acculturated alien Dalatoa, Danoa, Gudjiru, and Ngejim.

MS14. Kanuri. Specific data on the Kanuri, the dominant people of Bornu in northeastern Nigeria, including the kindred Beriberi, Koyam (Kai), and Manga (Mangawa).

MS15. Maba. Specific data on the Maba, the dominant people of Wadai (Ouadai) in the Republic of Chad, including the Kondongo and the subjugated Bandula, Fala (Bakka), Ganyanga, Kadjagse, Kadjanga (Abu Derreg), Kagba, Karanga, Kashmere, Kelingen, Kudu, Marfa, and Moyo.

MS16. Merarit. Specific data on the Merarit tribe of Wadai in the Republic of Chad, including the kindred Ali, Chale, Kubu, and Oro.

MS17. Mimi. Specific data on the Mimi (Mima, Mututu) tribe of Wadai.

MS18. Mubi. Specific data on the Mubi tribe of Wadai, including the kindred Karbo (Korbo, Kurbo).

MS19. Runga. Specific data on the Runga people of Dar Rounga in the Republic of Chad.

MS20. Songhai Specific data on the Songhai (Sonhrai) nation of the Republic of Mali, including the kindred Dendi and Dyerma (Zaberma).

MS21. Soninke Specific data on the Soninke or Sarakole nation of the Republic of Mali. For data on the kindred Diula and other mercantile peoples of West Africa see FA15.

MS22. Teda Specific data on the Teda (Tebu, Tibbu, Tubu) nation of Borku, Kanem, Kawar, and Tibesti in the east central Sahara, including the Bulgeda, Daza (Dazagade), Famalla (Haualla, Medela), Goran, Kecherda, Kreda (Karra), Wandala, and numerous other tribes. For data on the kindred Bideyat see MS5.

MS23. Timbuctoo. Specific data on the mercantile city of Timbuctoo (Tombouctou) in the Republic of Mali and on its inhabitants.

MS24. Trarza. Specific data on the Trarza, including the Brakna and Tasuma, a Berber nation of southwestern Mauritania now largely but not exclusively Arabic in language.

MS25. Tuareg Specific data on the Tuareg (Tawarik), a Berber nation of the west central Sahara, including the Ahaggar (the sample) (Ihaggaren, Hoggar, Kel Ahaggar), Air (Kel Air), Antessar (Kel Antessar), Aulliminden (Oulliminden), Azjer (Adjeur, Ajjer, Kel Azdjer), Ifora, Igwadaren (Iguaren), Imedreden, Irreganaten, Tadmekket (Kel Tademeket), Tengeredief, and Udalan (Wadalen) tribes. For data on the Inajenen Tuareg of Ghat see MT7.

MS26. Tuat. Specific data on the Zenata Berber inhabitants of the Tidekelt and Touat regions of southern Algeria.

MS27. Tukulor. Specific data on the Tukulor (Tekarir, Torado, Toucouleur) nation of Senegal.

MS28. Tungur. Specific data on the Tungur or Tundjer nation of Arabized Berbers who are scattered through Darfur, Kanem, and Wadai.

MS29. West Saharan Arabs. Specific data on the Aruissin, Berabish, Kunta, Regeibat, Tajakant, and other nomadic and caravan-protecting Arab tribes of southern former French Sudan, northeastern Mauritania, and southwestern Algeria. For data on the kindred Delim and Shuekh see MY4.

MS30. Wolof   Specific data on the Wolof (Djolof, Ouolof, Yollof) nation of Senegal.

MS31. Zenaga. Specific data on the Allush, Chorfa (Sirifu), Duaish (Idaouich), Girganke (Massin), and Mbarek (Oulad Mbarek), sedentary Zenaga Berber tribes, now largely but not exclusively Arabic in language, of Mauritania, including the related but nomadic Oulad Nasser and Tichit (Ahl Tichit).

MS32. Nemadi. Specific data on the Nemadi or hunting bands of the southwestern border of the Sahara.

MS33. Chad. General data on the modern Republic of Chad and its inhabitants.

MS34. Niger. General data on the modern Republic of Niger and its inhabitants.

MS35. Mali. General data on the modern Republic of Mali and its inhabitants.

MS36. Mauritania. General data on the modern Islamic Republic of Mauritania and its inhabitants.

MS37. Senegal. General data on the modern Republic of Senegal and its inhabitants.

Libya

MT1. Libya. General data on modern Libya and its inhabitants.

MT2. Historical Libya. Specific data on the history and recorded culture history of Libya.

MT3. Prehistoric Libya. Specific data on the prehistoric peoples and cultures of Libya.

MT4. Coastal Cyrenaica. Specific data on the Mediterranean coastal zone of Cyrenaica and Sirtica and their Arabic-speaking sedentary and semi-sedentary inhabitants.

MT5. Fezzan. Specific data on the sedentary and semi-sedentary inhabitants, basically Berber but largely Arabic in language, of Gatrun, Murzuch, Sebha, Semnu, and other oasis towns of Fezzan.

MT6. Gadames. Specific data on the Berber inhabitants of the oasis of Gadames in western Tripolitania.

MT7.	<u>Ghat</u>. Specific data on the oasis of Ghat (Gat) in southwestern Libya and its inhabitants, largely Tuareg of the Inajenen and related tribes. For data on other Tuareg tribes see MS25.

MT8.	<u>Khufra</u>. Specific data on the oasis of Khufra (Cufra) and its inhabitants. For data on the dominant Senussi sect see MT9.

MT9.	<u>Libyan Bedouin</u>. Specific data on the Arabic-speaking nomadic tribes of interior Libya and adjacent Egypt, including the Aulad Soliman, Harabi (with the Hasa), Hotman (Al-Hutman), Jibarna, Megarha (Megariha), Riah (Riyah), and Urfilla (Urfalla), on the related but semi-sedentary inhabitants of Forgha, Gialo, Sokna, Unianga, and Zella, and on the Senussi (Sanusi) sect which dominates the region.

MT10.	<u>Nafusa</u>. Specific data on the Berbers of Jebel Nafusa.

MT11.	<u>Tripolitanians</u>. Specific data on coastal Tripolitania and its inhabitants.

Tunisia

MU1.	<u>Tunisia</u>. General data on modern Tunisia and its inhabitants, and specific data on its French and other non-native inhabitants. For data on indigenous Tunisian culture see MU5.

MU2.	<u>Historical Tunisia</u>. Specific data on the history and recorded culture history of Tunisia from the Roman conquest (146 B.C.), through the Vandal, Arabic, and Turkish periods, to the beginning of French rule. For data on ancient Carthaginian civilization see MU3.

MU3.	<u>Carthaginians</u>. Specific data on the ancient Carthaginians, their culture, and their history from the founding of Carthage to its destruction in 146 B.C. For data on the Phoenicians see ME4.

MU4.	<u>Jerba</u>. Specific data on the island of Jerba (Djerba) and its Berber inhabitants.

MU5.	<u>Tunisians</u>. Specific data on the Arabic-speaking inhabitants of modern Tunisia and their culture.

Algeria

MV1.	<u>Algeria</u>. General data on modern Algeria and its inhabitants, and specific data on its French and other non-native inhabitants.

MV2.	<u>Historical Algeria</u>. Specific data on the history and recorded culture history of Algeria.

MV3.	<u>Prehistoric Algeria</u>. Specific data on the prehistoric peoples and cultures of Algeria.

MV4.	<u>Algerian Arabs</u>. Specific data on the Arabic-speaking peoples between the Atlas range and the Mediterranean in Algeria and adjacent eastern Morocco, including the Ulad Nail.

MV5. Chaamba. Specific data on the Chaamba tribe of camel-herding Arabs in the plateau region of central Algeria.

MV6. Kabyle   Specific data on the Kabyle nation of Berbers in coastal Algeria between Alger and Setif.

MV7. Mzab. Specific data on the Berber inhabitants of Ghardaia and adjacent oases.

MV8. Shawiya. Specific data on the Shawiya (Chaouia) nation of Berbers in the Aures Mountains.

MV9. Tuggurt. Specific data on the Berber inhabitants of the oasis of Tuggurt (Touggourt).

MV10. Wargla. Specific data on the Berber inhabitants of the Wargla (Ouargla) oasis, embracing the Beni Brahim, Beni Mezab, Beni Sisin, and Beni Waggin (Beni Ouagguin) tribes.

Morocco

MW1. Morocco. General data on modern Morocco and its inhabitants, either exclusive or inclusive of Tangier and Spanish Morocco. For specific data on Tangier and Spanish Morocco see MX1, on the Arab tribes of northeastern Morocco see MV4.

MW2. Medieval Morocco. Specific data on the history of Morocco, including Spanish Morocco, and on Moroccan Moorish culture from the coming of the Arabs (c. 700 A. D.) to the beginning of the modern period. For data on Moorish culture in Spain see EX3.

MW3. Ancient Morocco. Specific data on the history and culture history of Morocco, including Spanish Morocco, during the Carthaginian, Roman, and Vandal periods. For specific data on the Carthaginians see MU3, on Roman civilization see EI4, on the Vandals see MU2.

MW4. Prehistoric Morocco. Specific data on the prehistoric peoples and cultures of Morocco.

MW5. Beraber   Specific data on the nomadic or semi-nomadic tribes of the Beraber nation, including the Atta (Ait Atta), Buzid (Ait Buzid), Idrassen, Ndhir (Ait Ndhir, Beni Mtir), Seri (Ait Seri), Serruchen (Ait Tserrouchen), Sokham (Ait Chokham), Yafelman (Ait Jafelman), Yussi (Ait Youssi), Zaer, Zayan (the sample), and Zemur. For data on the sedentary Todga Beraber see MW12.

MW6. Drawa. Specific data on the Drawa (Drawi), sedentary Shluh Berbers along the Dra River in the desert region of southern Morocco, embracing the Fezwata, Ktawa, Mesgita, Mhammid, Seddrat, Ternata, Tinzulin, and Zerri tribes.

MW7. Fasi   Specific data on the inhabitants of the city of Fez and its environs.

MW8. Filala. Specific data on the Filala or Arabized Shluh Berbers in the Tafilelt oasis region.

MW9. Gharbya. Specific data on the Gharbya (Rarbya) or thoroughly Arabized Berbers in northwestern Morocco, including the related Ahsen (Beni Ahsen), Badua, Beni Malek, Fahsya, Khlot, Sofyan, and Tliq.

MW10. Marrakech Arabs. Specific data on the Abda, Chiadma, Dukkala, Fruga, Rehamna, Shawia, Sragna, Tadla, and other completely Arabized Berber tribes along the Atlantic coast from Rabat south to Mogador and inland to the city of Marrakech.

MW11. Shluh   Specific data on the Shluh (Chleuch) nation of sedentary Berbers in southern Morocco, comprising a very large number of small tribes. For data on other Berber peoples of the Shluh group see MW6, MW8, and MY6.

MW12. Todga. Specific data on the Todga (Ahl Todgha, Imazighen), including the related Dades (Ait Dades) and Imghun, who are sedentary riverain and oasis Berbers of the Beraber division.

MW13. Warain. Specific data on the Warain (Ait Warain, Beni Ouarain) Berbers of the Zenata group.

MW14. Znassen. Specific data on the Znassen (Beni Iznacen), including the Zekara, who are sedentary or semi-nomadic Zenata Berbers in northeastern Morocco.

Spanish Morocco

MX1. Spanish Morocco. General data on modern Spanish Morocco, including Tangier, and their inhabitants. For historical and prehistoric data see MW2-MW3.

MX2. Jebala. Specific data on the Jebala group of Arabized Riffian Berbers.

MX3. Rif   Specific data on the Rif nation, including the kindred
      Ghomara and Metalsa.

MX4. Senhaja.   Specific data on the Senhaja (Sanhadja), strongly Arabized
      Berbers of the Riffian group.

MX5. Tangier.   Specific data on the city and former international zone of
      Tangier and their inhabitants.

Rio de Oro

MY1. Rio de Oro.   General data on modern Spanish Sahara or Rio de Oro, in-
      cluding Ifni, and their inhabitants.

MY2. Historical Rio de Oro.   Specific data on the history and recorded cul-
      ture history of Rio de Oro and Ifni.

MY3. Prehistoric Rio de Oro.   Specific data on the prehistoric peoples and
      cultures of Rio de Oro and Ifni.

MY4. Delim.   Specific data on the Delim (Oulad Delim), including the Oulad
      Bu Seba and Shuekh (Oulad Chouekh), Arab nomads of Rio de Oro and
      adjacent Mauritania.

MY5. Imragen.   Specific data on the Imragen or fishing tribes of Berber
      origin along the coast of Rio de Oro and adjacent Mauritania.

MY6. Tekna.   Specific data on the Tekna (Tekena), Arabized Shluh Berbers of
      northern Rio de Oro, Tifni, and southwestern Morocco.

Middle East Islands

MZ1. Middle East Islands.   Specific data on Socotra and other minor islands
      off the coast of the Middle East.

MZ2. Bahrain Islands   Specific data on the islands of Bahrain in the
      Persian Gulf and their inhabitants.

MZ3. Canaries.   Specific data on the Canary Islands and their modern inhab-
      itants.

MZ4. Guanche   Specific data on the Guanche, an extinct Berber people
      of the Canary Islands.

MZ5. Cape Verde Islands.   Specific data on the Cape Verde Islands and their
      inhabitants.

MZ6. Madeira.   Specific data on the island of Madeira and its inhabitants.

N1. North America. General data on modern North America or the New
World in general, on any three or more of the political divisions
distinguished below, and on the non-aboriginal inhabitants of North
America north of Mexico. For data on the French Canadians see
NH5, on Latin Americans in general see S1, on other immigrant
groups see N6.

N2. Historical North America. General data on the history and culture history
of the European peoples in North America. For data on American
Indian history see N3, on Canadian history see NC3, on Mexican history see NU2, on South American history see S2, on United States history see NK2, on world history see W2.

N3. American Indians. General data on the Indians of North America or of the
New World as a whole, including historical data and materials on
acculturation. For general data on the Indians of South America see
S3.

N4. Prehistoric North America. General data on the prehistoric peoples and
cultures of aboriginal North America, including theories and evidence
concerning origins, spread, and cultural development.

N5. American Negroes. General data on the Negroes of North America or of
the New World as a whole, including historical materials. For data
on the slave trade see F1, on the Negroes of South America see S5,
on the Negroes of the southern states of the United States see NN6.

N6. Immigrant Americans. General data on immigration into North America
north of Mexico, and specific data on incompletely assimilated im-
migrant groups. For data on the French Canadians see NH5, on Latin
Americans see S1, on the Mexicans of the American Southwest see
NT4, on the New Amsterdam Dutch see NM12, on the Pennsylvania
Germans see NM13, on the Scotch Irish see ER5.

Alaska

NA1. Alaska. General data on modern Alaska and its people, and specific
data on its non-aboriginal inhabitants.

NA2. Historical Alaska. Specific data on the history of Alaska and of its non-
aboriginal inhabitants.

NA3. Alaskan Aborigines. General data on the aboriginal peoples of Alaska

and specific data on their acculturation. For data on the Athapaskan
peoples in general see ND3, on the Eskimo in general see ND2, on
the Northwest Coast Indians see NE3, on the Kutchin see ND10.

NA4. Prehistoric Alaska. Specific data on the prehistoric peoples and cultures of Alaska.

NA5. Ahtena. Specific data on the Ahtena (Ahtnakhotana, Midnoosky) tribe,
including the neighboring Nabesna.

NA6. Aleut   Specific data on the Aleutian Islands and the aboriginal
Aleut people.

NA7. Eyak (S3). Specific data on the Eyak tribe and their culture.

NA8. Ingalik. Specific data on the Ingalik tribe, including the neighboring
Koyukon (Coyukon, Kaiyukhotana, Ten'a) and Tanana (Tenankutchin).

NA9. North Alaska Eskimo. Specific data on the Eskimo tribes of northern
Alaska from Kotzebue Sound east to the Canadian border.

NA10. South Alaska Eskimo (C). Specific data on the Eskimo tribes of
southern Alaska from the Alaska Peninsula east to Prince William
Sound, including the Koniag of Kodiak Island.

NA11. Tanaina. Specific data on the Tanaina (Kenai, Knaiakhotana) tribe.

NA12. Tlingit   Specific data on the Tlingit (Kolosh) nation.

NA13. West Alaska Eskimo (S4). Specific data on the Eskimo tribes of
western Alaska from Kotzebue Sound south to Bristol Bay, including
those of Nunivak (the sample) and St. Lawrence Islands.

Greenland

NB1. Greenland. General data on modern Greenland and its people, and
specific data on its non-aboriginal inhabitants.

NB2. Historical Greenland. Specific data on the history and recorded culture
history of Greenland.

NB3. Prehistoric Greenland. Specific data on the prehistoric peoples and
cultures of Greenland.

NB4. Angmagsalik. Specific data on the Angmagsalik Eskimo of eastern
Greenland.

NB5. Polar Eskimo   Specific data on the Polar Eskimo (Arctic High-
       landers, Cape York Eskimo, Itanese, Smith Sound Eskimo) of
       northwestern Greenland.

NB6. West Greenland Eskimo. Specific data on the Eskimo of southwestern
       Greenland.

Canada

NC1. Canada. General data on modern Canada and its people, and specific
       data on Canadians of British descent. For data on the French
       Canadians see NH5, on incompletely assimilated immigrant groups
       see N6.

NC2. Historical Canada. General data on the history of Canada and the
       Canadian people.

NC3. Canadian Indians. General data on the Indians of Canada, including ma-
       terial on acculturation. For general data on the Indians of North
       America see N3, on the Athapaskan peoples see ND3, on the Eastern
       Woodland Indians see NM4, on the Eskimo peoples see ND2, on
       aboriginal prehistory see N4.

Northern Canada

ND1. Northern Canada. General data on northern Canada, embracing the
       territories of Franklin, Kewatin, Mackenzie, and Yukon, including
       historical information and specific data on its non-aboriginal inhab-
       itants.

ND2. Eskimo. General data on the Eskimo as a whole or on those of Canada,
       including information on acculturation. For data on the Yuit or
       Eskimo of Siberia see RY5.

ND3. Athapaskans. General data on the Athapaskan peoples of northern
       Canada, or on those of North America as a whole, or on the
       Mackenzie-Yukon culture area.

ND4. Prehistoric Northern Canada. Specific data on the prehistoric peoples
       and cultures of northern Canada.

ND5. Baffinland Eskimo. Specific data on the Eskimo of Baffinland, including
       the neighboring Iglulik and Southampton Island Eskimo (Sagdlirmiut).

ND6. Caribou Eskimo. Specific data on the Caribou Eskimo.

ND7. Chipewyan. Specific data on the Chipewyan Indians.

ND8. Copper Eskimo   Specific data on the Copper Eskimo of Victoria Island and Coronation Gulf.

ND9. Hare. Specific data on the Hare (Kawchodinne) Indians, including the neighboring Mountain tribe.

ND10. Kutchin   Specific data on the Kutchin (Loucheux) Indians, including the neighboring Han (Hankutchin) and Tutchone (Tutchonekutchin).

ND11. Mackenzie Eskimo. Specific data on the Mackenzie or Tchiglit Eskimo.

ND12. Nahane   Specific data on the Nahane Indians, embracing the Kaska (the sample), Tahltan, and Tsetsaut tribes.

ND13. Netsilik. Specific data on the Netsilik Eskimo.

ND14. Slave. Specific data on the Slave Indians, embracing the Dogrib (Thlingchadine), Satudene (Great Bear Lake Indians), Slave proper (Etchareottine), and Yellowknife (Tatsanottine) tribes.

British Columbia

NE1. British Columbia. General data on modern British Columbia and its people, and specific data on its non-aboriginal inhabitants.

NE2. Historical British Columbia. Specific data on the history of British Columbia and its non-aboriginal inhabitants.

NE3. Northwest Coast Indians. General data on the Indians of the Pacific coast from southern Alaska to northwestern California or on those in British Columbia. For general data on the Athapaskan Indians of British Columbia see ND3, on the Interior Salish tribes see NE12.

NE4. Prehistoric British Columbia. Specific data on the prehistoric peoples and cultures of British Columbia.

NE5. Bellabella. Specific data on the Bellabella tribe, including the Haisla and Heiltsuk.

NE6. Bellacoola. Specific data on the Bellacoola (Bilqula) tribe.

NE7. Carrier. Specific data on the Carrier (Takulli) tribe, including the Babine.

NE8. Chilcotin. Specific data on the Chilcotin tribe, including the detached Nicola.

NE9. Haida   Specific data on the Queen Charlotte Islands and on their aboriginal Haida inhabitants.

NE10. Kwakiutl   Specific data on the Kwakiutl tribe. For data on the kindred Bellabella see NE5.

NE11. Nootka   Specific data on the Nootka (Aht) tribe, including the kindred Makah of Cape Flattery in Washington.

NE12. Northeast Salish. Specific data on the northern Interior Salish tribes, embracing the Lillooet, northern Okanagon, Shuswap, and Thompson. For general data on the Plateau culture area see NR4.

NE13. Northwest Salish. Specific data on the Coast Salish tribes of British Columbia, embracing the Comox, Cowichan, Homalco, Klahuse, Muskwium, Nanaimo, Pentlatch, Sanetch, Seshelt, Slaiamun, and Squamish. For data on the Puget Sound Salish see NR15.

NE14. Sekani. Specific data on the Sekani tribe.

NE15. Tsimshian. Specific data on the Tsimshian tribe, including the kindred Gitksan and Niska.

Prairie Provinces

NF1. Prairie Provinces. General data on the modern Canadian provinces of Alberta, Manitoba, and Saskatchewan and their people, and specific data on their non-aboriginal inhabitants. For data on the Athapaskan peoples in general see ND3, on the Cree see NG4, on the Plains Indians see NQ4.

NF2. Historical Prairie Provinces. Specific data on the history of the prairie provinces and their non-aboriginal inhabitants.

NF3. Prehistoric Prairie Provinces. Specific data on the prehistoric peoples and cultures of the prairie provinces.

NF4. Assiniboin. Specific data on the Assiniboin (Stoney) tribe. For data on the kindred Dakota see NQ11.

NF5. Beaver. Specific data on the Beaver (Tsattine) tribe.

NF6. Blackfoot   Specific data on the Blackfoot (Siksika) tribe, including the kindred Blood and Piegan.

NF7. Dukhobors. Specific data on the Dukhobor sect and their culture.

NF8. Kutenai. Specific data on the Kutenai (Kootenay) tribe.

NF9. Sarsi. Specific data on the Sarsi (Sarcee) tribe.

Ontario

NG1. Ontario. General data on the modern province of Ontario and its people, and specific data on its non-aboriginal inhabitants. For general data on the Canadian Indians see NC3.

NG2. Historical Ontario. Specific data on the history of Ontario and its non-aboriginal inhabitants.

NG3. Prehistoric Ontario. Specific data on the prehistoric peoples and cultures of Ontario.

NG4. Cree. Specific data on the Cree nation, including the Maskegon and the Tete-de-Boule. For data on the Algonkian peoples in general see NM5.

NG5. Huron. Specific data on the Huron nation, including the Ataronchron, Tionontati (Tobacco nation), Wenrohonron, and Wyandot. For data on the Iroquoian peoples in general see NM8.

NG6. Ojibwa. Specific data on the Ojibwa nation, including the Bungi, Chippewa, Missisauga, Ottawa, and Saulteaux. For data on the Algonkian peoples in general see NM5.

Quebec

NH1. Quebec. General data on the modern province of Quebec and its inhabitants. For data on the Canadian Indians in general see NC3, on the Eastern Woodland Indians see NM4, on French Canadian culture see NH5.

NH2. Historical Quebec. Specific data on the history of Quebec and its non-aboriginal inhabitants.

NH3. Prehistoric Quebec. Specific data on the prehistoric peoples and cultures of Quebec.

NH4. Algonkin. Specific data on the Algonkin proper, including the Abitibi, Kitcisagi (Grand Lake Victoria Indians), Maniwaki (River Desert Indians), Nepissing, and Temiscaming. For data on the Algonkian peoples in general see NM5.

NH5. French Canadians   Specific data on the French-speaking inhabitants of Quebec, or of Canada as a whole, and their culture. For data on Canadians as a whole, or on Anglo-Canadians, see NC1.

NH6. Montagnais   Specific data on the Montagnais nation, including the Naskapi.

Newfoundland

NI1. Newfoundland. General data on the modern province of Newfoundland, including Labrador, and their people, and specific data on their non-aboriginal inhabitants.

NI2. Historical Newfoundland. Specific data on the history of Newfoundland and Labrador and their non-aboriginal inhabitants.

NI3. Prehistoric Newfoundland. Specific data on the prehistoric peoples and cultures of Newfoundland and Labrador.

NI4. Beothuk   Specific data on the aboriginal Beothuk of Newfoundland.

NI5. Labrador Eskimo. Specific data on the Eskimo of Labrador. For data on the Eskimo in general see ND2.

Maritime Provinces

NJ1. Maritime Provinces. General data on the modern maritime provinces of New Brunswick, Nova Scotia, and Prince Edward Island and their people, and specific data on their non-aboriginal inhabitants. For general data on the Canadian Indians see NC3, on the Eastern Woodland Indians see NM4.

NJ2. Historical Maritime Provinces. Specific data on the history and recorded culture history of the maritime provinces and their non-aboriginal inhabitants.

NJ3. Prehistoric Maritime Provinces. Specific data on the prehistoric peoples and cultures of the maritime provinces.

NJ4. Malecite. Specific data on the Malecite Indians, including the Etchimin and Passamaquoddy.

NJ5. Micmac   Specific data on the Micmac Indians.

NK1. United States. General data on the modern United States and its inhabitants. For data on the American Negroes see N5, on the Indians of the United States in general see N3, on incompletely assimilated immigrant groups in the United States see N6.

NK2. Historical United States. General data on the history and culture history of the United States since 1783.

NK3. Colonial United States. Specific data on the history and culture history, prior to 1783, of the colonies which ultimately united to form the United States. For American Indian prehistory see N4.

New England

NL1. New England. General data on the modern states of Connecticut, Maine, Massachusetts, New Hampshire, Rhode Island, and Vermont and their people, and specific data on their non-aboriginal inhabitants. For data on recent immigrant groups see N6, on the Algonkian Indians in general see NM5, on the Eastern Woodland Indians in general see NM4.

NL2. Historical New England. General data on the history and culture history of the New England states and former colonies and their non-aboriginal inhabitants.

NL3. Prehistoric New England. Specific data on the prehistoric peoples and cultures of New England.

NL4. Abnaki. Specific data on the Abnaki Indians, including the Arosagunta-cook, Kennebec, Norridgewock, Pennacook, Penobscot, Pocumtuc, and Wawenok.

NL5. Massachuset. Specific data on the Massachuset Indians, including the Nauset, Nipmuc, and Wampanoag.

NL6. Mohegan. Specific data on the Mohegan (Pequot) Indians, including the kindred Narraganset and Niantic. For data on the Mahican of western New England and eastern New York see NM10.

NL7. Historical Massachusetts Specific data on the history and culture history of the colony and state of Massachusetts and its non-aboriginal inhabitants.

NM1. Middle Atlantic States. General data on the modern states of Delaware, Maryland, New Jersey, New York, Pennsylvania, and West Virginia, on the District of Columbia, and on their people, and specific data on their non-aboriginal inhabitants. For data on recent immigrant groups see N6.

NM2. Historical Middle Atlantic States. Specific data on the history and culture history of the Middle Atlantic states and former colonies and their non-aboriginal inhabitants.

NM3. Prehistoric Middle Atlantic States. Specific data on the prehistoric peoples and cultures of the Middle Atlantic states.

NM4. Eastern Woodland Indians. General data on the Indian peoples and cultures, including material on acculturation, of the eastern United States and Canada. For data on the Algonkian Indians in general see NM5, on the American Indians in general see N3, on the Indians of the Southeast see NN3, on the Iroquoian Indians in general see NM8.

NM5. Algonkians. General data on the Algonkian-speaking Indian tribes and their culture and language.

NM6. Amish. Specific data on the Amish and related sects and their culture, including the Amish of other states as well as Pennsylvania. For data on the Pennsylvania Germans in general see NM13.

NM7. Delaware Specific data on the Delaware (Lenape) Indians, including the neighboring Metoac, Montauk, and Shinnecock of Long Island.

NM8. Iroquoians. General data on the Iroquoian-speaking Indian tribes and their language and culture, and specific data on the little-known Conestoga (Andaste, Susquehannock), Erie, and Neutral (Attiwandaron) tribes. For specific data on the Cherokee see NN8, on the Huron and Tionontati see NG5, on the Iroquois proper see NM9, on the Tuscarora see NN19.

NM9. Iroquois Specific data on the Iroquois nation proper, embracing the Cayuga, Mohawk, Oneida, Onondaga, and Seneca tribes, and on the Tuscarora after they joined the Iroquois League. For data on the earlier Tuscarora see NN19.

NM10. Mahican. Specific data on the Mahican Indians of the Hudson River valley, including the Wappinger of western Connecticut and

Massachusetts. For data on the Mohegan see NL6.

NM11. Nanticoke. Specific data on the Nanticoke Indians, including the Conoy
      or Piscataway.

NM12. New Amsterdam Dutch. Specific data on colonial New Amsterdam
      (later New York) and its inhabitants during the period of Dutch
      administration.

NM13. Pennsylvania Germans. Specific data on the so-called "Pennsylvania
      Dutch" and their culture. For data on the Amish see NM6, on German-
      Americans in general see N6.

Southeastern States

NN1. Southeastern States   General data on the states of Alabama,
     Florida, Georgia, Kentucky, Mississippi, North Carolina, South
     Carolina, Tennessee, and Virginia and their people since 1865, and
     specific data on the culture of their non-aboriginal inhabitants. For
     data pertaining exclusively to Negroes see NN6, to Mountain Whites
     see NN5.

NN2. Antebellum South. Specific data on the history and culture history of the
     southeastern states and former colonies prior to 1865.

NN3. Southeastern Indians. General data on the Indians of the Southeast or
     on the Muskhogean linguistic group. For data on the Eastern Wood-
     land Indians in general see NM4.

NN4. Prehistoric Southeast. Specific data on the prehistoric peoples and cul-
     tures of the southeastern states.

NN5. Mountain Whites. Specific data on the southern Appalachian mountaineers
     and their culture. For data on the Ozark mountaineers see N09.

NN6. Southern Negroes. Specific data on the modern Negro population of the
     southern states and on particular communities thereof. For data on
     the American Negroes in general see N5, on the slave trade see F1.

NN7. Calusa. Specific data on the Calusa Indians of southern Florida, includ-
     ing the Ais, Guacata, Jeaga, and Tekesta.

NN8. Cherokee   Specific data on the Cherokee Indians.

NN9. Chichasaw. Specific data on the Chichasaw Indians, including the
     Chakchiuma.

NN10. Choctaw. Specific data on the Choctaw Indians.

NN11. Creek   Specific data on the Creek (Muskogee) Indians, including the other tribes of the Creek Confederacy, i.e., the Alabama, Hitchiti, Koasati, and Yamasee. For data on the later Seminole see NN16.

NN12. Cusabo. Specific data on the Cusabo Indians, including the Ashipoo, Combahee, Edisto, Etiwaw, Kiawaw, Stono, Wapoo, and Wimbee, and on the neighboring Guale Indians.

NN13. Eastern Siouans. Specific data on the Siouan tribes of North and South Carolina, Virginia, and West Virginia, i.e., the Adshusheer, Backhook, Cape Fear, Catawba (Issa), Cheraw (Sara), Chonque, Congaree, Eno, Hassinunga, Hook, Keyauwee, Manahoac, Monacan, Mosopelea, Ocaneechi, Ofo, Ontponea, Peedee, Santee, Saponi, Sewee, Shackaconia, Shoccoree, Sissipahaw, Stegaraki, Sugaree, Tauxitania, Tegninateo, Tutelo, Ushpee, Waccamaw, Warrennuncock, Wateree, Waxhaw, Whonkenti, Winyaw, and Woccon. For data on the Biloxi of Mississippi see NN14, on the Siouans in general see NQ5.

NN14. Gulf Tribes. Specific data on the Southeastern Indians of the Gulf coast, i.e., the Apalachee, Biloxi (a Siouan tribe), Chatot, and Mobile (including the Moctobi, Naniba, Pascagoula, Pensacola, and Tomome).

NN15. Powhatan. Specific data on the Powhatan Indians, including the kindred Chickahominy, Pamlico, Pamunkey, Rappahannock, and Secotan. For data on the Algonkians in general see NM5.

NN16. Seminole   Specific data on the historical Seminole Indians, including the Creek-derived Seminole proper and the Hitchiti-derived Mikasuki. For data on the parent people see NN11.

NN17. Shawnee   Specific data on the Shawnee Indians. For data on the related Prairie Indians see NP4.

NN18. Timucua. Specific data on the Timucua Indians of northern Florida.

NN19. Tuscarora. Specific data on the Tuscarora Indians, including the kindred Meherrin and Nottaway. For data on the Iroquoians in general see NM8, on the Tuscarora subsequent to their joining the League of the Iroquois see NM9.

NN20. Yuchi. Specific data on the Yuchi (Uchi) Indians, including the Westo.

South Central States

N01. South Central States. General data on the modern states of Arkansas, Louisiana, Oklahoma, and Texas and their people, and specific data on their non-aboriginal inhabitants. For data pertaining exclusively to Negroes see NN6, to the Ozark mountaineers see N09.

N02. Historical South Central States. Specific data on the history of the south central states and their non-aboriginal inhabitants. For data on the Civil War and the events leading up to it see NN2.

N03. Prehistoric South Central States. Specific data on the prehistoric peoples and cultures of the south central states.

N04. Lower Mississippi Indians. General data on the Indian tribes of the lower Mississippi River region, and specific data on the Acolapissa, Atakapa, Huma, Tunica, and other lower Mississippi tribes not separately listed below. For data on the Natchez see N08, on the Quapaw see NQ12, on the Southeastern Indians in general see NN3.

N05. Caddo. Specific data on the Caddo (Ceni, Teja) Indians, including the kindred Adai, Hasinai, Hinai, and Natchitoches.

N06. Comanche   Specific data on the Comanche Indians.

N07. Karankawa. Specific data on the Karankawa Indians, including the neighboring Tonkawa.

N08. Natchez   Specific data on the Natchez Indians, including the kindred Avoyel and Taensa.

N09. Ozark Mountaineers. Specific data on the mountaineers of the Ozark Mountains and their culture. For data on the southern Appalachian mountaineers see NN5.

N010. Wichita. Specific data on the Wichita Indians, including the kindred Kichai and Waco.

East Central States

NP1. East Central States. General data on the modern states of Illinois, Indiana, Michigan, Ohio, and Wisconsin and their people, and specific data on their non-aboriginal inhabitants. For data on recent immigrant groups see N6.

NP2. Historical East Central States. Specific data on the history of the east central states and their non-aboriginal inhabitants.

NP3. Prehistoric East Central States. Specific data on the prehistoric peoples and cultures of the east central states.

NP4. Prairie Indians. General data on the Indians of the East Central states and on their culture, including materials on acculturation. For data on the Algonkians see NM5, on the Eastern Woodland Indians in general see NM4, on the Erie see NM8, on the Ojibwa and Ottawa see NG6, on the Plains Indians see NQ4, on the Shawnee see NN17.

NP5. Fox   Specific data on the Fox (Musquaki, Outagami) Indians.

NP6. Illinois. Specific data on the Illinois nation, including the Cahokia, Kaskaskia, Mascouten, Michigamea, Moingwena, Peoria, and Tamaroa tribes.

NP7. Kickapoo   Specific data on the Kickapoo Indians.

NP8. Menomini   Specific data on the Menomini Indians.

NP9. Miami. Specific data on the Miami Indians, including the Piankashaw and Wea.

NP10. Potawatomi. Specific data on the Potawatomi Indians.

NP11. Sauk. Specific data on the Sauk Indians.

NP12. Winnebago   Specific data on the Winnebago Indians.

West Central States

NQ1. West Central States. General data on the modern states of Iowa, Kansas, Minnesota, Missouri, Montana, Nebraska, North Dakota, South Dakota, and Wyoming and their people, and specific data on their non-aboriginal inhabitants. For data on the adjacent prairie provinces of Canada see NF1.

NQ2. Historical West Central States. Specific data on the history of the west central states and their non-aboriginal inhabitants.

NQ3. Prehistoric West Central States. Specific data on the prehistoric peoples and cultures of the west central states.

NQ4. Plains Indians. General data on the Indians of the west central states and on the Plains culture area as a whole. For data on the Assiniboin see NF4, on the Blackfoot see NF6, on the Commanche see NO6, on the

Plains Cree see NG4, on the Plains Ojibwa see NG6, on the Sarsi see NF9, on the Wichita see NO10.

NQ5. <u>Siouans</u>. General data on the language and culture of the Siouan-speaking Indians. For data on the Assiniboin see NF4, on the Biloxi see NN14, on the Eastern Siouans see NN13, on the Winnebago see NP12.

NQ6. <u>Arapaho</u>   Specific data on the Arapaho Indians.

NQ7. <u>Arikara</u>   Specific data on the Arikara Indians.

NQ8. <u>Cheyenne</u>   Specific data on the Cheyenne Indians.

NQ9. <u>Chiwere</u>   Specific data on the Chiwere Siouan tribes, embracing the Iowa, Missouri, and Oto.

NQ10. <u>Crow</u>   Specific data on the Crow or Apsaroke Indians.

NQ11. <u>Dakota</u>   Specific data on the Dakota or Sioux proper, embracing the Eastern Dakota (Mdewakanton, Santee, Sisseton, Wahpekute, and Wahpeton), the Western Dakota (Brule, Hunkpapa, Kuluwitcatca, Minneconjou, Oglala, Sans Arc, Teton, and Two Kettle), and the Yankton (with the Yanktonnai). The Teton will serve as the sample. For data on the kindred Assiniboin see NF4.

NQ12. <u>Dhegiha</u>   Specific data on the Dhegiha Siouan tribes, embracing the Kansa, Omaha (the sample), Osage, Ponca, and Quapaw.

NQ13. <u>Gros Ventre</u>   Specific data on the Gros Ventre (Atsina) Indians.

NQ14. <u>Hidatsa</u>   Specific data on the Hidatsa (Minitari) Indians.

NQ15. <u>Kiowa</u>. Specific data on the Kiowa Indians.

NQ16. <u>Kiowa Apache</u>   Specific data on the Kiowa Apache Indians.

NQ17. <u>Mandan</u>   Specific data on the Mandan Indians.

NQ18. <u>Pawnee</u>   Specific data on the Pawnee Indians.

NQ19. <u>Wind River</u>. Specific data on the Wind River Shoshone tribe.

<u>Northwestern States</u>

NR1. <u>Northwestern States</u>. General data on the modern states of Idaho,

Oregon, and Washington and their people, and specific data on their non-aboriginal inhabitants.

NR2. Historical Northwestern States. Specific data on the history of the northwestern states and their non-aboriginal inhabitants.

NR3. Prehistoric Northwestern States. Specific data on the prehistoric peoples and cultures of the northwestern states.

NR4. Plateau Indians   General data on the interior tribes of the northwestern states or on the Plateau culture area. For general data on the coastal tribes see NE3, on the Great Basin Indians see NT6. For specific data on the Kutenai see NF8, on the Northeast Salish see NE12.

NR5. Alsea. Specific data on the Alsea Indians, including the neighboring Kuitsh (Lower Umpqua), Siuslaw, and Yaquina.

NR6. Chinook. Specific data on the Chinook Indians, including the Clackamas, Clatsop, Kathlamet, Shoalwater Chinook, and Wahkiakum. For data on the Upper Chinook see NR23.

NR7. Coos. Specific data on the Coos tribe.

NR8. Flathead. Specific data on the Flathead (Salish proper) tribe. For data on other Interior Salish tribes see NE12 and NR19.

NR9. Kalapuya. Specific data on the Kalapuya tribe.

NR10. Klamath   Specific data on the Klamath tribe. For data on the linguistically kindred but culturally distinct Modoc see NS17.

NR11. Kwalhioqua. Specific data on the small and isolated Kwalhioqua and Tlatskanai tribes.

NR12. Nez Perce. Specific data on the Nez Perce (Sahaptin proper) tribe. For data on other Sahaptin tribes see NR18.

NR13. Northern Paiute   Specific data on the Paviotso or Northern Paiute Indians (the sample), including the Eastern Mono (Owens Valley Paiute) and Surprise Valley Paiute of California and numerous bands in Nevada and eastern Oregon.

NR14. Northern Shoshone. Specific data on the Northern Shoshone Indians, including the Fort Hall Shoshone, Hukundika, Lemhi, and Snake (Snake River Shoshone) as well as the neighboring but linguistically distinct Bannock. For data on the Western Shoshone see NT22, on the Wind River Shoshone see NQ19.

NR15. Puget Sound Salish. Specific data on the Coast Salish of the Puget Sound region, including the Chehalis, Copalis, Cowlitz, Dwamish, Humptulip, Klallam, Lummi, Nisqualli, Nootsak, Oyhut, Puyallup, Samamish, Samish, Satsop, Semiamo, Shoalwater Salish, Skagit, Snohomish, Snuqualmi, Songish, Sooke, Squaxon, and Twana. For data on the Coast Salish of British Columbia see NE13, on the Quinault see NR17, on the Tillamook see NR21.

NR16. Quileute. Specific data on the Quileute tribe, including the Chemakum and Ho. For data on the neighboring Makah see NE11.

NR17. Quinault   Specific data on the Quinault tribe, including the Queets.

NR18. Sahaptin   Specific data on the Sahaptin Indians, including the Klikitat (with the Mical and Taidnapam), Tenino (Warmsprings Sahaptin), Umatilla, Wallawalla (with the Palus and Wauyukma), and Yakima and likewise two ill-described neighboring Waiilatpuan tribes, the Cayuse and Molala. For data on the related Nez Perce see NR12.

NR19. Southeast Salish   Specific data on the southern Interior Salish Indians, embracing the Coeur d'Alene (Skitswish), Columbia (composed of the Chelan, Methow, Sinkaquaiius, Sinkiuse, and Wenatchi or Pisquow), Kalispel (with the Pend d'Oreille and Semteuse), Lake (Senijextee), Sanpoil (the sample tribe, including the Colville and Nespelem), Sinkaietk (southern Okanagon), and Spokan. For data on the kindred Flathead see NR8, on the Interior Salish tribes of British Columbia see NE12.

NR20. Takelma. Specific data on the Takelma tribe.

NR21. Tillamook. Specific data on the Tillamook Indians, including the Nehalem, Nestucca, and Siletz.

NR22. Tolowa. Specific data on the Tolowa Indians, including the kindred Chastacosta, Chetco, Coquille, Gallice, Tututni, and Umpqua.

NR23. Upper Chinook. Specific data on the Upper Chinook Indians, embracing the Wasco and Wishram. For data on the Lower and Middle Chinook see NR6.

NS1. California. General data on the modern state of California and its people, and specific data on its non-aboriginal inhabitants. For data on
the Mexicans of California see NT4, on other incompletely acculturated immigrant groups see N6.

NS2. Historical California. Specific data on the history and culture history
of California and its non-aboriginal inhabitants.

NS3. Prehistoric California. Specific data on the prehistoric peoples and cultures of California.

NS4. California Indians. General data on the Indians of California and on the
central and southern Californian culture areas. For data on the
Athapaskans see ND3, on the Great Basin Indians see NT6, on the
Northern Paiute see NR13, on the Northwest Coast Indians see NE3,
on the Southern Paiute see NT16, on the Tolowa see NR22, on the
Washo see NT20, on the Western Shoshone see NT22, on the Yuma
tribes of the Colorado River see NT15.

NS5. Achomawi. Specific data on the Achomawi tribe, including the kindred
Atsugewi.

NS6. Chimariko. Specific data on the Chimariko tribe.

NS7. Chumash. Specific data on the Chumash tribe, including the Indians of
the offshore islands of San Miguel, Santa Cruz, and Santa Rosa.

NS8. Costano. Specific data on the Costano Indians, including the neighboring
Esselen.

NS9. Diegueno Specific data on the Diegueno Indians, including the
kindred Akwaala, Kiliwa, and Pipai.

NS10. Gabrielino. Specific data on the Gabrielino Indians, including the related Fernandeno, Nicoleno, and Santa Catalina Islanders.

NS11. Hupa. Specific data on the Hupa tribe, including the kindred Chilula,
Tlelding, and Whilkut.

NS12. Karok. Specific data on the Karok tribe.

NS13. Kawaiisu. Specific data on the Kawaiisu Indians.

NS14. Luiseno. Specific data on the Luiseno Indians, including the kindred Agua Caliente, and Juaneno.

NS15. Maidu. Specific data on the Maidu Indians, including the related Nisenan.

NS16. Miwok. Specific data on the Miwok Indians, including the Olamentke or Coast Miwok.

NS17. Modoc. Specific data on the Modoc tribe. For data on the related Klamath see NR10.

NS18. Pomo   Specific data on the Pomo Indians.

NS19. Salina. Specific data on the Salina (Salinan) Indians.

NS20. Serrano. Specific data on the Serrano Indians, including the neighboring and related Ailliklik, Cahuilla, Cupeno, Kitanemuk, and Vanyuma.

NS21. Shasta. Specific data on the Shasta Indians.

NS22. Tubatulabal   Specific data on the Tubatulabal tribe.

NS23. Wailaki. Specific data on the Wailaki tribe, including the kindred Kato, Lassik, Mattole, Nongatl, and Sinkyone.

NS24. Wappo. Specific data on the Wappo tribe.

NS25. Western Mono. Specific data on the Western Mono tribe, who are culturally quite distinct from the Eastern Mono or Owens Valley Paiute (NR13).

NS26. Wintun   Specific data on the Wintun Indians, including the kindred Nomlaki, Patwin, and Wintu.

NS27. Wiyot. Specific data on the Wiyot tribe.

NS28. Yana. Specific data on the Yana Indians, including the kindred Yahi.

NS29. Yokuts   Specific data on the Yokuts nation.

NS30. Yuki. Specific data on the Yuki tribe, including the related Huchnom.

NS31. Yurok   Specific data on the Yurok Indians.

NT1. Southwestern States. General data on the modern states of Arizona, Colorado, Nevada, New Mexico, and Utah and their people, and specific data on their non-aboriginal inhabitants. For data on the Mexicans of the Southwest see NT4.

NT2. Historical Southwest. Specific data on the history and culture history of the southwestern states and of their non-aboriginal inhabitants.

NT3. Prehistoric Southwest. Specific data on the prehistoric peoples and cultures of the southwestern states.

NT4. Mexicans of the Southwest. Specific data on the Mexican immigrants in the southwestern states and California. For data on the Mexicans of Mexico see NU1.

NT5. Southwestern Indians. General data on the Indians of the Southwest culture area and of its component cultural provinces. For data on the Papago see NU28, on the Pima see NU29.

NT6. Great Basin Indians. General data on the Indians of the Great Basin culture area or on the Basin Shoshoneans. For data on the Northern Paiute see NR13, on the Northern Shoshone see NR14.

NT7. Acoma. Specific data on the Indians of Acoma and Laguna pueblos. For data on other Keresan pueblos see NT12.

NT8. Eastern Apache   Specific data on the Chiricahua (with the Gila or Mimbreno), Jicarilla, Lipan, and Mescalero (with the Faraon) tribes of Apache Indians. For data on the Western Apache see NT21, on the Navaho see NT13, on the Kiowa Apache see NQ16, on the Athapaskan Indians in general see ND3.

NT9. Hopi   Specific data on the Indians of the Hopi pueblos of Mishongnovi, Oraibi, Shipaulovi, Shongopovi, Sichomovi, and Walpi. For data on the associated pueblo of Hano see NT18.

NT10. Isleta. Specific data on the Indians of the Tiwa pueblos of Isleta, Isleta del Sur, Piro, Sandia, and Senecu del Sur. For data on the related peoples of Picuris and Taos see NT17.

NT11. Jemez. Specific data on the Indians of the Towa pueblos of Jemez and Pecos.

NT12. Keres   Specific data on the Indians of the Keresan pueblos of Cochiti, San Felipe, Santa Ana, Santo Domingo, and Zia (Sia). For data on the related peoples of Acoma and Laguna see NT7.

NT13. Navaho   Specific data on the Navaho (Navajo) nation. For data on the Athapaskan Indians in general see ND3.

NT14. Plateau Yumans   Specific data on the Havasupai (the sample), Keweyipaya (Southeastern Yavapai), Tolkepaya (Apache-Mohave, Western Yavapai), Walapai, and Yavapai (Mohave-Apache) tribes of Yuman Indians.

NT15. River Yumans   Specific data on the Cocopa (with the Halyikwami and Kohuana), Halchidhoma, Kamia, Kaveltcadom, Maricopa (the sample), Mohave, and Yuma tribes of Yuman Indians along the lower Colorado and Gila Rivers.

NT16. Southern Paiute. Specific data on the Southern Paiute tribes, including the Chemehuevi, Kaibab, Moapa, and Shivwits.

NT17. Taos   Specific data on the Indians of the Tiwa pueblos of Picuris and Taos. For data on the related Isleta people see NT10.

NT18. Tewa   Specific data on the Indians of the Tewa pueblos of Hano, Nambe, Pojoaque, San Ildefonso (the sample), San Juan, Santa Clara, Tano, and Tesuque.

NT19. Ute   Specific data on the Ute Indians.

NT20. Washo. Specific data on the Washo Indians.

NT21. Western Apache. Specific data on the Arivaipa, Carrizo, Cibecue, Pinaleno, San Carlos, Tonto, and White Mountain tribes of Apache Indians. For data on the Eastern Apache see NT8.

NT22. Western Shoshone. Specific data on the Western Shoshone tribes of Nevada, including the Gosiute and the Panamint (Koso) of California.

NT23. Zuni   Specific data on the Indians of Zuni pueblo.

NT24. Mormons. Specific data on the Mormons, including the Mormons of Utah and neighboring states.

Mexico

NU1. Mexico. General data on modern Mexico and its people, and specific data on its non-aboriginal and mixed or mestizo inhabitants. For data on Mexico southeast of the Isthmus of Tehuantepec see NV1, on

Mexicans in the United States see NT4, on Latin Americans in general see S1, on Latin American immigration see S6.

NU2. <u>Historical Mexico</u>. Specific data on the history and culture history of Mexico since the time of Cortez.

NU3. <u>Prehistoric Mexico</u>. Specific data on the prehistoric peoples and cultures of Mexico. For data on the prehistory of southeastern Mexico see NV3.

NU4. <u>Mexican Indians</u>. General data on the Indians of Mexico, including materials on acculturation. For data on the Mayan peoples see NV4, on Middle American civilization in general see NY1.

NU5. <u>Uto-Aztekans</u>. General data on the languages and culture of the Indians speaking Uto-Aztekan languages. For data on the Shoshonean tribes of the Great Basin see NT6.

NU6. <u>Acaxee</u>. Specific data on the Acaxee Indians, including the Hume and Xixime.

NU7. <u>Aztec</u> Specific data on the ancient Aztecs (Tenochca) and related Nahuan tribes of the Valley of Mexico, including the Colima and other Nahuan peoples of the Pacific slope, the Olmec and other Nahuan peoples of the Gulf coast, and the Ahululco and other Nahuan peoples on the Caribbean side of the Isthmus of Tehuantepec. For data on ancient Middle American civilization in general see NY1, on the Pipil see NV8.

NU8. <u>Cahita</u> Specific data on the Cahita nation, embracing the Baciroa, Conicari, Macoyahui, Mayo, Tepahue, and Yaqui tribes.

NU9. <u>Cazcan</u>. Specific data on the Cazcan Indians, including the neighboring Coca and Tehuexe.

NU10. <u>Chinantec</u>. Specific data on the Chinantec tribe.

NU11. <u>Choco</u>. Specific data on the Choco Indians, including the kindred Trique.

NU12. <u>Coahuiltec</u>. Specific data on the Coahuiltec Indians, embracing the Alasapa, Borrado, Comecrudo, Mescal, Orejon, Pakawa, Pampopa, Pausane, Pihuique, Sanipao, Tacame, Tilijayo, and Venado tribes.

NU13. <u>Cochimi</u>. Specific data on the Cochimi Indians of Lower California.

NU14. <u>Concho</u>. Specific data on the Concho tribe, including the Chinarra and Chizo.

NU15. Cora. Specific data on the Cora Indians, including the adjacent Tecual.

NU16. Guasave. Specific data on the Guasave Indians, including the Achire.

NU17. Huastec. Specific data on the Huastec nation. For data on the kindred Maya see NV4.

NU18. Huave. Specific data on the Huave tribe.

NU19. Huichol   Specific data on the Huichol tribe.

NU20. Jumano. Specific data on the Jumano tribe, including the Suma.

NU21. Matlatzinca. Specific data on the Matlatzinca tribe, including the kindred Mazahua.

NU22. Mazatec. Specific data on the Mazatec Indians, including the related "Popoloca" to the northwest. These Otomanguean Popoloca are not to be confused with the Mizocuavean Popoluca (see NU30).

NU23. Mixe   Specific data on the Mixe Indians, including the related Zoque.

NU24. Mixtec. Specific data on the Mixtec nation, including the related Amusgo and Chichatec.

NU25. Opata. Specific data on the Opata tribe, including the Heve (Eudeve) and Jova.

NU26. Otomi. Specific data on the Otomi nation. For data on the related but culturally backward Pame see NU27.

NU27. Pame. Specific data on the Pame Indians.

NU28. Papago   Specific data on the Papago Indians.

NU29. Pima   Specific data on the Pima nation, embracing the Nevome (Pima Bajo), Pima Alta, Sobaipuri, Ure, and Yecora tribes.

NU30. Popoluca. Specific data on the Popoluca Indians. For data on the unrelated Popoloca see NU22.

NU31. Seri   Specific data on the Seri tribe.

NU32. Tamaulipec. Specific data on the Tamaulipec Indians, including the adjacent Janambre.

NU33. Tarahumara   Specific data on the Tarahumara tribe.

NU34. Tarasco   Specific data on the Tarascan nation.

NU35. Tehueco. Specific data on the Tehueco Indians, including the neighboring
        Bamoa, Chinipa, Cinaloa, Comarito, Guasapar, Huite, Nio, Ocoroni,
        Oquero, Temori, Tubar, Varohio, Zoe, and Zuaque.

NU36. Tepehuan. Specific data on the Tepehuan Indians, including the re-
        lated Tepecano.

NU37. Tepoztlan   Specific data on the modern Mexican community of
        Tepoztlan.

NU38. Tequistlatec. Specific data on the Tequistlatec tribe.

NU39. Tlapanec. Specific data on the Tlapanec tribe. For data on the re-
        lated Subtiaba see SA18.

NU40. Totonac. Specific data on the Totonac nation.

NU41. Totorame. Specific data on the Totorame Indians, including the
        neighboring Mocorito and Tahue.

NU42. Waicuri. Specific data on the Waicuri (Guaicuri) of Lower California,
        including the neighboring Pericu.

NU43. Zacatec. Specific data on the Zacatec Indians, including the neighboring
        Guachichil and Lagunero.

NU44. Zapotec   Specific data on the Zapotec nation, including the kin-
        dred Chatino.

NU45. Chichimec. Specific data on the refugee Chichimec groups of north
        central Mexico.

                              Yucatan

NV1.   Yucatan. General data on the modern Mexican states southeast of the
        Isthmus of Tehuantepec, i.e., Campeche, Chiapas, Quintana Roo,
        Tabasco, and Yucatan, and their people, and specific data on their
        non-aboriginal and acculturated native inhabitants. For data on
        modern Mexico as a whole see NU1.

NV2.   Historical Yucatan. Specific data on the history and culture history of
        southeastern Mexico and its non-aboriginal inhabitants.

NV3.   Prehistoric Yucatan. Specific data on the prehistoric peoples and cul-
        tures of southeastern Mexico. For comparable data on British

Honduras see NX3.

NV4. Maya. General data on the Mayan-speaking peoples as a whole and specific data on the Maya of Yucatan and British Honduras at the time of the Spanish Conquest. For data on the modern Yucatec Maya see NV10, on ancient Middle American civilization in general see NY1.

NV5. Chiapanec. Specific data on the Chiapanec, an Otomanguean tribe in Chiapas.

NV6. Chol. Specific data on the ancient and modern Chol.

NV7. Chontal. Specific data on the ancient and modern Chontal.

NV8. Pipil. Specific data on the Pipil, a Nahuan people residing on the coast of Chiapas and in several enclaves farther south in Central America.

NV9. Tzeltal. Specific data on the Tzeltal of interior Chiapas, including the related Tzotzil. For data on the neighboring Mam see NW8.

NV10. Yucatec Maya Specific data on the post-Conquest and modern Maya of the Yucatan Peninsula and British Honduras, including the kindred Lacandon. For data on the Chorti see NW6.

Guatemala

NW1. Guatemala. General data on modern Guatemala and its people, and specific data on its non-aboriginal and acculturated or mestizo inhabitants. For data on Central America as a whole see SA1.

NW2. Historical Guatemala. Specific data on the history and culture history of Guatemala and its non-aboriginal inhabitants since the Spanish Conquest.

NW3. Prehistoric Guatemala. Specific data on the prehistoric peoples and cultures of Guatemala.

NW4. Guatemalan Indians. General data on the Indians of Guatemala or on the upland Mayan peoples, including materials on acculturation. For data on the Maya in general see NV4.

NW5. Cakchiquel. Specific data on the Cakchiquel nation.

NW6. Chorti. Specific data on the Chorti people of eastern Guatemala and adjacent Honduras.

NW7. Jacaltec. Specific data on the Jacaltec tribe, including the neighboring Chanabal, Chuj, and Kekchi.

NW8. Mam. Specific data on the Mam people of Guatemala and adjacent Chiapas, including the neighboring Chicomucaltec and Motozintlec.

NW9. Pokomam. Specific data on the Pokomam tribe, including the neighboring Pokonchi.

NW10. Quiche. Specific data on the Quiche nation, including the neighboring Aguacutec, Ixil, Tzutuhil, and Uzpantec.

NW11. San Pedro la Laguna   Specific data on the modern Indian community of San Pedro la Laguna in highland Guatemala.

British Honduras

NX1. British Honduras. General data on modern British Honduras or Belize and its peoples, and specific data on its non-aboriginal inhabitants. For data on Central America as a whole see SA1, on the Indians of British Honduras see NV4 and NV10.

NX2. Historical British Honduras. Specific data on the history of British Honduras and its non-aboriginal inhabitants.

NX3. Prehistoric British Honduras.. Specific data on the prehistoric peoples and cultures of British Honduras.

Middle America

NY1. Middle American Civilization. General data on the higher civilizations of native America, particularly of central and southeastern Mexico, Central America, and the Andean region of South America. For general data on the Central American Indians see SA2.

North American Islands

NZ1. North American Islands. General and specific data on Clipperton, Revilla Gigedo, and other lesser islands off the coast of North America. For data on the Aleutian Islands see NA6, on Baffin Island see ND5, on the Bahamas see SW1, on Cuba see SX1, on Greenland see NB1, on Iceland see EQ1, on Kodiak Island see NA10, on Newfoundland see NI1, on Nunivak and St. Lawrence Islands see

NA13, on Prince Edward Island see NJ1, on the Queen Charlotte
Islands see NE9, on Vancouver Island see NE1, on Victoria Island
see ND8.

NZ2.   Bermuda. Specific data on the island of Bermuda, its inhabitants, and
        its history.

NZ3.   St. Pierre and Miquelon. Specific data on the French islands of St.
        Pierre and Miquelon, their inhabitants, and their history.

01. <u>Oceania</u>. General data on modern Oceania, including Australia, Indonesia, and the Philippines, on its inhabitants, and on any three or more of the political divisions distinguished below. For general data on the Malayo-Polynesian peoples see 04.

02. <u>Historical Oceania</u>. General data on the history and recorded culture history of Oceania.

03. <u>Prehistoric Oceania</u>. General data on the prehistoric peoples and cultures of Oceania.

04. <u>Malayo-Polynesians</u>. General data on the Malayo-Polynesian or Austronesian peoples and their languages and culture. For data on the Formosan aborigines see AD4, on the Indonesians see 0B1, on the Malagasy see FY2, on the Malays see AN5, on the Malayo-Polynesian tribes of Indo-China see AM6, on the Melanesians see 0K2, on the Micronesians see 0R4, on the Polynesians see 0S2.

05. <u>Oceanic Negritos</u>. General data on the Negrito peoples of Southeast Asia and Oceania. For specific data on the Semang and other Negrito tribes of Malaya see AN7, on Andamanese Negritos see AZ2, on the Aeta or Zambales-Bataan Negritos of western Luzon see 0A4, on other Philippine Negritos see 0A31, and on other localized but unlisted groups see the respective area categories.

Philippines

0A1. <u>Philippines</u>   General data on the Philippine Islands and their modern inhabitants, and specific data on their non-aboriginal inhabitants.

0A2. <u>Historical Philippines</u>. Specific data on the history and recorded culture history of the Philippines.

0A3. <u>Prehistoric Philippines</u>. Specific data on the prehistoric peoples and cultures of the Philippine Islands.

0A4. <u>Aeta</u>   Specific data on the Aeta (Agta, Eta, Ita) or Zambales-Bataan Negritos of western Luzon. For data on other Philippine Negritos see 0A31.

0A5. <u>Apayao</u>   Specific data on the Apayao (Apayaw, Isneg) of northern Luzon, including the Magapta, Mandaya, Talifugo-Ripang, and Tawit.

0A6. <u>Ata</u>. Specific data on the Ata of Mindanao, including the kindred Dugbatang and Tugauanum.

0A7. <u>Bagobo</u>. Specific data on the Bagobo of Mindanao, including the Eto, Gianga (Gulanga), and Obo (Tagdapaya).

0A8. <u>Bajau</u>. Specific data on the Bajau (Badjo, Lutao) or Philippine Sea Gypsies. For data on the related Orang Laut of Indonesia see 0B4.

OA9. Batak.   Specific data on the Batak (Tinitian) of Palawan, a Veddoid people often mistakenly regarded as Negritos.

OA10. Bilaan.   Specific data on the Bilaan (Biraan, Tagalagad) of Mindanao, including the kindred Balud (Sarangani, Tumanao) and Buluan.

OA11. Bisayas Pagans.   Specific data on the pagan tribes of the Bisayas, including the Agtaa and Ati (Kalibugan, Montesco, Mundo).

OA12. Bontok.   Specific data on the Bontok (Bontoc Igorot, Guian, Itetapan) of northern Luzon.

OA13. Bukidnon.   Specific data on the Bukidnon tribe of Mindanao, including the kindred Banuauon (Bananaw).

OA14. Central Bisayan   Specific data on the Bisayan (Visayan) proper of the central Philippines, including the Aklan (Aklanon), Banton, Bohol, Hantik (Antique), Hiligaynon (Ilongo, Panayano), Hiniraya (Binukidnon), Samar-Leyte Bisayan (Waray-Waray), and Sugbuhanon (Cebuano, Sebuan).   For data on the Northwest Bisayan see OA30.

OA15. Central Mangyan.   Specific data on the central Mangyan tribes of Mindoro, embracing the Alangan, Bangon, Baribi, Batangan, Nauhan, Pula, and Tagaydan.   For data on other so-called Mangyan tribes see OA18 and OA23.

OA16. Coastal Moro.   Specific data on the maritime Moro tribes of the southwestern Philippines, including the Isamal, Jama Mapun (Cagayan Sulu), Samal, Sangil (Sangir), Taw Sug (Joloano, Sulu), and Yakan. For data on the inland Moro see OA22.

OA17. Dumagat.   Specific data on the Dumagat people of eastern Luzon, including the Alabat, Kalawat, Polillo, and Sierra Madre.

OA18. Hanunoo   Specific data on the Hanunoo (Hampangan, Minangyan) of Mindoro, including the kindred Buhid (Buid, Buhil) and pagan Ratagnon (Aradigi, Lactan, Latagnon).

OA19. Ifugao   Specific data on the Ifugao (Ifugaw) of northern Luzon, including the Kiangan, Lagawe, Mayoyao, Silipan, and Tokukan-Asin.

OA20. Igorot.   Specific data on the Igorot proper of northern Luzon, embracing the Ibaloi (Benguet Igorot, Inibiloi, Nabaloi), Kankanai (Lepanto Igorot), and pagan Gaddang.

0A21. Ilongot. Specific data on the Ilongot (Lingote) of northern Luzon, including the Abaka, Egongot, Ibalao, and Italon.

0A22. Inland Moro. Specific data on the inland Moro tribes of Mindanao, embracing the Lanao (with the Ilanun and Maranao) and Magindanao.

0A23. Iraya. Specific data on the Iraya of Mindoro, including the Alag-Bako, Dulangan, and Pagbahan.

0A24. Kalinga. Specific data on the Kalinga (Calinga) of northern Luzon, including the Ablig-Saligsig, Balbalasang-Ginaang, Kalagua, Lubuagan, Mangali-Lubo, and Nabayugan.

0A25. Kulaman. Specific data on the Kulaman (Culaman) of southern Mindanao.

0A26. Mamanua. Specific data on the Mamanua, a Veddoid tribe in Mindanao.

0A27. Mandaya. Specific data on the Mandaya of eastern Mindanao, including the Karaga, Magosan, Mansaka, and Pagsupan.

0A28. Manobo. Specific data on the Manobo (Debabaon, Libaganon), including the kindred Mangguangan.

0A29. Northern Filipinos. Specific data on the Christian Gaddang, Ibanag (Kagayan), Iloko (Ilocano), Isinai (Inmeas), and Ivatan (Batan) peoples of the northern Philippines.

0A30. Northwest Bisayan. Specific data on the northwestern Bisayan (Visayan) peoples, including the Agutaynon, Christian Ratagnon, Kalamian (Calamiano), and Kuyonon (Cuyo, Cuyuno). For data on the Bisayan proper see 0A14.

0A31. Philippine Negritos. General data on the Negrito tribes of the Philippines and specific data on Negrito groups other than the Aeta (see 0A4). The Ata (0A6), Batak (0A9), Bisayas Pagans (0A11), and Mamanua (0A26) are often incorrectly regarded as Negritos. For data on the Negritos of the Andaman Islands see AZ2, on the Negritos of Malaya see AN7.

0A32. Southern Filipinos. Specific data on the Christian Bikol (Vicol), Pampangan, Pangasinan, and Sambali (Sambal) peoples of southern and central Luzon.

0A33. Subanun Specific data on the Subanun (Subano) of western Mindanao, including the Malindang, Sibuguey, Sindangan, and Siokon.

0A34. Tagabili. Specific data on the Tagabili tribe of southern Mindanao.

0A35. Tagakaolo. Specific data on the Tagakaolo (Calagar, Kalagan) of southern Mindanao, including the kindred Loao.

0A36. Tagalog Specific data on the Tagalog nation of central Luzon and adjacent islands, including the Bataan, Batangan, Bulakan, Maynila, Palauan, Tanay-Paete, and Tayaba.

0A37. Tagbanua. Specific data on the Tagbanua of Palawan, including the Keney (Queney), Palawan, Silanganen (Bulalacauno), and Tangdulanen.

0A38. Tinggian. Specific data on the Tinggian (Itney, Tinguian) of northern Luzon.

0A39. Tiruray. Specific data on the Tiruray (Teduray) of southern Mindanao.

Indonesia

0B1. Indonesia. General data on modern Indonesia and its inhabitants. For data on the Malayo-Polynesian peoples in general see 04.

0B2. Historical Indonesia. General data on the history and recorded culture history of Indonesia and its peoples.

0B3. Prehistoric Indonesia. General data on the prehistoric peoples and cultures of Indonesia.

0B4. Orang Laut Specific data on the Orang Laut, Bajau (Badjo), or Sea Gypsies of Indonesia and Malaya. For data on the kindred Bajau of the Philippines see 0A8, on the Salon or Sea Gypsies of the Mergui Archipelago see AP8.

Borneo

0C1. Borneo. General data on the island of Borneo or Kalimantan, or on the part administered by Indonesia, and its inhabitants. For specific data on the British possessions in Borneo see 0C4.

0C2. Historical Borneo. General data on the history of Borneo and specific data on the history of former Dutch Borneo.

0C3. Prehistoric Borneo. Specific data on the prehistoric peoples and cultures of Borneo.

0C4. British Borneo. Specific data on British North Borneo, Brunei, and Sarawak, on their history, and on their modern economy, government, and non-aboriginal inhabitants.

0C5. Bahau. Specific data on the Bahau nation, including the Kayan and Kenya tribes.

0C6. Iban   Specific data on the Iban or Sea Dyak people.

0C7. Klamantan   Specific data on the Klamantan nation, including the Dusun, Kalabit, Milanau, and Murut tribes.

0C8. Land Dyak. Specific data on the Land Dyak people, including the Landak and Tayan.

0C9. Ngadju. Specific data on the Ngadju nation, including the Biadju, Katingan, Lawangan, Maanyan, and Ot Danom tribes.

0C10. Punan. Specific data on the Punan people, including the Basap, Bukit, and Bukitan.

Sumatra

0D1. Sumatra. General data on modern Sumatra, its offshore islands, and their inhabitants. For data on the true Malays see AN5.

0D2. Historical Sumatra. Specific data on the history and recorded culture history of Sumatra.

0D3. Prehistoric Sumatra. Specific data on the prehistoric peoples and cultures of Sumatra.

0D4. Atjehnese. Specific data on Atjeh and the Atjehnese people.

0D5. Batak   Specific data on the Batak nation and their country.

0D6. Enggano. Specific data on the island of Enggano and the Engganese people.

0D7. Gayo-Alas. Specific data on the Alas and Gayo tribes.

0D8. Kubu. Specific data on the Veddoid tribes of Sumatra, including the Akit, Benua, Kubu, Lubu, Mamak, and Sakai.

0D9. Mentawei   Specific data on the Mentawei Islands and the Mentaweian people.

0D10. Minangkabau   Specific data on the Minangkabau nation.

0D11. Nias. Specific data on the island of Nias and the aboriginal Niassans.

0D12. Redjang-Lampong. Specific data on the Lampong, Lebong, Pasemah, Redjang, and kindred Malay tribes of south Sumatra.

Java

0E1. Java. General data on the island of Java, including Madura, and their modern inhabitants, and specific data on their non-aboriginal inhabitants. For general data on modern Indonesia see 0B1.

0E2. Historical Java. Specific data on the history and recorded culture history of Java.

0E3. Prehistoric Java. Specific data on the prehistoric peoples and cultures of Java.

0E4. Badui. Specific data on the Badui people.

0E5. Javanese   Specific data on the Javanese nation and their culture.

0E6. Madura. Specific data on the island of Madura and the Madurese people.

0E7. Sundanese. Specific data on the Sundanese nation.

0E8. Tenggerese. Specific data on the Tenggerese people.

Lesser Sundas

0F1. Lesser Sundas. General data on the Lesser Sunda Islands and their modern inhabitants.

0F2. Historical Lesser Sundas. Specific data on the history and recorded culture history of the Lesser Sunda Islands. For specific data on Portuguese Timor and its history see 0F4.

0F3. Prehistoric Lesser Sundas. Specific data on the prehistoric peoples and cultures of the Lesser Sunda Islands.

0F4. Portuguese Timor. Specific data on Portuguese Timor, its history, and its modern economy, government, and non-aboriginal inhabitants.

For data on the native peoples of Timor see OF20.

OF5. Alor   Specific data on the islands of Alor and Solor and their inhabitants.

OF6. Babar. Specific data on the Babar Islands and their inhabitants.

OF7. Bali   Specific data on the island of Bali and the Balinese people, including the Bali Aga.

OF8. Damar. Specific data on the Damar and Roma Islands and their inhabitants.

OF9. Flores. Specific data on the island of Flores and its inhabitants, including the Manggarai, Ngada, Roka, and Sika.

OF10. Kisar. Specific data on the island of Kisar and its inhabitants.

OF11. Leti. Specific data on the islands of Lakor, Leti, and Moa and their inhabitants.

OF12. Lombok. Specific data on the island of Lombok and its inhabitants, including the Bodha and Sasak.

OF13. Nila. Specific data on the islands of Nila, Sema, and Teun and their inhabitants.

OF14. Roti. Specific data on the island of Roti and its inhabitants.

OF15. Savu. Specific data on the island of Savu and its inhabitants.

OF16. Sermata. Specific data on the islands of Luang and Sermata and their inhabitants.

OF17. Sumba. Specific data on the island of Sumba and its inhabitants.

OF18. Sumbawa. Specific data on the island of Sumbawa and its inhabitants, including the Bimanese, Do Donggo, and Sumbawanese.

OF19. Tanimbar. Specific data on the island of Tanimbar or Timorlaut and its inhabitants.

OF20. Timor. Specific data on the island of Timor and its inhabitants, including the Atoni, Belu, and Kupangese. For data on Portuguese Timor see OF4.

0F21. Wetar. Specific data on the island of Wetar and its inhabitants.

Celebes

0G1. Celebes. General data on Celebes or Sulawesi, its immediately offlying islands, and their modern inhabitants.

0G2. Historical Celebes. Specific data on the history and recorded culture history of Celebes.

0G3. Prehistoric Celebes. Specific data on the prehistoric peoples and cultures of Celebes.

0G4. Gorontalo. Specific data on the northern peninsula of Celebes and its inhabitants, including the Bolaang, Gorontalese, Minahasa, and Mongondou.

0G5. Loinang. Specific data on the eastern peninsula of Celebes, the Banggai Islands, and their inhabitants, including the Balantak, Banggai, Loinang, and Wana.

0G6. Makassar Specific data on the southwestern peninsula of Celebes and on the Buginese and Makassarese peoples.

0G7. Mori-Laki. Specific data on the southeastern peninsula of Celebes, its offlying islands, and their inhabitants, including the Bungku, Buton (Butung), Kabaena, Laki, Mori, and Muna.

0G8. Sadang. Specific data on the Sadang nation, including the Rongkong and Seko.

0G9. Sangirese. Specific data on the Sangir (Sanghihe) and Talaud (Talaur) Islands and their inhabitants.

0G10. Toala. Specific data on the Toala tribe.

0G11. Toradja Specific data on the Toradja nation of central Celebes, including the Besoa, Napu, Palu, Parigi, and Poso.

Moluccas

0H1. Moluccas. General data on the Molucca or Maluku Islands and their modern inhabitants.

0H2. Historical Moluccas. Specific data on the history and recorded culture history of the Moluccas.

OH3. <u>Prehistoric Moluccas.</u> Specific data on the prehistoric peoples and cultures of the Moluccas.

OH4. <u>Ambon.</u> Specific data on the island of Ambon and its inhabitants.

OH5. <u>Aru.</u> Specific data on the Aru Islands and their inhabitants, including the Aruese, Gungai, and Tungu.

OH6. <u>Banda.</u> Specific data on the Banda Islands and their inhabitants.

OH7. <u>Batjan.</u> Specific data on the Batjan Islands and their inhabitants.

OH8. <u>Buru.</u> Specific data on the island of Buru and its inhabitants.

OH9. <u>Ceram</u> Specific data on the island of Ceram and its inhabitants, including the Bonfia, Patalima, and Patasiwa.

OH10. <u>Ceramlaut.</u> Specific data on the island of Ceramlaut and its inhabitants.

OH11. <u>Goram.</u> Specific data on the Goram or Gorong Islands and their inhabitants.

OH12. <u>Halmahera.</u> Specific data on the islands of Halmahera and Morotai and their inhabitants.

OH13. <u>Kei.</u> Specific data on the Kei or Kai Islands and their inhabitants.

OH14. <u>Obi.</u> Specific data on the island of Obi and its inhabitants.

OH15. <u>Sula.</u> Specific data on the Sula Islands and their inhabitants.

OH16. <u>Ternate.</u> Specific data on the islands of Ternate and Tidore and their inhabitants.

OH17. <u>Watubela.</u> Specific data on the Watubela Islands and their inhabitants.

<u>Australia</u>

OI1. <u>Australia.</u> General data on modern Australia, including Tasmania, and their inhabitants, and specific data on the non-aboriginal Australian people and their culture. For data on the small island dependencies of Australia in the South Pacific see OI3.

OI2. Historical Australia. Specific data on the history and recorded culture history of Australia.

OI3. Norfolk Island. Specific data on Norfolk Island and other small island dependencies of Australia in the South Pacific, e.g., Cato, Lord Howe, and Macquarie Islands.

OI4. Prehistoric Australia. Specific data on the prehistoric peoples and cultures of Australia.

OI5. Australian Aborigines. General data on the Australian aborigines, including materials on acculturation, and specific data on particular tribes not separately listed below. For data on the Tasmanian aborigines see OI19.

OI6. Andedja. Specific data on the Andedja (Kular) tribe of Western Australia.

OI7. Arabana. Specific data on the Arabana (Arrabunna, Urabuna, Wangarabuna) tribe of South Australia.

OI8. Aranda Specific data on the Aranda (Arunta) tribe of central Australia.

OI9. Barkindji. Specific data on the Barkindji (Parkungi) tribe of New South Wales.

OI10. Dieri Specific data on the Dieri tribe of South Australia.

OI11. Kabikabi. Specific data on the Kabikabi (Dippil) tribe of Queensland.

OI12. Kamilaroi Specific data on the Kamilaroi tribe of New South Wales.

OI13. Karadjeri. Specific data on the Karadjeri tribe of Western Australia.

OI14. Kariera. Specific data on the Kariera tribe of Western Australia.

OI15. Kawadji. Specific data on the Kawadji tribe of Queensland.

OI16. Kurnai. Specific data on the Kurnai nation of Victoria, embracing the Brabralung, Braiakaulung, Bratauolung, Krauatungalung, and Tatungalung tribes.

OI17. Murngin Specific data on the Murngin (Wulamba) tribe of northeastern Arnhem Land, Northern Australia, embracing the Barlamomo, Yaernungo, Djinba, Ritarngo, Dai, and Yandjinung.

0118. Narrinyeri. Specific data on the Ngarkat and other tribes of the lower Murray River in South Australia known collectively as Narrinyeri.

0119. Tasmanians   Specific data on Tasmania and its aboriginal inhabitants.

0120. Tiwi   Specific data on the aborigines of Melville and Bathurst Islands, Northern Australia.

0121. Ualarai. Specific data on the Ualarai (Euahlayi, Uollaroi, Yualarai) tribe of New South Wales.

0122. Wikmunkan. Specific data on the Wikmunkan (Munkanu) tribe of Queensland.

0123. Wogait. Specific data on the Wogait tribe of Northern Australia.

0124. Worimi. Specific data on the Worimi (Kattang, Kutthung) tribe of New South Wales.

0125. Yiryoront   Specific data on the Yiryoront (Jirjoront) tribe of Queensland.

0126. Yungar   Specific data on the Kaneang (Kunyung), Koreng (Corine), Minang (Minung), Pibelmen (Biboulmoun, Peopleman), Pindjarup, Wardandi, Wheelman (Wiilmen), and kindred tribes of the Southwest Division of Western Australia.

New Guinea

0J1. New Guinea. General data on the island of New Guinea, its aboriginal inhabitants, and the so-called Papuan languages and cultures, and specific data on acculturation and on tribes not separately listed below. For data on the modern economy, government, and non-aboriginal inhabitants of New Guinea see 0J3, 0J4, and 0J5.

0J2. Prehistoric New Guinea. Specific data on the prehistoric peoples and cultures of New Guinea.

0J3. West Irian. Specific data on West Irian, formerly Netherlands New Guinea, its history, its non-aboriginal residents, and their activities.

0J4. Northeast New Guinea. Specific data on Northeast New Guinea, its history, its non-aboriginal residents, and their activities.

0J5. Papua. Specific data on Papua, its history, its non-aboriginal residents, and their activities.

0J6. Arapesh   Specific data on the Arapesh tribe of Northeast New Guinea.

0J7. Arfak. Specific data on the Arfak tribe of Geelvink Bay, Western New Guinea.

0J8. Banaro. Specific data on the Banaro tribe of Northeast New Guinea.

0J9. Biak. Specific data on Biak and other islands of the western Schouten group in Western New Guinea and on their aboriginal inhabitants.

0J10. Bukaua. Specific data on the Bukaua tribe of Huon Gulf, Northeast New Guinea.

0J11. Iatmul. Specific data on the Iatmul tribe of Northeast New Guinea.

0J12. Kiwai   Specific data on the Kiwai Papuans of the Fly River delta region in Papua.

0J13. Kwoma   Specific data on the Kwoma tribe of the Sepik River, Northeast New Guinea.

0J14. Mafulu. Specific data on the Mafulu tribe in Papua.

0J15. Mailu   Specific data on the Mailu people on the coast of Papua between Cape Rodney and Orangerie Bay.

0J16. Mapia. Specific data on the Mapia Islands north of Western New Guinea and on their inhabitants.

0J17. Marindanim   Specific data on the Marindanim nation, embracing the Kayakaya, Keraki, Merauke, Tugeri, and other tribes of southeastern Western New Guinea and adjacent Papua.

0J18. Monumbo. Specific data on the natives of Manam Island, Northeast New Guinea.

0J19. Motu. Specific data on the Toaripi and other Motuan-speaking tribes of the Port Moresby region of Papua.

0J20. Mount Hagen Tribes. Specific data on the Dika (Jika), Kenjiger, Kobe, Kulyi, Kumdi, Menembe, Mogei, Munjiger, Uga (Ulga), Yamkar, and other tribes of the Mount Hagen region, Northeast New Guinea.

0J21. Namau. Specific data on the Namau (Purari) tribe of the Purari River delta region of Papua.

0J22. Nuforese. Specific data on Noefoor (Noemfoor, Nvefoor) Island in Geelvink Bay, Western New Guinea, and its native inhabitants.

0J23. Orokaiva   Specific data on the Orokaiva tribe of Papua.

0J24. Torres Straits Islands   Specific data on the Torres Straits Islands south of New Guinea and on the Mabuiag, Miriam (the sample), and other indigenous inhabitants.

0J25. Waigeo. Specific data on Waigeo and neighboring islands northwest of Western New Guinea and their aboriginal inhabitants.

0J26. Waropen. Specific data on the Waropen tribe of Western New Guinea.

0J27. Wogeo   Specific data on Wogeo and other islands of the eastern Schouten group in Northeast New Guinea and their aboriginal inhabitants.

0J28. Yabim. Specific data on the Yabim (Jabim) tribe of the Finschhafen region, Northeast New Guinea.

0J29. Kapauku   Specific data on the Kapauku tribe of Western New Guinea.

0J30. Abelam. Specific data on the Maprik-speaking Abelam or Tshwosh (Tsosh, Bush Kanaka) of the Sepik district.

Melanesia

0K1. Melanesia. General data on Melanesia, its non-indigenous inhabitants, and the history of European exploration and economic and political penetration.

0K2. Melanesians. General data on the aboriginal inhabitants of Melanesia, their languages, and their culture. For data on the Malayo-Polynesian peoples as a whole see 04.

Massim

0L1. Massim. General data on the Massim region, especially on the islands immediately southeast of New Guinea, and specific data on the modern non-aboriginal residents of the region and their activities.

0L2. Historical Massim. Specific data on the history of the Massim region.

0L3. Prehistoric Massim. Specific data on the prehistoric peoples and cultures of the Massim region.

0L4. D'Entrecasteaux   Specific data on the D'Entrecasteaux Islands and their inhabitants, including Dobu (the sample), Fergusson, Goodenough, and Normanby Islands.

0L5. Louisades. Specific data on the Louisade Archipelago, including Rossel Island, and its inhabitants.

0L6. Trobriands   Specific data on the Trobriand Islands and their inhabitants.

Bismarck Archipelago

0M1. Bismarck Archipelago. General data on the Bismarck Archipelago and its inhabitants, and specific data on its non-aboriginal residents and their activities. For data on the Marqueen Islands see 0T4, on Nuguria see 0T5, on Nukumanu see 0T6.

0M2. Historical Bismarcks. Specific data on the history of the Bismarck Archipelago.

0M3. Prehistoric Bismarcks. Specific data on the prehistoric peoples and cultures of the Bismarck Archipelago.

0M4. Gazelle Peninsula. Specific data on the Gazelle Peninsula of New Britain and its inhabitants. For data on western New Britain and on New Britain in general see 0M8.

0M5. Kaniet. Specific data on the Kaniet or Anachoret Islands and their inhabitants.

0M6. Manus   Specific data on the Admiralty Islands and their inhabitants, including Manus (the sample).

0M7. Mussau. Specific data on Mussau or St. Matthias Island and its inhabitants.

0M8. New Britain. General data on the island of New Britain (Neu-Pommern) and specific data on western New Britain and its inhabitants. For data on the Gazelle Peninsula see 0M4.

0M9. New Hanover. Specific data on New Hanover or Lavongai Island and its inhabitants.

0M10. New Ireland   Specific data on the island of New Ireland (Neu-Mecklenburg) and its inhabitants, including the village of Lesu (the sample).

OM11. Ninigo. Specific data on the Ninigo Islands, including the Hermit Islands, and their inhabitants.

OM12. Tabar. Specific data on the Tabar Islands and their inhabitants.

OM13. Umboi. Specific data on Umboi Island and its inhabitants.

OM14. Vitu. Specific data on the Vitu Islands and their inhabitants.

OM15. Wuvulu   Specific data on Wuvulu (Matty) and Aua (Dourou) Islands and their inhabitants.

OM16. Nakanai. Specific data on the Nakanai of New Britain, including the Lakalai (West Nakanai).

Solomon Islands

ON1. Solomon Islands. General data on the Solomon Islands and their inhabitants and specific data on their non-aboriginal residents and their activities. For data on the Marqueen Islands see OT4, on Ontong Java see OT8, on Rennell and Bellona Islands see OT9, on Sikiana see OT10, on Tikopia see OT11.

ON2. Historical Solomons. Specific data on the history of the Solomon Islands.

ON3. Prehistoric Solomons. Specific data on the prehistoric peoples and cultures of the Solomon Islands.

ON4. Bougainville. Specific data on the island of Bougainville and its inhabitants. For data on the Melanesian tribes of northern Bougainville see ON6, on the Papuan tribes of southern Bougainville see ON5.

ON5. Buin   Specific data on the Papuan tribes of southern Bougainville.

ON6. Buka   Specific data on the island of Buka and its inhabitants, including the kindred tribes across Buka Passage in northern Bougainville.

ON7. Choiseul. Specific data on the island of Choiseul and its inhabitants.

ON8. Guadalcanal. Specific data on the island of Guadalcanal and its inhabitants, including also the adjacent Florida, Russell, Savo, and Tulagi Islands.

ON9. Malaita   Specific data on the island of Malaita, including smaller nearby islands, and their inhabitants.

ON10. New Georgia. Specific data on the island of New Georgia, including the nearby islands of Gonongga, Kolombangara, Nanguru, Rendova, Tetipari, Vella Lavella, and Wana Wana, and their inhabitants.

ON11. Nissan. Specific data on the Green Islands, including Nissan, and their
inhabitants.

ON12. San Cristobal. Specific data on the island of San Cristobal and its inhabitants.

ON13. Santa Cruz   Specific date on the Santa Cruz Islands and their inhabitants.

ON14. Shortlands. Specific data on the Shortland Islands, including Alu, Fauro,
and Mono, and their inhabitants.

ON15. Ulawa. Specific data on the island of Ulawa and its inhabitants.

ON16. Ysabel. Specific data on Ysabel (Santa Isabel) Island and its inhabitants.

New Hebrides

OO1. New Hebrides. General data on the New Hebrides and their inhabitants,
and specific data on their non-aboriginal residents and their
activities. For data on Aniwa and Erroman islands see OT2.

OO2. Historical New Hebrides. Specific data on the history of the New Hebrides.

OO3. Prehistoric New Hebrides. Specific data on the prehistoric peoples and
cultures of the New Hebrides.

OO4. Ambrym. Specific data on the island of Ambrym and its inhabitants.

OO5. Aneityum. Specific data on the island of Aneityum and its inhabitants.

OO6. Aurora. Specific data on Aurora or Maewo Island and its inhabitants.

OO7. Banks Islands   Specific data on the Banks Islands and their inhabitants.

OO8. Efate. Specific data on the island of Efate and its inhabitants.

OO9. Epi. Specific data on the island of Epi, including the Shepherd Islands,
and their inhabitants.

OO10. Eromanga. Specific data on the island of Eromanga and its inhabitants.

OO11. Espiritu Santo. Specific data on the island of Espiritu Santo and its
inhabitants.

0012. Malekula   Specific data on the island of Malekula and its inhabitants, including Atchin and Vao (the sample), the Nambas and the
various groups on the south portion of the island.

0013. Pentecost. Specific data on the island of Pentecost and its inhabitants.

0014. Tanna   Specific data on the island of Tanna and the Tannese people.

0015. Torres Islands. Specific data on the Torres Islands and their inhabitants.

New Caledonia

0P1. New Caledonia. General data on modern New Caledonia, including the
entire French colonial administrative area, and specific data on the
European, Asiatic, mixed, and acculturated inhabitants of New
Caledonia.

0P2. Historical New Caledonia. Specific data on the history and recorded culture history of New Caledonia.

0P3. Prehistoric New Caledonia. Specific data on the prehistoric peoples and
cultures of New Caledonia and its outlying islands.

0P4. Kanaka   Specific data on the Kanaka (Canaque) or aboriginal inhabitants of New Caledonia, including the Ile des Pins.

0P5. Loyalty Islands   Specific data on the Loyalty Islands and their
aboriginal inhabitants.

0P6. New Caledonian Outliers. Specific data on Avon, Chesterfield, Hunter,
Matthew, Sandy, Walpole, and other small outlying islands administered from New Caledonia.

Fiji

0Q1. Fiji. General data on the modern Fiji Islands and their inhabitants, and
specific data on the European, Asiatic, mixed, and acculturated
inhabitants.

0Q2. Historical Fiji. Specific data on the history of the Fiji Islands.

0Q3. Prehistoric Fiji. Specific data on the prehistoric peoples and cultures
of the Fiji Islands.

0Q4. Fijians. General data on the aboriginal Fijians and their culture.

0Q5. Kandavu. Specific data on the island of Kandavu and its inhabitants.

0Q6. Lau(H,Sl). Specific data on the Lau Islands and their inhabitants.

0Q7. Rotuma   Specific data on the island of Rotuma and its inhabitants.

0Q8. Vanua Levu. Specific data on the island of Vanua Levu and its inhab-
     itants.

0Q9. Viti-i-Loma. Specific data on the islands of Matuku, Moala, Nairai,
     Ngau, and Ovalau and their inhabitants.

0Q10. Viti Levu. Specific data on the island of Vitu Levu and its inhabitants.

0Q11. Yasawa. Specific data on the Yasawa Islands and their inhabitants.

Micronesia

0R1. Micronesia. General data on modern Micronesia under American ad-
     ministration, i.e., since 1945, and on its non-aboriginal, mixed,
     and acculturated inhabitants. For comparable data on the islands
     under British and Australian administration see 0R6 and 0R13.

0R2. Historical Micronesia   Specific data on the history of Micronesia,
     including the periods of Spanish, German, and Japanese hegemony.

0R3. Prehistoric Micronesia. Specific data on the prehistoric peoples and
     cultures of Micronesia.

0R4. Micronesians. General data on the aboriginal peoples, languages, and
     cultures of Micronesia as a whole or of the Caroline Islands in
     particular. For data on the Malayo-Polynesian peoples in general
     see 04, on the Polynesian outliers in Micronesia see 0T3 and 0T7.

0R5. Chamorro   Specific data on the aboriginal Chamorro of the Marianas
     Islands prior to 1900. For data on the modern Guamanians see 0R7.
     on the modern Marianas in general see 0R9.

0R6. Gilberts   Specific data on the Gilbert Islands, including Ocean
     Island (Banaba), and their inhabitants.

0R7. Guam   Specific data on Guam and the Guamanian people since 1900.
     For data on the earlier Chamorro see 0R5.

0R8. Kusaie   Specific data on the island of Kusaie and its inhabitants.

0R9. Marianas   Specific data on the Marianas or Ladrone Islands since

1900 and on their inhabitants, including the immigrant Carolinians. For data on the earlier Chamorro see 0R5, on modern Guam see 0R7.

0R10. Losap. Specific data on the islands of Losap and Nama and their inhabitants.

0R11. Marshalls   Specific data on the Marshall Islands and the Marshallese people.

0R12. Mokil. Specific data on the atolls of Mokil and Pingelap and their inhabitants.

0R13. Nauru   Specific data on the island of Nauru and its inhabitants.

0R14. Nomoi   Specific data on the Nomoi or Mortlock Islands, including the atolls of Etal, Lukunor, Namoluk, and Satawan, and their inhabitants.

0R15. Palau   Specific data on the Palau or Pelew Islands, including Angaur and Kayangel, and their inhabitants.

0R16. Ponape   Specific data on the island of Ponape, including the offlying Ant, Ngatik, Oroluk, and Pakin atolls, and their inhabitants.

0R17. Puluwat   Specific data on the atolls of Pulap, Pulusuk, Puluwat, and Satawal and their inhabitants.

0R18. Southwest Islands   Specific data on the islands of Merir, Pul, Sonsorol, and Tobi and their inhabitants.

0R19. Truk   Specific data on the atoll of Truk and its inhabitants, including the offlying Hall Islands (East Fayu, Murilo, and Nomwin) and the atoll of Nomonuito.

0R20. Ulithi. Specific data on the atoll of Ulithi, including neighboring Fais and Sorol, and their inhabitants.

0R21. Woleai   Specific data on the Central Caroline islands of Eauripik, Elato, Faraulep, Gaferut, Ifaluk (the sample), Lamotrek, Pikelot, West Fayu, and Woleai and their inhabitants.

0R22. Yap   Specific data on the island of Yap, including the offlying atoll of Ngulu, and their inhabitants.

Polynesia

OS1. <u>Polynesia</u>. General data on Polynesia, its non-indigenous inhabitants, and the history of European exploration and economic and political penetration.

OS2. <u>Polynesians</u>. General data on the aboriginal inhabitants of Polynesia as a whole or of Eastern Polynesia. For general data on the Malayo-Polynesian peoples see 04, on the Polynesian outliers see OT1, on Western Polynesia see OU1.

Polynesian Outliers

OT1. <u>Polynesian Outliers</u>. General data on the scattered islands in Melanesia and Micronesia occupied by Polynesian peoples and on their inhabitants.

OT2. <u>Aniwa</u>. Specific data on the New Hebrides islands of Aniwa and Erroman (Futuna) and their inhabitants.

OT3. <u>Kapingamarangi</u> Specific data on the atoll of Kapingamarangi (Greenwich) in the Carolines and its inhabitants.

OT4. <u>Marqueen</u>. Specific data on the Marqueen (Marken or Mortlock) Islands, including Tauu, in the Solomons and their inhabitants.

OT5. <u>Nuguria</u>. Specific data on Nuguria (Abgarris Islands) in the Bismarck Archipelago and its inhabitants.

OT6. <u>Nukumanu</u>. Specific data on Nukumanu (Tasman Islands) in the Solomons and its inhabitants.

OT7. <u>Nukuoro</u> Specific data on Nukuoro in the Carolines and its inhabitants.

OT8. <u>Ontong Java</u> Specific data on Ontong Java (Lord Howe Islands) in the Solomons and its inhabitants.

OT9. <u>Rennell</u>. Specific data on Rennell and Bellona Islands in the Solomons and their inhabitants.

OT10. <u>Sikiana</u>. Specific data on Sikiana (Stewart Islands) in the Solomons and its inhabitants.

OT11. <u>Tikopia</u> Specific data on the island of Tikopia, including Cherry Island, in the Santa Cruz group and their inhabitants.

Western Polynesia

OU1. Western Polynesia. General data on the Western Polynesian islands and their inhabitants. For data on the Polynesians as a whole see OS2.

OU2. Historical Western Polynesia. Specific data on the history of Western Polynesia.

OU3. Prehistoric Western Polynesia. Specific data on the prehistoric peoples and cultures of Western Polynesia.

OU4. American Samoa. Specific data on modern American Samoa and its administration. For data on the Samoan people and their aboriginal culture see OU8.

OU5. Ellice. Specific data on the Ellice Islands and their inhabitants.

OU6. Futuna. Specific data on Futuna (Horn Island) and its inhabitants.

OU7. Niue. Specific data on Niue (Savage Island) and its inhabitants.

OU8. Samoa. General data on the Samoan Islands and specific data on aboriginal Samoan culture.

OU9. Tonga   Specific data on the Tonga or Friendly Islands and their inhabitants.

OU10. Uvea   Specific data on Uvea (Wallis Island) and its inhabitants.

OU11. Western Samoa. General data on the modern nation of Western Samoa since its independence in 1962. For data on the Samoan people and their aboriginal culture, see OU8.

American Polynesia

OV1. American Polynesia. General data on the Polynesian islands administered by the United States and specific data on Baker, Howland, Johnston, and Wake Islands and on the northwestern islands of the Hawaiian chain (Laysan, Lisianski, Midway, Necker, and Nihoa). For data on American Samoa see OU4, on the Polynesians in general see OS2.

OV2. Hawaii. Specific data on modern Hawaii and its inhabitants.

OV3. Historical Hawaii. Specific data on the history and recorded culture history of Hawaii.

OV4. Prehistoric Hawaii. Specific data on the prehistoric peoples and cultures of the Hawaiian Islands.

OV5. Hawaiians. Specific data on the aboriginal Hawaiians and their culture.

OV6. Line Islands. General data on the Line Islands, including those administered or claimed by Great Britain, and specific data on Caroline, Christmas, Fanning, Flint, Jarvis, Malden, Palmyra, Starbuck, Vostok, and Washington Islands.

British Polynesia

OW1. British Polynesia. General data on the smaller Polynesian islands administered by Great Britain and specific data on Ducie, Henderson, and Oeno Islands. For data on the Ellice Islands see OU5, on Tonga see OU9.

OW2. Phoenix Islands. Specific data on the Phoenix Islands, including Canton and Enderbury.

OW3. Pitcairn. Specific data on Pitcairn Island and its inhabitants.

French Polynesia

OX1. French Polynesia. General data on the Polynesian islands administered by France and specific data on their non-aboriginal inhabitants. For data on Futuna see OU6, on the Polynesians in general see OS2, on modern Tahiti see OX8, on Uvea see OU10.

OX2. Historical French Polynesia. Specific data on the history of French Polynesia.

OX3. Prehistoric French Polynesia. Specific data on the prehistoric peoples and cultures of French Polynesia.

OX4. Australs. Specific data on the Austral or Tubuai Islands, including Morotiri and Rapa, and their inhabitants.

OX5. Gambier Islands. Specific data on the Gambier Islands, including Mangareva, and their inhabitants.

OX6. Marquesas   Specific data on the Marquesas Islands and their inhabitants.

OX7. Society Islands. Specific data on the Society Islands and their aboriginal inhabitants. For data on modern Tahiti see OX8.

OX8. Tahiti. Specific data on modern Tahiti and its inhabitants. For data on aboriginal Tahitian culture see OX7.

0X9. Tuamotu. Specific data on the Tuamotu or Paumotu Archipelago and its inhabitants.

Easter Island

0Y1. Easter Island. Specific data on Easter Island and its modern non-aboriginal, mixed, and acculturated inhabitants.

0Y2. Easter Islanders   Specific data on the aboriginal inhabitants of Easter Island and their culture.

New Zealand

0Z1. New Zealand   Specific data on modern New Zealand and its non-aboriginal, mixed, and acculturated inhabitants. For general data on the Polynesian islands administered by New Zealand see 0Z5.

0Z2. Historical New Zealand. Specific data on the history and recorded culture history of New Zealand.

0Z3. Prehistoric New Zealand. Specific data on the prehistoric peoples and cultures of New Zealand.

0Z4. Maori   Specific data on the aboriginal Maori of New Zealand and their culture.

0Z5. New Zealand Polynesia. General data on the Polynesian islands administered by New Zealand and specific data on Antipodes, Auckland, Bounty, Campbell, Kermadec, Palmerston (Stewart), and Suvorov Islands. For data on Niue see 0U7, on the Polynesians in general see 0S2, on Western Samoa see 0U8.

0Z6. Historical New Zealand Polynesia. Specific data on the history of the Polynesian islands administered by New Zealand.

0Z7. Prehistoric New Zealand Polynesia. Specific data on the prehistoric peoples and cultures of the Polynesian islands administered by New Zealand. For data on the prehistory of New Zealand itself see 0Z3.

0Z8. Chatham Islands. Specific data on the Chatham Islands and their inhabitants, including the aboriginal Moriori.

0Z9. Cook Islands   Specific data on the Cook or Hervey Islands, including Mangaia and Rarotonga, and their inhabitants.

0Z10. <u>Manihiki.</u> Specific data on the islands of Manihiki and Rakahanga and their inhabitants.

0Z11. <u>Pukapuka</u>   Specific data on Pukapuka (Danger Islands) and its <u>inhabitants.</u>

0Z12. <u>Tokelau.</u> Specific data on the Tokelau or Union Islands and their inhabitants.

0Z13. <u>Tongareva.</u> Specific data on Tongareva or the Penrhyn Islands and their inhabitants.

RUSSIA

R1. Soviet Union   General data on the Union of Soviet Socialist Republics, on the regions under Russian political control since 1918, or on any three or more of the regional divisions distinguished below. For general data on the Caucasus region see RH1, on European Russia see RA1, on Great Russia see RF1, on Russian Central Asia see RL1, on Siberia see RR1.

R2. Tsarist Russia. General and specific data on the history of Russia and the Russian Empire from Peter the Great to the Russian Revolution. For data on earlier Russian history see RA2.

R3. Circumpolar Culture. General data on the Circumpolar culture area. For general data on Eskimo culture see ND2, on northeastern Siberia see RY1, on northern Siberia see RU1.

European Russia

RA1. European Russia. General data on European as opposed to Asiatic Russia since 1700 A. D. For data on the German colonies in Russia see EL7, on Great Russia see RF1, on the Soviet Union in general see R1.

RA2. Historical Russia. Specific data on the history and recorded culture history of Russia prior to 1700. For data on Russian history from 1700 to 1918 see R2.

RA3. Prehistoric Russia. Specific data on the prehistoric peoples and cultures of European Russia exclusive of the Baltic countries, Caucasia, Karelia, and Moldavia.

RA4. Scyths   Specific data on the Scyths of southern Russia, especially as described by writers of classical antiquity.

Baltic Countries

RB1. Baltic Countries. General and specific data on Estonia, Latvia, and Lithuania and their peoples under Soviet rule. For historical and cultural data on the Estonians see RG4, on the Letts see RB4, on the Lithuanians see RB5, on the extinct Old Prussians see RB6.

RB2. Baltic Prehistory. Specific data on the prehistoric peoples and cultures of the Baltic countries.

RB3. Balto-Slavs. General data on the languages and culture of the Balto-Slavs. For data on the Indo-Europeans in general see E9, on the Letts see RB4, on the Lithuanians see RB5.

RB4. Letts   Specific data on Latvia prior to Soviet rule and on the Lettish people and their culture.

RB5. Lithuanians   Specific data on Lithuania prior to Soviet rule and on the Lithuanian people and their culture.

RB6. Old Prussians. General and specific data on the extinct Baltic people called the Old Prussians, and on their language and culture.

Belorussia

RC1. Belorussia   Specific data on Belorussia (White Russia) and its people. For historical and prehistoric data see R2, RA2, and RA3.

Ukraine

RD1. Ukraine   Specific data on the Ukraine or the Ukrainian Soviet Socialist Republic and its inhabitants since 1918. For earlier historic and prehistoric data see R2, RA2, and RA3.

RD2. Cossacks. Specific data on the pastoral Cossacks of eastern Ukraine and their culture. For data on Ukrainian culture in general see RD4.

RD3. Ruthenians   Specific data on the Ukrainians of the Carpathian Mountains, in particular on the Boiki, Hutsul, and Lemki tribes.

RD4. Ukrainians   General data on the Ukrainian people and specific data on the culture of the sedentary lowland Ukrainians.

Moldavia

RE1. Moldavia. Specific data on modern Moldavia or Bessarabia and its inhabitants under Soviet rule. For data on Rumanian culture see ED1, on the history and prehistory of Bessarabia see ED2 and ED3.

Great Russia

RF1. Great Russia. General and specific data on Great Russia or the Russian Soviet Federated Socialist Republic and its inhabitants since 1918. For data on the dependent Caucasic peoples see RH1, on European Russia in general see RA1, on the dependent Finnic peoples see RG1, on the history and prehistory of Great Russia see R2, RA2, and RA3.

RF2. Great Russians   Specific data on the Great Russian people and
        their culture.

RF3. Bashkir   Specific data on the Bashkir people and on the modern
     Bashkir Autonomous Soviet Socialist Republic.

RF4. European Kalmyk. Specific data on the Kalmyk (Kalmuck) people of
     the Caspian region. For data on the Kalmyk of western Mongolia
     see AH5.

RF5. Kazan Tatar   Specific data on the Tatars of the Kazan region and
        their culture.

RF6. Nogai. Specific data on the Nogai Tatars and their culture.

RF7. Chuvash   Specific data on the Chuvash people and culture and
     on the Chuvash Autonomous Soviet Socialist Republic.

RF8. Crimean Tatar. Specific data on the Crimean Tatars and their his-
        tory and culture.

Finno - Ugrians

RG1. Finno - Ugrians. General data on the languages and culture of the Finno-
     Ugrian peoples or on the Finnic peoples of European Russia. For
     specific data on the Finns see E01, on the Lapps see EP4, on the
     Magyars see EC1, on the Ostyak see RU3, on the Samoyed see RU4,
     on the Vogul see RU6.

RG2. Cheremis   Specific data on the Cheremis people and culture and
     on the modern Mari Autonomous Soviet Socialist Republic.

RG3. [Deleted]

RG4. Estonians   Specific data on the Estonian people and their culture,
     including the kindred Livonians, Vepses, and Votes, and on Estonia
     prior to Soviet rule. For data on the Baltic countries under Soviet
     rule see RB1.

RG5. Karelians. Specific data on Karelia and the Karelian people under Soviet
     rule. For data on Finland and Finnish culture see E01.

RG6. Mordva. Specific data on the Mordvinian people and culture and on the
     Mordva Autonomous Soviet Socialist Republic.

RG7. Votyak   Specific data on the Votyak (Udmurt) people and culture and on the Udmurt Autonomous Soviet Socialist Republic.

RG8. Zyryan   Specific data on the Zyryan (Komi) and Permian people and culture, on the Komi Autonomous Soviet Socialist Republic, and on the Komi-Permyak National Okrug.

Caucasia

RH1. Caucasia. General data on the Caucasus region and its peoples, either inclusive or exclusive of Transcaucasia, and on their condition under Soviet rule. For data on the Aissor see MA6.

RH2. Historical Caucasia. Specific data on the history and recorded culture history of the Caucasus region prior to 1918.

RH3. Prehistoric Caucasia. Specific data on the prehistoric peoples and cultures of the Caucasus region, including Armenia, Azerbaijan, and Georgia.

RH4. Adyge. Specific data on the Adyge (Adige) people and culture and on the modern Adyge Autonomous Oblast.

RH5. Cherkess   Specific data on the Cherkess or Circassian people and culture, on the modern Cherkess Autonomous Oblast, and on the related Termigoy and Abadzekh people.

RH6. Kabardin. Specific data on the Kabardin people and culture and on the modern Kabardian Autonomous Soviet Socialist Republic.

RH7. Kumyk. Specific data on the Kumyk (Kumik) people, including the Balkar and Karachai, and their culture.

RH8. Dagestan   Specific data on the Dagestan Autonomous Soviet Socialist Republic and on the Lezgin (Lesghin) peoples and cultures, including the Agul, Andi, Archin, Avar, Dargin (Hurkan), Didol, Djek, (with the Budukha, Khaput, and Khinalug), Kurin, Lek, (Kazikumuk), Rutul, Tabassaran, and Uden (Oudin.)

RH9. Osset   Specific data on the Osset people and culture and on the modern North Ossetian Autonomous Soviet Socialist Republic and the South Ossetian Autonomous Oblast.

Georgia

RI1.   Georgia. General data on the modern Georgian Soviet Socialist Republic
and its peoples. For data on the Georgians proper and their culture
see RI7.

RI2.   Historical Georgia. Specific data on the history and recorded culture
history of Georgia. For data on Georgian prehistory see RH3.

RI3.   Abkhaz   Specific data on the Abkhaz (Abchas) people and culture and
on the modern Abkhaz Autonomous Soviet Socialist Republic.

RI4.   Adzhar. Specific data on the Adzhar (Adshar) people and culture and on
the modern Adzhar Autonomous Soviet Socialist Republic.

RI5.   Chechen   Specific data on the Chechen people, including the Ingush.

RI6.   Khevsur. Specific data on the Khevsur (Chevsur) people, including the
kindred Pshav and Tush.

RI7.   Grusians   Specific data on the Grusians (Gruzinians) or Georgians
proper and their culture. For data on modern Georgia as a whole see
RI1.

RI8.   Gurians. Specific data on the Gurian people and their culture.

RI9.   Imeretin. Specific data on the Imeretin people and their culture.

RI10.   Laz   Specific data on the Laz or Chan (Dhan) people, including those
of Turkey.

RI11.   Mingrel. Specific data on the Mingrel (Megrel) people and their culture.

RI12.   Swan. Specific data on the Swan (Swanet) people and their culture.

Armenia

RJ1.   Armenia. General data on the modern Armenian Soviet Socialist Republic and its inhabitants.

RJ2.   Historical Armenia. Specific data on the history and recorded culture
history of Armenia and the Armenians. For prehistoric data see RH3.

RJ3.   Armenians   Specific data on the Armenian people and culture, including the Armenians of Iran, Iraq, and Turkey as well as of Armenia.

Azerbaijan

RK1. <u>Azerbaijan.</u> General data on the modern Azerbaydzhan Soviet Socialist Republic and its inhabitants.

RK2. <u>Historical Azerbaijan.</u> Specific data on the history and recorded culture history of Azerbaijan and the Azerbaijani. For prehistoric data see RH3.

RK3. <u>Azerbaijani</u> Specific data on the Azerbaijani (Azeri) people and culture, including the Azerbaijani and related sedentary Turkic peoples (e. g., the Kazvin) in Iran. For data on the Turkic peoples as a whole see RL4.

RK4. <u>Talysh.</u> Specific data on the Talysh (Talish) people and their culture.

RK5. <u>Tat.</u> Specific data on the Tat people and their culture.

Russian Central Asia

RL1. <u>Turkestan.</u> General data on Russian or Soviet Central Asia and its inhabitants.

RL2. <u>Historical Turkestan.</u> General data on the history and recorded culture history of Turkestan prior to 1918.

RL3. <u>Prehistoric Turkestan.</u> Specific data on the prehistoric peoples and cultures of Turkestan or Central Asia.

RL4. <u>Turkic Peoples.</u> General data on the Turkic peoples and their languages and culture. For specific data on the Altaian Tatars see RS2, on the Azerbaijani see RK3, on the Bashkir see RF3, on the Chuvash see RF7, on the Crimean Tatars see RF8, on the Kazan Tatars see RF5, on the Nogai Tatars see RF6, on the Ottoman Turks see M2, on the historical Seljuk Turks see M3, on the Turks of modern Turkey see MB1, on the Uigur see AI4, on the West Siberian Tatars see RT2, on the Yakut see RV2.

Turkmenistan

RM1. <u>Turkmenistan.</u> General and specific data on modern Turkmenistan or the Turkmen Soviet Socialist Republic and its inhabitants. For historical and prehistoric data see RL2 and RL3.

RM2. <u>Turcoman</u> Specific data on the Turcoman or Turkmen people, including those of Iran, and their culture.

Uzbekistan

RN1. Uzbekistan. General and specific data on modern Uzbekistan or the Uzbek Soviet Socialist Republic and its inhabitants. For historical and prehistoric data see RL2 and RL3.

RN2. Kara-Kalpak. Specific data on the Kara-Kalpak people and their culture.

RN3. Kipchak. Specific data on the Kipchak people and their culture.

RN4. Sart. Specific data on the sedentary and urban population of Uzbekistan and adjacent countries.

RN5. Uzbek   Specific data on the Uzbek (Uzbeg) people and their culture. For data on modern Uzbekistan in general see RN1.

Tadzhikstan

R01. Tadzhikstan. General and specific data on modern Tadzhikstan or the Tadzhik Soviet Socialist Republic and its inhabitants. For historical and prehistoric data see RL2 and RL3.

R02. Tadzhik   Specific data on the Tadzhik (Tadjik) people and culture, including those of Afghanistan and Iran as well as of Tadzhikstan.

Kirgizstan

RP1. Kirgizstan. General and specific data on modern Kirgizstan or the Kirgiz Soviet Socialist Republic and its inhabitants. For historical and prehistoric data see RL2 and RL3.

RP2. Kirgiz   Specific data on the Kirgiz (Kara-Kirgiz) people and their culture.

Kazakhstan

RQ1. Kazakhstan. General and specific data on modern Kazakhstan or the Kazakh Soviet Socialist Republic and its inhabitants. For historical and prehistoric data see RL2 and RL3.

RQ2. Kazak   Specific data on the Kazak (Kirgiz-Kaisak) people and their culture.

Siberia

RR1. Siberia. General data on modern Asiatic Russia and its peoples, either exclusive or inclusive of Russian Central Asia. For data on the Soviet Union as a whole see R1, on Russian Central Asia see RL1, on the Turkic peoples see RL4.

RR2. Historical Siberia. General and specific data on the history and re-corded culture history of Siberia prior to 1918.

RR3. Prehistoric Siberia. Specific data on the prehistoric peoples and cul-tures of Asiatic Russia or Siberia.

RR4. Sibiriak Specific data on the Sibiriak or immigrants or colonists from Europe into Siberia prior to 1918.

Altai Region

RS1. Altai Region. General and specific data on the modern Soviet autono-mous regions of Gorno-Altai, Khakas, and Tuva and their inhabitants. For historical and prehistoric data see RR2 and RR3.

RS2. Altaians. Specific data on the Sagai, Shor, Teleut, and other Tatar tribes of the Altai region and their culture.

RS3. Soyot Specific data on the Soyot (Uriankhai) people, including the Karagas, Tuva, and Kotan, and their cultures.

Central Siberia

RT1. Central Siberia. Specific data on the districts and inhabitants of central Siberia, particularly those along the route of the Trans-Siberian Railway from the Urals in the west to Lake Baikal in the east. For data on the European immigrants into this region prior to 1918 see RR4, on the history and prehistory of the region see RR2 and RR3.

RT2. West Siberian Tatar. Specific data on the Baraba, Chulyma, and other Tatar peoples in the region between Tobolsk and Tomsk. For data on the Altaian Tatars see RS2.

Northern Siberia

RU1. Northern Siberia. General and specific data on the modern national dis-tricts of Evenki, Nenets (in northeastern European Russia), Taimyr (Dolgano-Nenets) and Yamalo-Nenets National Okrugs and their in-habitants. For data on the Circumpolar culture area see R3, on the history and prehistory of northern Siberia see RR2 and RR3.

RU2. Ket   Specific data on the Ket (Yeniseians, Yenisei Ostyak) tribe
    and their culture.

RU3. Ostyak   Specific data on the Ostyak (Khanty) tribe and their culture,
    and general information on the Khanty-Mansi National Okrug.

RU4. Samoyed   Specific data on the Samoyed nation and their culture,
    including the Enets, Nenets, Nganasani, Selkup, and Yurak tribes,
    some of which extend into European Russia.

RU5. Tungus   General data on the Tungus nation and specific data on its
    western or Evenki division, including the Birar, Chapogir, Daur, the
    Even (Lamut), Evenki (Tungus proper), the Evenki National Okrug,
    Manegir, Orochon, and Solon tribes. For data on the eastern or
    Goldi division of the Tungus see RX3.

RU6. Vogul. Specific data on the Vogul (Mansi) tribe and their culture. For
    data on the Khanty-Mansi National Okrug see RU3.

Yakutia

RV1. Yakutia. General and specific data on the modern Yakut Autonomous
    Soviet Socialist Republic and its inhabitants. For historical and pre-
    historic data see RR2 and RR3.

RV2. Yakut   Specific data on the Yakut nation, including the Dolgan, and
    their culture.

RV3. Yukagir   Specific data on the Yukagir (Odul) tribe, including the
    kindred Chuvan, and their culture.

Russian Mongolia

RW1. Buryat Mongolia   General and specific data on the Buryat-Mongol
    Autonomous Soviet Socialist Republic, on the Aga ("Aginskiy") and Ust'-
    Orda ("Ust'-Ordynskiy") Buryat Mongol National Okrugs, on their in-
    habitants, and specific data on the Buryat or Northern Mongols and
    their culture. For data on Chinese Mongolia see AH1, on the history
    and prehistory of Buryat Mongolia see RR2 and RR3.

Southeast Siberia

RX1. Southeast Siberia. General data on the Amur River region, the adjacent
    Pacific coast, the island of Sakhalin, and their modern inhabitants.
    For data on the Ainu see AB6, on the Kurile Islands see RZ2, on the
    Sibiriak see RR4, on the history and prehistory of the region see RR2
    and RR3.

RX2. Gilyak   Specific data on the Gilyak (Nivkh) tribe and their culture.

RX3. Goldi   Specific data on the maritime Tungus tribes, including the Amgun, Goldi (Nanai), Kile, Negidal (Negda), Olcha (Ulcha), Orochi, Orok, Samagir, and Ude (Udekhe). For data on the inland Tungus tribes see RU5.

RX4. Birobidzhan. Specific data on the modern Jewish ("Evreyskaya") Autonomous Oblast and its inhabitants.

Northeast Siberia

RY1. Northeast Siberia. General and specific data on the peninsula of Kamchatka, on the modern Chukchee and Koryak National Okrugs, and on their inhabitants. For data on the Circumpolar culture area see R3, on the history and prehistory of northeastern Siberia see RR2 and RR3.

RY2. Chukchee   Specific data on the Chukchee (Luoravetlan) tribe and on the modern Chukchee (Chukotskiy) National Okrug.

RY3. Kamchadal   Specific data on the Kamchadal (Italmen) people and on the peninsula of Kamchatka.

RY4. Koryak   Specific data on the Koryak (Nymylan) tribe and on the modern Koryak National Okrug.

RY5. Yuit. Specific data on the Yuit or Siberian Eskimo and their culture. For data on the Eskimo in general see ND2.

Russian Islands

RZ1. Russian Islands. General and specific data on the islands off the coast of Russia, e. g., Commander (Komandorski) Islands, Franz Joseph Land, Kolguev Island, New Siberian Islands, Novaya Zemlya, and Wrangel Island. For data on the island of Sakhalin see RX1.

RZ2. Kuriles   Specific data on the Kurile Islands and their non-aboriginal inhabitants. For data on the aboriginal Ainu see AB6.

SOUTH AMERICA

S1. South America. General data on modern South America or on Latin
America as a whole, on their non-aboriginal and acculturated or
mestizo inhabitants, or on any three or more of the political
divisions distinguished below. For data on the New World as a whole
see N1.

S2. Historical South America. General data on the history and culture history
of the European peoples of South America or of Latin America as a
whole.

S3. South American Indians. General data on the Indians of South America,
including historical data and materials on acculturation. For data
on the Indians of the New World as a whole see N3, on the higher
aboriginal civilization of Middle America see NY1.

S4. Prehistoric South America. General data on the prehistoric peoples and
cultures of South America. For data and theories on American Indian
origins see N4.

S5. South American Negroes. General data on the Negroes of South America,
including historical materials. For data on the Negroes of the New
World as a whole see N5, on the slave trade see F1.

S6. Immigrant Latin Americans. General data on immigration into Latin
America, and specific data on incompletely assimilated immigrant
groups.

S7. West Indies. General data on the West Indies, their history, and their
modern inhabitants.

Central America

SA1. Central America. General data on Central America, its non-aboriginal
inhabitants, and their history. For specific data on British Honduras
see NX1, on Costa Rica see SA3, on El Salvador see SA5, on Guatemala
see NW1, on Honduras see SA7.

SA2. Central American Indians. General data on the Indians of Central America
or on the Circum-Caribbean culture area as a whole. For data on
the Maya see NV4, on native Middle American higher civilization see NY1,
on the Pipil see NV8.

SA3. Costa Rica   Specific data on Costa Rica, its non-aboriginal inhabitants, their history, and their culture.

SA4. Prehistoric Costa Rica. Specific data on the prehistoric peoples and cultures of Costa Rica.

SA5. El Salvador. Specific data on El Salvador, the Salvadoran people, their history, and their culture.

SA6. Prehistoric El Salvador. Specific data on the prehistoric peoples and cultures of El Salvador.

SA7. Honduras. Specific data on Honduras, its non-aboriginal inhabitants, their history, and their culture.

SA8. Prehistoric Honduras. Specific data on the prehistoric peoples and cultures of Honduras.

SA9. Nicaragua. Specific data on Nicaragua, its non-aboriginal inhabitants, their history, and their culture.

SA10. Prehistoric Nicaragua. Specific data on the prehistoric peoples and cultures of Nicaragua.

SA11. Chorotega. Specific data on the Chorotega (Choluteca) Indians, including the kindred Mangue and Orotina.

SA12. Garif. Specific data on the Garif or "Black Carib" people.

SA13. Jicaque. Specific data on the Jicaque (Xicaque) tribe.

SA14. Lenca. Specific data on the Lenca tribe.

SA15. Mosquito   Specific data on the Mosquito (Miskito) Indians, including the related Matagalpa, Sumo, and Ulva (Woolwa).

SA16. Paya. Specific data on the Paya tribe.

SA17. Rama. Specific data on the Rama Indians, including the kindred Guatuso (Corobici), Guetar, Suerre, and Voto.

SA18. Subtiaba. Specific data on the Subtiaba (Maribio) tribe. For data on the related Tlapanec see NU39.

SA19. Talamanca   Specific data on the Talamanca nation, embracing the Boruca, Bribri, Cabecar, Changuena, Coto, Dorasque, Quepo, and Terraba (Chirripo, Tirub) tribes.

Panama

SB1. **Panama.** General and specific data on modern Panama and its non-aboriginal and acculturated or mestizo inhabitants.

SB2. **Historical Panama.** Specific data on the history and culture history of Panama and the Panamanian people.

SB3. **Prehistoric Panama.** Specific data on the prehistoric peoples and cultures of Panama.

SB4. **Canal Zone.** Specific data on the Panama Canal, the Canal Zone, their history, and the life and activities of the inhabitants of the Canal Zone.

SB5. **Cuna** Specific data on the Cuna Indians.

SB6. **Guaymi.** Specific data on the Guaymi Indians. For data on the neighboring Talamanca see SA19.

Colombia

SC1. **Colombia** General data on modern Colombia and its people, and specific data on its non-aboriginal and acculturated or mestizo inhabitants.

SC2. **Historical Colombia.** Specific data on the history and culture history of Colombia and its non-aboriginal inhabitants.

SC3. **Colombian Indians.** General data on the Indians of Colombia or on the Chibchan tribes or culture area. For data on the Amazonian Indians see SL4, on the Andean area see SE3, on the Chinato see SS17, on the Circum-Caribbean area see SA2, on native Middle American civilization in general see NY1, on the Tucano see SQ19.

SC4. **Colombian Prehistory.** Specific data on the prehistoric peoples and cultures of Colombia.

SC5. **Achagua.** Specific data on the Arawakan-speaking Achagua, Caberre nd (Cabre), Cocaima, and Piapoco tribes of lowland Colombia.

SC6. **Betoi.** Specific data on the Betoi tribe, including the neighboring Airico, Jirara (Girara), Lucalia, and Situfa (Cituja).

SC7. **Cagaba** Specific data on the Cagaba tribe, including the kindred Buntigwa, Chimila, Ica, Kogi, Sanha, and Tairona. These Chibchan-speaking tribes of northern Colombia are sometimes known collectively as "Arhuaco."

SC8. <u>Carijona</u>. Specific data on the Cariban-speaking Carijona (Umaua) tribe.

SC9. <u>Cenu</u>. Specific data on the Chocoan-speaking Cenu tribes of northwestern Colombia, embracing the Abibe, Aburra, Ancerma, Antiocha, Bonda, Buritica, Calamari, Caramanta, Carex, Cartama, Catio, Cenufana, Evijico, Fincenu, Guazuzu, Mompox (Malebu), Nutabe, Pacabueye, Pancenu, Pemeo, Quinchia, Tahami, Tamalameque, Tolu, Turbaco (Turuaco), Urezo, Uruba, Yamaci, Yapel (Ayapel), and Zopia. For data on the Choco proper see SC12.

SC10. <u>Yupa</u>. Specific data on the Cariban-speaking Yupa, including the kindred Araucana, Chake (Motilones Mansos), Carare, Coanao (Guanao), Corbago, Itoto, Opon, Xiriguana, Yariqui, Irapa, Japreria, Macoita, Ovabre, Pariri, Shaparu, Viaksi, Wasama, Woshijpore and Yuco.

SC11. <u>Chibcha</u>. Specific data on the Chibcha (Muisca) nation, including the peripheral Chibchan-speaking Guane, Lache, Morcote, Tecua, and Tunebo (Tama).

SC12. <u>Choco</u>. Specific data on the Choco and Toro of the Pacific coast, including the little known Barbacoa and Yurimango farther south. For other Chocoan tribes of more advanced culture see SC9.

SC13. <u>Goajiro</u>   Specific data on the Arawakan-speaking Goajiro (Guajira) tribe of the Guajira Peninsula.

SC14. <u>Guahibo</u>. Specific data on the Guahibo and Chiricoa, migratory hunting tribes of the eastern savanna country.

SC15. <u>Paez</u>. Specific data on the Chibchan-speaking Paez Indians, including the kindred Andaqui, Coconuco, Guanaca, Moguex, Pijao (Pinao), Purace, Timana, and Yalcon (Cambi), of the southern highlands.

SC16. <u>Pantangoro</u>. Specific data on the Chibchan-speaking Pantangoro tribe of central Columbia, including the kindred Amani, Muzo, Naura, and Panche.

SC17. <u>Pasto</u>. Specific data on the Pasto (Coaiquer) Indians of southwestern Columbia, including the Abad, Camsa (Sebondoy), Guachicon, Ingano, Mastel, Papayanense, and Pataco.

SC18. <u>Puinave</u>. Specific data on the non-agricultural Puinave (Guaipunavo, Macu) tribes of eastern Colombia.

SC19. <u>Witoto</u>   Specific data on the Witoto (Uitoto) nation of south-eastern Colombia, including the kindred Andoke, Bora (Miranya),

Coeruna, Muenane, Nonoya, Ocaina, Orejon, and Resigero tribes.

SC20. Guayupe. Specific data on the Arawakan-speaking Choque, Eperigua, Guayupe (Guaypi), and Sae tribes of lowland Colombia.

Ecuador

SD1. Ecuador. General data on modern Ecuador and its people, and specific data on its non-aboriginal and acculturated or mestizo inhabitants. For general data on the Indians see SE3.

SD2. Historical Ecuador. Specific data on the history and culture history of Ecuador and its non-aboriginal inhabitants.

SD3. Prehistoric Ecuador. Specific data on the prehistoric peoples and cultures of Ecuador.

SD4. Canari. Specific data on the Canari tribe, including the kindred Puruhua.

SD5. Canelo. Specific data on the Canelo or Napo Indians. For data on the kindred Zaparo see SE22.

SD6. Cayapa   Specific data on the Chibchan-speaking Cayapa tribe.

SD7. Colorado   Specific data on the Chibchan-speaking Colorado (Tatchila) tribe.

SD8. Esmeralda. Specific data on the Chibchan-speaking Esmeralda tribe.

SD9. Jivaro   Specific data on the Jivaro Indians, including the kindred Aguaruna, Bracamoro, Huambisa, Malacata, and Palta.

SD10. Manta. Specific data on the Manta of coastal Ecuador, including the related Huancavilca, Puna, and Tumbez.

SD11. Quito. Specific data on the Chibchan-speaking Quito (Panzaleo) tribe, including the kindred Cara, Cofan, Quijo, and Yumbo tribes.

Peru

SE1. Peru   General data on modern Peru and its people, and specific data on its non-aboriginal and acculturated or mestizo inhabitants.

SE2. Historical Peru. Specific data on the history and culture history of Peru and its non-aboriginal inhabitants.

SE3. Peruvian Indians. General data on the Indians of Peru or on the Andean culture area. For data on native Middle American civilization in general see NY1, on the Amazonian Indians see SL4.

SE4. Peruvian Prehistory. Specific data on the prehistoric peoples and cultures of Peru.

SE5. Aguano. Specific data on the Aguano Indians, including the Chamicura, Cutinana, and Urarina (Itucale).

SE6. Amahuaca. Specific data on Panoan-speaking Amahuaca tribe, including the related Capanawa, Comobo, Maspo, Mochobo, Nianagua, Nocoman, Pichobo, Puyumanawa, Rema, Ruanagua, Soboyo, and Sensi.

SE7. Atsahuaca. Specific data on the Panoan-speaking Atsahuaca tribe, including the related Araca and Yamiaca.

SE8. Cahuapana. Specific data on the Cahuapana tribe, including the related Chaywita, Chebero (Xevero), Munichi, and Pambadeque.

SE9. Campa. Specific data on the Arawakan-speaking Campa (Anti) people, including the Amuesha and Chichiren.

SE10. Chama   Specific data on the Panoan-speaking Chama nation, embracing the Carabacho, Cashibo, Conibo, Setebo, and Shipibo tribes.

SE11. Cocama   Specific data on the Cocama (Ucayali) tribe, including the Cocamilla.

SE12. Encabellado. Specific data on the Tucanoan-speaking Encabellado (Angutera, Icaguate, Pioje), including the Correguaje, Coto (Orejon, Payagua), Sioni, and Tama.

SE13. Inca   Specific data on the Inca nation of highland Peru and their civilization at the time of the Spanish Conquest and during the period immediately following to ca. 1600 A.D.

SE14. Lama. Specific data on the Lama (Lamista) tribe, including the neighboring Alon, Amasifuin, Cascoasoa, Chedua, Cholon, Cholto, Cognomona, Cumbaza, Hibito (Xibito), Huatana, Nindaso, Nomona, Payanso, Suichichi, Tabalosa, and Zapaso.

SE15. Masco. Specific data on the Arawakan-speaking Masco tribe, including the Huachipari, Sirineri, Tuyuneri, and Amarakaeri.

SE16. Mayoruna. Specific data on the Panoan-speaking Mayoruna tribe.

SE17. Patagon. Specific data on the Patagon people, including the Bagua, Chachapoya, Chinchipe, Chirino, Copallin, Sacata, and Tabancal.

SE18. **Piro.** Specific data on the Arawakan-speaking Piro (Simirinch) tribe, including the Chontaquiro and Machiguenga.

SE19. **Tepqui.** Specific data on the extinct Tepqui people, including the Chunatahua, Chupacho, Chusco, Comanahua, Panatahua, Quidquidcana, Tingan, and Tulumayo.

SE20. **Yagua** Specific data on the Peban-speaking Yagua, including the kindred Peba and Yameo.

SE21. **Yunca.** Specific data on the extinct Yunca or Chimu nation of coastal Peru.

SE22. **Zaparo.** Specific data on the Zaparo nation, embracing the Andoa, Awishira, Coronado, Gae, Iquito, Maina, Pinche, Roamaina (Omuraina), Semigae, Zapa, and Zaparo tribes.

SE23. **Colonial Quechua.** Specific data on the Quechua-speaking peoples of Peru and Bolivia during the Spanish Colonial era, ca. 1600 to 1820 A.D. For pre-1600 A.D. Quechua see SE13 Inca.

SE24. **Modern Quechua.** Specific data on the Quechua-speaking peoples of Peru and Bolivia following 1820 A.D.

Bolivia

SF1. **Bolivia** General data on modern Bolivia and its people, and specific data on its non-aboriginal and acculturated or mestizo inhabitants. For specific data on the people of Sucre see SF22.

SF2. **Historical Bolivia.** Specific data on the history and culture history of Bolivia and its non-aboriginal inhabitants.

SF3. **Bolivian Indians.** General data on the Indians of Bolivia. For general data on the Amazonian Indians see SL4, on the Andean culture area see SE3, on the Chaco Indians see SK4.

SF4. **Bolivian Prehistory.** Specific data on the prehistoric peoples and cultures of Bolivia.

SF5. **Aymara** Specific data on the Aymara nation of highland Bolivia.

SF6. **Canichana.** Specific data on the Canichana tribe.

SF7. **Cayuvava.** Specific data on the Cayuvava tribe.

SF8. **Chane.** Specific data on the Arawakan-speaking Chane tribes.

SF9. **Chiquito.** Specific data on the Chiquito nation, including the Churapa, Gorgotoqui, Manasi, Penoqui, Pinoco, Siberi, Tamacoci, Tao, and Xaraye tribes.

SF10. Chiriguano. Specific data on the Chiriguano nation.

SF11. Guarayu. Specific data on the Guarayu and Pauserna (Araibayba, Carabere, Itatin) tribes.

SF12. Itonama. Specific data on the Itonama tribe.

SF13. Kitemoca. Specific data on the Chapacuran-speaking Kitemoca (Quitemo) and Napeca tribes.

SF14. Leco. Specific data on the Leco tribe, including the neighboring Apolista (Lapacho).

SF15. Mojo. Specific data on the Arawakan-speaking Mojo tribe, including the kindred Baure.

SF16. Mosetene. Specific data on the Mosetene (Amo, Rache) tribe, including the kindred Chimane.

SF17. Movima. Specific data on the Movima (Moyma) tribe.

SF18. Otuke. Specific data on the Otuke tribe, including the related Coraveca, Curave, Curucaneca, Curuminaca, and Tapii.

SF19. Pacaguara. Specific data on the Panoan-speaking Pacaguara tribe, including the related Capuibo, Caripuna, Chacobo, Jacaria, and Sinabo.

SF20. Saraveca. Specific data on the Arawakan-speaking Saraveca tribe, including the related Paiconeca and Paunaca.

SF21. Siriono. Specific data on the Siriono (Mbia) tribe.

SF22. Sucre. Specific data on the people of the modern city of Sucre and their culture.

SF23. Tacana. Specific data on the Tacana nation, embracing the Araona, Capechene, Cavina, Guacanahua, Maropo, Tacana, Tiatinagua, and Toromona tribes.

SF24. Uru. Specific data on the Uru (Puquina) tribe, including the kindred Chipaya.

SF25. Yuracare. Specific data on the Yuracare tribe.

Chile

SG1. Chile. General data on modern Chile and its people, and specific data on its non-aboriginal inhabitants. For data on the southern provinces of Aysen and Magallanes see SH1, on incompletely assimilated immigrant groups see S6.

SG2. Historical Chile. Specific data on the history and culture history of Chile and its non-aboriginal inhabitants.

SG3. Prehistoric Chile. Specific data on the prehistoric peoples and cultures of Chile.

SG4. Araucanians   Specific data on the Araucanian nation, embracing the Chilote, Huilliche, Mapuche, Pehuenche, and Picunche tribes.

SG5. Atacama. Specific data on the Atacama (Kunza) nation, including the Casavindo, Chango, and Cochinoca tribes.

SG6. Diaguita. Specific data on the Diaguita nation, including the Calchaqui.

Patagonia

SH1. Patagonia. General data on the Fuegian and Patagonian aborigines of southern South America and specific data on the geography and non-aboriginal inhabitants of the southern Chilean provinces of Aysen and Magallanes and the southern Argentinian territories of Chubut, Neuquen, Rio Negro, Santa Cruz, and Tierra del Fuego. For historical and prehistoric data see SG2, SG3, SI2, and SI3.

SH2. Alacaluf   Specific data on the Alacaluf tribe of Tierra del Fuego.

SH3. Chono. Specific data on the Chono tribe of southern Chile.

SH4. Ona   Specific data on the Ona (Shelknam) tribe of Tierra del Fuego, including the kindred Haush.

SH5. Tehuelche   Specific data on the Tehuelche or Patagonian people, including the kindred Poya.

SH6. Yahgan   Specific data on the Yahgan (Yamana) tribe of Tierra del Fuego.

Argentina

SI1. Argentina. General data on modern Argentina and its people, and specific data on its non-aboriginal inhabitants. For data on incompletely assimilated immigrant groups see S6, on the southern territories of

Chubut, Neuquen, Rio Negro, Santa Cruz, and Tierra del Fuego see SH1. on the Indians of the Gran Chaco see SK4.

SI2. Historical Argentina. Specific data on the history and culture history of Argentina and its non-aboriginal inhabitants.

SI3. Prehistoric Argentina. Specific data on the prehistoric peoples and cultures of Argentina.

SI4. Abipon Specific data on the Guaicuran-speaking Abipon (Mepene) tribe.

SI5. Comechingon. Specific data on the Comechingon nation, including the Indama and Sanaviron tribes.

SI6. Huarpe. Specific data on the Huarpe nation, embracing the Allentiac and Millcayac tribes.

SI7. Mataco Specific data on the Mataco (Mataguayo, Nocten) tribe.

SI8. Mocovi. Specific data on the Guaicuran-speaking Mocovi tribe.

SI9. Omaguaca. Specific data on the Omaguaca (Humahuaca) tribe, including the neighboring Ocloya.

SI10. Puelche. Specific data on the Puelche (Genakin, Pampa) tribe, including the kindred Het (Chechehet and Diuihet) and Querandi tribes.

SI11. Timbu. Specific data on the Timbu (Atambi) tribe, including the neighboring Carcarana, Chana-Mbegua, Chana-Timbu, Colastine, Coronda, Mbegua, and Quiloaza.

SI12. Toba Specific data on the Guaicuran-speaking Toba (Natekebit) tribe, including the kindred Aguilot, Cocolot, and Pilaga.

SI13. Tonocote. Specific data on the Tonocote tribe, including the neighboring Matara.

SI14. Vilela. Specific data on the Vilela nation, embracing the Atalala, Chunupe, Lule, Ocole, Omoampa (Umuampa), Pasain, Vacaa, Yecoanita, and Yooc tribes.

Uruguay

SJ1. Uruguay. General data on modern Uruguay and its people, and specific data on its non-aboriginal inhabitants.

SJ2. Historical Uruguay. Specific data on the history and culture history of Uruguay and its non-aboriginal inhabitants.

SJ3. Prehistoric Uruguay. Specific data on the prehistoric peoples and cultures of Uruguay.

SJ4. Chandule. Specific data on the Chandule (Chandri) tribe of the islands of the La Plata estuary.

SJ5. Charrua. Specific data on the Charrua nation, embracing the Bohane, Chana, Charrua, Minuane (Guenoa), and Yaro tribes.

Paraguay

SK1. Paraguay. General and specific data on modern Paraguay and its non-aboriginal, mixed, and acculturated inhabitants.

SK2. Historical Paraguay. Specific data on the history and culture history of Paraguay and its non-aboriginal inhabitants.

SK3. Prehistoric Paraguay. Specific data on the prehistoric peoples and cultures of Paraguay.

SK4. Chaco Indians. General data on the Indians of Paraguay or of the Gran Chaco in general, including the Bolivian and Argentinian Chaco. For data on the Guarani see SM4.

SK5. Ashluslay. Specific data on the Matacoan-speaking Ashluslay (Chulupi) tribe.

SK6. Choroti Specific data on the Matacoan-speaking Choroti (Zolota) tribe.

SK7. Guana Specific data on the Arawakan-speaking Guana (Chana) tribes, including the Echoaladi, Kinikinao, Layana, Niguecactemic, and Terena.

SK8. Guayaki. Specific data on the Tupi-Guarani-speaking Guayaki tribe.

SK9. Maca. Specific data on the Matacoan-speaking Maca (Cochaboth, Enimaga) tribe.

SK10. Mascoi Specific data on the Mascoi nation, embracing the Angaite, Kaskiha, Lengua, Mascoi, Sanafana, and Sapuki tribes.

SK11. Mbaya Specific data on the Mbaya (Caduveo, Guaicuru) nation.

SK12. Payagua. Specific data on the Guaicuran-speaking Payagua (Cadigue) tribe, including the kindred Agaz (Magach).

SK13. Tapiete. Specific data on the Tapiete (Tapii) tribe.

SK14. Zamuco. Specific data on the Zamuco nation, embracing the Chamacoco, Guaranoca, Moro, Morotoco, Poturero, and Tsirakua tribes.

Brazil

SL1. Brazil   General data on modern Brazil and its people. For data on incompletely assimilated immigrant groups see S6.

SL2. Historical Brazil. Specific data on the history and recorded culture history of Brazil and its non-aboriginal inhabitants.

SL3. Prehistoric Brazil. Specific data on the prehistoric peoples and cultures of Brazil.

SL4. Brazilian Indians. General data on the Indians of Brazil, including materials on acculturation, or on the lowland or Amazonian Indians as a whole. For data on the Arawakan linguistic group see SR6, on the Cariban linguistic group see SR7, on the Ge linguistic group see SL5, on the Tupi-Guarani linguistic group see SL6.

SL5. Ge. General data on the languages and culture of the Indians of the Ge linguistic stock.

SL6. Tupi-Guarani. General data on the languages and culture of the Indians of the Tupi-Guarani linguistic stock.

South Brazil

SM1. South Brazil. Specific data on the southern Brazilian states of Parana, Rio Grande do Sul, and Santa Catarina and their non-aboriginal, mixed, and acculturated inhabitants. For general data on the Indians see SL4, for prehistoric data see SL3.

SM2. Aweikoma   Specific data on the Aweikoma (Botocudo, Bugre, Santa Catarina Caingang, Shokleng) tribe.

SM3. Caingang   Specific data on the scattered tribes of the Caingang nation, also variously known as Caagua, Chiqui, Coroado, Dorin, Gualacho, Guayana, Ingain, and Taven. For data on the Santa Catarina Caingang or Aweikoma see SM2.

SM4. Guarani   Specific data on the Guarani (Caingua, Carijo) nation, including the Apapocuva, Arechane, Carima, Cayua, Cheiru, Chiripa, Guarambare, Guayana, Itatin, Ivapare, Mbya, Oguauiva, Pan, Taioba, Tanygua, Tape, Taruma, and Tobatin tribes. For data on the Tupi-Guarani peoples in general see SL6.

East Brazil

SN1. East Brazil. Specific data on the eastern Brazilian states of Espirito Santo, Minas Gerais, Rio de Janeiro, and São Paulo and their non-aboriginal, mixed, and acculturated inhabitants. For general data on the Indians see SL4, for prehistoric data see SL3, for data on the Tupinamba see S09.

SN2. Botocudo   Specific data on the Botocudo (Aimore, Borun) nation, comprising the Arana, Crecmun, Crenak, Gutucrac, and Nadache tribes.

SN3. Guaitaca   Specific data on the Guaitaca (Waitaca) tribe.

SN4. Mashacali. Specific data on the Mashacali tribe, including the neighboring Caposho, Cumanasho, Macuni, Malali, Moshosho, and Paname.

SN5. Patasho. Specific data on the Patasho tribe.

SN6. Puri. Specific data on the Puri tribe, including the related Coroado and Coropa.

SN7. Tupi. Specific data on the Tupi nation, including the Amoipira, Tobajara, and Tupina. For data on the kindred Tupinamba see S09, on the Tupi-Guarani peoples in general see SL6.

Northeast Brazil

S01. Northeast Brazil   Specific data on the northeastern Brazilian states of Alagoas, Baia, Ceará, Maranhão, Paraíba, Pernambuco, Piauí, Rio Grande do Norte, and Sergipe and their non-aboriginal, mixed, and acculturated inhabitants. For general data on the Indians see SL4, for prehistoric data see SL3, for data on the Ge peoples see SL5, on the Tupi-Guarani peoples see SL6.

S02. Camacan. Specific data on the Camacan tribe, including the related Catathoy, Cutasho, Masacara, and Menian.

S03. Cariri. Specific data on the Cariri nation, embracing the Camuru, Dzubucua, Kipea, and Sapuya tribes, and on the neighboring and little-known Carapoto, Fulnio (Carnijo, Fornio), Natu, Pancararu, Shoco, Shucuru, and Tusha.

S04. <u>Guaja</u>. Specific data on the Guaja tribe.

S05. <u>Tarairu</u>. Specific data on the Tarairu people, including the Acriu, Anace, Caratiu, Jandoin, Juca, and Payacu.

S06. <u>Tenetehara</u>   Specific data on the Tenetehara nation, embracing the Guajajara, Tembe, and Urubu tribes.

S07. <u>Teremembe</u>. Specific data on the Teremembe tribe.

S08. <u>Timbira</u>   Specific data on Timbira (Canella, Cran) nation, comprising the Apanyecra, Craho, Crepumcateye, Creye, Cricati, Cucoecamecra, Gaioes, Kencateye, Porecamecra, Pucobye, Ramcocamecra (Capiecran), Shacamecra, and Timbira tribes and the presumably kindred Jeico and Pimenteira. For data on the Apinaye or Western Timbira see SP3.

S09. <u>Tupinamba</u>   Specific data on coast-dwelling Tupinamba nation, embracing the Caete, Potiguara, Tamoyo, Timimino, Tupinamba, and Tupinikin tribes. For data on the kindred Tupi of the interior see SN7.

S010. <u>Gamella</u>. Specific data on the Gamella tribe.

S011. <u>Bahia Brazilians</u>.   Specific data on the inhabitants of the city of Bahia (Salvador) and of the surrounding Reconcavo.

<u>Mato Grosso</u>

SP1. <u>Mato Grosso</u>. Specific data on the Brazilian states of Goiaz and Mato Grosso and their non-aboriginal, mixed, and acculturated inhabitants. For general data on the Indians see SL4, on the Ge peoples see SL5, on the Tupi-Guarani peoples see SL6, for prehistoric data see SL3.

SP2. <u>Apiaca</u>. Specific data on the Tupi-Guarani-speaking Apiaca tribe, including the related Cayabi and Tapanyuna.

SP3. <u>Apinaye</u>   Specific data on the Ge-speaking Apinaye or Western Timbira <u>tribe</u>. For data on the Timbira proper or Eastern Timbira see S08.

SP4. <u>Arawine</u>. Specific data on the Tupi-Guarani-speaking Arawine tribe.

SP5. <u>Arikem</u>. Specific data on the Tupi-Guarani-speaking Arikem (Ahopovo) <u>tribe</u>.

SP6. <u>Aueto</u>. Specific data on the Tupi-Guarani-speaking Aueto tribe, including the kindred Arauiti, Camayura, and Manitsaua (Mantizula).

SP7. Bacairi   Specific data on the Cariban-speaking Bacairi tribe.

SP8. Bororo   Specific data on the Ge-speaking Bororo nation, including
     the Acione, Aravira, Biriune, and Umotina tribes.

SP9. Caraja. Specific data on the Caraja tribe, including the related Javahe
     and Shambioa.

SP10. Cawahib. Specific data on the Tupi-Guarani-speaking Cawahib
      (Cabahiba) tribe, including the related Itogapuk, Mialat, Paranawat,
      Parintintin, Ramarama, Taipeshishi, Takwatip, and Tupi-Cawahib.

SP11. Cayapo. Specific data on the Ge-speaking Cayapo proper or Southern
      Cayapo, including the neighboring Opaye and Oti. For data on the
      Coroa or Northern Cayapo see SP13.

SP12. Chapacura. Specific data on the Chapacura (Tapacura) nation, embracing
      the Chapacura, Cujuna, Curnana, Huanyam (Pawumwa), Jaru, Matama,
      More (Itene), Quitemoca, Rocorona, Tora, Urunamacan, and Urupa
      tribes.

SP13. Coroa. Specific data on the Ge-speaking Coroa (Northern Cayapo)
      nation, including the Cayamo, Cradaho, Gorotire, and Pau d'Arco
      tribes. For data on the Cayapo proper or Southern Cayapo see SP11.

SP14. Guachi. Specific data on the Guaicuran-speaking Guachi tribe.

SP15. Guato   Specific data on the Guato tribe.

SP16. Macurap. Specific data on the Tupi-Guarani-speaking Macurap tribe,
      including the kindred Amniapa, Arua, Guaratagaja, and Wayoro.

SP17. Nambicuara   Specific data on the Nambicuara nation, including the
      Anunze, Cocozu, and Uaintacu tribes.

SP18. Waura. Specific data on the Arawakan-speaking Waura, and on the related
      Custenau, Mehinacu (Minaco), and Yaulapiti tribes.

SP19. Paressi   Specific data on the Arawakan-speaking Paressi nation,
      embracing the Cashiniti, Cozarini (Cabishi), Iranche, and Uaimare
      tribes.

SP20. Sherente   Specific data on the Ge-speaking Sherente (Cherente)
      tribe, including the kindred Shavante (Chavante, Crixa, Puxiti,
      Tapacua).

SP21. <u>Suya</u>. Specific data on the Ge-speaking Suya tribe.

SP22. <u>Tapirape</u>   Specific data on the Tupi-Guarani-speaking Tapirape tribe, including the neighboring Canoeiro.

SP23. <u>Trumai</u>   Specific data on the Trumai tribe.

SP24. <u>Yabuti</u>. Specific data on the Yabuti (Japuti) tribe, including the neighboring Aricapu, Aruashi, Cabishinana, Canoa, Huari (Massaca), Kepikiriwat, Mure, Palmella, Purubora, Sanamaica, and Tupari.

SP25. <u>Yaruma</u>. Specific data on the Cariban-speaking Yaruma tribe, including the kindred Apalakire, Kalapalo, Kuikuru, Mariape, Nahuqua, Naravute, and Tsuva.

Amazonia

SQ1. <u>Amazonia</u>   Specific data on the Brazilian states of Amazonas and Pará and the territory of Acre and on their non-aboriginal, mixed, and acculturated inhabitants. For general data on the Amazonian Indians see SL4, on the Arawakan peoples see SR6, on the Cariban peoples see SR7, on the Tupi-Guarani peoples see SL6.

SQ2. <u>Amanaye</u>. Specific data on the Tupi-Guarani-speaking Amanaye tribe, including the related Anambe, Cuperob, Jacunda, Pacaja, Paracana, Tapiraua (Anta), and Turiwara.

SQ3. <u>Apalai</u>. Specific data on the Cariban-speaking Apalai tribe, including the kindred Apurui.

SQ4. <u>Arara</u>. Specific data on the Cariban-speaking Arara (Apiaca) tribe, including the kindred Aracaju.

SQ5. <u>Arua</u>. Specific data on the Arawakan-speaking Arua of Marajó Island.

SQ6. <u>Cashinawa</u>   Specific data on the Panoan-speaking Cashinawa, including the related Ararawa (Arara), Canamari, Catukina, Contanawa, Curina, Cuyanawa, Espino, Marinawa, Nawa, Nucuini, Pacanawa, Sacuva, Saninawa, Shanindawa, Shipinawa, Taminawa, Tushinawa, Yauavo, and Yura.

SQ7. <u>Catukina</u>   Specific data on the Catukina nation, embracing the Bandiapa, Burue, Canamari, Catawishi, Catukina, Catukino, Mangeroma (Tucun-Dyapa), Parawa, and Tawari tribes.

SQ8. <u>Emerillon</u>. Specific data on the Tupi-Guarani-speaking Emerillon, including the related Culiana, Guayapi (Paikipiranga, Wayapi),

Oyampi, and Uara-Guacu.

SQ9. Ipurina. Specific data on the Arawakan-speaking Ipurina (Kangiti, Hypurina), including the related Canamari, Casharari, Catiana, Cujigeneri, Cuniba, and Maniteneri.

SQ10. Macu. Specific data on the migratory Macu Indians.

SQ11. Manao. Specific data on the Arawakan-speaking Manao tribe, including the related Cayuishaua, Juri, Pase, and Uainuma.

SQ12. Maue. Specific data on the Tupi-Guarani-speaking Maue tribe, including the related Andira, Apanto, Arapium, Maragua, and Tupinambarana.

SQ13. Mundurucu   Specific data on the Tupi-Guarani-speaking Mundurucu tribe.

SQ14. Mura. Specific data on the Mura tribe, including the neighboring Matanawi and Piraha.

SQ15. Omagua. Specific data on the Tupi-Guarani-speaking Omagua (Agua, Compeba, Umaua) tribe.

SQ16. Palikur. Specific data on the Arawakan-speaking Palikur (Wasa) tribe, including the kindred Marawan (Maraon).

SQ17. Paumary. Specific data on the Paumary (Purupuru) tribe, including the kindred Yuberi.

SQ18. Yanoama. Specific data on the migratory Yanoama, including the Sanema (Guaharibo), the Nabudub, Pubmatari and Taclaudub, the Waica, the Casapare (Shiriana), the Karime, Samatari, Surara, and Pakidai.

SQ19. Tucano   Specific data on the Tucano nation, embracing the Arapaso, Bara, Buhagana, Carapana, Cubeo, Cueretu, Desana, Macuna, Pamoa (Tatuyo), Piratapuyo, Tucano, Tuyuca, Uaina, Uanana, Uasona, Yahuna, and Yapua (Japua) tribes.

SQ20. Tucuna   Specific data on the Tucuna (Ticuna) tribe.

SQ21. Wairacu. Specific data on the Arawakan-speaking Wairacu tribe, including the kindred Marawa.

SQ22. Waiwai. Specific data on the Cariban-speaking Waiwai tribe, including the kindred Atroahy, Bonari, Carabinana, Cashuena, Catawian, Chikena, Crichana, Guacara, Ichu, Paraviyana, Pauxi, Pishauco,

Puricoto, Purucuato, Saluma, Sapara, Waimiry, Wayumara, and
Yauaperi.

SQ23. Yamamadi. Specific data on the Arawakan-speaking Yamamadi tribe,
including the kindred Araua, Culino (Curia, Curina), Madiha,
Pamana, Sewaco, and Sipo.

SQ24. Yuma. Specific data on the Yuma tribe, including the neighboring Arara.

SQ25. Yurimagua. Specific data on the Yurimagua tribe, including the neighboring Aizuare, Curuzirari, Ibanoma, Paguana, and Soliman.

SQ26. Yuruna. Specific data on the Tupi-Guarani-speaking Yuruna (Juruna)
tribe, including the kindred Arupai, Asurini, Curuaya, Shipaya
(Achipoya, Chipaya), and Tacunyape.

SQ27. Barauna. Specific data on the Arawakan-speaking Barauna of north-
western Amazonia, and on the related Arekena, Avane, Baniwa, Bare,
Cariaya, Carutana, Catapolitani, Caua, Curipaco, Guinau, Huhuteni,
Ipeca, Maipure, Parauana, Pauishana, Siusi, and Tariana tribes of
Brazil, Venezuela, and Colombia.

SQ28. Tapajo. Specific data on the Tapajo tribe.

Guiana

SR1. Guiana. General data on the geography, history, and peoples of Guiana.

SR2. British Guiana. Specific data on British Guiana, its history, and its non-
aboriginal inhabitants.

SR3. French Guiana. Specific data on French Guiana, its history, and its
non-aboriginal inhabitants.

SR4. Surinam. Specific data on Surinam or Dutch Guiana, its history, and
its non-aboriginal inhabitants.

SR5. Prehistoric Guiana. Specific data on the prehistoric peoples and cultures
of Guiana.

SR6. Arawakan Indians. General data on the Arawakan-speaking Indians of
South America, their languages, and their culture.

SR7. Cariban Indians. General data on the Cariban-speaking Indians of South
America, their languages, and their culture.

SR8. Bush Negroes   Specific data on the Bush Negro peoples of Guiana.
For data on the South American Negroes in general see S5.

SR9. Carib   Specific data on the true Carib (Culina, Galibi), including the closely related Acawai, Acuria, and Waica.

SR10. Locono. Specific data on the Locono or true Arawak people.

SR11. Macusi. Specific data on the Cariban-speaking Macusi tribe.

SR12. Rucuyen. Specific data on the Cariban-speaking Rucuyen nation, em-
bracing the Acokwa, Amicuana, Aramagoto, Aramisho, Caran,
Comayana, Cusari, Custumi, Diau (Trio), Garipon, Macapa,
Nourage, Oyaricoulet, Pianacoto, Pino, Oyana (Rucuyen proper),
Taira, Tocoyen, Tonayena, Upurui, Yao, and Yapacoye tribes.

SR13. Wapishana   Specific data on the Arawakan-speaking Wapishana
tribe, including the kindred Amariba, Atorai, Maopityan, and Taruma.

Venezuela

SS1. Venezuela   General data on modern Venezuela and its people, and
specific data on its non-aboriginal, mixed, and acculturated inhabitants. For data on the islands of Aruba, Bonaire, and Curacao see
SZ2.

SS2. Historical Venezuela. Specific data on the history and culture history of
Venezuela and its non-aboriginal inhabitants.

SS3. Prehistoric Venezuela. Specific data on the prehistoric peoples and cultures of Venezuela.

SS4. Venezuelan Indians. General data on the Indians of Venezuela. For general data on the Arawakan Indians see SR6, on the Cariban Indians
see SR7, on the Circum-Caribbean area as a whole see SA2.

SS5. Auake. Specific data on the nomadic Auake, Caliana, Maracana, and the
Macu of the Rio Auary (Sierra Pacaraima).

SS6. Cariña. Specific data on the Cariban-speaking Cariña.

SS7. Caquetio. Specific data on the Arawakan-speaking Caquetio and Paraujano
tribes.

SS8. Caraca. Specific data on the Caraca tribe, including the neighboring
Arvaco, Chagaragoto, Mariche, Meregoto, Tacarigua, Tarma,
Teque, and Toramaina.

SS9. Cumana. Specific data on the Cariban-speaking Cumana tribe, including
the kindred Chaima (Sayma), Core, Cuaga, Cumanagoto, Palenque
(Guarina), Pariagoto, Piritu, and Tumuza.

SS10. Gayon. Specific data on the non-agricultural Gayon tribe.

SS11. Guamontey. Specific data on the non-agricultural Guamontey (Guaiqueri) tribe, including the neighboring Atapaima, Atature, Colorado, Dazaro, Guamo, Guarico, Maiba (Amayba), Masparro, Payure, Taparita, Tayaga, and Yagui.

SS12. Jirajara. Specific data on the Jirajara tribe, including the related Aticare, Ayoman, Ciparicoto, Coyon, Guiba, and Xagua. For data on the kindred but culturally backward Gayon see SS10.

SS13. Bari. Specific data on the Chibchan-speaking Bari nation, embracing the Aratoma, Bubure (Coronado), Cuprigueri, Dobokubi, Kunaguanasaya, Mape (Motilones Bravos), Pemeno, Quiriquire, and Tomoporo.

SS14. Otomac Specific data on the Otomac tribe, including the kindred Pao and Saruro.

SS15. Saliva. Specific data on the Saliva nation, embracing the Ature, Piaroa, and Maco (Macu of the Rio Ventuari).

SS16. Pemon. Specific data on the Cariban-speaking Pemon tribe, including the Taulipang (Arecuna), Camaracoto and Teweya.

SS17. Timote. Specific data on the Timote tribe, the related Coromocho, Cuica, and Miguri, and the neighboring Charaqua, Chinato, Chitarera, Quenago, Sunesua, Tequia (Cercada), and Zorca, all characterized by cultures of derivative Andean type.

SS18. Warao Specific data on the Warao (Warrau, Guarauno) tribe of the Orinoco delta region, including the Mariusa, Winikina and Farute.

SS19. Yaruro Specific data on the Yaruro tribe.

SS20. Makiritare. Specific data on the Cariban-speaking Makiritare (Soto), including the Yecuana, Decuana, Cunahana, and Maioncon.

SS21. Panare. Specific data on the Cariban-speaking Panare tribe.

SS22. Yabarana. Specific data on the Yabarana tribe, including the Curasicana and Wociare.

SS23. Cariniaco. Specific data on the Cariban-speaking Cariniaco tribe, including the kindred Arebato, Arigua, Cuacua, Mapoye, Pareca, Quiriquiripa and Waruwadu.

Lesser Antilles

ST1. Lesser Antilles. General data on the Lesser Antilles, their history, and their modern inhabitants. For data on the aboriginal inhabitants see ST12 - ST14, on Aruba, Bonaire, and Curacao see SZ2.

ST2. Barbados. Specific data on the British island of Barbados.

ST3. British Virgin Islands. Specific data on the British islands of Anegada, Tortola, and Virgin Gorda. For data on the American Virgin Islands see ST10.

ST4. Dominica. Specific data on the British island of Dominica.

ST5. Guadeloupe. Specific data on the French island of Guadeloupe, including the lesser islands of Les Saintes, Marie Galante, St. Barthelemy, and (French) St. Martin.

ST6. Leeward Islands. Specific data on the British islands of Anguilla, Antigua, Barbuda, Montserrat, Nevis, Redonda, St. Kitts, and Sombrero.

ST7. Martinique. Specific data on the French island of Martinique.

ST8. St. Eustatius. Specific data on the Dutch island of St. Eustatius, including the lesser islands of Saba and (Dutch) St. Martin.

ST9. Trinidad. Specific data on the island of Trinidad, including the lesser island of Tobago.

ST10. Virgin Islands. Specific data on the American (formerly Danish) islands of St. Croix, St. John, and St. Thomas.

ST11. Windward Islands. Specific data on the British Islands of Grenada, the Grenadines, St. Lucia, and St. Vincent.

ST12. Prehistoric Lesser Antilles. Specific data on the prehistoric peoples and cultures of the Lesser Antilles.

ST13. Callinago   Specific data on the aboriginal Callinago (Calino, Island Carib) of the Lesser Antilles. For data on the Cariban peoples in general see SR7, on Circum-Caribbean culture see SA2.

ST14. Igneri. Specific data on the aboriginal Igneri of Trinidad and Tobago. For data on the Arawakan peoples in general see SR6.

Puerto Rico

SU1. Puerto Rico   Specific data on modern Puerto Rico and the Puerto Rican people, including data on the islands of Vieques and Culebra.

SU2. Historical Puerto Rico. Specific data on the history and culture history of Puerto Rico and its non-aboriginal inhabitants prior to the twentieth century.

SU3. Prehistoric Puerto Rico. Specific data on the prehistoric peoples and cultures of Puerto Rico. For data on the Igneri see ST14, on the Tainan Boriqueno see SV5.

Hispaniola

SV1. Hispaniola. General data on the island of Hispaniola and its history.

SV2. Dominican Republic. Specific data on Santo Domingo or the Dominican Republic, its history, and the Dominican people.

SV3. Haiti   Specific data on Haiti, its history, and the Haitian people, including data on the island of Gonave. For data on the American Negroes in general see N5 and S5.

SV4. Prehistoric Hispaniola. Specific data on the prehistoric peoples and cultures of Hispaniola.

SV5. Taino   Specific data on the Taino aborigines of Hispaniola and eastern Cuba, on the related Boriqueno of Puerto Rico, and on other peoples of similar culture throughout the Greater Antilles. For data on the Arawakan peoples in general see SR6, on Circum-Caribbean culture see SA2.

Bahamas

SW1. Bahamas. Specific data on the geography and modern inhabitants of the Bahamas, whose principal component islands are Aklin, Andros, Caicos, Cat, Crooked, Eleuthera, French (Plana), Grand Bahama, Great Abaco, Great Exuma, Great Guana, Great Inagua, Little Inagua, Long, Mayaguana, Nassau, Rum, Samana (Atwood), San Salvador (Watling), and Turks.

SW2. Historical Bahamas. Specific data on the history and culture history of the Bahamas and their non-aboriginal inhabitants.

SW3. Prehistoric Bahamas. Specific data on the prehistoric peoples and cultures of the Bahamas. For data on the Lucayo see SX5.

Cuba

SX1. Cuba. Specific data on modern Cuba and the Cuban people.

SX2. Historical Cuba. Specific data on the history and culture history of Cuba and its non-aboriginal inhabitants prior to the twentieth century.

SX3. Prehistoric Cuba. Specific data on the prehistoric peoples and cultures of Cuba.

SX4. Ciboney. Specific data on the aboriginal Ciboney of western Cuba, including the presumably related aborigines of the southwestern peninsula of Hispaniola.

SX5. Sub-Taino. Specific data on the Sub-Taino aborigines of central and eastern Cuba and Jamaica, on the related Lucayo of the Bahamas, and on other peoples of similar culture throughout the Greater Antilles. For data on the Arawakan peoples in general see SR6.

Jamaica

SY1. Jamaica. Specific data on modern Jamaica and the Jamaican people, including data on the Cayman Islands.

SY2. Historical Jamaica. Specific data on the history and culture history of Jamaica and its non-aboriginal inhabitants.

SY3. Prehistoric Jamaica. Specific data on the prehistoric peoples and cultures of Jamaica. For data on the aboriginal Subtaino people see SX5.

South American Islands

SZ1. South American Islands. General data on the Cocos, Juan Fernandez, Malpelo, Sala y Gomez, San Felix, South Georgia, South Orkney, South Sandwich, South Shetland, [Brazilian] Trinidad, and other lesser islands off the coast of South America. For data on the Bahamas see SW1, on the Lesser Antilles see ST1.

SZ2. Curacao. Specific data on the Dutch islands of Aruba, Bonaire, and Curacao in the Caribbean, their history, and their modern inhabitants. For data on the aboriginal Caquetio Indians see SS7.

SZ3. Falkland Islands. Specific data on the Falkland Islands.

SZ4. Galapagos Islands. Specific data on the Galapagos Islands.

SZ5. Nueva Esparta. Specific data on the Venezuelan state of Nueva Esparta, comprising the islands of Margarita, La Tortuga, and their outliers. For data on Venezuela as a whole see SS1.

Ababda, MR9
Ababua, FO8
Abaco, Great, SW1
Abad, SC17
Abaduma, FS5
Abadzekh, RH5
Abagaza, FR5
Abaha, FO42
Abahela, FS5
Abaka, FJ18, OA21
Abaluhya, FL4
Abam, FF4
Abangba, FO29
Abango, FI7
Abanyai, FS5
ABARAMBO, FO5
Abashankwe, FS5
Abatonga, FS5
Abchas, RI3
Abda, MW10
Abdullab, MQ15
Abe, FA25
Abelam, OJ30
Abgarris Islands,
  OT5
Abibe, SC9
Abiji, FA25
ABIPON, SI4
Abire, FJ20
Abisa, FQ5
Abitibi, NH4
ABKHAZ, RI3
Abkhaz A.S.S.R., RI3
Ablig-Saligsig, OA24
ABNAKI, NL4
Abo, FF40, FH14
Abol, FJ21
ABOR, AR2
Abron, FE8
Abu Derreg, MS15
Abu Garein, FJ11
Abu Ghussun, MQ5
Abu Gunuk, FJ11
Abu Hadid, MQ4
Abure, FA5
Aburra, SC9
Abu Seida, FJ11
Abu Semen, MS8
Abu Tubr, MQ4
Abyssinia, MP1
Acawai, SR9
ACAXEE, NU6
ACHAGUA, SC5
Achang, AP6
Achawa, FT7
Aceh, OD4
Achewa, FR4
Achikunda, FR4
Achikuya, FI33
Achipeta, FR4
Achipoya, SQ26
Achire, NU16
ACHOLI, FK4
ACHOMAWI, NS5
Achwabo, FT5
Acilowe, FT5
Acione, SP8
Acokwa, SR12
Acolapissa, NO4
ACOMA, NT7
Acre, SQ1
Acriu, SO5
Aculo, FE7
Acuria, SR9
ADA, FF4
Ada, FJ16
Adai, NO5
Adangme, FE6
Adele, FA35
ADEN, MM1
Aden Colony, MM1
Aden Protectorate,
  MM2
Adham, AM35

Adige, RH4
Adja, FA18
Adjao, FT7
Adjeur, MS25
Adjumba, FI23
Admiralty Islands,
  OM6
Adshar, RI4
Ad Sheikh, MN9
Adshusheer, NN13
Adsoa, FT7
Aduma, FI12
Adun, FF17
ADYGE, RH4
Adyge Autonomous Oblast,
  RH4
ADZHAR, RI4
Adzhar A.S.S.R., RI4
AETA, OA4
AFAR, MN4
AFARS-ISSIS TERRITORY,
  MO6
Afawa, FF46
Afema, FA5
Afghan, AU4
AFGHANISTAN, AU1
Afghanistan, Historical,
  AU2
Afghanistan, Prehistoric,
  AU3
Afitti, FJ11
AFO, FF5
AFRICA, F1
AFRICAN ISLANDS, FZ1
Africa, Prehistoric,
  F3
Afrikanders, FX7
Afusara, FF31
Aga Buryat Mongol
  National Okrug,
  RW1
Agar, FJ12
AGARIA, AW23
Agariya, AW23
Agatu, FF27
Agaz, SK12
Aghem, FF39
Aginskiy Buryat Mongol
  National Okrug,
  RW1
Agola, FA36
Agonglin, FA18
Agta, OA4
Agtaa, OA11
Agua, SQ15
Agua Caliente, NS14
Aguacutec, NW10
Agua Jews, MP9
AGUANO, SE5
Aguaruna, SD9
Aguilot, SI12
Agul, RH8
Agutaynon, OA30
Ahaggar, MS25
Ahamda, MQ15
Ahanta, FA5
Aheria, AW45
Ahioko, FP4
Ahl Tichit, MS31
Ahl Todgha, MW12
AHOM, AR3
Ahopovo, SP5
Ahsen, MW9
Aht, NE11
AHTENA, NA5
Ahtnakhotana, NA5
Ahululco, NU7
Aike, FF27
Ailliklik, NS20
Aimol, AR8
Aimore, SN2
Ainamwanga, FN21
AINU, AB6
Air, MS25

Airico, SC6
Ais, NN7
AISSOR, MA6
Ait Atta, MW5
Ait Buzid, MW5
Ait Chokham, MW5
Ait Dades, MW12
Ait Jafelman, MW5
Ait Ndhir, MW5
Ait Seri, MW5
Ait Tserrouchen, MW5
Ait Warain, MW13
Ait Youssi, MW5
Aizo, FA18
Aizuare, SQ25
Ajawa, FT7
Ajiba, FJ6
Ajie, FK8, OP4
Ajjer, MS25
Ajmer, AW15
Ajukru, FA25
Ajure, FF34
Akaju, FF22
Akalai, FI14
Akale, FJ20
Akamba, FL9
Akapless, FA5
Akasele, FA10
Akela, FO19
Akelle, FI14
AKHA, AO4
Akhous, FA36
Akikiyu, FL10
Akit, OD8
Aklan, OA14
Aklanon, OA14
Aklin, SW1
Akposo, FA35
Akum, FK12
Akunakuna, FF60
Akwaala, NS9
Akwapim, FE12
Akyem, FE12
Ala, MP13
Alaba, MP15
Alabama, NN1, NN11
Alabat, OA17
ALACALUF, SH2
Alag-Bako, OA23
Alagoas, SO1
Alagya, FA25
ALAK, AM14
Alakong, AM15
Alangan, OA15
Alas, OD7
Alasapa, NU12
Alashan, AH5
ALASKA, NA1
Alaska, Historical,
  NA2
ALASKAN ABORIGINES,
  NA3
Alaska, Prehistoric,
  NA4
Alawa, FN5
ALAWITES, MD7
ALBANIA, EG1
Albania, Historical,
  EG2
Albanians, EG1
Albania, Prehistoric,
  EG3
Alberta, NF1
Aldabra, FZ1
Alendu, FO25
ALEUT, NA6
Aleutian Islands,
  NA6
ALGERIA, MV1
Algeria, Historical,
  MV2
ALGERIAN ARABS, MV4
Algerians, MV1, MV4
Algeria, Prehistoric,
  MV3

ALGONKIANS, NM5
ALGONKIN, NH4
Al-Hutman, MT9
Ali, MS16
Aliab, FJ12
Aliane, FA36
Aliyan, FA36
Alkatcho, NE7
Allentiac, SI6
Allush, MS31
Alomwe, FT5
Alon, SE14
Alonda, FQ5
ALOR, OF5
Alsace, EW10
ALSATIANS, EW10
ALSEA, NR5
ALTAIANS, RS2
ALTAI REGION, RS1
Alu, ON14
Aluena, FP14
Alui, FQ9
Alunda, FO27, FQ5
Alungu, FQ5
ALUR, FK5
Alwer, FO17
Amadi, FO5
AMAHUACA, SE6
Amalozwi, FS5
Amambwe, FQ5
AMAMI, AC4
Aman, FJ15
AMANAYE, SQ2
Amandebele, FS4
Amani, SC16
Amap, FF32
Amar, MP8
Amarakaeri, SE15
Amarar, MR9
Amariba, SR13
Amarna, MQ15
Amaro, MP14
Amarro, MP7
Amasifuin, SE14
Amaswazi, FU2
Amaxosa, FX17
Amayba, SS11
Amazonas, SQ1
AMAZONIA, SQ1
Amazonian Indians,
  SL4
Amazulu, FX20
AMBA, FO6
Ambaca, FP6
Ambala, FO30
Ambamba, FI12
Ambaquista, FP6
Ambete, FI12
AMBO, FX8
Ambo, FQ8
Amboim, FP6
AMBON, OH4
AMBRYM, OO4
Ambuella, FP12
Ambunda, FP12
Ambundu, FP6
Ambunu, FO17
AMERICAN INDIANS,
  N3
AMERICAN NEGROES,
  N5
AMERICAN POLYNESIA,
  OV1
AMERICAN SAMOA, OU4
Americans, Immigrant,
  N6
American Virgin Islands,
  ST10
Amgun, RX3
AMHARA, MP5
Ami, AD16
Amicuana, SR12
AMISH, NM6
Amniapa, SP16

Amo, SF16
Amoipira, SN7
Amput, FO17
Amsterdam, FZ1
Amubenge, FO8
Amuesha, SE9
Amusgo, NU24
Amwimbe, FL5
Ana, FA6
Anace, SO5
Anachoret Islands,
  OM5
ANAG, MQ4
Anaguta, FF31
Anakatza, MS5
Anambe, SQ2
Anang, FF25
ANATOLIAN GREEKS,
  MB6
Ancerma, SC9
ANCIENT ASIA MINOR,
  MB2
ANCIENT EGYPT, MR5
ANCIENT ETHIOPIA,
  MP3
ANCIENT HEBREWS, MF7
ANCIENT MACEDONIANS,
  EH8
ANCIENT MESOPOTAMIA,
  MH5
ANCIENT MOROCCO, MW3
ANCIENT PERSIA, MA4
ANCIENT SPARTANS,
  EH9
Andamanese Negritos,
  AZ2
ANDAMANS, AZ2
Andaqui, SC15
Andaste, NM8
Andean culture area,
  SE3
ANDEDJA, OI6
Andembu, FP6, FP14
Andh, AW46
Andhra Pradesh, AW17
Andi, RH8
Andira, SQ12
Andoa, SE22
Andoke, SC19
Andombe, FP15
Andoni-Ibeno, FF25
Andorobo, FL6
ANDORRA, EX7
Andros, SW1
Andumbo, FI12
Anegada, ST3
ANEITYUM, OO5
Anfillo, MP19
Angaite, SK10
Angami, AR13
ANGAS, FF6
Angaur, OR15
Angbandi, FO36
Anglo, FA17
Anglo-Canadians, NC1
Anglo-Egyptian Sudan,
  FJ1, MQ1
ANGMAGSALIK, NB4
ANGOLA, FP2
Angola, Prehistoric,
  FP19
Angola, Traditional,
  FP3
Angoni, FR5
Anguilla, ST6
Angul, FO17
Angutera, SE12
Anhwei, AF14
ANIWA, OT2
Ankutshu, FO47
Ankwe, FF6
Anna, MS5
Annam, AM11

Annia, MP13
Anno, FA5
Annobon, FZ1
Ant, OR16
Anta, SQ2
Antaifasina, FY16
Antaifasy, FY16
Antaimoro, FY7
Antaimorona, FY7
ANTAISAKA, FY17
Antaiva, FY19
ANTAMBAHOAKA, FY15
Antanala, FY8
Antandroy, FY13
ANTANKARANA, FY9
ANTANOSY, FY14
Antarctic, W5
ANTEBELLUM SOUTH,
  NN2
ANTEIFASY, FY16
ANTEIMORO, FY7
Antessar, MS25
Anti, SE9
Antigua, ST6
Antimerina, FY5
Antiocha, SC9
Antipodes Islands,
  OZ5
Antique, OA14
Antisianaka, FY12
ANUAK, FJ4
Anunze, SP17
Anyang, FF53
Anyanja, FR4
Anyassa, FR4
Anyi, FA5
ANYI-BAULE, FA5
Ao, AR13
Apache, NQ16, NT8,
  NT21
Apache, Eastern, NT8
Apache, Kiowa, NQ16
Apache-Mohave, NT14
Apache, Western, NT21
Apalachee, NN14
APALAI, SQ3
Apalakire, SP25
Apanto, SQ12
Apanyecra, SO8
Apapocuva, SM4
Apa Tani, AR11
APAYAO, OA5
Apayaw, OA5
Apfuru, FI7
APIACA, SP2
Apiaca, SQ4
APINAYE, SP3
Apingi, FI30
Apolista, SF14
Apono, FI30
Appalachian mountaineers,
  NN5
Apsaroke, NQ10
Apurui, SQ3
ARABANA, OI7
Arabia, MJ1-MJ3
Arabia, Eastern, MK1
Arabia, Historical,
  MJ2
Arabian Peninsula,
  MJ1
Arabia, Prehistoric,
  MJ3
Arabia, South, ML2,
  ML3
ARABIC EGYPT, MR3
ARABS, M10
Arabs, Algerian, MV4
Arabs, Bagdad, MH3
Arabs, Chad, MS9
Arabs, Kordofan, MQ10
Arabs, Maritime, MK2
Arabs, Marrakech,
  MW10

Arabs, Marsh, MH13
Arabs, Nile, MQ14
Arabs, Palestinian,
  MG1
Arabs, West Saharan,
  MS29
Araca, SE7
Aracaju, SQ4
Aradigi, OA18
Arago, FF27
Araibayba, SF11
Araka, FF38
Aramagoto, SR12
Aramisho, SR12
Arana, SN2
Aranadan, AW63
ARANDA, OI8
Araona, SF23
Arap, AM6
ARAPAHO, NQ6
Arapaso, SQ19
ARAPESH, OJ6
Arapium, SQ12
ARARA, SQ4
Arara, SQ6, SQ24
Ararawa, SQ6
Aratoma, SS13
Araua, SQ23
Araucana, SC10
ARAUCANIANS, SG4
Arauiti, SP6
Aravira, SP8
Arawak, SR10
ARAWAKAN INDIANS,
  SR6
ARAWINE, SP4
Arbore, FL7
Archin, RH8
Arctic, W5
Arctic Highlanders,
  NB5
Arebato, SS23
Arechane, SM4
Arecuna, SS16
Aregwa, FF16
Arekena, SQ27
ARFAK, OJ7
ARGENTINA, SI1
Argentina, Historical,
  SI2
Argentina, Prehistoric,
  SI3
Argentinian Chaco,
  SK4
Argobba, MP5
Arhuaco, SC7
Ari, FA25
Aricapu, SP24
Arigua, SS23
ARIKARA, NQ7
ARIKEM, SP5
Arin, RU2
Arivaipa, NT21
Arizona, NT1
Arkansas, NO1
ARMENIA, RJ1
Armenia, Historical,
  RJ2
ARMENIANS, RJ3
Armenian S.S.R., RJ1
Arna, MS12
Aro, FF4, FL7
Arosaguntacook, NL4
Arrabunna, OI7
ARU, OH5
ARUA, SQ5
Arua, SP16
Aruashi, SP24
Aruba, SZ1
Aruese, OH5
Aruissin, MS29
Arund, FO27
Arunta, OI8
Arupai, SQ26

Arusha, FL7, FL12
Arussi, MP13
Arvaco, SS8
Aryans, AQ5
Asa, FL6
Asan, RU2
ASCENSION, FZ2
Asena, FR4
Asenga, FQ5
Asen-Twifo, FE12
Ashaku, FF56
Ashango, FI19
Ashanti, FE12
Ashipoo, NN12
ASHLUSLAY, SK5
Ashogo, FI30
ASIA, A1
Asia, Historical,
  A2
Asia, Prehistoric,
  A3
ASIATIC ISLANDS, AZ1
Asiatic Russia, RR1
Asimba, RI30
Asolongo, FO21
Assale, MS9
ASSAM, AR1
Assamese, AR1, AR3
Assini, FA5
ASSINIBOIN, NF4
Assumbo-Ambele, FF22
Assyrians, MA6
Asu, FN4
Asur, AW46
Asurini, SQ26
ATA, OA6
ATACAMA, SG5
Atakapa, NO4
ATAKPAME, FA6
Atalala, SI14
Atambi, SI11
Atapaima, SS11
Ataronchron, NG5
Atature, SS11
ATAYAL, AD8
Atayfat, MS9
Atchin, OO12
Atembu, FP6
Aten, FF9
ATHAPASKANS, ND3
Atharaka, FL5
Athens, Periclean,
  EH11
Ati, OA11
Aticare, SS12
Atjeh, OD4
ATJEHNESE, OD4
Atonga, FS5
Atoni, OF20
Atorai, SR13
Atroahy, SQ22
ATSAHUACA, SE7
Atsi, AP6
Atsina, NQ13
Atsokwe, FP4
Atsugewi, NS5
Atta, MW5
Attaqua, FX13
Attie, FA5
Attiwandaron, NM8
Ature, SS15
Atwood, SW1
Atwot, FJ12
Atyuti, FE8
Aua Island, OM15
AUAKE, SS5
Aucaner, SR8
Auckland Islands,
  OZ5
Auen, FX10
Aueti, SP6
Aueto, SP6
Aulad Hamayd, MQ10
Aulad Hamid, MS9

Aulad Sliman, MS9
Aulad Soliman, MT9
Aulliminden, MS25
AURORA, OO6
Aushi, FQ5
AUSTRALIA, OI1
Australia, Historical,
OI2
AUSTRALIAN ABORIGINES,
OI5
Australians, OI1
Australia, Prehistoric,
OI4
AUSTRALS, OX4
AUSTRIA, EK1
Austria, Historical,
EK2
Austria-Hungary, EK2
Austria, Prehistoric,
EK3
Austronesians, O4
Avane, SQ27
Avar, RH8
Avausi, FQ5
Avikam, FA25
Avon, OP6
Avoyel, NO8
Avukaya, FJ19
Awamba, FO6
Awasira, FQ5
AWEIKOMA, SM2
Awemba, FQ5
Awisa, FQ5
Awishira, SE22
Awiwa, FN21
AWIYA, MP6
Awoen, FA36
Aworo, FF62
Awouhen, FA36
Awuna, FE7
Ayan, FA36
Ayaon, FA36
Ayapel, SC9
AYMARA, SF5
Ayo, FT7
Ayoman, SS12
Aysen, SH1
Ayu, FF45
AZANDE, FO7
Azen, FA36
AZERBAIJAN, RK1
Azerbaijan, Historical,
RK2
AZERBAIJANI, RK3
Azerbaydzhan S.S.R.,
RK1
Azeri, RK3
Azimba, FR4
Azjer, MS25
Azna, MS12
AZORES, EZ2
AZTEC, NU7

Baamba, FO6
Babai, FO9
Babaie, FO43
Babali, FO9
Babalia, FI16
Babangi, FI7, FO13
BABAR, OF6
Babati, FO8
Babemba, FQ5
Babembe, FO21
Babeo, FO8
Babeyru, FO11
Babi, FI4
Babimbi, FH12
Babindi, FO20
Babine, NE7
Babinga, FH4, FI4
Babinja, FO8
Babinji, FO23
Babira, FO11
Babisa, FQ5

Babochi, FI7
Baboma, FO43
Babouisse, FI19
Babudja, FS5
Babudjue, FO15
Babudu, FO14
Babuende, FO21
Babui, FO15
Babukur, FO33
Babundu, FO17
Babur, FF12
Babuya, FO15
Babvanuma, FO38
BABWA, FO8
Babwile, FQ5
BACAIRI, SP7
Bachake, FI17
BACHAMA, FF7
Bachapin, FV6
Bachila, FQ5
Bachoko, FP4
Baciroa, NU8
Backhook, NN13
Bacuisso, FP7
BADAGA, AW50
Badagri, FF62
Badiaranke, FA36
Badinga, FO17
BADITU, MP7
Badjo, OA8, OB4
Badjok, FP4
Badjue, FH21
Badua, MW9
BADUI, OE4
Baduma, FI12, FS5
Badyaranke, FA36
Badyo, FO29
Badzing, FO17
Baele, MS5
Baenya, FO45
Baer, FJ14
BAFFINLAND ESKIMO,
ND5
Bafia, FH10
Bafiote, FI34
Bafo, FF40
Bafuleri, FO10
Bafumbum, FF51
Bafungwi, FS5
Bafuru, FI7
Bafut, FF51
Bafute, FH24
BAGA, FA7
Bagam, FF51
Baganda, FK7
BAGDAD ARABS, MH3
Bagengele, FO45
Bagesu, FK13
BAGGARA, MQ5
Bagielle, FH4
BAGIRMI, MS4
Bagishu, FK13
Bagisu, FK13
Bagiuni, MO5
Bagobo, OA7
Bagua, FO18, SE17
Baguana, FO17
Bagunda, FH21, FO29
Bahama, Grand, SW1
BAHAMAS, SW1
Bahamas, Historical,
SW2
Bahamas, Prehistoric,
SW3
Bahamba, FO6, FO47
Bahanga, FL4
Bahariya, MR12
BAHAU, OC5
Bahavu, FO10
Bahelia, AW45
Bahenga, FR6
Bahia, SO11
BAHIA BRAZILIANS,
SO11

BAHNAR, AM15
Bahnar Chams, AM22
Baholo, FP5
Baholoholo, FO18
Bahonde, FO22
Bahonga, FQ5
BAHRAIN, MZ2
Bahuku, FO38
Bahumbu, FO30
Bahungana, FO17
Bahushi, FQ5
Bahutu, FO42
Bai, FI28, FJ20, FO43
Baia, FJ16, SO1
BAIGA, AW24
Baila, FQ6
Bailundo, FP13
Bainuk, FB6
Bait, AH5
BAJAU, OA8
Bajau, OB4
Baji, FF41
Bajia, FO43
Bajun, MO5
Baka, FJ18
Bakahonde, FQ7
Bakalahari, FV4
Bakalanga, FO15
Bakale, FI14
Bakango, FO8
Bakaunde, FQ7
Bakela, FO19
Bakelle, FI14
Baker Island, OV1
Bakerewe, FN10
Bakete, FO20
Bakgotlha, FV6
Bakhtiari, MA12
Bakielle, MH4
Bakinike, FI12
Bakioko, FP4
Bakka, MS15
BAKO, MP8
Bakoba, FV5
Bakoko, FH12
Bakondjo, FO22
Bakongo, FO21
Bakoroka, FP7
Bakosi, FF40
Bakota, FI17
Bakougni, FO50
Bakuando, FP15
Bakuba, FO23
Bakuise, FP7
Bakulia, FL8
Bakum, FH11
Bakumbu, FO11
Bakunda, FO15
Bakundu, FF41
Bakuruthse, FV6
Bakusu, FL4, FO47
Bakuti, FO19, FO32
Bakutshu, FO32
Bakutu, FO32
Bakwange, FO45
Bakwe, FD7
Bakwele, FF43, FH20
Bakwena, FV6
Bakwese, FO28
Bakwili, FF43, FH20
Bakxatla, FV6
Bakyiga, FK6
Balala, FQ8
Balamba, FQ8
Balanga, FO19
Balantak, OG5
Balante, FB6
Balbalasang-Ginaang,
OA24
Balda, FH15
Bale, FO13, FO25
BALEARICS, EZ3
Balega, FO25
Balegga, FO41

Balemba, FX19
Balembe, FO41
Balembo, FJ20
Balendu, FO25
Balenge, FI26
Balengora, FO11
Balenje, FQ6
Balese, FO31
BALI, FO9
BALI, OF7
Bali, FF51
Bali Aga, OF7
Balika, FO9
Balinese, OF7
Balinga, FO32
BALKAN PEOPLES, E13
Balkar, RH7
Balobedu, FX14
Baloch, AT2
Balochasi, FP8
Baloi, FI7
Balolo, FO32
Balom, FH10
Balonda, FQ5
Balori, FO17
Balovale, FP14
BALTI, AV2
BALTIC COUNTRIES,
RB1
BALTIC PREHISTORY,
RB2
BALTO-SLAVS, RB3
Balua, FO28
Baluba, FO27
BALUCHI, AT2
Balud, OA10
Balue, FF41
Balui, FI7
Baluimbe, FP9
Balukolwe, FQ10
Balumba, FO15
Balumbo, FI19
Balunda, FO27
Balung, FF40, FH19
Bamakoma, FQ9
Bamanga, FO29
Bamangala, FO12
Bamangwato, FV6
Bamasasa, FQ10
Bamba, FI12, FO21
Bambagani, FO20
Bambala, FO30
Bambamba, FI12
Bambao, FI17
BAMBARA, FA8
Bambata, FO21
Bambe, FL13
Bamberawa, FF14
Bambete, FI12
Bamboko, FF43
Bambole, FO19, FO35
Bambuba, FO31
Bambuli, FO19
Bambunda, FO17
Bambuti, FO4
Bambwela, FQ10
Bamendzo, FH19
Bamfumu, FI33
Bamfunuka, FI33
BAMILEKE, FH19
Bamoa, NU35
Bamputu, FO17
Bamum, FF51
BANA, FI5
Bana, FH19
Banaba, OR6
Banabuddu, FO14
Banaka, FI26
Banana, FH23
Bananaw, OA13
Banande, FO22
Banano, FP13
BANARO, OJ8
Banbunu, FI33

BANDA, FI6
BANDA, OH6
Bandaka, FO9
Bandala, MQ11
Bandassa, FI17
Bandawa, FF59
Bandem, FH19
Bandempo, FP14
Bandi, FD4
Bandiapa, SQ7
Bandjambi, FI17
Bandjo, FI11
Bandombe, FP15
Bandomo, FI17
Bandula, MS15
Bandumbo, FI12
Bandya, FX8
Banen, FH10
Banend, FH10
Banfungunu, FI33
Banga, FF64
Bangala, FO12, FP10
Bangambue, FP18
Bangandu, FI22, FO35
Bangangte, FH19
Bangangulu, FI33
Bangba, FO29
Bangbele, FO29
Bang Chan, AO7
Bange, FO8
Bangelima, FO8
Banggai, OG5
Banggai Islands, OG5
BANGI, FI7
Bangili, FI7
Bango, FO13
Bangobango, FO27
Bangodi, FO17
Bangombe, FO32
Bangomo, FI14
Bangon, OA15
Bangongo, FO30
Bangove, FI19
Bangu, FH19
Banguie, FI17
Banguli, FO17
Bangumbi, FP17
Bangwa, FH19
Bangwaketse, FV6
Bangwe, FI14
Bani, FF51
Baniabungu, FO10
Banianeka, FP18
Banianga, FO22
Baninga, FO32
Baniwa, SQ27
Banjabi, FI12
Banjadi, FO17
Banjanja, FS5
Banjogi, AR4
Banju, FH19
Bankalawa, FF31
BANKS ISLANDS, OO7
Bankundu, FO32
Bankutshu, FO47
Banmana, FA8
Ban Manus, AW45
Bannock, NR14
Banoho, FI26
Banso, FF51
Banton, OA14
Bantu, FX5
Bantu, Interlacustrine,
  FK1
Bantu Kavirondo, FL4
Banuauon, OA13
Banunu, FI33
Banyai, FS5
Banyali, FO38
Banyamwezi, FN18
Banyang, FF53
Banyangi, FF53
Banyankole, FK11
Banyaruanda, FO42

Banyika, FN21
Banyin, FH10
Banyoro, FK11
Banyoro-Wassongora,
  FO38
Banyun, FB6
Banza, FI6
Banzari, FO17
BANZIRI, FI8
Baole, FL7
Bapea, FH10
Bapedi, FX16
Bapende, FO39
Bapere, FO11
Bapindi, FO46
Bapindji, FI30
Bapopoie, FO29
Bapoto, FO40
Bapou, FI17
Bapubi, FI30
Bapuko, FI26
Bapuni, FI30
BARA, FY13
Bara, SQ19
Baraba, RT2
Barabaig, FN26
BARABRA, MR8
Barama, FI19, SR9
Barambo, FO5
Bararetta, FL7
BARAUNA, SQ27
Barawa, FF31
Barbacoa, SC12
BARBADOS, ST2
Barbuda, ST6
Bare, FF11, SQ27
BAREA, MN5
Barega, FO41
Barein, FI31
BARGU, FA9
Bargwe, FS5
BARI, FJ5
BARI, SS13
Bari, FJ20
Bariba, FA9
Baribi, OA15
BARKINDJI, OI9
Barlamomo, OI17
Barolong, FV6
Barombi, FF41
Baron, FF6
Barondo, FF41
Baronga, FT6
Barotse, FQ9
Barozi, FQ9
Barozwi, FS5
Baru, AM16
Barundi, FO42
Barutse, FQ9
Barwe, FS5
Basa, FF8
Basakata, FO43
Basakomo, FF8
Basala, FQ6
Basanga, FI27, FQ7
Basap, OC10
BASARI, FA10
Basele, FP6
Basengere, FO32
Bashankwe, FS5
Basheke, FI29
Bashera, FF61
BASHI, FO10
Bashikongo, FO21
Bashilele, FO24
Bashilongo, FO21
Bashinshe, FP10
BASHKIR, RF3
Bashkir A.S.S.R.,
  RF3
Bashukulompo, FQ6
Basiba, FN8
Basin Shoshoneans,
  NT6

Basiri, FJ20
Basisiu, FI14
Basketo, MP26
Basoko, FO44
Basolongo, FO21
Basonde, FO28
Basongo, FO30
Basongola, FO45
Basongo-Meno, FO16
Basossi, FF40
Basotho, FW2
BASSA, FF8
Bassa, FD7, FH12
Bassa-Komo, FF8
Bassa-Nge, FF29
Bassari, FA36
Basseri, MA13
Bassonge, FO27
Basu, FH19
Basuku, FO46
Basukuma, FN18
Basumbe, FP6
Basundi, FO21
Basungwe, FS5
Basuto, FW2
Basutoland, FW1
Bata, FF12
Bataan, OA36
Batabwa, FQ5
Batahin, MQ15
BATAK, OA9
BATAK, OD5
Batambwa, FQ5
Batan, OA29
Batanga, FF41, FI26
Batangan, OA15, OA36
Batcham, FH19
Batchangui, FI12
Batchokwe, FP4
Batchopi, FT4
Bategue, FI33
Bateke, FI33
Bateso, FK12
Batete, FO43
Batetela, FO47
Bathonga, FT6
Bati, FH10, FO8
Batitu, FO32
BATJAN, OH7
Batlaping, FV6
Batlaro, FV6
Batlokwa, FV6
Batoka, FQ12
Batonga, FQ12, FR6
Batongtu, FH19
Batonka, FQ12, FS5
Batoro, FK11
Batotela, FQ12
Batswa, FT6
Batta, FO21
Batu, FF63
Batumbuka, FR6
Batumbwe, FO18
Batutsi, FO42
Batwa, FO42
Batwana, FV6
Baule, FA5
Baunga, FQ5
Baure, SF15
Baushanga, FQ10
Baushi, FF36
Bavenda, FX19
Bavili, FI34
Bavumbu, FO30
Bavungo, FI19
Bawgott, FL13
Bawongo, FO24
BAYA, FI9
Bayaka, FI19, FO49
Bayan Tala, AH6
Bayangela, FO50
Bayansi, FO17
Baye, FO43

Bayei, FV5
Bayeke, FO27
Baygo, MQ7
Bayit, AH5
Bayombe, FO50
Bayot, FA14
Bayugu, FI23, FO29
Baza, FF12
Bazaa, MQ10
Bazanche, FE8
Bazezuru, FS5
Bazimba, FO41, FO45,
  FR4
Bazombo, FO21
BEA, FH5
BEAVER, NF5
Beba, FF58
Bechuana, FV6
Bechuanaland, FV1
Bedanga, FI31
Bedayria, MQ10
Bede, FF50
Bedia, AW46
Bedik, FA36
BEDOUIN, MJ4
Bedouin, Egyptian,
  MR11
Bedouin, Iraq, MH8
Bedouin, Jordanian,
  MG2
Bedouin, Libyan, MT9
Bedouin, Syrian, MD5
Befang, FF58
Begbak, FH10
Bego, MQ7
BEHAVIOR THEORY, W3
Behr, FJ14
BEIR, FJ6
Beit Asgede, MN9
BEJA, MR9
Bekom, FF39
Belen, MN6
Belgian Congo, FO1
BELGIUM, EV1
Beli, FJ18
Belize, NX1
BELLABELLA, NE5
BELLACOOLA, NE6
Belle, FD7
Bellona Island, OT9
BELORUSSIA, RC1
Belu, OF20
BEMBA, FQ5
Bembance, FI14
Bembe, FO21, FO41
Bena, FN9
Bena Kalundwe, FO27
Bena Kanioka, FO27
Bena Kazembe, FQ5
Bena Lulua, FO27
Bende, FN18
Bene, FH9
Benga, FI26
Bengal, AW20
Bengal, East, AS1
BENGAL TRIBES, AW49
Bengal, West, AW20
Bengela, FP10
Benguet Igorot, OA20
Beni Ahsen, MW9
Beni Amer, MR9
Beni Brahim, MV10
Beni Gerar, MQ10
Beni Helba, MQ5
Beni Iznacen, MW14
Beni Malek, MW9
Beni Mezab, MQ5
Beni Mtir, MW5
Benin, FF21
Beni Omran, MQ10
Beni Ouagguin, MV10
Beni Ouarain, MW13
Beni Selim, MQ5
Beni Sisin, MV10

Beni Waggin, MV10
Benimukuni, FQ6
Benua, OD8
BEOTHUK, NI4
BERABER, MW5
Berabish, MS29
BERBERS, M11
Ber Dser, AE11
BERGDAMA, FX9
Beri, FJ4
Beriberi, MS14
BERMUDA, NZ2
Berom, FF9
BERTA, FJ7
Berti, MS5
Besikongo, FO21
Besimbo, FH11
Besoa, OG11
Besom, FH21
Besorube, FA9
Bessarabia, RE1
Bete, FD7, FF17
Betie, FA5
Betjek, FH12
BETOI, SC6
Betsi, FH9
BETSILEO, FY11
BETSIMISARAKA, FY4
BEZANOZANO, FY19
Bhaca, FX20
Bhar, AW45
Bharaiya, AW48
Bharia, AW46
Bhatra, AW32
BHIL, AW25
Bhilala, AW25
Bhogta, AW46
Bhoksa, AW45
Bhopal, AW4
Bhuia, AW28
BHUINAR, AW27
Bhuinhar, AW27
BHUIYA, AW28
Bhuksha, AW45
Bhumia, AW46
BHUMIJ, AW29
BHUTAN, AK2
Biadju, OC9
Biafada, FB6
Biafar, FB6
BIAK, OJ9
Biakum, FH21
Biboulmoun, OI26
Bichari, MR9
BIDEYAT, MS5
Bidjuk, FH21
Bienesho, MP10
Bifra, FB6
Bigola, FA36
BIHAR, AW2
Bihe, FP13
BIJOGO, FB4
Bikol, Christian,
  OA32
BILAAN, OA10
Bilin, MN6
Biloxi, NN14
Bilqula, NE6
Bilwana, FN18
Bimanese, OF18
Bimbi, FH12
Bimbia, FH7
Bimbundu, FP13
Bindi, FO20
Binga, FI15
Bini, FF21
Binjhwar, AW46
Binji, FO23
Binna, FF64
Bintukua, SC7
Binukidnon, OA14
Binza, FO8
Bira, FJ17
BIRA, FO11

Biraan, OA10
Birar, RU5
BIRHOR, AW26
Biri, FJ20
Birifor, FE4
Biriune, SP8
Birjia, AW46
BIRKED, MQ6
BIROBIDZHAN, RX4
BIROM, FF9
Birra, FJ10
Bisa, FA12, FQ5
Bisayan, Central,
  OA14
Bisayan, Northwest,
  OA30
BISAYAS PAGANS, OA11
Bisharin, MR9
BISMARCK ARCHIPELAGO,
  OM1
Bismarcks, Historical,
  OM2
Bismarcks, Prehistoric,
  OM3
Bison Horn, AW32
Bissagos Islands,
  FB4
Bitare, FF63
Biti, FJ18
Biya, MP8
Biyan, FA36
Biye, MP8
Bizhi, FQ6
Bjakuk, FH21
Bla, AM17
BLACK AFRICA, F2
Black Bobo, FA11
Black Carib, SA12
BLACKFOOT, NF6
Black Jews, MP9
Black Ndebele, FX18
Black Thai, AL3
Bliss-Karone, FA14
Blo, AM35
Blood, NF6
Bo, FF40
Boale, FH9
Bobai, FJ11, FO43
Bobangi, FI7
Bobenge, FO8
BOBO, FA11
Bobofing, FA11
Bobo-oule, FA11
Bobo-zbe, FA11
Bobwa, FO8
Boda, MP8
Bodha, OF12
Bodho, FJ14
Bodiman, FH7
Bodo, AR6
Boers, FX7
Bofi, FI9
Boghorom, FF61
BOGO, MN6
Bogoto, FI9
Bohane, SJ5
Bohemia, EB2
Bohol, OA14
Boiki, RD3
Boka, FI22
Bokaka, FI22
Bokala, FO32
Bokete, FO32
Boki, FF17
Bokiba, FI17
Boko, FF13
Bola, FB6
Bolaang, OG4
Bole, FO32
Bolendu, FO32
BOLEWA, FF10
Bolia, FO32
Boliba, FJ19
BOLIVIA, SF1

Bolivia, Historical,
  SF2
Bolivian Chaco, SK4
BOLIVIAN INDIANS,
  SF3
Bolivian Prehistory,
  SF4
Bolki, FF12
Bolo, FO35
BOLOKI, FO12
Bolombo, FO44
Bolongo, FO32
Boma, FJ6, FO43
Bomali, FI27
Bomam, FH21
BOMBAY, AW3
BOMBAY TRIBES, AW47
Bombesa, FO13
Bomitaba, FI22
Bomome, FH21
Bomvana, FX17
Bonaire, SZ2
Bonangando, FH7
Bonari, SQ22
Bonda, SC9
Bondei, FN28
Bondjo, FI11
BONDO, AW30
Bondo Poroja, AW30
Bonfia, OH9
Bonga, FI22
Bongili, FI22
Bongiri, FI22
BONGO, FJ8
Bongo, FP6
Boni, SR8
BONINS, AZ3
Bonkeng, FH7
Bonkesse, FO16
Bonom, AM30
Bontoc Igorot, OA12
BONTOK, OA12
Booli, FO32
Bor, FJ12, FJ14
Bora, AW45, SC19
Boram, FF6
Boran, FL7
Borana, FL7
Bori, FJ4, FO32
Boriqueno, SV5
Borku, MS22
BORNEO, OC1
Borneo, British, OC4
Borneo, Dutch, OC2
Borneo, Historical,
  OC2
Borneo, North, OC4
Borneo, Prehistoric,
  OC3
Borom, FF9
BORORO, SP8
Bororo, MS11
Borrado, NU12
Borrom, FF61
Boruca, SA19
Borun, SN1
Bosaka, FO32
Bosanga, FI27
Bosha, MP27
Boshi, FI7
Boska, FJ11
Bosre, AM29
Bota, FI22
Botel Tobago, AD17
BOTOCUDO, SN2
Botocudo, SM2
BOTSWANA, FV1
Botswana, Historical,
  FV2
Botswana, Prehistoric,
  FV3
Boua, FA11
BOUGAINVILLE, ON4

Bounty Islands, OZ5
Bouvet, FZ1
Boya, FJ10
Boyela, FO19
BOZO, MS6
Brabralung, OI16
Bracamoro, SD9
Brahui, AT2
Braiakaulung, OI16
Brakna, MS24
Bram, FB6
Brandenburg, EL12
Brao, AM14
Brariga, FN26
Brass, FF30
Bratauolung, OI16
BRAZIL, SL1
Brazil, East, SN1
Brazil, Historical,
  SL2
Brazilian Indians,
  SL4
Brazilians, Bahia,
  SO11
Brazil, Northeast,
  SO1
Brazil, Prehistoric,
  SL3
Brazil, South, SM1
BRETONS, EW8
Bribri, SA19
Brinya, FA25
Britain, ES1-ES4,
  ES8
Britain, Early Modern,
  ES4
Britain, Prehistoric,
  ES8
BRITISH BORNEO, OC4
BRITISH COLUMBIA,
  NE1
British Columbia,
  Historical, NE2
British Columbia,
  Prehistoric, NE4
British Empire, ES1
British Guiana, SR2
BRITISH HONDURAS,
  NX1
British Honduras,
  Historical, NX2
British Honduras,
  Prehistoric, NX3
BRITISH INDIA, AQ2
British Isles, ES1
British North Borneo,
  OC4
BRITISH POLYNESIA,
  OW1
British Southern Cameroons,
  FH1
British Togoland,
  FE1
BRITISH VIRGIN ISLANDS,
  ST3
Broi, FH8
Brong, FE8
BRU, AM16
Brule, NQ11
Brunei, OC4
BUA, FI10
Bua, FA11
Buamba, FO6
Bubangi, FI7
BUBI, FG3
Bubure, SS13
Buchamai, FI17
Budeh, AM39
Budip, AM39
BUDJA, FO13
Budja, FS5
BUDU, FO14
Budukha, RH8
BUDUMA, MS7

Buginese, OG6
Bugre, SM2
Buhagana, SQ19
Buhid, OA18
Buhil, OA18
Buid, OA18
Builsa, FE7
BUIN, ON5
Bujawa, FF32
Bujeba, FH5
Buji, FF32
BUKA, ON6
Bukanda, FQ8
BUKAUA, OJ10
BUKIDNON, OA13
Bukit, OC10
Bukitan, OC10
Buku, FI26
BULA, FF11
Bula, MP20
Bulach, AM39
Bulai, FF12
Bulakan, OA36
BULALA, MS8
Bulalacauno, OA37
BULGARIA, EE1
Bulgaria, Historical,
  EE2
Bulgarians, EE1
Bulgaria, Prehistoric,
  EE3
Bulgeda, MS22
Buli, FH7
Bulia, FL8
Bulo, AM39
Bulom, FC8
Bulu, FH9
Buluan, OA10
Bum, FF5, FH16
Bumali, FI27
Bumbe, FI9
Bumbon, FH21
Buna, MP20
Bunda, FO17
Bunga, FN20
Bungi, NG6
Bungku, OG7
Bungu, FN21
Buni, FJ25
Bunlap, OO13
Buno, FI22
Buntigwa, SC7
Bunu, FF62
BUNUN, AD10
BURA, FF12
Bura, MP8
Buraka, FI8
Burama, FB6
Buritica, SC9
Burji, MP17
Burkeneji, FL12
Burle, MP8
BURMA, AP1
Burma, Historical,
  AP2
Burmans, AP4
Burma, Prehistoric,
  AP3
Burma, Union of, AP14
BURMESE, AP4
Burrum, FF61
BURU, OH8
Burue, SQ7
Burum, FF9
BURUN, FJ9
BURUNDI, FO52
Burunge, FN5
Burungi, FN5
BURUSHO, AV7
Buryat, RW1
Buryat Mongol A.S.S.R.,
  RW1
BURYAT MONGOLIA, RW1
BUSA, FF13

Busanse, FA12
BUSANSI, FA12
Bush Kanaka, OJ30
BUSH NEGROES, SR8
BUSHMEN, FX10
Bushongo, FO23
Businka, SC7
Busintana, SC7
Bussa, MP17
Busso, FI21
BUTA, FF14
Butawa, FF14
Bute, FH24
Buton, OG7
Butung, OG7
BUYE, FO15
Buzi, FD8
Buzid, MW5
Bviri, FJ20
BWAKA, FI11
Bwari, FO41
Bwende, FO21
Bwile, FQ5
Bwisi, FI19
Bwol, FF6
Bworo, MP21
Byrre, FH16
BYZANTINE CIVILIZATION,
  EH3

Caagua, SM3
Cabahiba, SP10
Cabecar, SA19
Caberre, SC5
Cabinda, FO21, FP1
Cabishi, SP19
Cabishinana, SP24
Cabrai, FA22
Cabre, SC5
CADDO, NO5
Cadigue, SK12
Caduveo, SK11
Caete, SO9
CAGABA, SC7
Cagayan Sulu, OA16
CAHITA, NU8
Cahokia, NP6
CAHUAPANA, SE8
Cahuilla, NS20
Caicos, SW1
CAINGANG, SM3
Caingang, Santa Catarina,
  SM2
Caingua, SM4
CAKCHIQUEL, NW5
Calagar, OA35
Calamari, SC9
Calamiano, OA30
Calchaqui, SG6
Caliana, SS5
CALIFORNIA, NS1
California, Historical,
  NS2
CALIFORNIA INDIANS,
  NS4
California, Prehistoric,
  NS3
Calinga, OA24
Calino, ST13
CALLINAGO, ST13
CALUSA, NN7
CAMACAN, SO2
Camaracoto, SS16
Camayura, SP6
Camba, SF1
Cambi, SC15
CAMBODIA, AM4
Cambodians, AM4
CAMEROON, FH1
Cameroon, Colonial,
  FH2
Cameroon, Prehistoric,
  FH25

CAMEROON PYGMIES,
  FH4
Cameroon, Traditional,
  FH3
Cameroons, British
  Southern, FH1
Cameroun, French,
  FH1
Camma, FI23
CAMPA, SE9
Campbell Island, OZ5
Campeche, NV1
Camsa, SC17
Camuru, SO3
CANADA, NC1
Canada, Historical,
  NC2
CANADIAN INDIANS,
  NC3
Canadians, NC1
CANAL ZONE, SB4
Canamari, SQ6-SQ7,
  SQ9
Canaque, OP4
CANARI, SD4
CANARIES, MZ3
Canary Islands, MZ3
Canella, SO8
CANELO, SD5
CANICHANA, SF6
Canoa, SP24
Canoeiro, SP22
Canton, OW2
Capanawa, SE6
Capechene, SF23
CAPE COLORED, FX11
Cape Fear, NN13
Cape Hottentot, FX13
Cape Nguni, FX17
CAPE VERDE ISLANDS,
  MZ5
Cape York Eskimo,
  NB5
Capiecran, SO8
Caposho, SN4
Capuibo, SF19
CAQUETIO, SS7
Cara, SD11
Carabacho, SE10
Carabere, SF11
Carabinana, SQ22
CARACA, SS8
CARAJA, SP9
Caramanta, SC9
Caran, SR12
Carapana, SQ19
Carapoto, SO3
Carare, SC10
Caratiu, SO5
Carcarana, SI11
Carex, SC9
Cariaya, SQ27
CARIB, SR9
CARIBAN INDIANS, SR7
Carib, Black, SA12
Carib, Island, ST13
CARIBOU ESKIMO, ND6
Carijo, SM4
Carima, SM4
CARINA, SS6
CARINIACO, SS23
Caripuna, SF19
CARIRI, SO3
Carnijo, SO3
Caroline Island, OV6
Caroline Islands,
  OR4
Carolines, Central,
  OR21
Ca-Rong, AM25
CARRIER, NE7
Carrizo, NT21
Cartama, SC9

CARTHAGINIANS, MU3
Carutana, SQ27
Casapare, SQ18
Casavindo, SG5
Cascoasoa, SE14
Casharari, SQ9
Cashibo, SE10
CASHINAWA, SQ6
Cashiniti, SP19
Cashuena, SQ22
CASPIAN IRANIANS,
  MA7
Cat, FJ14, SW1
CATALANS, EX9
Catalonia, EX9
Catapolitani, SQ27
Catathoy, SO2
Catawba, NN13
Catawian, SQ22
Catawishi, SQ7
Catiana, SQ9
Catio, SC9
Cato Island, OI3
CATUKINA, SQ7
Catukina, SQ6
Catukino, SQ7
Caua, SQ27
CAUCASIA, RH1
Caucasia, Historical,
  RH2
Caucasia, Prehistoric,
  RH3
Cau Ma, AM29
Cavina, SF23
Cawahib, SP10
Cayabi, SP2
Cayamo, SP13
CAYAPA, SD6
CAYAPO, SP11
Cayapo, Northern,
  SP13
Cayapo, Southern,
  SP11
CAYMAN ISLANDS, SZ6
Cayua, SM4
Cayuga, MN9
Cayuishaua, SQ11
Cayuse, NR18
CAYUVAVA, SF7
CAZCAN, NU9
Ceara, SO1
Cebuano, OA14
CELEBES, OG1
Celebes, Historical,
  OG2
Celebes, Prehistoric,
  OG3
CELTIC IRISH, ER4
CELTIC PEOPLES, E10
Ceni, NO5
CENTRAL AFRICAN REPUBLIC,
  FI35
Central African Republic,
  Colonial, FI36
Central African Republic,
  Prehistoric, FI38
Central African Republic,
  Traditional, FI37
CENTRAL AMERICA, SA1
CENTRAL AMERICAN INDIANS,
  SA2
Central Asia, Russian,
  RL1, RR1
CENTRAL BISAYAN, OA14
Central Bushmen, FX10
Central Carolines,
  OR21
CENTRAL CHINA, AF14
CENTRAL MANGYAN, OA15
CENTRAL SIBERIA, RT1
CENTRAL THAI, AO7
CENTRAL TRIBES, AW46
CENU, SC9
Cenufana, SC9

CERAM, OH9
CERAMLAUT, OH10
Cercada, SS17
Cewa, FR4
CEYLON, AX1
Ceylon, Historical, AX2
Ceylon, Prehistoric, AX3
CHAAMBA, MV5
Chachapoya, SE17
Chacobo, SF19
CHACO INDIANS, SK4
CHAD, MS33
Chad, MQ2, MQ3
CHAD ARABS, MS9
Chad-Hamite, FF46
Chagaragoto, SS8
CHAGGA, FN4
Chagos, AZ1
Chahar Mongols, AH6
Chaima, SS9
Chainoqua, FX13
Chakalle, FE7
Chakchiuma, NN9
Chake, FI17, SC10
Chakma, AR4
CHAKOSSI, FA13
Chale, MS16
CHAM, AM5
CHAMA, SE10
Chamacoco, SK14
Chamar, AW19
CHAMBA, FF15
Chamba, FA10
Chamicura, SE5
CHAMORRO, OR5
Chan, RI10
Chana, SJ5, SK7
Chana-Mbegua, SI11
Chana-Timbu, SI11
Chanabal, NW7
Chandri, SJ4
CHANDULE, SJ4
CHANE, SF8
Chang, AR13
Changi, FI12
Chango, SG5
Changuena, SA19
Chaobon, AM7
Chaonam, AP8
Chao-uda, AH6
Chaouia, MV8
CHAPACURA, SP12
Chapogir, RU5
Chara, FF32, MP26
Charaqua, SS17
Chariguriqua, FX13
CHARRUA, SJ5
Chastacosta, NR22
CHATHAM ISLANDS, OZ8
Chatino, NU44
Chatot, NN14
Chattisgarh, AW46
Chavante, SP20
CHAWAI, FF16
Chaywita, SE8
Chebero, SE8
Chebleng, FL13
CHECHEN, RI5
Chedua, SE14
Chehalis, NR15
Cheiru, SM4
CHEJU-DO, AA4
Cheke, FF12
Chekiang, AF15
Chelan, NR19
Chemakum, NR16
Chemehuevi, NT16
CHENCHU, AW51
Cheraw, NN13
Chere, FJ20
CHEREMIS, RG2

Cherente, SP20
CHERKESS, RH5
Cherkess Autonomous
   Oblast, RH5
Chero, AW46
CHEROKEE, NN8
Cherry Island, OT11
Chesterfield, OP6
Chetco, NR22
Cheva, FR4
Chewa, FR4
CHEYENNE, NQ8
Cheykye, MQ14
Chiadma, MW10
Chiang, AE3
CHIAPANEC, NV5
Chiapas, NV1
Chibak, FF12
CHIBCHA, SC11
Chibchan, SC3
Chiboque, FP4
Chichatec, NU24
CHICHIMEC, NU45
Chichiren, SE9
Chickahominy, NN15
CHICKASAW, NN9
Chicomucaltec, NW8
CHIGA, FK6
Chikena, SQ22
Chikunda, FR4
Chikuyu, FP18
CHILCOTIN, NE8
CHILE, SG1
Chile, Historical, SG2
Chile, Prehistoric, SG3
Chilote, SG4
Chilula, NS11
Chimane, SF16
CHIMARIKO, NS6
Chimbaro, FE8
Chimila, SC7
Chimu, SE21
CHIN, AP5
Chin, AF4, AF8
CHINA, AF1
China, Central, AF14
China, East, AF15
China, Greater, AE1
China, North, AF12
China, Northwest, AF13
CHINANTEC, NU10
China, Peoples' Republic of, AF18
China, Prehistoric, AF10
Chinarra, NU14
China, South, AF17
China, Southwest, AF16
Chinato, SS17
Chinchipe, SE17
Chinese, AF1, AF18
CHINESE REGIONAL CULTURES, AF11
Chinese Thai, AE7
Chinese Turkestan, AI1
CHING, AF2
Chinge, FP10
Chinghai, AF13
Chingpaw, AP6
CHIN-HAN, AF8
Chinipa, NU35
CHINOOK, NR6
Chinook, Upper, NR23
Chipaya, SF24, SQ26
Chipeta, FR4
CHIPEWYAN, ND7
Chippewa, NG6
Chiqui, SM3
CHIQUITO, SF9

Chiri, FI32
Chiricahua, NT8
Chiricoa, SC14
CHIRIGUANO, SF10
Chirino, SE17
Chiripa, SM4
Chirripo, SA19
Chisenga, FQ5
Chitarera, SS17
Chitimacha, NO4
CHITTAGONG, AR4
CHIWERE, NQ9
Chizo, NU14
Chleuh, MW11
Chobo, FN13
CHOCO, NU11
CHOCO, SC12
CHOCTAW, NN10
Chodhara, AW47
CHOISEUL, ON7
Chokobo, FF32
CHOKWE, FP4
CHOL, NV6
Cholon, SE14
Cholto, SC10
Choluteca Indians, SA11
Chong, AM7
CHONO, SH3
Chonque, NN13
CHONTAL, NV7
Chontaquiro, SE18
Chonyi, FL14
CHOPI, FT4
Choque, SC20
Chorfa, MS31
CHOROTEGA, SA11
CHOROTI, SK6
CHORTI, NW6
Chota Nagpur, AW46
Chou, AF9
CHRAU, AM17
Christian Bikol, OA32
Christian Gaddang, OA29
Christian Ratagnon, OA30
Christians, Syrian, AW11
Christmas Island, OV6
Chru, AM18
Chuabo, FT5
Chuang, AL3
Chubut, SH1
Chugach, NA13
Chuj, NW7
CHUKA, FL5
CHUKCHEE, RY2
Chukchee National Okrug, RY1, RY2
Chulupi, SK5
Chulyma, RT2
CHUMASH, NS7
Chumbuli, FE8
Chunatahua, SE19
Chung-chia, AL3
Chungwe, FN9
Chunupe, SI14
Chupacho, SE19
Churapa, SF9
Churi, MP22
CHURU, AM18
Chusco, SE19
Chuvan, RV3
CHUVASH, RF7
Chuvash A.S.S.R., RF7
Chwampo, FT5
Cibecue, NT21
CIBONEY, SX4
Cic, FJ12
Cil, AM31
Cilenge, FP15

Cinaloa, NU35
Cipala, FP6
Ciparicoto, SS12
Cipeta, FP6
Cipungu, FP17
Circassians, RH5
Circum-Caribbean culture area, SA2
CIRCUMPOLAR CULTURE, R3
Cisama, FP6
Cisanje, FP6
Cituja, SC6
Ciwere, FR5
Clackamas, NR6
Clatsop, NR6
CLIMACTIC SPAIN, EX2
Clipperton, NZ1
Coahuiltec, NU12
Coaiquer, SC17
Coanao, SC10
COASTAL CYRENAICA, MT4
COASTAL MORO, OA16
Coast Miwok, NS16
Coast Salish, NE13, NR15
Coast Yuki, NS30
Coca, NU9
Cocaima, SC5
COCAMA, SE11
Cocamilla, SE11
Cochaboth, SK9
COCHIMI, NU13
Cochinchina, AM11
Cochinoca, SG5
Cochiti, NT12
Cocolot, SI12
Coconuco, SC15
Cocopa, NT15
Cocos, SZ1
COCOS ISLANDS, AZ8
Cocozu, SP17
Coeruna, SC19
Coeur d'Alene, NR19
Cofan, SD11
Cognomona, SE14
Colastine, SI11
Colima, NU7
COLOMBIA, SC1
Colombia, Historical, SC2
COLOMBIAN INDIANS, SC3
COLOMBIAN PREHISTORY, SC4
COL. CAMEROON, FH2
COL. CENTRAL AFRICAN REPUBLIC, FI36
COL. CONGO-BRAZZAVILLE, FI40
COL. DAHOMEY, FA39
COL. EQUATORIAL GUINEA, FG2
COL. GABON, FI44
COL. GAMBIA, FC12
COL. GHANA, FE2
COL. GUINEA, FA43
COL. IVORY COAST, FA47
COL. KENYA, FL2
COL. MADAGASCAR, FY2
COL. MALAWI, FR2
COL. NIGERIA, FF2
COL. QUECHUA, SE23
COL. RUANDA-URUNDI, FO53
COL. SIERRA LEONE, FC2
COL. TANGANYIKA, FN2
COL. TOGO, FA51
COL. UGANDA, FK2

COL. UNITED STATES, NK3
COL. UPPER VOLTA, FA55
COL. ZAIRE, FO2
COL. ZAMBIA, FQ2
COLORADO, SD7
Colorado, NT1, SS11
Columbia, NR19
Colville, NR19
Comanahua, SE19
COMANCHE, NO6
Comarito, NU35
Comayana, SR12
Combahee, NN12
COMECHINGON, SI5
Comecrudo, NU12
Commander Islands, RZ1
Comobo, SE6
Comoro Islands, FZ3
COMOROS, FZ3
Comox, NE13
Compeba, SQ15
CONCHO, NU14
Conestoga, NM8
Congaree, NN13
Congo, Belgian, FO1
CONGO-BRAZZAVILLE, FI39
Congo-Brazzaville, Colonial, FI40
Congo-Brazzaville, Prehistoric, FI42
Congo-Brazzaville, Traditional, FI41
Congo, Democratic Republic of, FO1
Congo-Kinshasa, FO1
Congo, Middle, FI39
Congo, Moyen, FI39
Coniagui, FA36
Conibo, SE10
Conicari, NU8
Connecticut, NL1
Conoy, NM11
Contanawa, SQ6
CONTEMPORARY MACEDONIANS, EF8
COOK ISLANDS, OZ9
COORG, AW5
COOS, NR7
Copalis, NR15
Copallin, SE17
COPPER ESKIMO, ND8
Copts, MR10
Coquille, NR22
CORA, NU15
Coraveca, SF18
Corbago, SC10
Core, SS9
Corine, OI26
Corma, MP22
CORNISH, ES9
COROA, SP13
Coroado, SM3, SN6
Coroados Island, FZ4
Corobici, SA17
Coroca, FP7
Coromocho, SS17
Coronado, SE22, SS13
Coronda, SI11
Coropa, SN6
Correguaje, SE12
CORSICA, EZ4
Corsicans, EZ4
COSSACKS, RD2
COSTA RICA, SA3
Costa Rica, Prehistoric, SA4

COSTANO, NS8
Cote d'Ivoire, FA46
Coto, SA19, SE12
Cowichan, NE13
Cowlitz, NR15
Coyon, SS12
Coyukon, NA8
Cozarini, SP19
Cradaho, SP13
Craho, SO8
Cran, SO8
Crecmun, SN2
CREE, NG4
CREEK, NN11
Crenak, SN2
Crepumcateye, SO8
CRETE, EZ5
Creye, SO8
Cricati, SO8
Crichana, SQ22
CRIMEAN TATAR, RF8
Crixa, SP20
Croatia, EF4
CROATS, EF4
Crooked, SW1
CROSS-CULTURAL RESEARCH, W6
CROSS RIVER TRIBES, FF17
CROW, NQ10
Crozet, FZ1
CUA, AM19
Cuacua, SS23
Cuaga, SS9
Cuamato, FX8
CUBA, SX1
Cuba, Historical, SX2
Cubans, SX1
Cuba, Prehistoric, SX3
Cubeo, SQ19
Cucoecamecra, SO8
Cueretu, SQ19
Cufra, MT8
Cuica, SS17
Cujigeneri, SQ9
Cujuna, SP12
Culaman, OA25
Culebra, SU1
Culiana, SQ8
Culina, SR9
Culino, SQ23
CUMANA, SS9
Cumana, SP12
Cumanagoto, SS9
Cumanasho, SN4
Cumbaza, SE14
CUNA, SB5
Cunahana, SS20
Cuniba, SQ9
Cupeno, NS20
Cuperob, SQ2
Cuprigueri, SS13
CURACAO, SZ2
Curasicana, SS22
Curave, SF18
Curia, SQ23
Curina, SQ6, SQ23
Curipaco, SQ27
Curuaya, SQ26
Curucaneca, SF18
Curuminaca, SF18
Curuzirari, SQ25
CUSABO, NN12
Cusari, SR12
CUSHITES, M12
Custenau, SP18
Custumi, SR12
Cutasho, SO2
Cutinana, SE5
Cuyanawa, SQ6
Cuyo, OA30
Cuyono, OA30

Cypriotes, MC1
CYPRUS, MC1
Cyprus, Prehistoric, MC2
Cyrenaica, Coastal, MT4
CZECHOSLOVAKIA, EB1
Czechoslovakia, Prehistoric, EB3
Czechs, EB1

Daarood, MO4
Daba, FH15
Dabosa, FJ25
Dades, MW12
Dadio, MQ7
Da Dong, AM29
Dadzo, MQ7
Dafi, FA15
Dafla, AR11
Daga, AW47
DagaaWiili, FE4
Dagaba, FE4
DAGARI, FE4
Dagana, MS9
Dagbamba, FE5
DAGESTAN, RH8
DAGOMBA, FE5
DAGU, MQ7
Dagu, MQ16
DAGUR, AG5
Dahomean, FA18
DAHOMEY, FA38
Dahomey, Colonial, FA39
Dahomey, Prehistoric, FA41
Dahomey, Traditional, FA40
Dahuni, OL1
Dahur Mongols, AG5
Dai, OI17
Dair, FJ11
DAITO, AC5
Daju, MQ7
DAKA, FF18
Dakakari, FF36
Dakhla, MR12
DAKOTA, NQ11
Dakpa, FI28
Dalatoa, MS13
Dama, FH6, FL11
Damao, AY5
Damaqua, FX13
DAMAR, OF8
Damara, FX12
Damara, Mountain, FX9
Damboma, FI17
Damot, MP6
Dan, FA29
Danagla, MR8
Danakil, MN4
Danes, EM1
Danger Islands, OZ11
Danoa, MS13
Darassa, MP23
DARD, AV3
Dargin, RH8
Dar Hamid, MQ10
DARI, FH6
Dariganga Mongols, AH4
Darkhat Mongols, AH4
Dathanaich, FL7
Datoga, FN26
Daur, RU5
Daur Mongols, AG5
Daurawa, MS12
Daya, FI28
Daza, MS22
Dazagade, MS22
Dazaro, SS11
De, FD7

Debabaon, OA28
Debri, FJ11
Decuana, SS20
Deforo, FA16
Degha, FE7
Dei, FD7
Dekakire, MS9
DELAWARE, NM7
Delaware, NM1
Delhi, AW6
DELIM, MY4
Dembo, FJ14, FP6
Democratic Republic of Congo, FO1
Democratic Republic of Vietnam, AM12
Denawa, FF46
Dendi, FI8, MS20
DENGESE, FO16
Denkawi, FJ12
DENMARK, EM1
Denmark, Historical, EM2
Denmark, Prehistoric, EM3
D'ENTRECASTEAUX, OL4
Dera, FF19
Deressia, FI32
Desana, SQ19
Dey, FD7
Dhan, RI10
Dhanwar, AW46
Dhartu, AW45
DHEGIHA, NQ12
Dhimal, AR6
Dhodia, AW47
Dhruva, AW32
Dhuri, MP22
Dia, FO43
DIAGUITA, SG6
Dialonke, FA33
Diamat, FA14
Dian, FA26
DIANDER, FA37
Diau, SR12
Dibo, FF52
Dibombari, FH7
Dibum, FH19
DIDINGA, FJ10
Didol, RH8
Die, AM23
DIEGUENO, NS9
DIERI, OI10
Difale, FA22
Digguel, MQ5
Digil, MO4
Digo, FL14
Dika, OJ20
DILLING, FJ11
Dima, MP8
Dime, MP8
Dimuk, FF6
Dindje, FI28
DINGA, FO17
DINKA, FJ12
Diol, AL3
DIOLA, FA14
Diongor, FI16
Dippil, OI11
Dir, MO4
Dirma, MP22
District of Columbia, NM1
Diu, AY5
Diuihet, SI10
DIULA TRIBES, FA15
Diwala, FH7
Djakka, FO49
Djallonke, FA33
Djarso, MP13
Djebel, MQ16
Djedj, FA18
Djek, RH8
DJENNE, MS10

Djennenke, MS10
Djerba, MU4
Djinba, OI17
Djompra, FF65
Djuka, SR8
Do, FO26
Dobokubi, SS13
Dobu Island, OL4
Do Donggo, OF18
Dodoso, FK8
Dodoth, FK8
Doe, FN27
Dogom, FA16
DOGON, FA16
DOGRA, AV6
Dogrib, ND14
Doko, FO34, MP26
Dokwa, FV6
Dolgan, RV2
Dolgano-Nenets, RU1
Dollong, FF61
Dolot, MP22
Dombe, FP15
Dombo, AW46
DOMINICA, ST4
DOMINICAN REPUBLIC, SV2
Dompago, FA9
Donga, FF15
Dongotono, FJ17
Donyiro, FJ25
Dor, FJ8
Dorasque, SA19
Dorbet, AH5
Dorin, SM3
Dorla, AW32
Dormo, FI32
DOROBO, FL6
Dorosie, FA26
Dorsse, MP26
Dorze, MP26
Dourou Island, OM15
Dravidian, AQ1
DRAWA, MW6
Drawi, MW6
DRUZE, MD6
Duaish, MS31
DUALA, FH7
Dubab, MQ10
Dubasiin, MQ15
Dubla, AW47
Ducie Island, OW1
Duga, FO5
Dugbatang, OA6
Dukawa, FF36
DUKHOBORS, NF7
Dukkala, MW10
Dulangan, OA23
Dulman, FJ11
DUMA, FI12
Duma, FS5
DUMAGAT, OA17
DUMBO, FF20
Dume, MP8
Duru, FH18
Duruma, FL14
Durumba, FL14
Dusadh, AW45
Dusun, OC7
DUTCH, ET4
Dutch Borneo, OC2
Dutch Guiana, SR4
Dutch, New Amsterdam, NM12
Dutch New Guinea, OJ3
Dutch, Pennsylvania, NM13
Dwamish, NR15
Dyak, Land, OC8
Dyak, Sea, OC6
Dyalonke, FA33
Dyamu, FE7
Dyan, FA26

Dyerma, MS20
Dyiwat, FA14
Dyur, FJ14
Dzakhachin, AH5
Dzalia, FO35
Dzem, FH20
Dzing, FO17
Dzubucua, SO3
Dzungle, FF51

EARLY ENGLAND, ES7
EARLY GERMANS, EL4
EARLY HISTORIC MIDDLE EAST, M5
EARLY IBERIA, EX4
EARLY ICELANDERS, EQ2
EARLY INDIA, AQ4
EARLY JAPAN, AB3
EARLY MODERN BRITAIN, ES4
EARLY MODERN EUROPE, E3
EARLY MODERN FRANCE, EW2
EARLY MODERN GERMANY, EL2
EARLY MODERN ITALY, EI2
EARLY SCOTLAND, ES6
East Africa, Portuguese, FT2
East Bengal, AS1
EAST BRAZIL, SN1
EAST CENTRAL STATES, NP1
East Central States, Historical, NP2
East Central States, Prehistoric, NP3
EAST CHINA, AF15
EASTER ISLAND, OY1
EASTER ISLANDERS, OY2
EASTERN APACHE, NT8
Eastern Arabia, MK1
Eastern Dakota, NQ11
Eastern Lao, AM8
Eastern Mono, NR13
Eastern Polynesia, OS2
EASTERN SIOUANS, NN13
Eastern Sudan, Historical, MQ2
Eastern Sudan, Prehistoric, MQ3
Eastern Timbira, SO8
EASTERN WOODLAND INDIANS, NM4
EAST EUROPEAN GERMANS, EL7
East Fayu, OR19
EAST GERMANY, EL11
East Hottentot, FX13
EAST PAKISTAN, AS1
EAST PANJAB, AW6
East Panjab States Union, AW6
Eauripik, OR21
Ebga, FF62
Ebrie, FA25
Echira, EI19
Echoaladi, SK7
ECUADOR, SD1
Ecuador, Historical, SD2
Ecuador, Prehistoric, SD3
E-de, AM35
Edisto, NN12
Ediye, FG3
EDO, FF21
Edsin Gol, AH5
EFATE, OO8

Efik, FF25
Efu, FF41
Egabo, FF62
Egesminde, NB6
Eghap, FF51
Egongot, OA21
Egye, FK8
EGYPT, MR1
EGYPTIAN BEDOUIN, MR11
EGYPTIAN OASES, MR12
Egyptians, MR1, MR13
Egypt, Prehistoric, MR7
Ehinga, FP17
EIGHTEENTH DYNASTY EGYPT, MR6
Eile, MO5
Eire, ER1
Ejagham, FF22
Ekeita, FJ6
Ekela, FO19
Eket, FF25
Ekiti, FF62
EKOI, FF22
Ekonda, FO32
Ekota, FO32
Ekuri, FF60
El Amira, FJ21
Elanga, FO32
Elato, OR21
Elburgu, FL12
Eleuthera, SW1
Elgeyu, FL13
Elgonyi, FL13
Elgume, FL17
Elgumi, FK12
El Haraza, MQ4
Elinga, FO32
ELLICE, OU5
Elmolo, FL12
Elong, FF40
EL SALVADOR, SA5
El Salvador, Prehistoric, SA6
Emberre, FL5
Embu, FL5
EMERILLON, SQ8
ENCABELLADO, SE12
Enderbury, OW2
Endo, FL13
Enenga, FI23
Enets, RU4
Engganese, OD6
ENGGANO, OD6
England, ES4, ES5, ES7
England, Early, ES7
Enimaga, SK9
Eno, NN13
Enyong, FF25
Epan, AM35
Eperigua, SC20
EPI, OO9
Equatorial Africa, French-Speaking, FI1
EQUATORIAL AFRICAN PEOPLES, FI2
EQUATORIAL AFRICAN PYGMIES, FI4
Equatorial Africa, Prehistoric, FI3
EQUATORIAL GUINEA, FG1
Equatorial Guinea, Colonial, FG2
Equatorial Guinea, Traditional, FG4
Erabu, AC6
Eravalan, AW64
Eraykat, MS9
Erenga, MQ16
Erie, NM8

ERITREA, MN1
Eritrea, Historical, MN2
Eritrea, Prehistoric, MN3
Ermbeli, MQ16
Ernadu, AW63
Erokh, FN5
EROMANGA, OO10
Erroman, OT2
ERUKA, AW52
Erukala, AW52
Esela, FP6
Esele, FP6
Eshikongo, FO21
Esimbi, FF58
ESKIMO, ND2
Eskimo, Baffinland, ND5
Eskimo, Cape York, NB5
Eskimo, Caribou, ND6
Eskimo, Copper, ND8
Eskimo, Labrador, NI5
Eskimo, Mackenzie, ND11
Eskimo, North Alaska, NA9
Eskimo, Nunivak, NA13
Eskimo, Polar, NB5
Eskimo, Siberian, RY5
Eskimo, Smith Sound, NB5
Eskimo, South Alaska, NA10
Eskimo, Southampton Island, ND5
Eskimo, Tchiglit, ND11
Eskimo, West Alaska, NA13
Eskimo, West Greenland, NB6
ESMERALDA, SD8
Eso, FO44
Espino, SQ6
Espirito Santo, SN1
ESPIRITU SANTO, OO11
Essel, FH21
Esselen, NS8
Estonia, RB1, RG4
ESTONIANS, RG4
Eta, OA4
Etal, OR14
Etchareottine, ND14
Etchimin, NJ4
ETHIOPIA, MP1
Ethiopia, Prehistoric, MP4
Etiwaw, NN12
Eto, OA7
Eton, FH9
Etruscans, EI5
Etsako, FF21
Euahlayi, OI21
Eudeve, NU25
Eunda, FX8
EUROPE, E1
EUROPEAN ISLANDS, EZ1
EUROPEAN JEWS, EI4
EUROPEAN KALMYK, RF4
EUROPEAN RUSSIA, RA1
Europe, Early Modern, E3
Evale, FX8
Even, RU5
Evenki, RU1, RU5
Evenki National Okrug, RU5
Evijico, SC9
EWE, FA17

Ewumi, FI26
Ewuni, FH7
Exuma, Great, SW1
EYAK, NA7
Eyarra, FH7

Fadnia, MQ15
Faeroe Islands, EZ1
Fagdelu, FJ5
Fagnia, FI10
Fahsya, MW9
Fais, OR20
Fajulu, FJ5
Fala, MS15
FALASHA, MP9
FALI, FH8
FALKLAND ISLANDS,
  SZ3
Famalla, MS22
Fan, FH9
Fanda, FJ11
FANG, FH9
Fanning Island, OV6
Fanti, FE12
Fanyan, FI10
Farafra, MR12
Faraon, NT8
Faraulep, OR21
Farquhar, FZ1
Farute, SS18
FASI, MW7
Fauro, ON14
Fayu, East, OR19
Fayu, West, OR21
Fazoglo, FJ7
Federation of French
  Equatorial Africa,
  FI1
Federation of French
  West Africa, FA1
Federation of Malaya,
  AN1
Federation of Malaysia,
  AN8
Felata, MS11
FELLAHIN, MR13
Felup, FA14
Fergusson Island,
  OL4
Fernandeno, NS10
Fernando Po, FG1
Fernando Po, Prehistoric,
  FG5
Fertit, MQ11
FEUDAL JAPAN, AB2
Feyadicha, MR8
Fez, MW7
Fezara, MQ10
Fezwata, MW6
FEZZAN, MT5
FIA, FH10
FIJI, OQ1
FIJIANS, OQ4
Fiji, Historical,
  OQ2
Fiji, Prehistoric,
  OQ3
FILALA, MW8
Fincenu, SC9
Fingo, FX20
FINLAND, EO1
Finland, Historical,
  EO2
Finland, Prehistoric,
  EO3
FINNO-UGRIANS, RG1
Finns, EO1
FIOME, FN5
FIPA, FN6
Five Dynasties, AF5
Fjort, FI34
FLATHEAD, NR8
FLEMINGS, EV2
Flemish, EV2

Flint Island, OV6
FLORENTINES, EI8
FLORES, OF9
Florida, NN1
Florida Island, ON8
Fo, FF40
Fogny, FA14
FON, FA18
Fondang, FH19
For, MQ8
Forawa, MQ8
Forgha, MT9
Fori, FJ4
FORMER FRENCH INDIA,
  AY2
FORMER PORTUGUESE
  INDIA, AY5
FORMOSA, AD1
Formosa, Historical,
  AD2
FORMOSAN ABORIGINES,
  AD4
Formosa, Prehistoric,
  AD3
Fornio, SO3
Fort Hall Shoshone,
  NR14
FOX, NP5
FRANCE, EW1
France, Early Modern,
  EW2
France, Prehistoric,
  EW6
Franklin, ND1
FRANKS, EW4
Franz Joseph Land,
  RZ1
French, SW1
French Cameroun, FH1
FRENCH CANADIANS,
  NH5
French Equatorial
  Africa, Federation
  of, FI1
FRENCH GUIANA, SR3
French Guinea, FA42
FRENCH POLYNESIA,
  OX1
French Polynesia,
  Historical, OX2
French Polynesia,
  Prehistoric, OX3
FRENCH REGIONAL CULTURES,
  EW7
French Somaliland,
  MO6
FRENCH-SPEAKING EQUATORIAL
  AFRICA, FI1
FRENCH-SPEAKING WEST
  AFRICA, FA1
FRENCH SWISS, EJ4
French West Africa,
  Federation of, FA1
Friendly Islands,
  OU9
Frisians, ET5
Fruga, MW10
Fuegian aborigines,
  SH1
Fujiga, FJ14
Fukien, AF17
Fulah, MS11
Fulakunda, FA19
FULANI, MS11
Fulbe, MS11
Fulero, FO10
Fulilwa, FR6
Fulirwa, FR6
Fulnio, SO3
Fulse, FA28
Fumbum, FF51
Fumu, FI33
Fung, FJ7
Fungom, FF51

Fungor, FJ21
Fungwe, FR6, FS5
Fur, MQ8
Furu, FI7
Fut, FF51
FUTAJALONKE, FA19
Futuna, OT2
FUTUNA, OU6

GA, FE6
Gaaliin, MQ14
Gabar, MA8
Gaberi, FI32
Gabin, FF12
GABON, FI43
Gabon, Colonial, FI44
Gabon, Prehistoric,
  FI46
Gabon, Traditional,
  FI45
GABR, MA8
GABRIELINO, NS10
GADABA, AW31
GADAMES, MT6
Gaddang, OA20
Gaddang, Christian,
  OA29
Gade, FF24
Gae, SE22
Gaferut, OR21
Gagu, FA21
Gaida, MS5
Gaioes, SO8
Gala, FN18
Galab, FL7
Galaganza, FN18
Galambawa, FF46
GALAPAGOS ISLANDS,
  SZ4
Galibi, SR9
Galim, FH14
GALLA, FL7
Galla, MN10, MP13,
  MP15, MP17, MP18,
  MP23, MP25
Gallice, NR22
Galoa, FI23
Gam, FF51
Gamba, FJ20
GAMBIA, FC11
Gambia, Colonial,
  FC12
Gambia, Prehistoric,
  FC14
Gambia, Traditional,
  FC13
GAMBIER ISLANDS, OX5
Gamergu, FF47
GAMELLA, SO10
Gamilla, FJ7
Gamit, AW47
Gamta, AW47
Gamti, AW47
Gamuia, MQ14
Gan, FA5, FA26, FK4
Ganagana, FF52
Ganawa, FF37
Ganawuri, FF9
GANDA, FK7
Ganda, FP15
Gane, FH23
Gangi, FN20
Ganguella, FP16
Ganyanga, MS15
Ganza, FJ15
Gao Empire, FA2
Gar, AM31
Garasia, AW48
Garavos Island, FZ4
Gardulla, MP17
GARIF, SA12
Garipon, SR12
GARO, AR5
Garo, MP27

Gat, MT7
Gatrun, MT5
Gauar, FH15
GAULS, EW5
Gaya, FL11
Gayi, MP8
Gayo, OD7
GAYO-ALAS, OD7
GAYON, SS10
Gaza, FR5
GAZELLE PENINSULA,
  OM4
GBANDE, FD4
Gbandi, FD4, FO36
Gbanziri, FI8
GBARI, FF23
Gbaya, FI9, FJ16
GE, SL5
Geleba, FL7
Gemaab, MQ14
Gemira, MP10
Genakin, SI10
Gengele, FO45
Gengle, FF48
Genya, FO45
GEORGIA, RI1
Georgia, NN1
Georgia, Historical,
  RI2
GEORGIAN S.S.R., RI1
GEORGIAN BRITAIN,
  ES3
Georgians, RI7
Georgia, South, SZ1
Gerawa, FF46
German Democratic
  Republic, EL11
GERMANIC PEOPLES,
  E11
GERMAN REGIONAL CULTURES,
  EL6
Germans, Early, EL4
Germans, Pennsylvania,
  NM13
Germans, Sudeten,
  EL9
GERMAN SWISS, EJ5
GERMANY, EL1
Germany, East, EL11
Germany, Early Modern,
  EL2
Germany, Prehistoric,
  EL5
Germany, West, EL10
Gerumawa, FF46
Geshu, FK13
Geso, FO44
Gesu, FK13
Ghana, Colonial, FE2
Ghana Empire, FA2
Ghana, Prehistoric,
  FE14
Ghana, Traditional,
  FE3
GHARBYA, MW9
Ghardaia, MV7
Ghasi, AW46
GHAT, MT7
Gheg, EG1
Ghodiat, MQ10
Ghormara, MX3
Giaka, FO49
Gialo, MT9
Gianga, OA7
GIBRALTAR, EX10
Gidder, FH15
Gidhia, AW45
Gidole, MP17
Gikuyu, FL10
Gila, NT8
Gilaki, MA7
GILBERTS, OR6
GILYAK, RX2
Gimaa, MQ14

Gimiab, MQ14
GIMIRA, MP10
Gimma, MP18, MQ14
Gio, FA29
Girange, FL11
Girara, SC6
Girganke, MS31
Giriama, FL14
Giryama, FL14
Gishu, FK13
Gisiga, FH15
GISU, FK13
Gitksan, NE15
Gizii, FL8
Glai, AM33
Glebo, FD7
Glidyi, FA17
Goa, AY5, FO45
GOAJIRO, SC13
Gobawein, MO5
Gobir, MS12
Gobu, FI6
Gofa, MP26
GOGO, FN7
Goiaz, SP1
GOLA, FD5
Gola, FF48
Golar, AM15
Gold Coast, FE1
GOLDI, RX3
Golo, FJ20
Goma, FO15
Gomani, FR5
Gomaro, MP14
Gombe, FO12
Gombo, FP18
Gonaqua, FX13
Gonave, SV3
GOND, AW32
Gond Bards, AW32
Gond, Maria, AW32
Gond, Muria, AW32
Gonga, MP14
Gongicho, MP14
Gonja, FE8
Gonongga, ON10
Goodenough Island,
   OL4
GORAM, OH11
Goram, FF6
Goran, MS22
Gorgotoqui, SF9
Goringhaiqua, FX13
Gorno-Altai, RS1
Goroa, FN5
Gorong Islands, OH11
Gorontalese, OG4
GORONTALO, OG4
Gorotire, SP13
Gorowa, FN5
Gosiute, NT22
Goths, EL4
Gotta, AW32
Gough Island, FZ9
Goum, FA18
Gova, FS5
Gowa, FQ12
Gowaze, MP17
GRAECO-ROMAN EGYPT,
   MR4
GRAECO-ROMAN IRAQ,
   MH4
GRAECO-ROMAN JEWS,
   MF6
GRAECO-ROMAN PERSIA,
   MA3
Gran Chaco, SK4
Grand Bahama, SW1
Grand Lake Victoria
   Indians, NH4
Grassia, AW48
Great Abaco, SW1
GREAT BASIN INDIANS,
   NT6

Great Bear Lake Indians,
   ND14
GREAT BRITAIN, ES1
GREATER CHINA, AE1
GREATER INDIA, AQ1
Great Exuma, SW1
Great Guana, SW1
Great Inagua, SW1
GREAT RUSSIA, RF1
GREAT RUSSIANS, RF2
Grebo, FD7
GREECE, EH1
Greece, Prehistoric,
   EH7
GREEK REGIONAL CULTURES,
   EH12
Greeks, EH1-EH6
Greeks, Anatolian,
   MB6
Green Islands, ON11
GREENLAND, NB1
Greenland, Historical,
   NB2
Greenland, Prehistoric,
   NB3
Greenwich, OT3
Grenada, ST11
Grenadines, ST11
Grigriqua, FX13
GROS VENTRE, NQ13
Grunshi, FE7
GRUSI, FE7
GRUSIANS, RI7
Gruzinians, RI7
Guacanahua, SF23
Guacara, SQ22
Guacata, NN7
GUACHI, SP14
Guachichil, NU43
Guachicon, SC17
GUADALCANAL, ON8
GUADELOUPE, ST5
Guaharibo, SQ18
GUAHIBO, SC14
Guaicuri, NU42
Guaicuru, SK11
Guaipunavo, SC18
Guaiqueri, SS11
GUAITACA, SN3
GUAJA, SO4
Guajajara, SO6
Guajira, SC13
Guala, FA31
Gualacho, SM3
Guale, NN12
GUAM, OR7
Guamanians, OR7
Guamo, SS11
GUAMONTEY, SS11
GUANA, SK7
Guanaca, SC15
Guana, Great, SW1
Guanao, SC10
GUANCHE, MZ4
Guane, SC11
GUANG, FE8
Guarambare, SM4
GUARANI, SM4
Guaranoca, SK14
Guaratagaja, SP16
Guarauno, SS18
GUARAYU, SF11
Guarico, SS11
Guarina, SS9
Guasapar, NU35
GUASAVE, NU16
GUATEMALA, NW1
Guatemala, Historical,
   NW2
GUATEMALAN INDIANS,
   NW4
Guatemala, Prehistoric,
   NW3
GUATO, SP15

Guatuso, SA17
GUAYAKI, SK8
Guayana, SM3, SM4
Guayapi, SQ8
GUAYMI, SB6
Guaypi, SC20
GUAYUPE, SC20
Guazuzu, SC9
Gudiela, MP15
Gudjiru, MS13
Gudo, FF12
Guenoa, SJ5
Guere, FA29
Guerze, FD6
Guetar, SA17
Guha, FO18
Guhayna, MQ15
Guian, OA12
GUIANA, SR1
Guiana, British, SR2
Guiana, Dutch, SR4
Guiana, French, SR3
Guiana, Prehistoric,
   SR5
Guiba, SS12
Guimr, MQ16
Guinau, SQ27
GUINEA, FA42
GUINEA COAST PEOPLES,
   FA4
Guinea, Colonial,
   FA43
Guinea, Equatorial,
   FG1, FG2, FG4
Guinea, French, FA42
Guinea, Portuguese,
   FB2, FB3, FB7
Guinea, Prehistoric,
   FA45
Guinea, Traditional,
   FA44
Gujarat, AW7
GUJARATI, AW7
GULA, FI13
Gulai, FI28
Gulanga, OA7
Gule, FJ15
GULF TRIBES, NN14
Gulfan, FJ11
Gulud, FJ21
Gumus, FJ15
Gun, FA18
Gundi, FH21
Gungai, OH5
Gungawa, FF36
Gur, FJ14
Gura, FJ9
Gurabo, MP14
GURAGE, MP11
Guraghe, MP11
Gure, FF35
Gurensi, FE10
GURIANS, RI8
GURKHA, AK4
Gurkha, FF6
GURMA, FA20
GURO, FA21
GUSII, FL8
Gutu, FN14
GUYANA, SR2
Gutucrac, SN2
Guzai, MP24
Gwa, FA25
Gwamaa, MQ10
Gwana, FJ15
GWANDARA, FF24
Gwari, FF23
Gwe, FL4
Gweabo, FD7
Gwembe Tonga, FQ12
Gwere, FK7
Gwin, FA31
Gye, FK8
GYPSIES, E15

Ha, FO42
Habab, MN9
Habau, AM6
Habbania, MQ5
Habe, FA16
Haddendowa, MR9
Haderuma, AC9
HADHRAMAUT, MM2
Hadia, MP15
Hadimu, FM2
Hadzapi, FN11
HAIDA, NE9
HAINAN, AE2
Haisla, NE5
HAITI, SV3
Haitians, SV3
HAKKA, AE8
Hakka, AD7
Haku, FP6
HALANG, AM20
Halang Doan, AM23
Halchidhoma, NT15
Halenga, MR9
Hall Islands, OR19
HALMAHERA, OH12
Halyikwami, NT15
Hamama, MU5
Hamar, MQ10
Hamasien, MP24
Hamba, FO47
Hambukushu, FP11
Hamites, M9
HAMITO-SEMITES, M9
Hampangan, OA18
Hamran, MQ15
Han, AF8, ND10
Hancumqua, FX13
Handa, FF64
Hanga, FL4
Hankutchin, ND10
Hano, NT18
Hantik, OA14
HANUNOO, OA18
Hanya, FP15
Harabi, MT9
Harappa, AQ6
HARARI, MP12
HARE, ND9
Haruro, MP26
Hasa, MT9
Hasania, MQ14
Hasinai, NO5
Hassinunga, NN13
Hatsa, FN11
Haualla, MS22
Haukoin, FX9
HAUSA, MS12
Haush, SH4
Haute-Volta, FA54
Havasupai, NT14
Havu, FO10
HAW, AE14
HAWAII, OV2
HAWAIIANS, OV5
Hawaii, Historical,
   OV3
Hawaii, Prehistoric,
   OV4
Hawawir, MQ9
Hawazma, MQ10
Hawiye, MO4
HAYA, FN8
Hayo, FL4
HAZARA, AU5
Heard, FZ1
Hebrews, Ancient,
   MF7
Hebrides, ES10
HEHE, FN9
Heia, FN8
Heiban, FJ21
Heikum, FX10
Heiltsuk, NE5
Heimad, MQ5

Helai, MO5
HELLENIC GREECE, EH5
HELLENISTIC GREECE,
  EH4
Hemat, MQ5
Henderson Island,
  OW1
Henga, FR6
Her, FA14
Hera, FS5
HERERO, FX12
Hermit Islands, OM11
Hervey Islands, OZ9
Hessequa, FX13
Het, SI10
Heve, NU25
Hewa, FR6
Hewe, FR6
Hiao, FT7
Hibito, SE14
HIDATSA, NQ14
Hiechware, FX10
High Germans, E11
HIGHLAND SCOTS, ES10
Hiji, FF12
Hiligaynon, OA14
Hill Jarawa, FF31
Hill Reddi, AW59
Himachal Pradesh,
  AW14
Himba, FX12
Hina, FF55
Hinai, NO5
Hindu, AW1
Hinga, FP17
Hiniraya, OA14
Hinnaro, MP14
HISPANIOLA, SV1
Hispaniola, Prehistoric,
  SV4
HIST. AFGHANISTAN,
  AU2
HIST. ALASKA, NA2
HIST. ALBANIA, EG2
HIST. ALGERIA, MV2
HIST. ARABIA, MJ2
HIST. ARGENTINA, SI2
HIST. ARMENIA, RJ2
HIST. ASIA, A2
HIST. AUSTRALIA, OI2
HIST. AUSTRIA, EK2
HIST. AZERBAIJAN,
  RK2
HIST. BAHAMAS, SW2
HIST. BISMARCKS, OM2
HIST. BOLIVIA, SF2
HIST. BORNEO, OC2
HIST. BOTSWANA, FV2
HIST. BRAZIL, SL2
HIST. BRITISH COLUMBIA,
  NE2
HIST. BRITISH HONDURAS,
  NX2
HIST. BULGARIA, EE2
HIST. BURMA, AP2
HIST. CALIFORNIA,
  NS2
HIST. CANADA, NC2
HIST. CAUCASIA, RH2
HIST. CELEBES, OG2
HIST. CEYLON, AX2
HIST. CHILE, SG2
HIST. COLOMBIA, SC2
HIST. CUBA, SX2
HIST. DENMARK, EM2
HIST. EAST CENTRAL
  STATES, NP2
HIST. EASTERN SUDAN,
  MQ2
HIST. ECUADOR, SD2
HIST. ERITREA, MN2
HIST. FIJI, OQ2
HIST. FINLAND, EO2
HIST. FORMOSA, AD2

HIST. FRENCH POLYNESIA,
  OX2
HIST. GEORGIA, RI2
HIST. GREENLAND, NB2
HIST. GUATEMALA, NW2
HIST. HAWAII, OV3
HIST. HUNGARY, EC2
HIST. INDOCHINA, AM2
HIST. INDONESIA, OB2
HIST. IRELAND, ER2
HIST. JAMAICA, SY2
HIST. JAVA, OE2
HIST. KOREA, AA2
HIST. LEBANON, ME2
HIST. LESOTHO, FW2
HIST. LESSER SUNDAS,
  OF2
HIST. LIBERIA, FD2
HIST. LIBYA, MT2
HIST. MALAYA, AN2
HIST. MANCHURIA, AG2
HIST. MARITIME PROVINCES,
  NJ2
HIST. MASSACHUSETTS,
  NL7
HIST. MASSIM, OL2
HIST. MEXICO, NU2
HIST. MICRONESIA,
  OR2
HIST. MIDDLE ATLANTIC
  STATES, NM2
HIST. MOLUCCAS, OH2
HIST. MONGOLIA, AH2
HIST. NETHERLANDS,
  ET2
HIST. NEW CALEDONIA,
  OP2
HIST. NEW ENGLAND,
  NL2
HIST. NEW HEBRIDES,
  OO2
HIST. NEW ZEALAND,
  OZ2
HIST. NEW ZEALAND
  POLYNESIA, OZ6
HIST. NEWFOUNDLAND,
  NI2
HIST. NILOTIC SUDAN,
  FJ3
HIST. NORTH AMERICA,
  N2
HIST. NORTHWESTERN
  STATES, NR2
HIST. NORWAY, EP2
HIST. OCEANIA, O2
HIST. ONTARIO, NG2
HIST. PALESTINE, MF2
HIST. PANAMA, SB2
HIST. PARAGUAY, SK2
HIST. PERU, SE2
HIST. PHILIPPINES,
  OA2
HIST. POLAND, EA2
HIST. PORTUGAL, EY2
HIST. PRAIRIE PROVINCES,
  NF2
HIST. PUERTO RICO,
  SU2
HIST. QUEBEC, NH2
HIST. RUMANIA, ED2
HIST. RUSSIA, RA2
HIST. RYUKYUS, AC2
HIST. SAHARA AND SUDAN,
  MS2
HIST. SIBERIA, RR2
HIST. SINKIANG, AI2
HIST. SOLOMONS, ON2
HIST. SOMALILAND,
  MO2
HIST. SOUTH AFRICA,
  FX2
HIST. SOUTH AMERICA,
  S2
HIST. SOUTH ARABIA,
  ML2

HIST. SOUTH CENTRAL
  STATES, NO2
HIST. SOUTHWEST, NT2
HIST. SUMATRA, OD2
HIST. SWAZILAND, FU3
HIST. SWEDEN, EN2
HIST. SWITZERLAND,
  EJ2
HIST. SYRIA, MD2
HIST. THAILAND, AO2
HIST. TIBET, AJ2
HIST. TUNISIA, MU2
HIST. TURKESTAN, RL2
HIST. UNITED STATES,
  NK2
HIST. URUGUAY, SJ2
HIST. VENEZUELA, SS2
HIST. WEST CENTRAL
  STATES, NQ2
HIST. WESTERN POLYNESIA,
  OU2
HIST. YUCATAN, NV2
HIST. YUGOSLAVIA,
  EF2
HIST. ZANZIBAR, FM3
Hitchiti, NN11
HITTITES, MB4
Hlengwe, FT6
Hlubi, FX20
HO, AW33
Ho, AE4, AE14, FA17,
  NR16
Ho Drong, AM15
Hodrung, AM6
Hoggar, MS25
Hoit, AH5
Holland, ET1
Holli, FF62
Holma, FF12
HOLO, FP5
HOLOHOLO, FO18
Hom, FF39
Homalco, NE13
Hombo, FO27
HOMERIC GREECE, EH6
Homr, FI13
Hona, FF12
Honan, AF12
HONDURAS, SA7
Honduras, Prehistoric,
  SA8
HONG KONG, AY3
Honja, FQ5
Hook, NN13
Hopei, AF12
HOPI, NT9
Horn Island, OU6
Horohoro, FK11
Hoshut, AH5
Hotman, MT9
Hottentot, FX13
Houni, AE4
Hova, FY5
Howland Island, OV1
HRE, AM21
HROY, AM22
Hsifan, AE3
Huachipari, SE15
Huailu, OP4
Huambisa, SD9
Huambo, FP13
Huana, FO17
Huancavilca, SD10
Huanyam, SP12
Huari, SP24
HUARPE, SI6
HUASTEC, NU17
Huatana, SE14
HUAVE, NU18
Hubu, FA19
Huchnom, NS30
Huela, FA15
Huhuteni, SQ27
HUICHOL, NU19

Huilla, FP18
Huilliche, SG4
Huite, NU35
Hukundika, NR14
Hukwe, FX10
Huma, NO4
Humahuaca, SI9
Humba, FL12
Humbe, FP17
Humbu, FO30
Hume, NU6
Humptulip, NR15
Humr, MQ5
Hunan, AF14
Hunde, FO22
Hungarians, EC1
HUNGARY, EC1
Hungary, Historical,
  EC2
Hungary, Prehistoric,
  EC3
Hungu, FO21
Hungwe, FI17
Hunkpapa, NQ11
Hunter, OP6
Hunza, AV7
HUPA, NS11
Hupeh, AF14
Hurkan, RH8
HURON, NG5
Hurutshe, FV6
Husaynat, MQ14
Husseinat, MQ14
Hutsul, RD3
Hutu, FO42
Hwei, AE13
Hwing, AM35
HYDERABAD, AW8
Hypurina, SQ9

IATMUL, OJ11
Ibadan, FF62
Ibalao, OA21
Ibaloi, OA20
IBAN, OC6
Ibanag, OA29
Ibanoma, SQ25
Ibara, FY13
Ibea, FH5
Iberia, EX4, EX5
Iberia, Early, EX4
Iberia, Prehistoric,
  EX5
IBIBIO, FF25
IBO, FF26
Ica, SC7
Icaguate, SE12
ICELAND, EQ1
Icelanders, Early,
  EQ2
Ichu, SQ22
Idaho, NR1
Idakho, FL4
Idaouich, MS31
Idio, FO7
IDOMA, FF27
Idrassen, MW5
Ie, AC7
Ifaluk, OR21
Ife, FF62
Ifni, MY1-MY3
Ifora, MS25
IFUGAO, OA19
Ifugaw, OA19
IGALA, FF28
Igara, FF28
IGBIRA, FF29
Igbo, FF17, FF26
Igbolo, FF62
Igbona, FF62
Iglulik, ND5
Ignahatom, FJ25
IGNERI, ST14
IGOROT, OA20

Kachuba, MP22
Kadai, AL3
Kadan, AW64
KADAR, AW54
KADARA, FF34
Kadei, FH11
Kadero, FJ11
Kadjagse, MS15
Kadjanga, MS15
Kado, FA16
Kadohadacho, NO5
Kadu Kurumba, AW56
Kadugli, FJ21
Kaffa, MP14
KAFFICHO, MP14
Kaffir, FX17
Kafima, FX8
Kafir, AU6
Kaga, MQ4
Kagayan, OA29
Kagba, MS15
Kagoma, FF38
Kagoro, FA8, FF38
Kaguru, FN22
Kahgalu, MA12
KAHUGU, FF35
Kai, MS14
Kaibab, NT16
Kai Islands, OH13
Kaiyukhotana, NA8
Kajaja, FJ21
Kaje, FF38
KAKA, FH11
Kaka, FF20
Kakalelwa, FL4
Kakamega, FL4
Kakanda, FF29
Kakeroma, AC4
Kakongo, FO21
Kakuak, FJ5
Kakwa, FJ5
Kalabari, FF30
Kalabit, OC7
Kalagan, OA35
Kalagua, OA24
KALAI, FI14
Kalamian, OA30
Kalanga, FO15, FS5
Kalapalo, SP25
KALAPUYA, NR9
Kalawat, OA17
Kalay, FI14
Kalega, FO41
Kaleri, FF45
Kali, FH6
Kalibugan, OA11
Kaliko, FO26
Kalimantan, OC1
KALINGA, OA24
Kalispel, NR19
Kalmuck, AH5, RF4
KALMYK, AH5
Kalmyk, RF4
Kalo, AM16
Kaluchazi, FP8
Kaluena, FP14
Kalunda, FO27
Kalyo-Kengyu, AR13
Kam, FF18
Kamanga, FR6
Kamantan, FF38
KAMAR, AW34
Kamas, RU4
Kamasia, FL13
Kamassian Samoyeds, RU4
Kamasya, FL13
KAMBA, FL9
KAMBATA, MP15
Kambe, FL14
KAMBERI, FF36
Kambonsenga, FQ8
KAMCHADAL, RY3
Kamchatka, RY1, RY3

Kami, FN27
Kamia, NT15
KAMILAROI, OI12
Kamkam, FH14
Kamuku, FF36
Kamum, FJ14
KANADA, AW10
KANAKA, OP4
Kanakanabu, AD11
Kankuama, SC7
Kanakura, FF19
Kanawa, MS12
Kanda, FI30
KANDAVU, OQ5
Kandawire, FR6
KANDH, AW35
Kandha, AW35
Kaneang, OI26
Kanem, MS22
KANEMBU, MS13
Kangeju, FN11
Kangharia, AW45
Kangiti, SQ9
Kangu, FH8
KANIET, OM5
Kanike, FI12
Kanikkaran, AW64
Kanjaga, FE7
Kanjar, AW45
Kankanai, OA20
Kansa, NQ12
Kansas, NQ1
Kansu, AF13
KANURI, MS14
Kao, FJ21
KAONDE, FQ7
KAPAUKU, OJ29
Kapeta, FJ6
KAPINGAMARANGI, OT3
Kapsiki, FF12
Kara, FI15, FN10
Karachai, RH7
KARADJERI, OI13
Karaga, OA27
Karagas, RS3
Karakal, AY2
KARA-KALPAK, RN2
Kara-Kirgiz, RP2
KARAMOJONG, FK8
Karanga, FS5, MS15
KARANKAWA, NO7
Karbo, MS18
Kare, FH16, FJ20
KAREKARE, FF37
Karelia, RG5
KARELIANS, RG5
KAREN, AP7
KARIERA, OI14
Karime, SQ18
Karimojong, FK8
Karo, MP22
KAROK, NS12
Karoko, FJ10
Karoma, MP22
Karra, MS22
Kasena, FE7
Kasha, FJ11
Kashgai, MA13
Kashioko, FP4
Kashmere, MS15
KASHMIR, AV1
KASHMIRI, AV4
Kasinji, FP10
Kaska, ND12
Kaskaskia, NP6
Kaskiha, SK10
Kassanga, FB6
Kasseng, AM14
Kassonke, FA27
Kasuba, AW63
KATAB, FF38
Katang, AM14
Kathlamet, NR6
Katingan, OC9

Katkari, AW47
Katla, FJ21
Kato, NS23
Katsenawa, MS12
Kattang, OI24
KATU, AM24
Katul, MQ4
Kauma, FL14
Kavalan, AD4
Kaveltcadom, NT15
Kaw, AO4
Kawa, AP12
KAWADJI, OI15
Kawahla, MQ10
KAWAIISU, NS13
Kawalib, FJ21
Kawar, AW46, MS22
Kawasma, MQ15
Kawchodinne, ND9
Kawendi, FQ5
Kayah, AP7
KAYONG, AM25
Kayakaya, OJ17
Kayan, OC5
Kayangel, OR15
Kayla, MP9
KAZAK, RQ2
Kazakh S.S.R., RQ1
KAZAKHSTAN, RQ1
KAZAN TATAR, RF5
Kazikumuk, RH8
Kazvin, RK3
Kdrao, AM35
Keaka, FF22
Kebbawa, MS12
Kecherda, MS22
Kederu, FJ19
Kedi, FK12
Keeling Islands, AZ8
KEI, OH13
Keiga Girru, FJ24
Kekchi, NW7
KELA, FO19
Kel Ahaggar, MS25
Kel Air, MS25
Kel Antessar, MS25
Kel Azdjer, MS25
Kele, FI14, FJ7
Keliko, FO26
Kelingen, MS15
Kel Tademeket, MS25
KEMANT, MP16
Kenai, NA11
Kenana, MQ15
Kencateye, SO8
Keney, OA37
KENGA, FI16
Kenga, FF13
Kengawa, FF13
Kenjiger, OJ20
Kennebec, NL4
Kentu, FF33
Kentucky, NN1
Kenuzi, MR8
KENYA, FL1
Kenya, FI16, OC5
Kenya, Colonial, FL2
Kenya, Traditional, FL3
Kenye, FN25
Kenyi, FK7
Kepere, FH16
Kepikiriwat, SP24
Keraki, OJ17
KERALA, AW11
Kerala, AW64
Kerama, AC7
KERES, NT12
KEREWE, FN10
Kerguelen, FZ1
Kermadec Islands, OZ5
Kerrarish, MR8
Kerre, MP22

Kerriat, MQ9
KET, RU2
KETE, FO20
Ketu, FF62
Keura, MP7
Kewatin, ND1
Keweyipaya, NT14
Keyauwee, NN13
Keyu, FL13
KGALAGADI, FV4
Kgatla, FV6
Khaha, FX14
Khakas, RS1
KHALKA, AH4
Khamir, MN7
Kha Mou, AM26
KHAMSEH, MA10
KHAMTA, MN7
Khanty, RU3
Khanty-Mansi National Okrug, RU3
Khaput, RH8
Kharga, MR12
KHARIA, AW36
Khavi, FL4
Khawalla, MQ15
Khayo, FL4
Kherwar, AW46
KHEVSUR, RI6
Khinalug, RH8
Khlot, MW9
Khmer, AM4
KHMU, AM26
KHOISAN PEOPLES, FX6
Khoit, AH5
Khon Muang, AO6
Khoshut, AH5
Khous, FA36
Khozzam, MS9
Khua, AM19
KHUFRA, MT8
Khumbi, FP17
Khumi, AR4
Khurutshe, FV6
Khutu, FN27
Khyen, AP5
Kian, FA11
Kiangan, OA19
Kiangsi, AF14
Kiangsu, AF15
Kiawaw, NN12
Kiba, FI17
Kibala, FP6
Kibet, MQ5
Kibo, FF9
Kibyen, FF9
Kichai, NO10
Kichepo, MP22
KICKAPOO, NP7
Kiga, FK6
Kika, AC4
KIKUYU, FL10
Kil, AM31
Kilba, FF12
Kile, RX3
Kilenge, FP15
Kilinga, FA9
Kiliwa, NS9
Kilwa, FN13
Kim, FI5
Kimbande, FP9
Kimbu, FN18
KIMBUNDU, FP6
Kimr, MQ16
KINDIGA, FN11
KINGA, FN12
Kinikinao, SK7
Kioko, FP4
KIOWA, NQ15
KIOWA APACHE, NQ16
Kipala, FP6
KIPCHAK, RN3
Kipea, SO3

Kipsigis, FL13
Kipungu, FP17
Kira, MP22 .
Kirdi, MQ5
KIRGIZ, RP2
Kirgiz-Kaisak, RQ2
Kirgiz S.S.R., RP1
KIRGIZSTAN, RP1
Kisa, FL4
Kisama, FP6
Kisanji, FP6
KISAR, OF10
Kisi, FN12
Kisii, FL8
KISSI, FA23
Kita, AC5
Kitako, AC8
Kitanemuk, NS20
Kitara, FK11
Kitcisagi, NH4
KITEMOCA, SF13
Kitosh, FL4
Kiturika, FN13
KIWAI, OJ12
Kiwai Papuans, OJ12
Kiziba, FN8
Kiziere, FI24
Klahuse, NE13
Klallam, NR15
KLAMANTAN, OC7
KLAMATH, NR10
Klikitat, NR18
Knaiakhotana, NA11
Koalib, FJ21
Koasati, NN11
KOBA, FV5
Kobaba, FL7
Kobe, OJ20
Kobiana, FB6
Koch, AR6
Kochoqua, FX13
Kodoro, FJ11
Kofa, FF12
Kogi, SC7
Kogo, FF41, FJ15
Koho, AM27
Kohuana, NT15
Koi, AW32
Koitur, AW32
Koke, FI10
KOKO, FH12
KOL, AW37
Kolam, AW46
Kolbila, FH18
Kole, FF41
Kolguev Island, RZ1
Koli, AW47
Kololo, FQ9
Kolombangara, ON10
Kolosh, NA12
Kolta, AW45
KOM, FF39
Kom, AR8
KOMA, FJ15
Komandorski Islands,
  RZ1
Kombe, FF41, FI26
Komi, RG7
Komi A.S.S.R., RG8
Komi-Permyak National
  Okrug, RG8
Komo, FJ15
Komono, FA31
Kona, FF33
Konda-Dora, AW46
Konda-Reddi, AW59
Konde, FN17
Kondh, AW35
Kondongo, MS15
KONGO, FO21
Koniag, NA10
Koniagui, FA36
KONJO, FO22
KONKOMBA, FA24

KONO, FC4
Konongo, FN18
KONSO, MP17
Konta, AW59, MP26
Kony, FL13
Konyak, AR13
Kootenay, NF8
Kora, FX13
Korana, FX13
KORANKO, FC5
Korbo, MS18
KORDOFAN ARABS, MQ10
KOREA, AA1
Korea, Historical,
  AA2
Korea, North, AA5
Koreans, AA1
Korea, Peoples Democratic
  Republic of, AA5
Korea, Prehistoric,
  AA3
Korea, Republic of,
  AA6
Korea, South, AA6
Koreng, OI26
Koriuk, FJ17
KORKU, AW38
Korma, MP22
Koro, FF34
KOROCA, FP7
Korofawa, FF33
Korongo, FJ21
Korop, FF17
Korwa, AW38
KORYAK, RY4
Koryak National Okrug,
  RY1, RY4
KOSHIKI, AB8
Koso, NT22
Kosova, FL8
KOSSI, FF40
Kot, RU2
KOTA, AW55
KOTA, FI17
Kotan, RS3
Kotofo, FH18
KOTOKO, FH13
Kotokoli, FA34
Kotopo, FH18
Koya, AW32
Koyam, MS14
Koyra, MP7
Koyukon, NA8
Kpa, AM35
Kpankpam, FA24
Kpe, FF43
KPELLE, FD6
Krachi, FE8
Krahn, FD7
Kran, FD7
Krao, FD7
Krauatungalung, OI16
KRECH, FJ16
Kreda, MS22
Kredi, FJ16
Kreish, FJ16
Krim, FC8
KRU, FD7
Ktawa, MW6
Kualuthi, FX8
Kuambi, FX8
Kuang, FI21
Kuanyama, FX8
KUBA, FO23
Kuba, FV5
Kubja, FJ11
KUBU, OD8
Kubu, MS16
Kuchino, AB9
Kuchinoyerabu, AB9
Kudawa, FF46
Kudia, FI13
Kudu, MS15
Kudubi, AW63

Kuen, AM31
Kugama, FF48
Kui, AM7
Kuikuru, SP25
Kuitsh, NR5
Kuka, MS8
Kuki, AR8
KUKI-LUSHAI, AR8
Kuku, FJ5
Kuku Nor, AH5
Kukuruku, FF21
Kukwe, FN17
KULAMAN, OA25
Kulango, FA26
Kular, OI6
Kullo, MP26
Kulu, FF59
Kuluwitcatca, NQ11
Kulya, FL8
Kulyi, OJ20
Kum, FK8
Kumam, FK12
Kumba, FF48
Kumbe, FH7, FI26
Kumdi, OJ20
Kumik, RH7
Kumu, FO11
KUMYK, RH7
Kunabemba, FH21
Kunaguanasaya, SS13
KUNAMA, MN8
Kunante, FB6
Kunda, FO15
KUNDU, FF41
Kundu, FO32
Kung, FI21, FX10
Kunnuvan, AW63
Kunta, MS29
Kunya, FE8
Kunyi, FO50
Kunyung, OI26
Kunza, SG5
Kuoy, AM7
Kupangese, OF20
KURAMA, FF42
Kuravan, AW64
Kurbo, MS18
KURD, MA11
Kuria, FL8
KURILES, RZ2
Kurin, RH8
KURNAI, OI16
Kuroba, FA5
Kurtatchi, ON6
Kurukh, AW39
KURUMBA, AW56
Kurumba, FA28
KUSAIE, OR8
Kusasi, FE10
Kusu, FO47
KUTCH, AW9
KUTCHIN, ND10
KUTENAI, NF8
Kuti, FO32
Kutin, FH18
Kutshu, FO32
Kutsung, AE3
Kutthung, OI24
Kutu, FO32
KUWAIT, MI1
Kuyonon, OA30
Kuyu, FI7
Kwafi, FL12
Kwahu, FE12
KWAKIUTL, NE10
Kwakwa, FA25
KWALHIOQUA, NR11
Kwanda, FQ9
Kwando, FP15
Kwangare, FP11
Kwange, FO45
Kwangsi, AF17
Kwangtung, AF17
Kwanyime, FP18

Kwara, MP16
Kwaya, FN25
Kweichow, AF16
Kwele, FH20
Kwena, FV6
Kwere, FN27
Kwese, FO28
KWIRI, FF43
Kwise, FP7
Kwisso, FP7
Kwolla, FF6
KWOMA, OJ13
Kwotto, FF29
Kyama, FA25
Kyatu, FF33
Kyoungtha, AR4

La arua, AD11
LaBhu, AE11
Labrador, NI1
Labrador Eskimo, NI5
Labwor, FK4
Lacandon, NV10
LACCADIVES, AZ4
Lache, SC11
Lactan, OA18
Ladak, AJ4
Ladaki, AJ4
Ladrone Islands, OR9
Lafit, FJ17
Lafofa, FJ21
Lagawe, OA19
LAGOON TRIBES, FA25
Laguna, NT7
Lagunero, NU43
Lahawiin, MQ15
LAHU, AP13
Lahul, AJ4
Laikipiak, FL12
Laka, FI18, FX18
Lakalai, OM16
Lake, NR19
LAKESIDE TONGA, FR7
Lakher, AR8
Laki, OG7
LAKKA, FI18
Lako, FL13
Lakor, OF11
Lala, FF64, FQ8
Lalia, FO35
LAMA, SE14
LAMBA, FQ8
Lambya, FN21
Lame, FH6
LAMET, AM28
Lamista, SE14
Lamotrek, OR21
Lampong, OD12
Lamut, RU5
Lanao, OA22
Landak, OC8
LAND DYAK, OC8
LANDUMA, FB5
Langa, FX18
Langi, FN16
LANGO, FK9
Lango, FJ17
Lannathai, AO6
Lao, AM8
Lao, Eastern, AM8
LAOS, AM8
Laotian Thai, AM8
Laotians, AM8
Lao, Western, AO6
Lapacho, SF14
LAPPS, EP4
Laro, FJ21
Lashi, AP6
Lassik, NS23
Lat, AM27
Latagnon, OA18
LATE MODERN EUROPE,
  E2
Latin America, S1,
  S2

Mahria, MS9
Mahungo, FO21
Maiba, SS11
MAIDU, NS15
MAILU, OJ15
Maina, SE22
Maine, NL1
Maioncon, SS20
Maipure, SQ27
Maiye, FV5
Maji, MP10
Maka, FH20
Makah, NE11
Makalaka, FS5
Makaraka, FO7
Makari, FH13
MAKASSAR, OG6
Makassarese, OG6
Makere, FO29
Makie, FH20
MAKIRITARE, SS20
Makoa, FY18
Makololo, FQ9
Makoma, FQ9
MAKONDE, FN13
Makoroko, FP7
Ma Ku, AO9
MAKUA, FT5
Makua, FI7
Makuango, FO21
Makurma, MP22
Makwangare, FP11
Mala-Arayan, AW64
Malabar, AW11
Malabu, FF12
Malacata, SD9
Malagasy Republic,
  FY1
MALAITA, ON9
Malali, SN4
Malama, FL4
Malamkiravan, AW64
Mala Pantaram, AW64
Malapulayan, AW64
Malasar, AW63
Malavettan, AW64
MALAWI, FR1
Malawi, Colonial,
  FR2
Malawi, Prehistoric,
  FR8
MALAYA, AN1
Malaya, Historical,
  AN2
Malaya, Prehistoric,
  AN3
Malayarayan, AW64
MALAYO-POLYNESIANS,
  O4
MALAYS, AN5
Malays, OD12
MALAYSIA, AN8
Malay, Thai, AO8
Malden Island, OV6
MALDIVES, AZ5
Malebu, SC9
MALECITE, NJ4
MALEKULA, OO12
Malele, FO29
Malemba, FP6
Malepa, FX19
MALER, AW40
MALI, MS35
Mali, FI13
Mali Empire, FA2
Malika, FO9
Malila, FN21
Malimba, FH7
Malindang, OA33
MALINKE, FA27
Malkan, FJ7
Malo, MP26
Malobale, FP14
Malochazi, FP8

Mal Paharia, AW46
Malpelo, SZ1
MALSER, AW57
MALTA, EZ6
Maltese, EZ6
Malto, AW40
Maluku Islands, OH1-OH3
MAM, NW8
Mama, FF45
Mamak, OD8
MAMANUA, OA26
Mamassani, MA12
Mambanga, FO29
Mambari, FP13
Mambere, FO29
MAMBILA, FH14
Mamboe, FQ9
Mambukushu, FP11
Mambunda, FP12
Mambwe, FQ5
Mambwela, FQ10
Mamidja, FX14
Mampoko, FI7
MAMPRUSI, FE9
Mamun, FI13
Mamvu, FO31
Man, AE6
Manageir, FJ14
Manahoac, NN13
Manala, FX18
Manam Island, OJ18
MANAO, SQ11
Manasi, SF9
Manasir, MQ14
Mancho, MP10
MANCHU, AG4
MANCHURIA, AG1
Manchuria, Historical,
  AG2
Manchuria, Prehistoric,
  AG3
MANDAEANS, MH11
MANDALA, MQ11
MANDAN, NQ17
MANDARA, FF47
MANDAYA, OA27
Mandaya, OA5
Mandingo, FA27
Mandinka, FA27
Mandino, FA27
Mandja, FI20
Mandjak, FB6
MANDJIA, FI20
Mandyak, FB6
Mandyako, FB6
Manegir, RU5
Manga, FO29, MS14
Mangaia, OZ9
Mangali-Lubo, OA24
Manganja, FR4
Mangara, FO12
Mangareva, OX5
Mangati, FN26
Mangawa, MS14
Mangba, FO29
Mangbei, FI24
MANGBETU, FO29
Mangeroma, SQ7
Manggarai, OF9
Mangguangan, OA28
Mangoni, FR5
Mangue, SA11
Mangyan, OA15, OA18,
  OA23
MANIHIKI, OZ10
Manipuri, AR9
Maniteneri, SQ9
Manitoba, NF1
Manitsaua, SP6
Maniwaki, NH4
Mankagne, FB6
Mankanya, FB6
Mankoya, FQ10
Mannan, AW64

MANOBO, OA28
Mansaka, OA27
Mansi, RU6
MANTA, SD10
Manta, FF22
Mantizula, SP6
Manundi, FN14
MANUS, OM6
MANX, ES12
Manyanga, FO21
Manyika, FS5
MAO, MP19
Mao, AR13
Maopityan, SR13
MAORI, OZ4
Mape, SS13
MAPIA, OJ16
Mapoch, FX18
Mapoye, SS23
Mapuche, SG4
Mara, FE13
Maracana, SS5
Marachi, FL4
Maragoli, FL4
Maragua, SQ12
Marais, FH7
Marajo Island, SQ5
Marakwet, FL13
Maram, AR13
Marama, FL4
Maranao, OA22
Maranhao, SO1
Maraon, SQ16
MARATHI, AW12
MARAVI, FR4
Marawa, SQ21
Marawan, SQ16
Marba, FI5
MARCUS, AZ6
Marfa, MS15
Margarita, SZ5
Margi, FF12
Mari A.S.S.R., RG2
Maria, MN9, MR9
Maria Gond, AW32
MARIANAS, OR9
Mariape, SP25
Maribio, SA18
Mariche, SS8
Maricopa, NT15
Marie Galante, ST5
Marille, FL7
Marinawa, SQ6
MARINDANIM, OJ17
Marion, FZ1
MARITIME ARABS, MK2
MARITIME PROVINCES,
  NJ1
Maritime Provinces,
  Historical, NJ2
Maritime Provinces,
  Prehistoric, NJ3
Maritu, MP22
Mariusa, SS18
Marka, FA15
Marken Islands, OT4
Marle, FL7
Marma, AR4
Maropo, SF23
Marotse, FQ9
MARQUEEN, OT4
MARQUESAS, OX6
MARRAKECH ARABS, MW10
Marshallese, OR11
MARSHALLS, OR11
Marsh Arabs, MH13
MARTINIQUE, ST7
Maru, AP6
Marule, FJ6
Marungu, FQ5
Maryland, NM1
MASA, FI21
Masaba, FK13
Masacara, SO2

MASAI, FL12
MASALIT, MQ12
Masango, MP20
MASCO, SE15
MASCOI, SK10
Mascouten, NP6
MASHACALI, SN4
Mashasha, FQ10
Masheba, FR4
Mashona, FS5
Mashongo, MP20
Mashukolumbwe, FQ6
Masikoro, FY6
Maskegon, NG4
Masmadje, FI16
Masparro, SS11
Maspo, SE6
Massaca, SP24
MASSACHUSET, NL5
Massachusetts, Historical,
  NL7
MASSIM, OL1
Massim, Historical,
  OL2
Massim, Prehistoric,
  OL3
Massin, MS31
Massubia, FQ11
Mastel, SC17
Masupia, FQ11
Matabele, FS4
MATACO, SI7
Mataguayo, SI7
MATAKAM, FH15
Matalgalpa, SA15
Matama, SP12
Matamba, FP6
Matambwe, FN13
Matanawi, SQ14
Matara, SI13
Matawara, FS5
Matchioko, FP4
MATENGO, FN14
MATLATZINCA, NU21
MATO GROSSO, SP1
Matoka, FQ12
Matotela, FQ12
Matthew, OP6
Mattole, NS23
Mattuvan, AW64
Matty Island, OM15
Matuku, OQ9
Matumbi, FN13, FN20
Matumbuka, FR6
Mau, FA15, MP19
MAUE, SQ12
Maune, FX18
Mauri, MS12
MAURITANIA, MS36
MAURITIUS, FZ4
Mavia, FT5
Maviha, FT5
Mawia, FT5
Mawken, AP8
MAYA, NV4
Mayaguana, SW1
Maya, Highland, NW4
Mayaka, FO49
Maya, Yucatec, NV10
Maynila, OA36
Mayo, NU8
Mayogu, FO29
Mayombe, FO50
MAYORUNA, SE16
Mayoyao, OA19
Mazahua, NU21
Mazanderani, MA7
MAZATEC, NU22
Mazi, MP10
Mazitu, FN14
Mazizuru, FS5
Mbae, FO29
Mbagani, FO20
Mbai, FI28

Mbailundu, FP13
Mbaka, FI11, FP6
MBALA, FO30
Mbala, FQ6
Mbalantu, FX8
Mbali, FP13
Mbamba, FO21
Mbande, FP9
Mbandja, FI6, FX8
Mbandyeru, FX12
Mbang, FH19
MBANGALA, FP10
Mbao, FI17
Mbarek, MS31
Mbarike, FF65
Mbata, FO21
Mbato, FA25
MBAYA, SK11
Mbegua, SI11
Mbegumba, FJ20
Mbelwa, FR5
Mbembe, FF20
Mbenbe, FF17
Mbere, FH16
Mberidi, FJ14
Mbesa, FO13
Mbete, FI12
Mbia, SF21
Mbimu, FH21
Mbo, FF40
Mboi, FF64
Mboke, FF43
Mboko, FI7
Mbole, FO32
Mbondjo, FI11
Mbondo, FP6
Mbonge, FF41
Mboshi, FI7
Mbowe, FQ9
Mbuba, FO31
Mbudja, FO13
MBUGU, FN15
MBUGWE, FN16
Mbui, FP6
Mbuila, FP18
Mbuin, FA31
Mbuiyi, FP6
MBUKUSHU, FP11
Mbula, FF11
Mbulu, FN5
Mbulunge, FN5
MBUM, FH16
Mbumbung, FH21
MBUNDA, FP12
MBUNDU, FP13
Mbundu, FP6
Mbunga, FN20
Mbunu, FI33, FO17
Mburikem, FF51
Mbuti, FO4
Mbwe, FI14
Mbwela, FP12, FQ10
Mbwera, FQ10
Mbya, SM4
Mdewakanton, NQ11
Mdur, AM35
Meban, FJ9
Medela, MS22
MEDIEVAL ENGLAND,
  ES5
MEDIEVAL ETHIOPIA,
  MP2
MEDIEVAL EUROPE, E4
MEDIEVAL FRANCE, EW3
MEDIEVAL GERMANY,
  EL3
MEDIEVAL ITALY, EI3
MEDIEVAL MOROCCO,
  MW2
MEDIEVAL PERSIA, MA2
Medje, FO29
Megarha, MT9
Megariha, MT9
Megrel, RI11

Meherrin, NN19
Mehinacu, SP18
Meidob, MQ13
MEITHEI, AR9
Mekan, MP22
Mekei, FH9
Mekyibo, FA5
MELANESIA, OK1
MELANESIANS, OK2
Menam, AM23
MENDE, FC7
Mendsime, FH20
Menembe, OJ20
Menian, SO2
Menka, FF58
MENOMINI, NP8
Mensa, MN9
MENTAWEI, OD9
Mentawei Islands,
  OD9
Meo, AE5, AW48
Mepene, SI4
Mer, AW48
MERARIT, MS16
Merat, AW48
Merauke, OJ17
Merdu, MP22
Mere, FJ16
Meregoto, SS8
MERGUI, AP8
MERINA, FY5
Merir, OR18
Meru, FL5, FN4
Merzu, MP22
Mesakin, FJ21
Mesallania, MQ14
Mescal, NU12
Mescalero, NT8
Mesgita, MW6
Mesme, FI32
Mesopotamia, MA4,
  MH4-MH6
Mesopotamia, Prehistoric,
  MH6
Messira, FQ5
Messiria, MQ5
Meta, FF58
Metalsa, MX3
Metcho, FF20
Methow, NR19
Metoac, NM7
Metsha, MP18
MEXICAN INDIANS, NU4
MEXICANS OF THE SOUTHWEST,
  NT4
MEXICO, NU1
Mexico, Historical,
  NU2
Mexico, Prehistoric,
  NU3
Mfioti, FI34
Mfumte, FF20
Mfumungu, FI33
Mfute, FH24
Mgharba, MS9
Mhammid, MW6
Mialat, SP10
MIAMI, NP9
MIAO, AE5
Mical, NR18
Michigamea, NP6
Michigan, NP1
MICMAC, NJ5
MICRONESIA, OR1
Micronesia, Historical,
  OR2
MICRONESIANS, OR4
Micronesia, Prehistoric,
  OR3
Middle American Civilization,
  NY1
MIDDLE ATLANTIC STATES,
  NM1
Middle Atlantic States,
  Historical, NM2

Middle Atlantic States,
  Prehistoric, NM3
Middle Chinook, NR6
Middle Congo, FI39
MIDDLE EAST, M1
MIDDLE EAST-ARABIC
  PERIOD, M3
Middle East, Early
  Historic, M5
MIDDLE EAST-GRAECO-ROMAN
  PERIOD, M4
MIDDLE EAST ISLANDS,
  MZ1
MIDDLE EAST-TURKISH
  PERIOD, M2
Midnoosky, NA5
MIDOBI, MQ13
Midogo, MS8
Midway, OV1
Mien, MP22
Miguri, SS17
Mihavani, FT5
Mijikenda, FL14
Mikasuki, NN16
MIKEA, FY18
MIKIR, AR10
Milanau, OC7
Millcayac, SI6
Miltu, FI32
Mima, MS17
Mimbreno, NT8
MIMI, MS17
Mina, AW48
Minaco, SP18
Minahasa, OG4
Minami, AC5
Minamiko, AC8
Minang, OI26
MINANGKABAU, OD10
Minangyan, OA18
Minas Gerais, SN1
MINCHIA, AE11
Mindassa, FI17
Mindumbo, FI12
MING, AF3
Mingat, AH5
MINGREL, RI11
Minianka, FA31
Minitari, NQ14
Min-nan, AD5
Minneconjou, NQ11
Minnesota, NQ1
MINOAN CIVILIZATION,
  EH10
MINOR ASIATIC COLONIES,
  AY1
Minuane, SJ5
Minung, OI26
Minungu, FP4
Minyombo, FH21
Mirafab, MQ14
Miranya, SC19
MIRI, AR11
Miri, FJ21
Miriam, FF6, OJ24
Mirzapur, AW46
Misaje, FF20
MISHMI, AR12
Mishongnovi, NT9
Mishulundu, FQ9
Miskito Indians, SA15
Misorongo, FO21
Missanga, FI27
Missisauga, NG6
Mississippi, NN1
Missouri, NQ1, NQ9
MITABA, FI22
Mitsogo, FI30
MITTU, FJ18
Mituku, FO41
MIWOK, NS16
MIXE, NU23
MIXTEC, NU24
MIYAKO, AC6

Mizocuavean Popoluca,
  NU30
MNONG, AM31
Mo, FE7
Moa, OF11
Moala, OQ9
Moapa, NT16
Moba, FA24
Mobale, FO13
Mobanghi, FO8
Mobango, FO13
Mobati, FO8
Mobengo, FO8
Mobile, NN14
Mocha, MP14
Mochebo, FI14
Mochobo, SE6
Mocorito, NU41
MOCOVI, SI8
Moctobi, NN14
Modern Assyrians,
  MH12
MODERN QUECHUA, SE24
Modgel, FI32
MODOC, NS17
Mogamaw, FF58
Mogei, OJ20
Mogh, AR4
Mogogodo, FL12
Moguex, SC15
MOGUL INDIA, AQ3
Mogum, FI13
Mogwandi, FO36
Mohave, NT15
Mohave-Apache, NT14
Mohawk, NM9
MOHEGAN, NL6
Mohilla, FP18
MOI-KHA, AM9
Moingwena, NP6
MOJO, SF15
MOKIL, OR12
Mokuk, FH9
Molala, NR18
MOLDAVIA, RE1
Molima, OL4
Molingi, FI26
Molucca Islands, OH1-OH3
MOLUCCAS, OH1
Moluccas, Historical,
  OH2
Moluccas, Prehistoric,
  OH3
Mombati, FO8
Mombera, FR5
Mombesa, FO13
Mombutu, FO31
Mompox, SC9
MOMVU, FO31
MON, AP9
Monacan, NN13
Monachi, NS25
Monbutto, FO29
Mondari, FJ5
Mondjembo, FI11
Mong, FJ12
Mongalla, FO12
Mongandu, FO35
Mongelima, FO8
MONGO, FO32
MONGOLIA, AH1
Mongolia, Buryat,
  RW1
Mongolia, Historical,
  AH2
Mongolia, Inner, AH6
Mongolian People's
  Republic, AH7
Mongolia, Outer, AH7
Mongolia, Prehistoric,
  AH3
Mongolia, Russian,
  RW1

Mongols, AE9, AG5,
AH1-AH7, RW1
Mongondou, OG4
MONGUOR, AE9
MON-KHMER, AL2
Mono, FH6, ON14
Mono, Eastern, NR13
MONOM, AM30
Mono, Western, NS25
MONTAGNAIS, NH6
Montana, NQ1
Montauk, NM7
MONTENEGRINS, EF5
Montesco, OA11
Montoil, FF6
Montserrat, ST6
MONUMBO, OJ18
MOORISH SPAIN, EX3
Mopoi, FO29
Moquisse, FP7
Moravia, EB2
Morcote, SC11
MORDVA, RG6
Mordva A.S.S.R., RG6
Mordvinians, RG6
More, SP12
Morea, MS5
Moreb, FJ21
Mori, OG7
MORI-LAKI, OG7
Moriori, OZ8
MORMONS, NT24
Moro, FJ21, SK14
MOROCCO, MW1
Morocco, Prehistoric,
MW4
Morocco, Spanish,
MW1, MX1
Moro, Coastal, OA16
Moro, Inland, OA22
Moron, FJ11
Morotai, OH12
Morotiri, OX4
Morotoco, SK14
Mortlock Islands,
OR14, OT4
MORU, FJ19
Moru Kodo, FJ18
Moru Misa, FJ19
Moru Wadi, FJ18
Morwa, FF38
Mosengele, FO32
MOSETENE, SF16
Moshinji, FP10
Moshosho, SN4
Moso, NE12
Mosopelea, NN13
MOSQUITO, SA15
MOSSI, FA28
Mossilongi, FO21
Mota, OO7
Motilones Bravos,
SS13
Motilones Mansos,
SC10
Motozintlec, NW8
MOTU, OJ19
Mou, AM26
Moundan, FI24
Mountain, ND9
Mountain Damara, FX9
MOUNTAIN WHITES, NN5
MOUNT HAGEN TRIBES,
OJ20
MOVIMA, SF17
Moyen Congo, FI39
Moyma, SF17
Moyo, MS15
MOZAMBIQUE, FT2
Mozambique, Prehistoric,
FT8
Mozambique, Traditional,
FT3
Mpangu, FO21

Mpangwe, FH9
Mpezeni, FR5
Mpondo, FX17
MPONGWE, FI23
Mputu, FO17
Mrabri, AO9
Mrashi, FL4
Mru, AM17, AR4
MT. ATHOS, EH13
Mubali, FO9
MUBI, MS18
Mubi, FF12
Mucusso, FP11
Mudsau, FT7
Muduvan, AW64
Muenane, SC19
Muenyi, FQ9
Mufa, FI13
Muffo, FH15
Muhanha, FP15
Muhumbe, FP17
Muisca, SC11
Muiza, FQ5
Mujano, FT7
Mujua, FT7
Mukulehe, FH15
Muleng, FF12
Mulfa, FI13
Muluena, FP14
Mum, FF51
Mumbake, FF15
MUMUYE, FF48
Muna, OG7
Munano, FP13
MUNDA, AW41
MUNDANG, FI24
Mundar, FJ5
Mundo, OA11
Mundombe, FP15
MUNDU, FO33
MUNDURUCU, SQ13
Munga, FF18
Mungo, FH7
Munhaneca, FP18
Munichi, SE8
Munjiger, OJ20
Munkanu, OI22
Munshi, FF57
MUONG, AM10
Mupinda, FP6
MURA, SQ14
Murdia, MS5
Mure, SP24
Muria, AW32
Muria Gond, AW32
Murilo, OR19
Murle, FJ6
MURNGIN, OI17
Murro, MQ5
Murse, MP22
Mursia, MP22
Murut, OC7
Murutu, MP22
Murzu, MP22
Murzuch, MT5
Muscat, MK1
Museki, FI29
MUSGU, FH17
Musha, MP22
Mushikongo, FO21
Muskhogean, NN3
Muskogee, NN11
Muskwium, NE13
Musquaki, NP5
MUSSAU, OM7
Musso, AP13
Mussoi, FI5
Musugoi, FH15
Musuk, FH17
Musurongo, FO21
Mutair, MJ4
Muthuvan, AW64
Mutsaya, FI33
Mututu, MS17
Muzo, SC16

Mverodi, FJ14
Mvumba, FH5
Mwanga, FQ9
Mwariba, FN17
Mwei, FH9
Mwelle, FH9, FH12
Mwelya, FN12
Mwenyi, FQ9
Mwera, FN13
Mweru, FL5
Mwimbe, FL5
Myao, FT7
Mysore, AW10
MZAB, MV7

Nabaloi, OA20
Nabayugan, OA24
Nabesna, NA5
Nabudub, SQ18
Nadache, SN2
Nafana, FA31
NAFUSA, MT10
NAGA, AR13
Naga, FJ15
Nagar, AV7
Nago, FF62
NAHANE, ND12
Nahsi, AE12
Nahuan, NU7, NV8
NAHUA PEOPLES, NU46
Nahuqua, SP25
Naika, AW47
Naikda, AW47
Nairai, OQ9
Najo, MP10
NAKANAI, OM16
Nakano, AB9
Nakaza, MS5
Naked Rengma, AR13
NAKHI, AE12
Nalu, FB6
Nama, FF56, FX13,
OR10
Namainga, FQ12
Namaqua, FX13
NAMAU, OJ21
Namba, FA9
Nambas, OO12
Nambe, NT18
NAMBICUARA, SP17
NAMIBIA, FX23
Namibia, Prehistoric,
FX4
Namibia, Traditional,
FX23
Namnam, FE10
Namoluk, OR14
NAMSHI, FH18
Nanai, RX3
Nanaimo, NE13
Nan-chao, AF6
Nande, FO22
NANDI, FL13
Nangire, FI32
Nanguru, ON10
Naniba, NN14
NANKANSE, FE10
Nankwila, FN18
Nano, FP13
NANTICOKE, NM11
Nanumba, FE5
Nanzela, FQ6
Nao, MP10
Napeca, SF13
Napo Indians, SD5
Napore, FJ25
Napu, OG11
Naravute, SP25
Narene, FX14
Naron, FX10
Narraganset, NL6
NARRINYERI, OI18
Naskapi, NH6
Nassau, SW1

Nata, FN25
NATAL INDIANS, FX15
Natal Nguni, FX20
NATCHEZ, NO8
Natchitoches, NO5
Natekebit, SI12
Natioro, FA31
Natu, SO3
Nauhan, OA15
Naura, SC16
NAURU, OR13
Nauset, NL5
NAVAHO, NT13
Navajo, NT13
Nawa, SQ6
Nawaiba, MS9
Nawuru, FE8
NAYADI, AW58
Nayak, AW47
Nayar, AW11
Nchumbulung, FE8
Nchumuru, FE8
Ndaka, FO9
Ndali, FN21
Ndam, FI32
Ndamba, FN20
Ndara, FI28
Ndasa, FI17
Ndau, FS5
Nde, FF22
NDEBELE, FS4
Ndebele, Black, FX18
Ndebele, Rhodesian,
FS4
Ndebele, Transvaal,
FX18
Ndemba, FP6
NDEMBU, FP14
Ndemi, FI28
Ndendehule, FN14
Ndengereko, FN27
Ndengese, FO16
Ndenie, FA5
Ndhir, MW5
Ndiki, FH10
Ndo, FL13, FO26
Ndob, FF51
NDOGO, FJ20
Ndogobessol, FH12
NDOKO, FO34
NDOMBE, FP15
Ndomme, FH22
Ndomo, FI17
Ndonde, FN13
Ndonga, FX8
Ndoren, FH14
NDORO, FF49
Ndorobo, FL6
N'Doute, FA37
Ndsime, FH20
Ndugo, FJ20
Nduka, FI28
Ndumbo, FI12
Ndumu, FI12
Ndundulu, FQ9
Ndut, FA37
Ndyau, FP18
Ndzundza, FX18
Near East, M1
Nebraska, NQ1
Necker, OV1
Negda, RX3
Negidal, RX3
Negritos, Andamanese,
AZ2
Negritos, Malayan,
AN7
Negritos, Oceanic,
O5
Negritos, Philippine,
OA31
Negritos, Zambales-Bataan,
OA4
Negroes, Bush, SR8

Negroes, of North America, N5
Negroes, of the New World, N5
Negroes, slave trade, F1
Negroes, of South America, S5
Negroes, of Southern United States, NN6
NEGROID SOMALILAND PEOPLES, MO5
Negye, FK8
Nehalem, NR21
NEMADI, MS32
Nenets, RU1, RU4
NEOLITHIC EUROPE, E7
NEOLITHIC MIDDLE EAST, M7
NEPAL, AK1
Nepalese, AK1
Nepissing, NH4
Nespelem, NR19
Nestorians, MH12
Nestucca, NR21
NETHERLANDS, ET1
Netherlands, Historical, ET2
Netherlands New Guinea, OJ3
Netherlands, Prehistoric, ET3
NETSILIK, ND13
Neu-Mecklenburg, OM10
Neu-Pommern, OM8
Neuquen, SH1
Neutral, NM8
Nevada, NT1
Nevia, FP18
Nevis, ST6
Nevome, NU29
NEW AMSTERDAM DUTCH, NM12
NEW BRITAIN, OM8
New Brunswick, NJ1
NEW CALEDONIA, OP1
New Caledonia, Historical, OP2
NEW CALEDONIAN OUTLIERS, OP6
New Caledonia, Prehistoric, OP3
NEW ENGLAND, NL1
New England, Historical, NL2
New England, Prehistoric, NL3
NEWFOUNDLAND, NI1
Newfoundland, Historical, NI2
Newfoundland, Prehistoric, NI3
NEW GEORGIA, ON10
NEW GUINEA, OJ1
New Guinea, Netherlands, OJ3
New Guinea, Northeast, OJ4
New Guinea, Prehistoric, OJ2
New Guinea, Western, OJ3
New Hampshire, NL1
NEW HANOVER, OM9
NEW HEBRIDES, OO1
New Hebrides, Historical, OO2
New Hebrides, Prehistoric, OO3
NEW IRELAND, OM10
New Jersey, NM1
New Mexico, NT1
New Siberian Islands, RZ1

New World, N1
New York, NM1
NEW ZEALAND, OZ1
New Zealand, Historical, OZ2
NEW ZEALAND POLYNESIA, OZ5
New Zealand Polynesia, Historical, OZ6
New Zealand Polynesia, Prehistoric, OZ7
New Zealand, Prehistor OZ3
NEZ PERCE, NR12
Ngabre, FI32
Ngachopo, MP22
Ngada, OF9
NGADJU, OC9
Ngala, FH13, FO12
Ngaloi, FI23
Ngama, FI28
Ngambue, FP18
Ngamo, FF37
Nganasani, RU4
Nganda, FP15
Ngandjera, FX8
NGANDU, FO35
Ngandu, FI9
Ngangela, FP16
Ngangte, FH19
Ngangulu, FI33
Ngarkat, OI18
Ngata, FO32
Ngatik, OR16
Ngau, OQ9
NGBANDI, FO36
Ngbanya, FE8
Ngbele, FO29
Nge, FF29
Ngeh, AM14
Ngejim, MS13
Ngelima, FO8
Ngell, FF9
Ngemba, FF58
NGERE, FA29
Nghie, FI17
Ngiaka, FO49
Ngie, FF58
Ngindo, FN13
Ngiri, FI7
Ngiye, FK8
NGIZIM, FF50
Ngoli, FO17
Ngolo, FF41
Ngombe, FO12, FO32, FP18
Ngomwia, FN5
NGONDE, FN17
Ngongo, FO30
NGONI, FR5
NGONYELU, FP16
Ngonzellu, FP16
Ngoteng, FH19
Ngove, FI19
Nguangua, FX8
Ngulu, FN28, OR22
Ngumba, FH5
NGUMBI, FP17
Ngumbi, FI26
Ngumbu, FQ5
Ngundi, FI22
Nguni, Cape, FX17
Nguni, South, FX17
Nguru, FN28, FT5
Nguruimi, FN25
Ngwaketse, FV6
Ngwato, FV6
Ngwo, FF58
Ngwoi, FF36
Nha Heun, AM14
Nhang, AL3
Nhemba, FP16
Niam-Niam, FO7
Nianagua, SE6

Niantic, NL6
Niapu, FO29
NIAS, OD11
Niassans, OD11
NICARAGUA, SA9
Nicobarese, AZ7
NICOBARS, AZ7
Nicola, NE8
Nicoleno, NS10
Nidu, FF33
Nielim, FI10
Nieniegue, FA11
Nienige, FA11
NIGER, MS34
Nigeria, Colonial, FF2
Nigeria, Prehistoric, FF66
Nigeria, Traditional, FF3
Niguecactemic, SK7
Nihoa, OV1
NIKA, FL14
Nikaroma, MP22
Nikoroma, FJ10
NILA, OF13
NILE ARABS, MQ14
NILOTES, FJ2
Nilotic Kavirondo, FL11
NILOTIC SUDAN, FJ1
Nilotic Sudan, Historical, FJ3
Nilotic Sudan, Prehistoric, FJ26
Nindaso, SE14
Nindi, FN14
Ningawa, FF46
NINIGO, OM11
Ninzam, FF45
Nio, NU35
Nioniosse, FA28
Nipmuc, NL5
Nisenan, NS15
Niska, NE15
Nisqualli, NR15
NISSAN, ON11
NIUE, OU7
Nivkh, RX2
Njabeta, FH10
Njambi, FI17
Njamus, FL12
Njanja, FS5
Njanti, FH10
Njao, FS5
Njawi, FI12
Njei, FF12
NJEM, FH20
Njie, FK8
Njokon, FH19
Njungene, FF51
Nkafa, FF12
Nki, FF17
Nkomi, FI23
Nkossi, FF40
Nkoya, FQ10
Nkumbe, FP17
Nkumm, FF22
Nkundo, FO32
Nkundu, FO32
Nkutshu, FO47
Noar, AM23
Nocoman, SE6
Nocten, SI7
Noefoor Island, OJ22
Noemfoor Island, OJ22
NOGAI, RF6
Nogai Tatars, RF6
Noko, FI26
Nole, MP13
Nome, FE13
Nomlaki, NS26
NOMOI, OR14
Nomona, SE14

Nomonuito, OR19
Nomwin, OR19
Non, FA37
None, FA37
Nong, AM31
Nongatl, NS23
Nono, MS10
Nonoya, SC19
NOOTKA, NE11
Nootsak, NR15
Nop, AM27
NORFOLK ISLAND, OI3
Normanby Island, OL4
Norridgewock, NL4
North Africa, M1
NORTH ALASKA ESKIMO, NA9
NORTH AMERICA, N1
North America, Historical, N2
NORTH AMERICAN ISLANDS, NZ1
North America, Prehistoric, N4
Northern Canada, Prehistoric, ND4
North Carolina, NN1
NORTH CHINA, AF12
North Dakota, NQ1
NORTHEAST BRAZIL, SO1
NORTHEAST NEW GUINEA, OJ4
NORTHEAST SALISH, NE12
NORTHEAST SIBERIA, RY1
Northern Bushmen, FX10
NORTHERN CANADA, ND1
Northern Cayapo, SP13
Northern Dynasties, AF7
NORTHERN FILIPINOS, OA29
NORTHERN IRELAND, ER5
Northern Mongols, RW1
NORTHERN PAIUTE, NR13
Northern Rhodesia, FQ1
NORTHERN SHOSHONE, NR14
NORTHERN SIBERIA, RU1
NORTHERN TRIBES, AW45
NORTH KOREA, AA5
North Ossetian A.S.S.R., RH9
NORTH VIETNAM, AM12
NORTHWEST BISAYAN, OA30
NORTHWEST CHINA, AF13
NORTHWEST COAST INDIANS, NE3
NORTHWESTERN STATES, NR1
Northwestern States, Historical, NR2
Northwestern States, Prehistoric, NR3
NORTHWEST SALISH, NE13
NORWAY, EP1
Norway, Historical, EP2
Norway, Prehistoric, EP3
Norwegians, EP1
Nosu, AE4
Nottaway, NN19
Nourage, SR12
Nova Scotia, NJ1

Novaya Zemlya, RZ1
NSAW, FF51
Nsenga, FR4
Nsungli, FF51
Ntem, FF51
Nthali, FR6
Ntomba, FO32
Ntribu, FA34
Ntum, FH9
Nua, AE7
NUBA, FJ21
Nuba, FJ11, MQ4
Nubians, MR8
Nucuini, SQ6
NUER, FJ22
NUEVA ESPARTA, SZ5
NUFORESE, OJ22
NUGURIA, OT5
NUKUMANU, OT6
NUKUORO, OT7
Numana, FF45
Nunamiut, NA9
Nung, AL3, AP6
Nungu, FF45
Nungula, FF44
Nunivak Eskimo, NA13
Nunu, FI33, MS10
Nunuma, FE7
NUPE, FF52
NURI, AU6
Nusan, FX10
Nutabe, SC9
Nvefoor Island, OJ22
Nwanati, FT6
Nyai, FS5
Nyakwai, FJ25
Nyakyusa, FN17
Nyala, FL4
Nyamang, FJ11
Nyamba, FP16
Nyamusa, FJ18
Nyamwanga, FN21
NYAMWEZI, FN18
NYANEKA, FP18
Nyanga, FO22
Nyangatom, FJ25
Nyangbara, FJ5
Nyangeya, FJ25
NYANGI, FF53
Nyangori, FL13
Nyanja, FR4
Nyankole, FK11
NYARI, FO38
Nyaro, FJ21
Nyasa, FR4
NYATURU, FN19
Nyengo, FQ9
Nyetto, FJ11
Nyifwa, FL11
Nyiha, FN21
Nyika, FL14
Nyikoromo, MP22
Nyilam, MP20
Nyilem, FI10
Nyima, FJ11
Nymylan, RY4
Nyole, FL4
Nyong, FI26
NYORO, FK11
Nyuli, FK7
NZAKARA, FI25
Nzari, FO17
NZIMU, FH21
Nzofo, FO28
Nzombo, FO21

Oako, FP6
Obamba, FI12
Obang, FF22
OBI, OH14
Obo, OA7
Ocaina, SC19
Ocaneechi, NN13

Ocean Island, OR6
OCEANIA, O1
Oceania, Historical, O2
Oceania, Prehistoric, O3
OCEANIC NEGRITOS, O5
Ocloya, SI9
Ocole, SI14
Ocoroni, NU35
Ododop, FF17
Odul, RV3
Oeno Island, OW1
Ofo, NN13
Oghoriok, FJ17
Ogi, FJ19
Oglala, NQ11
Oguauiva, SM4
Ogu Uku, FF26
Ohio, NP1
Oirat, AH5
OJANG, MP20
OJIBWA, NG6
Okafima, FX8
Okak, FH9
Okanagon, NE12, NR19
Okanda, FF29, FI30
Okiek, FL6
OKINAWA, AC7
Okino, AC5
Okinoyerabu, AC4
Okkalinga, AW10
Oklahoma, NO1
Okoiyong, FF17
Okpoto, FF29
Olam, MP20
Olamentke, NS16
Olcha, RX3
OLD PRUSSIANS, RB6
Old World, W1
Olemba, FO47
Oli, FH7
Olmec, NU7
Olot, AH5
Olulumo, FF22
OMAGUA, SQ15
OMAGUACA, SI9
Omaha, NQ12
Oman, MK1
Omand, FH10
Ombalantu, FX8
Ombandya, FX8
Ombarandu, FX8
Ombe, FP6
Omeng, FH10
Omoampa, SI14
Omuraina, SE22
ONA, SH4
Ondo, FF62
Ondonga, FX8
Ondri, FJ19
Oneida, NM9
Ongandjera, FX8
Ongom, FI14
Ongono, FI14
Onguangua, FX8
Onitsha Ibo, FF26
Onondaga, NM9
ONTARIO, NG1
Ontario, Historical, NG2
Ontario, Prehistoric, NG3
ONTONG JAVA, OT8
Ontponea, NN13
OPATA, NU25
Opaye, SP11
Opon, SC10
Oquero, NU35
Oraibi, NT9
ORANG LAUT, OB4
ORAON, AW39
Ordos, AH6

Oregon, NR1
Orejon, NU12, SC19, SE12
ORISSA, AW13
ORKNEYS, EZ7
Orkney, South, SZ1
Oro, MS16
Orochi, RX3
Orochon, RU5
Orogniro, FJ25
Orok, RX3
OROKAIVA, OJ23
Oroluk, OR16
Orotina, SA11
Orri, FF17
Orungu, FI23
Osage, NQ12
Oshopong, FF17
Osieba, FH9
OSSET, RH9
OSTYAK, RU3
Ostyak Samoyeds, RU4
Ostyak, Yenisei, RU2
OSUMI, AB9
Ot Danom, OC9
Oti, SP11
Oto, NQ9
OTOMAC, SS14
Otomanguean, NV5
Otomanguean Popoloca, NU22
OTOMI, NU26
Otoro, FJ21
Ottawa, NG6
Ottoman Turks, M2
OTUKE, SF18
Ouadai, MS15
Ouagadougou, FA28
Ouargla, MV10
Oudin, RH8
Oulad Bu Seba, MY4
Oulad Chouekh, MY4
Oulad Delim, MY4
Oulad Mbarek, MS31
Oulad Nasser, MS31
Oulliminden, MS25
Ouo, FA36
Ouolof, MS30
Outagami, NP5
OUTER MONGOLIA, AH7
Ovabre, SC10
Ovah, FY5
Ovaherero, FX12
Ovahinga, FP17
Ovakuangari, FP11
Ovakuanyama, FX8
Ovakumbi, FP17
Ovalau, OQ9
Ovambo, FX8
Ovamguambi, FX8
Ovandonga, FX8
Ovangandyera, FX8
Ovanguuruze, FX8
Ovanyaneka, FP18
Ovimbali, FP13
Ovimbundu, FP13
Owens Valley Paiute, NR13
Owerri Ibo, FF26
Oy, AM14
Oyampi, SQ8
Oyana, SR12
Oyaricoulet, SR12
Ovhut, NR15
Oyo, FF62
OZARK MOUNTAINEERS, NO9

Pabir, FF12
Pacabueye, SC9
PACAGUARA, SF19
Pacaja, SQ2
Pacanawa, SQ6

PACOH, AM32
Padang, FJ12
Padebu, FD7
PAEZ, SC15
Pagbahan, OA23
Pagsupan, OA27
Paguana, SQ25
PAHARI, AW14
Pahuin, FH9
Paiconeca, SF20
Paiema, FF9
PAI-I, AE7
Paikipiranga, SQ8
Paiute, Northern, NR13
Paiute, Owens Valley, NR13
Paiute, Southern, NT16
Paiute, Surprise Valley, NR13
PAIWAN, AD13
Pakawa, NU12
Pakho, AM32
Pakhtun, AU4
Pakidai, SQ18
Pakin, OR16
PAKISTAN, AT1
Palauan, OA36
PALAUNG, AP10
Palawan, OA37
Palenque, SS9
PALEOLITHIC EUROPE, E8
PALEOLITHIC MIDDLE EAST, M8
Palestine, MF1-MF3
Palestine, Historical, MF2
Palestine, Prehistoric, MF3
Palestinian Arabs, MG1
PALIKUR, SQ16
Paliyan, AW64
Palmella, SP24
Palmerston Island, OZ5
Palmyra Island, OV6
Palta, SD9
Palu, OG11
Palus, NR18
Pamana, SQ23
Pambadeque, SE8
Pambia, FJ20
PAME, NU27
Pamlico, NN15
Pamoa, SQ19
Pampa, SI10
Pampangan, OA32
Pampopa, NU12
Pamunkey, NN15
Pan, SM4
PANAMA, SB1
Panama Canal, SB4
Panama, Historical, SB2
Panama, Prehistoric, SB3
Paname, SN4
Panamint, NT22
Panapanayan, AD15
PANARE, SS21
Panatahua, SE19
Panayano, OA14
Pancararu, SO3
Pancenu, SC9
Panche, SC16
Pandikeri, FK10
Pangasinan, OA32
Pang-hse, AE13
Pango, FO21
Pangwa, FN12

Paniyan, AW63
Panjab, AW6
Panjab, East, AW6
Panjabi, West, AT3
Pankho, AR4
PANTANGORO, SC16
PANTHAY, AE13
Panturani, AW64
Panzaleo, SD11
Pao, SS14
PAPAGO, NU28
Papayanense, SC17
Pape, FH18
PAPUA, OJ5
Papuans, OJ1
Papuans, Kiwai, OJ12
Para, SQ1
Paracana, SQ2
PARAGUAY, SK1
Paraguay, Historical,
  SK2
Paraguay, Prehistoric,
  SK3
Paraiba, SO1
Paraiya, SW46
Parana, SM1
Paranawat, SP10
Parauana, SQ27
Paraujano, SS7
Paraviyana, SQ22
Parawa, SQ7
Pardha, AW32
Pare, FN4
Pareca, SS23
PARESSI, SP19
Parhaiya, AW46
Pari, FJ4
Pariagoto, SS9
Parigi, OG11
Parintintin, SP10
Pariri, SC10
PARISIANS, EW9
Parja, AW32
Parkungi, OI9
PARSI, AW21
Pasain, SI14
Pascagoula, NN14
Pase, SQ11
Pasemah, OD12
PASHTUN, AU4
Passamaquoddy, NJ4
PASTO, SC17
Pataco, SC17
PATAGON, SE17
PATAGONIA, SH1
Patagonian aborigines,
  SH1
Patagonians, SH5
Patalima, OH9
PATASHO, SN5
Patasiwa, OH9
PATHAN, AT4
Patiala, AW6
Patwin, NS26
Pau d'Arco, SP13
Pauishana, SQ27
PAUMARY, SQ17
Paumotu Archipelago,
  OX9
Paunaca, SF20
Pausane, NU12
Pauserna, SF11
Pauxi, SQ22
Paviotso, NR13
Pawaria, AW45
PAWNEE, NQ18
Pawumwa, SP12
PAYA, SA16
Payacu, SO5
Payagua, SK12
Payagua, SE12
Payanso, SE14
Payure, SS11
Pazeh, AD4

Pear, AM7
Peba, SE20
Pecos, NT11
PEDI, FX16
Peedee, NN13
Pehuenche, SG4
PEI-CHAO, AF7
Pelew Islands, OR15
Pemba, FM1
Pemeno, SS13
Pemeo, SC9
PEMON, SS16
PENDE, FO39
Pend d'Oreille, NR19
Penin, FH10
Pennacook, NL4
Pennsylvania, NM1
Pennsylvania Dutch,
  NM13
PENNSYLVANIA GERMANS,
  NM13
Penobscot, NL4
Penoqui, SF9
Penrhyn Islands, OZ13
Pensacola, NN14
PENTECOST, OO13
Penti, AE4
Pentlatch, NE13
Penya, FN21
Peopleman, OI26
Peoples Democratic
  Republic of Korea,
  AA5
PEOPLES REPUBLIC,
  AF18
Peoples Republic of
  China, AF18
Peoria, NP6
PEPEL, FB6
Pequot, NL6
Pere, FH16, FO11
PERICLEAN ATHENS,
  EH11
Pericu, NU42
Permians, RG8
Pernambuco, SO1
Persia, MA2-MA4
PERU, SE1
Peru, Historical,
  SE2
PERUVIAN INDIANS,
  SE3
PERUVIAN PREHISTORY,
  SE4
Peske, FH8
Petsu, AE11
Peul, MS11
Phalaborwa, FX14
PHILIPPINE NEGRITOS,
  OA31
Philippine Sea Gypsies,
  OA8
PHILIPPINES, OA1
Philippines, Historical,
  OA2
Philippines, Prehistoric,
  OA3
Phi Tong Luang, AO9
PHNONG, AM7
PHOENICIANS, ME4
PHOENIX ISLANDS, OW2
Phoka, FR6
Phuthai, AO6
Pianacoto, SR12
Piankashaw, NP9
Piapoco, SC5
Piaroa, SS15
Piaui, SO1
Pibelmen, OI26
Pibor, FJ6
Pichobo, SE6
Picunche, SG4
Picuris, NT17
Piegan, NF6

Pihuique, NU12
Pijao, SC15
Pikelot, OR21
Pilaga, SI12
Pilapila, FA9
PIMA, NU29
Pima Alta, NU29
Pima Bajo, NU29
Pimbwe, FN6
Pimenteira, SO8
Pinaleno, NT21
Pinao, SC15
Pinche, SE22
Pinda, FP6
Pindi, FO46
Pindjarup, OI26
Pindji, FO46
Pingelap, OR12
Ping-pu, AD4
Pino, SR12
Pinoco, SF9
Pioje, SE12
Pipai, NS9
PIPIL, NV8
Piraha, SQ14
Piratapuyo, SQ19
Piritu, SS9
PIRO, SE18
Piro, NT10
Piscataway, NM11
Pishauco, SQ22
Pisquow, NR19
PITCAIRN, OW3
Piti, FF32
Plains Bira, FO11
Plains Cree, NG4
PLAINS INDIANS, NQ4
Plains Jarawa, FF31
Plains Ojibwa, NG6
Plana, SW1
PLATEAU INDIANS, NR4
Plateau Tonga, FQ12
PLATEAU YUMANS, NT14
Pnong, AM7
Pocumtuc, NL4
Podogo, FH15
Podokwo, FH15
Podzo, FT5
POGORO, FN20
Pojoaque, NT18
Pojulu, FJ5
Pok, FL13
Poka, FR6
POKOMAM, NW9
POKOMO, FL15
Pokonchi, NW9
Pokot, FL13
POLAND, EA1
Poland, Historical,
  EA2
Poland, Prehistoric,
  EA3
POLAR ESKIMO, NB5
POLAR REGIONS, W5
Poles, EA1
Polillo, OA17
POLISH JEWS, EA4
POLYNESIA, OS1
Polynesia, American,
  OV1
Polynesia, British,
  OW1
Polynesia, Eastern,
  OS2
Polynesia, French,
  OX1, OX2, OX3
Polynesia, New Zealand,
  OZ5, OZ6, OZ7
POLYNESIAN OUTLIERS,
  OT1
POLYNESIANS, OS2
Polynesia, Western,
  OU1, OU2, OU3
POMO, FI27, NS18

PONAPE, OR16
Ponca, NQ12
Pondichery, AY2
Pondo, FX17
Ponek, FH10
Ponend, FH10
Pongo, FF36, FH7,
  FI23
Popo, FA18
Popoi, FO29
Popoloca, NU22
POPOLUCA, NU30
Porecamecra, SO8
Porja, AW63
Poroto, FR21
Porr, AM7
PORTUGAL, EY1
Portugal, Historical,
  EY2
Portuguese, EY1
Portuguese East Africa,
  FT2
PORTUGUESE GUINEA,
  FB2
Portuguese Guinea,
  Prehistoric, FB7
Portuguese Guinea,
  Traditional, FB3
PORTUGUESE TIMOR,
  OF4
Portuguese West Africa,
  FP2
Poso, OG11
POTAWATOMI, NP10
Potiguara, SO9
POTO, FO40
Poturero, SK14
Pove, FI30
POWHATAN, NN15
Poya, SH5
PRAIRIE INDIANS, NP4
PRAIRIE PROVINCES,
  NF1
Prairie Provinces,
  Historical, NF2
Prairie Provinces,
  Prehistoric, NF3
Preh, AM31
PREHIST. AFGHANISTAN,
  AU3
PREHIST. AFRICA, F3
PREHIST. ALASKA, NA4
PREHIST. ALBANIA,
  EG3
PREHIST. ALGERIA,
  MV3
PREHIST. ANGOLA, FP19
PREHIST. ARABIA, MJ3
PREHIST. ARGENTINA,
  SI3
PREHIST. ASIA, A3
PREHIST. AUSTRALIA,
  OI4
PREHIST. AUSTRIA,
  EK3
PREHIST. BAHAMAS,
  SW3
PREHIST. BISMARCKS,
  OM3
PREHIST. BORNEO, OC3
PREHIST. BOTSWANA,
  FV3
PREHIST. BRAZIL, SL3
PREHIST. BRITAIN,
  ES8
PREHIST. BRITISH COLUMBIA,
  NE4
PREHIST. BRITISH HONDURAS,
  NX3
PREHIST. BULGARIA,
  EE3
PREHIST. BURMA, AP3
PREHIST. CALIFORNIA,
  NS3

PREHIST. CAMEROON, FH25
PREHIST. CAUCASIA, RH3
PREHIST. CELEBES, OG3
PREHIST. CENTRAL AFRICAN REPUBLIC, FI38
PREHIST. CEYLON, AX3
PREHIST. CHILE, SG3
PREHIST. CHINA, AF10
PREHIST. CONGO-BRAZZAVILLE, FI42
PREHIST. COSTA RICA, SA4
PREHIST. CUBA, SX3
PREHIST. CYPRUS, MC2
PREHIST. CZECHOSLOVAKIA, EB3
PREHIST. DAHOMEY, FA41
PREHIST. DENMARK, EM3
PREHIST. EAST CENTRAL STATES, NP3
PREHIST. EASTERN SUDAN, MQ3
PREHIST. ECUADOR, SD3
PREHIST. EGYPT, MR7
PREHIST. EL SALVADOR, SA6
PREHIST. EQUATORIAL AFRICA, FI3
PREHIST. ERITREA, MN3
PREHIST. ETHIOPIA, MP4
PREHIST. FERNANDO PO, FG5
PREHIST. FIJI, OQ3
PREHIST. FINLAND, EO3
PREHIST. FORMOSA, AD3
PREHIST. FRANCE, EW6
PREHIST. FRENCH POLYNESIA OX3
PREHIST. GABON, FI46
PREHIST. GAMBIA, FC14
PREHIST. GERMANY, EL5
PREHIST. GHANA, FE14
PREHIST. GREECE, EH7
PREHIST. GREENLAND, NB3
PREHIST. GUATEMALA, NW3
PREHIST. GUIANA, SR5
PREHIST. GUINEA, FA45
PREHIST. HAWAII, OV4
PREHIST. HISPANIOLA, SV4
PREHIST. HONDURAS, SA8
PREHIST. HUNGARY, EC3
PREHIST. IBERIA, EX5
PREHIST. INDIA, AQ6
PREHIST. INDOCHINA, AM3
PREHIST. INDONESIA, OB3
PREHIST. IRAN, MA5
PREHIST. IRELAND, ER3
PREHIST. ITALY, EI6
PREHIST. IVORY COAST, FA49
PREHIST. JAMAICA, SY3
PREHIST. JAPAN, AB4

PREHIST. JAVA, OE3
PREHIST. KOREA, AA3
PREHIST. LEBANON, ME3
Prehist. Lesotho, FX4
PREHIST. LESSER ANTILLES, ST12
PREHIST. LESSER SUNDAS, OF3
PREHIST. LIBERIA, FD10
PREHIST. LIBYA, MT3
PREHIST. MADAGASCAR, FY22
PREHIST. MALAWI, FR8
PREHIST. MALAYA, AN3
PREHIST. MANCHURIA, AG3
PREHIST. MARITIME PROVINCES, NJ3
PREHIST. MASSIM, OL3
PREHIST. MESOPOTAMIA, MH6
PREHIST. MEXICO, NU3
PREHIST. MICRONESIA, OR3
PREHIST. MIDDLE ATLANTIC STATES, NM3
PREHIST. MOLUCCAS, OH3
PREHIST. MONGOLIA, AH3
PREHIST. MOROCCO, MW4
PREHIST. MOZAMBIQUE, FT8
Prehist. Namibia, FX4
PREHIST. NETHERLANDS, ET3
PREHIST. NEW CALEDONIA, OP3
PREHIST. NEW ENGLAND, NL3
PREHIST. NEWFOUNDLAND, NI3
PREHIST. NEW GUINEA, OJ2
PREHIST. NEW HEBRIDES, OO3
PREHIST. NEW ZEALAND, OZ3
PREHIST. NEW ZEALAND POLYNESIA, OZ7
PREHIST. NIGERIA, FF66
PREHIST. NILOTIC SUDAN, FJ26
PREHIST. NORTH AMERICA, N4
PREHIST. NORTHERN CANADA, ND4
PREHIST. NORTHWESTERN STATES, NR3
PREHIST. NORWAY, EP3
PREHIST. OCEANIA, O3
PREHIST. ONTARIO, NG3
PREHIST. PALESTINE, MF3
PREHIST. PANAMA, SB3
PREHIST. PARAGUAY, SK3
PREHIST. PHILIPPINES, OA3
PREHIST. POLAND, EA3
PREHIST. PORTUGUESE GUINEA, FB7
PREHIST. PRAIRIE PROVINCES, NF3
PREHIST. PUERTO RICO, SU3

PREHIST. QUEBEC, NH3
PREHIST. RHODESIA, FS6
PREHIST. RUANDA-URUNDI, FO55
PREHIST. RUMANIA, ED3
PREHIST. RUSSIA, RA3
PREHIST. RYUKYUS, AC3
PREHIST. SAHARA AND SUDAN, MS3
PREHIST. SIBERIA, RR3
PREHIST. SINKIANG, AI3
PREHIST. SOLOMONS, ON3
PREHIST. SOMALILAND, MO3
PREHIST. SOUTH AMERICA, S4
PREHIST. SOUTH ARABIA, ML3
PREHIST. SOUTH CENTRAL STATES, NO3
PREHIST. SOUTHEAST, NN4
PREHIST. SOUTHERN AFRICA, FX4
PREHIST. SOUTHWEST, NT3
Prehist. South West Africa, FX4
PREHIST. SUMATRA, OD3
Prehist. Swaziland, FX4
PREHIST. SWEDEN, EN3
PREHIST. SWITZERLAND, EJ3
PREHIST. SYRIA, MD3
PREHIST. TANGANYIKA, FN29
PREHIST. THAILAND, AO3
PREHIST. TIBET, AJ3
PREHIST. TOGO, FA53
PREHIST. TURKESTAN, RL3
PREHIST. TURKEY, MB3
PREHIST. UGANDA, FK15
PREHIST. UPPER VOLTA, FA57
PREHIST. URUGUAY, SJ3
PREHIST. VENEZUELA, SS3
PREHIST. WEST AFRICA, FA3
PREHIST. WEST CENTRAL STATES, NQ3
PREHIST. WESTERN POLYNESIA, OU3
PREHIST. YUCATAN, NV3
PREHIST. YUGOSLAVIA, EF3
PREHIST. ZAIRE, FO56
PREHIST. ZANZIBAR, FM4
PRIMATE BEHAVIOR, W4
Prince Edward, FZ1
Prince Edward Island, NJ1
Principe, FZ7
Prong, AM31
PROTOHISTORIC EUROPE, E6
PROTOHISTORIC ITALY, EI5
PROTOHISTORIC MIDDLE EAST, M6
Providence, FZ1

Pru, AM27
PRUSSIANS, EL8
Prussians, Old, RB6
Pshav, RI6
Pu, FI17
Pubi, FI30
Pubmatari, SQ18
Pucobye, SO8
Pudu, FD7
PUELCHE, SI10
Puerto Ricans, SU1
PUERTO RICO, SU1
Puerto Rico, Historical, SU2
Puerto Rico, Prehistoric, SU3
PUGET SOUND SALISH, NR15
Puguma, AD15
PUINAVE, SC18
PUKAPUKA, OZ11
PUKU, FI26
Pul, OR18
Pula, OA15
Pulap, OR17
Pulusuk, OR17
PULUWAT, OR17
Puna, SD10
PUNAN, OC10
Pungu, FP17
Puno, FI30
Puquina, SF24
Purace, SC15
Purari, OJ21
PURI, SN6
Puricoto, SQ22
Purubora, SP24
Purucuato, SQ22
Puruhua, SD4
Purupuru, SQ17
Puthai, AL3
Putu, FD7
Puxiti, SP20
Puyallup, NR15
PUYUMA, AD15
Puyumanawa, SE6
Pwo, AP7
Pyem, FF9
PYGMIES, FO4
Pygmies, Cameroon, FH4
Pygmies, Equatorial African, FI4
Pygmies, Zambian, FQ4
Pyuma, AD15

Qara, MP16
QASHGAI, MA13
QATAR, MK3
Qemant, MP16
Quapaw, NQ12
QUEBEC, NH1
Quebec, Historical, NH2
Quebec, Prehistoric, NH3
Quechua, Colonial, SE23
Quechua, Modern, SE24
Quechua, SE13, SE23, SE24
Queen Charlotte Islands, NE9
Queets, NR17
Quelpart, AA4
Quenago, SS17
Queney, OA37
Quepo, SA19
Querandi, SI10
QUICHE, NW10
Quidquidcana, SE19
Quijo, SD11
Quilengue, FP15

QUILEUTE, NR16
Quiloaza, SI11
Quimbande, FP9
QUINAULT, NR17
Quinchia, SC9
Quintana Roo, NV1
Quioco, FP4
Quipungu, FP17
Quiriquire, SS13
Quiriquiripa, SS23
Quissama, FP6
Quissanje, FP6
Quitemo, SF13
Quitemoca, SP12
QUITO, SD11

Rabai, FL14
Rache, SF16
RAGLAI, AM33
Rahanwin, MO4
Rakahanga, OZ10
RAJASTHAN, AW15
RAJASTHAN TRIBES,
  AW48
Rajhwar, AW46
Raji, AW45
Rajput, AW15
RAMA, SA17
Rama, FI19
Ramarama, SP10
Ramba, FN19
Rambia, FN21
Ramcocamecra, SO8
Rangi, FN16
Ranon, OO4
Rapa, OX4
Rappahannock, NN15
Rarbya, MW9
Raroians, OX9
Rarotonga, OZ9
Rashad, FJ21
Ratagnon, OA18
Ratagnon, Christian,
  OA30
Rawalta, AW45
Rawat, AW48
Red Bobo, FA11
Red Thai, AL3
REDDI, AW59
Redjang, OD12
REDJANG-LAMPONG, OD12
Redonda, ST6
REGA, FO41
Regeibat, MS29
Rehamna, MW10
Rema, SE6
Rendile, FL7
Rendova, ON10
RENGAO, AM34
Rengma, AR13
RENNELL, OT9
Republic of Korea,
  AA6
Republic of Singapore,
  AN9
Republic of Vietnam,
  AM13
Republique Centrafricaine,
  FI35
Reshe, FF36
Reshiat, FL7
Resigero, SC19
Reungao, AM34
REUNION, FZ5
Revilla Gigedo, NZ1
RHADE, AM35
Rhode Island, NL1
RHODESIA, FS2
Rhodesian Ndebele,
  FS4
Rhodesia, Northern,
  FQ1
Rhodesia, Prehistoric,
  FS6

Rhodesia, Southern,
  FS2
Rhodesia, Traditional,
  FS3
Riah, MT9
Ribam, FF32
Ribanawa, FF32
Ribe, FL14
Rien, AM27
RIF, MX3
Rio Auary, SS5
Rio Grande do Norte,
  SO1
Rio Grande do Sul,
  SM1
Rio de Janeiro, SN1
Rio Muni, FG1, FG2,
  FG4, FH25
Rio Negro, SH1
Rio de Oro, MY1
Rio Ventuari, SS15
Ripere, FH16
Riseighat, MQ5
Ritarngo, OI17
RIVER YUMANS, NT15
Riyah, MT9
Rizaykat, MQ5
Rlam, AM31
Roamaina, SE22
Rocorona, SP12
Rodriguez Island,
  FZ4
Roglai, AM33
Roh, AM15
Roka, OF9
Rolong, FV6
Roma Island, OF8
Romance peoples, E12
ROMAN EUROPE, E5
ROMAN ITALY, EI4
Romans, EI4, EI9
Romans, Imperial,
  EI9
Ron, FF6
Ronga, FT6
Rongkong, OG8
Rori, FN9
Rossel Island, OL5
ROTI, OF14
ROTUMA, OQ7
Rozi, FQ9
Rozwi, FS5
Ruanagua, SE6
Ruanda, FO42
Ruanda-Urundi, Colonial,
  FO53
Ruanda-Urundi, Prehistoric,
  FO55
Ruanda-Urundi, Traditional,
  FO54
Rubatab, MQ14
RUCUYEN, SR12
Rufaa, MQ15
Rufiji, FM2
RUKAI, AD14
Rukuba, FF32
Rum, SW1
Rumada, FF46
Rumai, AP10
RUMANIA, ED1
Rumania, Historical,
  ED2
Rumanians, ED1
Rumania, Prehistoric,
  ED3
Rumbi, FO29
RUNDI, FO42
RUNGA, MS19
Rungu, FI23
Rungwa, FN6
RURAL IRISH, ER6
Ruri, FN25
Rusia, FL7
Russell Islands, ON8

Russia, R1-RZ2
Russia, Historical,
  RA2
Russian S.F.S.R.,
  RF1
Russian Central Asia,
  RL1, RR1
Russian Empire, R2
RUSSIAN ISLANDS, RZ1
Russian Mongolia,
  RW1
Russia, Prehistoric,
  RA3
RUTHENIANS, RD3
Ruton, FI28
Rutul, RH8
Ruvu, FN28
RWALA, MD4
RWANDA, FO51
RYUKYUS, AC1
Ryukyus, Historical,
  AC2
Ryukyus, Prehistoric,
  AC3

Saaroa, AD11
Sab, MO4
Saba, FI16, ST8
Sabaeans, MH11
Sabah, AN8, OC4
Sabderat, MN9
Sabei, FL13
Sacata, SE17
Sacuva, SQ6
SADANG, OG8
Sae, SC20
Safaliba, FE13
Safen, FA37
SAFWA, FN21
Safwi, FA5
Sagada Igorot, OA20
Sagai, RS2
Sagala, FN22
SAGARA, FN22
Sagdlirmiut, ND5
Saha, SC7
Sahanga, FI8
SAHAPTIN, NR18
Sahaptin, NR12
SAHARA AND SUDAN,
  MS1
Sahara and Sudan,
  Historical, MS2
Sahara and Sudan,
  Prehistoric, MS3
Sahara, Spanish, MY1
Saharia, AW43
Sahel, MU5
Saho, MN4
Saint Barthelemy,
  ST5
Saint Croix, ST10
SAINTE MARIEN, FY20
SAINT EUSTATIUS, ST8
SAINT HELENA, FZ6
Saint John, ST10
Saint Kitts, ST6
Saint Lawrence Island,
  NA13
Saint Lucia, ST11
Saint Martin, ST5,
  ST8
Saint Matthias Island,
  OM7
Saint Paul, FZ1
SAINT PIERRE AND MIQUELON,
  NZ3
Saint Thomas, ST10
Saint Vincent, ST11
Saisiat, AD9
SAISIYAT, AD9
SAKAI, AN6
Sakai, OD8
SAKALAVA, FY6

SAKATA, FO43
Sakhalin, RX1
Saku, FN17
Sala, FQ6
Sala y Gomez, SZ1
Salamat, MS9
SALINA, NS19
Salinan, NS19
Salish, NE12, NE13,
  NR8, NR15, NR19
SALIVA, SS15
Salon, AP8
Saluma, SQ22
Salvador, SO11
Salvadorans, SA5
Samaale, MO4
Samagir, RX3
Samal, OA16
Samamish, NR15
Samana, SW1
SAMARITANS, MG3
Samar-Leyte Bisayan,
  OA14
Samatari, SQ18
Sambal, OA32
Sambali, OA32
Sambara, FN24
Samburu, FL12
Samia, FL4
Samish, NR15
SAMO, FA30
SAMOA, OU8
Samoa, American, OU4
Samoa, Western, OU11
SAMOYED, RU4
Samre, AM7
Sanafana, SK10
Sanamaica, SP24
Sanaviron, SI5
San Carlos, NT21
SAN CRISTOBAL, ON21
Sandawe, FN23
Sande, FO7
Sandia, FN12, NT10
Sandwich, South, SZ1
Sandy, OP6
Sanema, SQ18
Sanetch, NE13
San Felipe, NT12
San Felix, SZ1
SANGA, FI27
Sanga, FQ7
Sangawa, FF32, FF35
Sanghihe Islands,
  OG9
Sangil, OA16
Sangir, OA16
Sangir Islands, OG9
SANGIRESE, OG9
Sango, FI8
Sangtam, AR13
Sangu, FN9
Sanha, SC7
Sanhadja, MX4
Sania, FL7
San Ildefonso, NT18
Saninawa, SQ6
Sanipao, NU12
San Juan, NT18
Sanka, SC7
San-kuo, AF6
SAN-KUO TO NAN-CHAO,
  AF6
San Miguel, NS7
SAN PEDRO LA LAGUNA,
  NW11
Sanpoil, NR19
San Salvador, SW1
Sans Arc, NQ11
Santa, AE9
Santa Ana, NT12
Santa Catalina Islanders,
  NS10
Santa Catarina, SM1

Santa Catarina Caingang, SM2
Santa Clara, NT18
SANTA CRUZ, ON13
Santa Cruz, NS7, SH1
Santa Isabel Island, ON16
SANTAL, AW42
Santa Rosa, NS7
Santchuan, AE9
Santee, NN13, NQ11
Santo Domingo, NT12, SV2
Sanusi, MT9
Sanwi, FA5
Sanye, FL7
Saoch, AM7
Sao Paulo, SN1
Saora, AW43
SAO THOME, FZ7
Sapara, SQ22
Sapo, FD7
Saponi, NN13
Sapuki, SK10
Sapuya, SO3
SARA, FI28
Sara, NN13
Sarae, MP24
SARAKATSANI, EH14
Sarakole, MS21
Saramacca, SR8
Saramo, FN27
Sarangani, OA10
SARAVECA, SF20
Sarawak, AN8, OC4
Sarcee, NF9
SARDINIA, EZ8
Sari, FH18
SARSI, NF9
SART, RN4
Saruro, SS14
Sarwa, FI32
Sasak, OF12
Saskatchewan, NF1
Satawal, OR17
Satawan, OR14
Satsop, NR15
Satudene, ND14
SAUDI ARABIA, MJ1
SAUK, NP11
Saulteaux, NG6
Savage Island, OU7
SAVARA, AW43
Savo Island, ON8
SAVU, OF15
Sayan, AM23
Sayir, FF61
Sayma, SS9
Scandinavians, E11
Schouten Islands, OJ9, OJ27
Scotch-Irish, ER5
Scotland, Early, ES6
Scots, ES6, ES10
SCYTHS, RA4
Sea Dyak, OC6
Sea Gypsies, AP8, OA8, OB4
Sebei, FL13
Sebha, MT5
Sebondoy, SC17
Sebuan, OA14
Secotan, NN15
SEDANG, AM36
Seddrat, MW6
Segeju, FM2
Seiyawa, FF61
SEKANI, NE14
SEKE, FI29
Sekiani, FI29
Seko, OG8
Sele, FP6
Selim, MQ5
Seljuk Turks, M3

Selkup, RU4
Selle, FP6
Selong, AP8
Selya, FN17
Sema, AR13, OF13
SEMANG, AN7
Semiamo, NR15
Semigae, SE22
SEMINOLE, NN16
Semites, M9
Semnu, MT5
Semteuse, NR19
Sena, FR4
Seneca, NM9
Senecu del Sur, NT10
SENEGAL, MS37
Senga, FQ5, FR4
Sengele, FO32
SENHAJA, MX4
Seniang, OO12
Senijextee, NR19
Senoi, AN6
Sensi, SE6
SENTO, AC8
SENUFO, FA31
Senussi, MT9
Serae, MP24
Serbia, EF6
SERBS, EF6
Sere, FJ20
SERER, FA32
Sergipe, SO1
SERI, NU31
Seri, MW5
Seria, FN17
SERMATA, OF16
SERRANO, NS20
Serruchen, MW5
Serva, FJ11
Sesan, AM6
Seshelt, NE13
Setebo, SE10
Sewaco, SQ23
Sewe, FH18
Sewee, NN13
SEYCHELLES, FZ8
Sgaw, AP7
Shacamecra, SO8
Shackaconia, NN13
Shaikia, MQ14
Shake, FI29
SHAMBALA, FN24
Shambioa, SP9
SHAN, AP11
Shan, AE7
Shang, AF9
Shanga, FF13, FS5
Shangalla, FJ7
Shangana-Tonga, FT6
Shangawa, FF13
SHANG-CHOU, AF9
Shango, FI19
Shanindawa, SQ6
Shanjo, FQ9
Shankwe, FS5
Shanshan, FJ11
Shansi, AF12
SHAN-THAI, AL3
Shantung, AF12
Shaparu, SC10
SHASHI, FN25
SHASTA, NS21
Shat, MQ16
Shatt, FJ14
Shavante, SP20
Shawia, MW10
SHAWIYA, MV8
SHAWNEE, NN17
She, MP10
Sheka, MP14
Shelknam, SH4
Shenable, MQ10
Shensi, AF13
Shepherd Islands, OO9

SHERBRO, FC8
Shere, FI32
SHERENTE, SP20
Sheri, FJ20
SHETLANDS, EZ9
Shetland, South, SZ1
Shifr, FJ11
Shiho, MN4
Shikuya, FI33
Shila, FQ5
SHILLUK, FJ23
Shilluk-Luo, FJ14
Shilma, FJ11
Shilongol, AH6
Shimba, FX12
SHINASHA, MP21
Shindu, AR4
Shinje, FP10
Shinnecock, NM7
Shioko, FP4
Shipaulovi, NT9
Shipaya, SQ26
Shipibo, SE10
Shipinawa, SQ6
Shira, FI19
Shirawa, FF50
Shirazi, FM2
Shiriana, SQ18
Shivwits, NT16
SHLUH, MW11
Shoa Galla, MP25
Shoalwater Chinook, NR6
Shoalwater Salish, NR15
Shoccoree, NN13
Shoco, SO3
SHOGO, FI30
Shokleng, SM2
SHONA, FS5
Shongopovi, NT9
Shor, RS2
SHORTLANDS, ON14
Shoshoneans, Basin, NT6
Shoshone, Northern, NR14
Shoshone, Snake River, NR14
Shoshone, Western, NT22
Shoshone, Wind River, NQ19
Shucuru, SO3
Shuekh, MY4
SHUKRIA, MQ15
Shukuriye, MQ15
Shuli, FK4
SHURI, MP22
Shuswap, NE12
Shuwa, MS9
Shuwaywat, MQ10
Sia, FA15, NT12
Siam, AO1
Siamese, AO1
Siberi, SF9
SIBERIA, RR1
Siberia, Central, RT1
Siberia, Historical, RR2
Siberian Eskimo, RY5
Siberia, Northern, RU1
Siberia, Prehistoric, RR3
Siberia, Southeast, RX1
SIBIRIAK, RR4
Sibuguey, OA33
Sichomovi, NT9
SICILIANS, EI10
Sicily, EI1
SIDAMO, MP23

Siena, FA31
Sierra Leone, Colonial, FC2
Sierra Leone, Traditional, FC3
Sierra Madre, OA17
Sierra Pacaraima, SS5
Sifan, AE3
SIHANAKA, FY12
Sika, OF9
Sikang, AF16
SIKIANA, OT10
Sikisi, FL13
SIKKIM, AK3
Sikkimese, AK3
Sikon, FD7
Siksika, NF6
SILA, MQ16
Silanganen, OA37
Siletz, NR21
Silingol, AH6
Silipan, OA19
Sillok, FJ7
Simaa, FQ9
Simba, FI30
Simbiti, FL8
Simbo, ON10
Simirinch, SE18
Sinabo, SF19
Sinai Peninsula, MR11
Sindangan, OA33
SINDHI, AT5
SINGAPORE, AN9
Singapore, AN1
Singpho, AP6
SINKIANG, AI1
Sinkiang, Historical, AI2
Sinkiang, Prehistoric, AI3
Sinkiuse, NR19
Sinkquaiius, NR19
Sinkyone, NS23
SINO-TIBETAN BORDER, AE3
Siokon, OA33
Sioni, SE12
SIOUANS, NQ5
Siouans, Eastern, NN13
Sioux, NQ11
Sipo, SQ23
Sip Song Pannas, AE7
Sirifu, MS31
Sirineri, SE15
SIRIONO, SF21
Sirtica, MT4
Sisala, FE7
Siska, FR6
Sisseton, NQ11
Sissipahaw, NN13
Sisya, FR6
Siti, FE7
Situfa, SC6
Siusi, SQ27
Siuslaw, NR5
Sivokakmeit, NA13
SIWANS, MR14
Skagit, NR15
Skitswish, NR19
Slaiamun, NE13
SLAVE, ND14
SLAVIC PEOPLES, E16
Slavs, South, EF1
Slovakia, EB2
Slovaks, EB1
SLOVENES, EF7
Slovenia, EF7
Smith Sound Eskimo, NB5

Snake, NR14
Snake River Shoshone,
NR14
Snohomish, NR15
Snuqualmi, NR15
SO, AM37
Soai, AM7
Soba, FL8
Sobaipuri, NU29
Soboyo, SE6
Soce, FA27
SOCIETY ISLANDS, OX7
Socotra, MM3
Sofi, FJ18
Sofyan, MW9
Soga, FK7
Soghaua, MS5
Sokham, MW5
Sokile, FN17
Sokna, MT9
SOKO, FO44
SOKORO, FI31
Sokwia, FK13
Soliman, MS9, SQ25
SOLOMON ISLANDS, ON1
Solomons, Historical,
ON2
Solomons, Prehistoric,
ON3
Solon, RU5
Solongo, FO21
Solor, OF5
SOMALI, MO4
Somaliland, Historical,
MO2
Somaliland, Prehistoric,
MO3
SOMALI REPUBLIC, MO1
Somba, FA9
Sombrero, ST6
SOMRAI, FI32
Sonde, FO28
Songe, FO27
SONGHAI, MS20
Songhay Empire, FA2
Songish, NR15
Songo, FO30, FP6
SONGOLA, FO45
Songomeno, FO16
Sonhrai, MS20
SONINKE, MS21
Sonjo, FN25
Sonsorol, OR18
Sooke, NR15
Sop, AM29
Sorol, OR20
Sorotua, FP7
Soso, FA33
Sosse, FA27
Sossi, FF40
SOTHO, FW2
Sotho, Transvaal,
FX16
Soto, SS20
Soussou, FA33
SOUTH AFRICA, FX1
South Africa, Historical,
FX2
South Africa, Traditional,
FX3
SOUTH ALASKA ESKIMO,
NA10
SOUTH AMERICA, S1
South America, Historical,
S2
SOUTH AMERICAN INDIANS,
S3
SOUTH AMERICAN ISLANDS,
SZ1
SOUTH AMERICAN NEGROES,
S5
South America, Prehistoric,
S4
Southampton Island
Eskimo, ND5

South Arabia, ML2,
ML3
South Arabia, Historical,
ML2
South Arabia, Prehistoric,
ML3
SOUTH BRAZIL, SM1
South Carolina, NN1
SOUTH CENTRAL STATES,
NO1
South Central States,
Historical, NO2
South Central States,
Prehistoric, NO3
SOUTH CHINA, AF17
South Dakota, NQ1
SOUTHEAST ASIA, AL1
SOUTHEASTERN INDIANS,
NN3
SOUTHEASTERN STATES,
NN1
Southeastern Yavapai,
NT14
SOUTHEAST SALISH,
NR19
Southeast, Prehistoric,
NN4
SOUTHEAST SIBERIA,
RX1
Southern Africa, Prehistoric,
FX4
Southern Bushmen,
FX10
Southern Cayapo, SP11
Southern Dynasties,
AF6
SOUTHERN FILIPINOS,
OA32
Southern Lunda, FP14
SOUTHERN NEGROES,
NN6
SOUTHERN PAIUTE, NT16
Southern Rhodesia,
FS2
SOUTHERN THAI, AO8
SOUTHERN YEMEN, MM3
South Georgia, SZ1
South Kanara, AW18
SOUTH KOREA, AA6
SOUTH NGUNI, FX17
South Orkney, SZ1
South Ossetian Autonomous
Oblast, RH9
South Sandwich, SZ1
South Shetland, SZ1
South Slavs, EF1
SOUTH VIETNAM, AM13
South West Africa,
FX22
South West Africa,
Prehistoric, FX4
SOUTHWEST CHINA, AF16
SOUTHWESTERN INDIANS,
NT5
SOUTHWESTERN STATES,
NT1
Southwest, Historical,
NT2
SOUTHWEST ISLANDS,
OR18
Southwest, Prehistoric,
NT3
Soviet Central Asia,
RL1
SOVIET UNION, R1
Sowe, FN9
SOYOT, RS3
SPAIN, EX1
Spanish Morocco, MW1,
MX1
SPANISH REGIONAL CULTURES,
EX6
SPANISH SAHARA, MY1
Sparta, EH9

Spartans, Ancient,
EH9
Spiti, AJ4
SPITZBERGEN, EZ10
Spokan, NR19
Spreewald District,
EL12
Squamish, NE13
Squaxon, NR15
Sragna, MW10
Sre, AM27
Stalo, NE13
Starbuck Island, OV6
Stegaraki, NN13
Stewart Island, OZ5
Stewart Islands, OT10
STIENG, AM39
Stoney, NF4
Stono, NN12
Suba, FL8
Subano, OA33
SUBANUN, OA33
SUBIA, FQ11
Subiya, FQ11
SUB-TAINO, SX5
SUBTIABA, SA18
Subu, FH7
Subya, FQ11
SUCRE, SF22
SUDAN, MQ1
Sudan, FJ1, FJ3, FJ26,
MQ2, MQ3, MS1-MS3
SUDETEN GERMANS, EL9
Suerre, SA17
SUEZ CANAL, MR15
Suga, FH14
Sugaree, NN13
Sugbuhanon, OA14
Sui, AF5
Suichichi, SE14
SUI-SUNG, AF5
Suk, FL13
Suka, FL5
SUKU, FO46
Sukuma, FN18
Sukur, FF12
SULA, OH15
Sulawesi, OG1
Sulu, OA16
Sulu, Cagayan, OA16
Suma, NU20
SUMATRA, OD1
Sumatra, Historical,
OD2
Sumatra, Prehistoric,
OD3
SUMBA, OF17
SUMBAWA, OF18
Sumbawanese, OF18
Sumbe, FP6
Sumbwa, FN18
SUMERIANS, MH9
Sumo, SA15
SUNDANESE, OE7
Sundi, FO21
Sunesua, SS17
Sung, AF5
Sungor, MQ16
Sungu, FO47
Sura, FF6
Surara, SQ18
Suri, MP22
SURINAM, SR4
Surma, MP22
Suro, MP22
Surprise Valley Paiute,
NR13
Susquehannock, NM8
SUSU, FA33
Suvorov Island, OZ5
Suwanose, AB9
SUYA, SP21
Svan, RI12
SWAHILI, FM2

SWAN, RI12
Swanet, RI12
SWAZI, FU2
SWAZILAND, FU1
Swaziland, Historical,
FU3
Swaziland, Prehistoric,
FX4
SWEDEN, EN1
Sweden, Historical,
EN2
Sweden, Prehistoric,
EN3
Swedes, EN1
Sweta, FL8
SWITZERLAND, EJ1
Switzerland, Historical,
EJ2
Switzerland, Prehistoric,
EJ3
SURAI, MH12
Syeba, FH9
Synteng, AR7
SYRIA, MD1
Syria, Historical,
MD2
SYRIAN BEDOUIN, MD5
Syrian Christians,
AW11
Syrians, MD1
Syria, Prehistoric,
MD3
Szechwan, AF16

Taaisha, MQ5
Ta-ang, AP10
Tabak, FJ11
Tabalosa, SE14
Tabancal, SE17
TABAR, OM12
Tabasco, NV1
Tabassaran, RH8
Tabi, FJ13
Tabwa, FQ5
Tacame, NU12
TACANA, SF23
Tacarigua, SS8
Tachoni, FL4
Taclaudub, SQ18
Tacunyape, SQ26
Tadjik, RO2
Tadjoni, FL4
Tadla, MW10
Tadmekket, MS25
TADZHIK, RO2
Tadzhik S.S.R., RO1
TADZHIKSTAN, RO1
Taelba, MQ5
Taensa, NO8
TAGABILI, OA34
TAGAKAOLO, OA35
Tagalagad, OA10
Tagali, FJ21
TAGALOG, OA36
Tagaydan, OA15
TAGBANUA, OA37
Tagdapaya, OA7
Tagoy, FJ21
Tagu, MQ7
Tahami, SC9
TAHITI, OX8
Tahltan, ND12
Tahue, NU41
Taidnapam, NR18
Taifasy, FY16
Taimoro, FY7
Taimyr National Okrug,
RU1
TAINO, SV5
Taioba, SM4
Taipeshishi, SP10
Taira, SR12
Tairona, SC7
Taisaka, FY17

Taita, FL16
TAIWAN, AD6
Taiwan, AD1
TAIWAN HAKKA, AD7
TAIWAN HOKKIEN, AD5
Tajakant, MS29
TAKELMA, NR20
Takulli, NE7
Takwatip, SP10
Talaing, AP9
TALAMANCA, SA19
Talaud Islands, OG9
Talaur Islands, OG9
Tali, AE11, FH16
Talifugo-Ripang, OA5
Talish, RK4
TALLENSI, FE11
Talodi, FJ21
TALYSH, RK4
Tama, FK7, MQ16, SC11, SE12
Tamacoci, SF9
Tamalameque, SC9
Tamaroa, NP6
TAMAULIPEC, NU32
Tamba, FP6
Tambaro, MP15
Tamberma, FA9
Tambo, FN21
TAMIL, AW16
Taminawa, SQ6
Tamoyo, SO9
Tampolense, FE7
TANAINA, NA11
TANALA, FY8
Tanana, NA8
Tanay-Paete, OA36
Tandruy, FY13
Tane, FI28
Tanega, AB9
Tang, AF5, FF51
Tanga, FF41, FI26
TANGALE, FF54
Tanganyika, FN1, FN2
Tanganyika, Colonial, FN2
Tanganyika, Prehistoric, FN29
Tanganyika, Traditional, FN3
Tangdulanen, OA37
TANGIER, MX5
Tangier, MW1, MX1
Tangkhul, AR13
TANGUT, AJ5
TANIMBAR, OF19
Tankara, FY9
Tankarana, FY9
Tankay, FY19
TANNA, OO14
Tannekwe, FX10
Tannese, OO14
Tano, NT18
Tanosy, FY14
Tanusi, FY14
Tanygua, SM4
TANZANIA, FN30
Tao, SF9
TAOS, NT17
Tapacua, SP20
Tapacura, SP12
TAPAJO, SQ28
Tapanyuna, SP2
Taparita, SS11
Tape, SM4
TAPIETE, SK13
Tapii, SF18, SK13
TAPIRAPE, SP22
Tapiraua, SQ2
Taqagmiut, NI5
Tara, FA11
TARAHUMARA, NU33
TARAIRU, SO5
Tarama, AC6

TARASCO, NU34
Tareumiut, NA9
Tariana, SQ27
Tarma, SS8
Tarok, FF61
Taroma, AD14
Taruma, SM4, SR13
Tasman Islands, OT6
Tasmania, OI1
TASMANIANS, OI19
Tasoni, FL4
Tasuma, MS24
TAT, RK5
Tatars, RF5, RF6, RF8, RS2, RT2
Tatchila, SD7
Tatog, FN26
TATOGA, FN26
Tatsanottine, ND14
Tatungalung, OI16
Taturu, FN26
Tatuyo, SQ19
Taulipang, SS16
Tau-Oi, AM16
Taurawa, FF32
Tauu, OT4
Tauxitania, NN13
Taven, SM3
Taveta, FL16
Tavgi Samoyeds, RU4
Tawana, FV6
Tawara, FS5
Tawari, SQ7
Tawarik, MS25
Tawit, OA5
Taw Sug, OA16
Tayaba, OA36
Tayaga, SS11
Tayal, AD8
Tayan, OC8
Tazarawa, MS12
Tchiglit Eskimo, ND11
Tebu, MS22
Tecua, SC11
Tecual, NU15
TEDA, MS22
Tedshiwo, MP14
Teduray, OA39
Tefasi, FY16
Tegessie, FA26
Tegninateo, NN13
Tegwe, FI33
TEHUECO, NU35
TEHUELCHE, SH5
Tehuexe, NU9
Teis-um-Danab, FJ24
TEITA, FL16
Teja, NO5
Tekarir, MS27
TEKE, FI33
Tekena, MY6
Tekesta, NN7
Tekna, MY6
Tele, FI28
Teleut, RS2
TELUGU, AW17
TEM, FA34
Temba, FA34
Tembe, SO6
Tembu, FX17
Teme, FF48
TEMEIN, FJ24
Temiscaming, NH4
TEMNE, FC9
Temori, NU35
Temoro, FY7
Temuru, FY7
Tena, NA8
Tenankutchin, NA8
TENDA, FA36
Tenda Boeni, FA36
Tenda-Dounka, FA36
Tenda Mayo, FA36
Tendanke, FA36

Tenda-Niokolo, FA36
Tende, FL8
TENETEHARA, SO6
Tengeredief, MS25
TENGGERESE, OE8
Tenino, NR18
Tennessee, NN1
Tenochca, NU7
Tepahue, NU8
Tepecano, NU36
TEPEHUAN, NU36
Tepes, FJ25
Tepeth, FJ25
TEPOZTLAN, NU37
TEPQUI, SE19
Teque, SS8
Tequia, SS17
TEQUISTLATEC, NU38
TERA, FF55
Terawia, MS5
Terayfia, MQ10
Terema, MP22
TEREMEMBE, SO7
Terena, SK7
Terik, FL13
Termigoy, RH5
Terna, FJ10, MP22
Ternata, MW6
TERNATE, OH16
Terraba, SA19
Tesaka, FY17
TESO, FK12
Tesuque, NT18
Tete, FO43
Tete-de-Boule, NG4
TETELA, FO47
Tetipari, ON10
Teton, NQ11
Teun, OF13
Teuso, FJ25
Teuth, FJ25
Teve, FS5
TEWA, NT18
Teweya, SS16
Texas, NO1
Thabina, FX14
Thado, AR8
Thai, AO1
Thai, Black, AL3
Thai, Central, AO7
Thai, Chinese, AE7
Thai Isan, AO6
Thai Islam, AO8
Thailand, AO1
Thailand, Historical, AO2
Thailand, Prehistoric, AO3
Thai, Laotian, AM8
Thai Malay, AO8
Thai, Red, AL3
Thai, Southern, AO8
Thai, White, AL3
Thakur, AW47
Thang, FJ12
Thanta Pulayan, AW64
THAO, AD12
Tharaka, FL5
Tharu, AW45
The Gambia, FC11
Thembu, FX17
Thin, AM38
Thlingchadine, ND14
Tho, AL3
Thompson, NE12
THONGA, FT6
Three Kingdoms, AF6
Thuak, MP22
Thuri, FJ14, MP22
Tian, FA11
Tiapi, FB5
Tiatinagua, SF23
Tibbu, MS22
Tibesti, MS22

TIBET, AJ1
Tibetans, West, AJ4
Tibet, Historical, AJ2
Tibet, Prehistoric, AJ3
Tichit, MS31
Ticuna, SQ20
Tid, MP22
Tidore, OH16
Tie, FI28
Tienga, FF13
Tierra del Fuego, SH1
Tigon, FF56
TIGONG, FF56
TIGRE, MN9
TIGRINYA, MP24
Tigritian, MN9
TIKAR, FH22
TIKOPIA, OT11
Tilijayo, NU12
TILLAMOOK, NR21
Tilma, MP22
Tima, FJ21
Timana, SC15
TIMBIRA, SO8
Timbira, Eastern, SO8
Timbira, Western, SP3
TIMBU, SI11
TIMBUCTOO, MS23
Timimino, SO9
TIMOR, OF20
Timorlaut, OF19
Timor, Portuguese, OF4
TIMOTE, SS17
TIMUCUA, NN18
Tin, AM38
Tindiga, FN11
Tingan, SE19
TINGGIAN, OA38
Tinguelin, FH8
Tinguian, OA38
Tinitian, OA9
Tinzulin, MW6
Tionontati, NG5
Tippera, AR4
Tira, FJ21
Tiramandi, FJ21
Tiriki, FL4
Tirma, MP22
Tirmaga, MP22
Tirub, SA19
TIRURAY, OA39
TIV, FF57
Tiwa, NT10, NT17
TIWI, OI20
TLAPANEC, NU39
Tlatskanai, NR11
Tlelding, NS11
Tlhaping, FV6
Tlharu, FV6
TLINGIT, NA12
Tliq, MW9
Tlokwa, FV6
TOALA, OG10
Toaripi, OJ19
TOBA, SI12
Tobacco, NG5
Tobajara, SN7
Tobatin, MN4
Tobelorese, OH12
Tobi, OR18
Tocoyen, SR12
Tod, MP22
TODA, AW60
TODGA, MW12
Tofoke, FO44
TOGO, FA50
Togo, Colonial, FA51
Togoland, British, FE1

Togo, Prehistoric, FA53
Togo, Traditional, FA52
Toi, FJ10
Toka, FQ12
Tokara, AB9
Tokara Islands, AB9
TOKELAU, OZ12
Tokukan-Asin, OA19
Tokuno, AC4
Tokwa, FV6
Tolakka, FI18
Tolkepaya, NT14
Tollo, FO43
Tolo, AM15
TOLOWA, NR22
Tolu, SC9
TOMA, FD8
Tomam, MQ10
Tombo, FA16
Tomboji, FS5
Tombouctou, MS23
Tomome, NN14
Tomoporo, SS13
Tonayena, SR12
TONGA, FQ12
TONGA, OU9
Tonga, FR6, FS5, FT4
Tonga, Gwembe, FQ12
Tonga, Lakeside, FR7
Tonga, Plateau, FQ12
TONGAREVA, OZ13
Tongwe, FN18
Toni, FH9
Tonkawa, NO7
Tonkin, AM11
TONOCOTE, SI13
Tonto, NT21
Topoke, FO44
TOPOTHA, FJ25
Tora, SP12
TORADJA, OG11
Torado, MS27
Toramaina, SS8
Torgut, AH5
Tornasi, FJ7
Toro, FK11, FN19, SC12
Toromona, SF23
TORRES ISLANDS, OO15
TORRES STRAITS ISLANDS, OJ24
Tortola, ST3
Tortuga, SZ5
Tosc, EG1
To Sung, AM15
Totela, FQ12
TOTONAC, NU40
TOTORAME, NU41
Tou, AM29
Toucouleur, MS27
Touggourt, MV9
Towa, NT11
TRAD. ANGOLA, FP3
TRAD. CAMEROON, FH3
TRAD. CENTRAL AFRICAN REPUBLIC, FI37
TRAD. CONGO-BRAZZAVILLE, FI41
TRAD. DAHOMEY, FA40
TRAD. EQUATORIAL GUINEA, FG4
TRAD. GABON, FI45
TRAD. GAMBIA, FC13
TRAD. GHANA, FE3
TRAD. GUINEA, FA44
TRAD. IVORY COAST, FA48
TRAD. KENYA, FL3
TRAD. LIBERIA, FD3
TRAD. MADAGASCAR, FY3

TRAD. MOZAMBIQUE, FT3
TRAD. NAMIBIA, FX23
TRAD. NIGERIA, FF3
TRAD. PORTUGUESE GUINEA FB3
TRAD. RHODESIA, FS3
TRAD. RUANDA-URUNDI, FO54
TRAD. SIERRA LEONE, FC3
TRAD. SOUTH AFRICA, FX3
TRAD. TANGANYIKA, FN3
TRAD. TOGO, FA52
TRAD. UGANDA, FK3
TRAD. UPPER VOLTA, FA56
TRAD. ZAIRE, FO3
TRAD. ZAMBIA, FQ3
Transcaucasia, RH1
TRANSVAAL NDEBELE, FX18
Transvaal Sotho, FX16
TRARZA, MS24
Travancore-Cochin, AW11
TRAVANCORE TRIBES, AW64
TRIBAL INDIA, AW22
Tring, AM27
Trinidad, ST9
TRINIDAD AND TOBAGO, ST9
Trinidad [Brazilian], SZ1
Trio, SR12
TRIPOLITANIANS, MT11
Trique, NU11
TRISTAN DA CUNHA, FZ9
TROBRIANDS, OL6
TRUCIAL OMAN, MK4
TRUK, OR19
TRUMAI, SP23
Tsaidam, AH5
Tsalisen, AD14
TSARIST RUSSIA, R2
Tsattine, NF5
Tsaya, FI33
Tserekwe, FX10
Tsetsaut, ND12
Tsha, FA6
Tshopi, FT4
Tshwosh, OJ30
TSIMIHETY, FY10
TSIMSHIAN, NE15
Tsin, AF6
Tsirakua, SK14
Tsivokwe, FP4
Tsokwe, FP4
Tsono, AD11
Tsoo, AD11
Tsosh, OJ30
Tsotso, FL4
TSOU, AD11
Tsowu, AD11
TSUSHIMA, AB10
Tsuva, SP25
TSWANA, FV6
TUAMOTU, OX9
TUAREG, MS25
Tuareg, Inajenen, MT7
TUAT, MS26
Tubar, NU35
TUBATULABAL, NS22
Tubindi, FO20
Tubishe, FO23
Tubu, MS22
Tubuai Islands, OX4
TUBURI, FH23
TUCANO, SQ19
TUCUNA, SQ20

Tucun-Dyapa, SQ7
Tugauanum, OA6
Tugen, FL13
Tugeri, OJ17
TUGGURT, MV9
Tujen, AE9
Tuken, FL13
Tukete, FO20
Tukubba, FO23
TUKULOR, MS27
Tukum, FF56
Tula, FF54
Tulagi Island, ON8
TULAMA, MP25
Tulishi, FJ21
Tullishi, FJ21
TULU, AW18
Tulumayo, SE19
Tulwena, FP14
Tumak, FI32
Tumanao, OA10
Tumba, FO32
Tumbab, MQ10
Tumbez, SD10
TUMBUKA, FR6
Tumbwe, FO18
Tumeli, FJ21
Tumet, AH6
Tuminungu, FP4
Tumtum, FJ21
Tumuk, FJ21
Tumuza, SS9
Tundjer, MS28
Tunebo, SC11
Tung, AL3
Tungu, OH5
TUNGUR, MS28
TUNGUS, RU5
Tunia, FI10
Tunica, NO4
TUNISIA, MU1
Tunisia, Historical, MU2
TUNISIANS, MU5
Tunni Torre, MO5
Tupari, SP24
Tupende, FO39
TUPI, SN7
Tupi-Cawahib, SP10
TUPI-GUARANI, SL6
Tupina, SN7
TUPINAMBA, SO9
Tupinambarana, SQ12
Tupinikin, SO9
Tur, FF12, FJ12
Tura, FA29
Turbaco, SC9
TURCOMAN, RM2
Turi, AW46
Turiwara, SQ2
TURKANA, FL17
TURKESTAN, RL1
Turkestan, Chinese, AI1
Turkestan, Historical, RL2
Turkestan, Prehistoric, RL3
TURKEY, MB1
Turkey, Prehistoric, MB3
TURKIC PEOPLES, RL4
Turkic Proto-Bulgars, EE2
TURKISH EGYPT, MR2
TURKISH GREECE, EH2
TURKISH IRAQ, MH2
Turkmen, RM2
TURKMENISTAN, RM1
Turkmen S.S.R., RM1
Turks, MB1, SW1
Turks, Ottoman, M2
Turks, Seljuk, M3
Turon, FJ11

Turruba, FO27
Turu, FN19
Turuaco, SC9
Turuka, FA31
Turumba, FO44
TUSCARORA, NN19
Tuscarora, NM9
Tush, RI6
Tusha, SO3
Tushinawa, SQ6
Tutchone, ND10
Tutchonekutchin, ND10
Tutelo, NN13
Tutsi, FO42
Tututni, NR22
Tuva, RS1, RS3
Tuyuca, SQ19
Tuyuneri, SE15
Twa, FO42, FQ4
Twana, NR15
TWI, FE12
Two Kettle, NQ11
Tyikuyu, FP18
Tyrolese, EK4
TZELTAL, NV9
TZOTZIL, NV11
Tzutuhil, NW10

Uaimare, SP19
Uaina, SQ19
Uaintacu, SP17
Uainuma, SQ11
UALARAI, OI21
Uanana, SQ19
Uara-Guacu, SQ8
Uasona, SQ19
Ubangi-Shari, FI35
Ucayali, SE11
Uchi, NN20
Udalan, MS25
Ude, RX3
Udekhe, RX3
Uden, RH8
Udio, FI28
Udmurt, RG7
Udmurt A.S.S.R., RG7
Udok, FJ15
Uga, OJ20
Uganda, Colonial, FK2
Uganda, Prehistoric, FK15
Uganda, Traditional, FK5
Uge, FF17
Uggi, FJ19
UIGUR, AI4
Uitoto, SC19
Ujang, MP20
Uji Island, AB8
Ukara, FN10
Ukelle, FF17
UKRAINE, RD1
UKRAINIANS, RD4
Ukrainian S.S.R., RD1
Ukualuthi, FX8
Ukuambi, FX8
Ulad Nail, MV4
Ulanjab, AH6
ULAWA, ON15
Ulcha, RX3
Ulga, OJ20
ULITHI, OR20
Ullatan, AW64
Ulva, SA15
Ulu, FJ9
Umatilla, NR18
Umaua, SC8, SQ15
Umbete, FI12
UMBOI, OM13
Um Durrag, MQ4
Umiro, FK9
Umotina, SP8

Umpqua, NR22
Umpqua, Lower, NR5
Umuampa, SI14
Unga, FQ5
Ungu, FN21
Unia, MS5
Unianga, MT9
Union Islands, OZ12
UNION OF BURMA, AP14
Union of South Africa, FX1
Union of Soviet Socialist Republics, R1
UNITED NATIONS, W7
United Provinces, AW19
UNITED STATES, NK1
United States, Colonial, NK3
United States, Historical, NK2
Uollaroi, OI21
Uotsuri, AC8
Upper Chinook, NR23
UPPER VOLTA, FA54
Upper Volta, Colonial, FA55
Upper Volta, Prehistoric, FA57
Upper Volta, Traditional, FA56
Upurui, SR12
Urabuna, OI7
Urala, AW64
Urali, AW64
Urarina, SE5
Urdus, AH6
Ure, NU29
Urezo, SC9
Urfalla, MT9
Urfilla, MT9
Urhobo, FF21
Uriankhai, AH5, RS3
Urku, FF59
URU, SF24
Uru, FF36
Uruba, SC9
Urubu, SO6
URUGUAY, SJ1
Uruguay, Historical, SJ2
Uruguay, Prehistoric, SJ3
Urunamacan, SP12
Urundi, FO52
Urupa, SP12
Ushi, FQ5
Ushpee, NN13
Ust-Orda Buryat Mongol National Okrug, RW1
Ust-Ordynskiy Buryat Mongol National Okrug, RW1
Utah, NT1
UTE, NT19
UTO-AZTEKANS, NU5
UTTAR PRADESH, AW19
UVEA, OU10
Uyanga, FF17
Uzbeg, RN5
UZBEK, RN5
UZBEKISTAN, RN1
Uzbek S.S.R., RN1
Uzpantec, NW10

Vabembe, FO41
Vacaa, SI14
Vachioko, FP4
Vachopi, FT4
Vaduma, FS5
Vagala, FE7
VAI, FD9
Vakaranga, FS5

Vakuanano, FP13
Vakuanyama, FX8
Vakuise, FP7
Valega, FO41
Valenge, FT4
Valley Tonga, FQ12
Valuchazi, FP8
Valuheke, FP7
Valuimbe, FP9
Valunda, FO27
Valwena, FP14
Vamuila, FP18
Vancouver Island, NE1
Vandals, EL4
Vandau, FS5
Vangangela, FP16
Vankumbe, FP17
VANUA LEVU, OQ8
Vanyaneka, FP18
Vanyuma, NS20
Vao, OO12
Varama, FI19
Varli, AW44
Varohio, NU35
Vasawa, AW47
Vasorontu, FP7
VATICAN CITY, EI11
Vatoka, FT4
Vatonga, FT4
Vatyipungu, FP17
Vazezuru, FS5
VAZIMBA, FY21
VEDDA, AX5
Velao, FT7
Vella Lavella, ON10
Venado, NU12
VENDA, FX19
Vende, FN18
VENEZUELA, SS1
Venezuela, Historical, SS2
VENEZUELAN INDIANS, SS4
Venezuela, Prehistoric, SS3
Vepses, RG4
Vere, FF48
Vermont, NL1
Vezo, FY6
Viaksi, SC10
Vicol, OA32
Victoria Island, ND8
Vieques, SU1
VIETNAM, AM11
Vietnam, Democratic Republic of, AM12
Vietnam, North, AM12
Vietnam, Republic of, AM13
Vietnam, South, AM13
VIKINGS, EP5
VILELA, SI14
VILI, FI34
Vindhya Pradesh, AW4
Vinza, FO42
Virgin Gorda, ST3
Virginia, NN1
VIRGIN ISLANDS, ST10
Virgin Islands, American, ST10
Virgin Islands, British, ST3
Visayan, OA14, OA30
VITI-I-LOMA, OQ9
VITI LEVU, OQ10
VITU, OM14
Viye, FP13
VLACHS, EH15
VOGUL, RU6
Volcano Islands, AZ3
Vonum, AD10
Vostok Island, OV6
Votes, RG4

Voto, SA17
VOTYAK, RG7
Vuahuha, FO18
Vugusu, FL4
Vungo, FI19
Vungu, FN21
Vyetre, FA5

WA, AP12
Wabali, FO9
Wabargwe, FS5
Wabembe, FO41
Wabena, FN9
Wabende, FN18
Wabondei, FN28
Wa Boni, MO5
Wabuddu, FO14
Wabuyu, FO15
Wabwari, FO41
Waccamaw, NN13
Wachanzi, FO17
Waco, NO10
Wadai, MS15
Wadalen, MS25
Wadia, FO43
Wadigo, FL14
Wadoe, FN27
Wadschagga, FN4
Waduma, FS5
Waduruma, FL14
Waenya, FO45
Wafipa, FN6
Wafulero, FO10
Wafungwe, FR6
Wagadugu, FA28
Waganda, FK7
Wageia, FL11
Wagenia, FO45
Wagiliama, FL14
Wagogo, FN7
Wagoma, FO15
Wa Gosha, MO5
Waguha, FO18
Waha, FO42
Wahaiao, FT7
Wahaya, FN8
Wahehe, FN9
Wahenga, FR6
Wahera, FS5
Wahkiakum, NR6
Wahorohoro, FO18
Wahpekute, NQ11
Wahpeton, NQ11
Waica, SQ18, SR9
WAICURI, NU42
Waiilatpuan, NR18
WAILAKI, NS23
Waimiry, SQ22
WAIRACU, SQ21
Waitabwa, FQ5
Waitaca, SN3
WAIWAI, SQ22
Waiyao, FT7
Waja, FF54
Wajita, FN25
Wajote, FL7
Waka, FF48
Wakaguru, FN22
Wakalanga, FS5
Wakamanga, FR6
Wakamba, FL9
Wakami, FN27
Wakarra, FN10
Wake Island, OV1
Wakerewe, FN10
Wakikuyu, FL10
Wakondjo, FO22
Wakua, FT5
Wakumu, FO11
Wakusu, FO47
Wakutu, FN27
Wakwere, FN27

Wala, FE13
Walaitza, MP26
Walako, FL4, FL13
Walamba, FQ8
WALAMO, MP26
Walapai, NT14
Walega, MP18
Walendu, FO25
Walengola, FO11
Walese, FO31
Wali, FJ11
Walia, FH23
Walika, FO9
Walimi, FN19
Wallawalla, NR18
Wallis Island, OU10
WALLOONS, EV3
Walo, FF59
Walomwe, FT5
Walpi, NT9
Waluba, FO27
Waluguru, FN27
Walumbi, FO29
Walungu, FQ5
Wamakonde, FN13
Wamakua, FT5
Wamatumbi, FN20
Wamba, FN21
Wambanga, FO29
Wambu, FP13
Wambudjga, FS5
Wambugu, FN15
Wambugwe, FN16
Wambulu, FN5
Wambunga, FN20
Wamfumu, FI33
Wamia, FK12
Wampanoag, NL5
WAMOLE, FE13
Wamuera, FN13
Wana, OG5
Wanande, FO22
Wana Wana, ON10
Wandaka, FO9
Wandala, FF47, MS22
Wandamba, FN20
Wanderobo, FJ25
Wandonde, FN13
Wandorobbo, FL6
Wandya, FN21
Wanga, FL4
Wangala, FO12
Wangandi, FO36
Wanganga, FR4
Wangarabuna, OI7
Wangata, FO32
Wangindo, FN13
Wangomwia, FN5
Wangonde, FN17
Wangoni, FR5
Wangoroine, FN25
Wanguru, FN28
Waniaturu, FN19
Waninga, FO32
Wanji, FN12
Wanjika, FN21
Wanyabungu, FO10
Wanyamwezi, FN18
Wanyanga, FO22
Wanyanja, FR4
Wanyassa, FR4
Wanyika, FL14, FS5
Wapare, FN4
WAPISHANA, SR13
Wapodzo, FT5
Wapogoro, FN20
Wapokomo, FL15
Wapoo, NN12
Waporoporo, FK11
Wappinger, NM10
WAPPO, NS24
War, FF51
Wara, FA31

WARAIN, MW13
Warambia, FN21
Warangi, FN16
WARAO, SS18
Waray-Waray, OA14
Wardai, FL7
Wardandi, OI26
Warega, FO41
WARGLA, MV10
Wa Ribi, MO5
Warizwi, FS5
Warjawa, FF46
WARLI, AW44
Warmsprings Sahaptin,
  NR18
WAROPEN, OJ26
Warrau, SS18
Warrennuncock, NN13
Warumbi, FO29
Warundi, FO42
Warungu, FQ5
Waruri, FN25
Waruwa, FO15
Waruwadu, SS23
Wasa, FE12, SQ16
Wasagara, FN22
Wasama, SC10
Wasaramo, FN27
Wasco, NR23
Wasegua, FN28
Wasena, FR4
Washambala, FN24
Washangwe, FS5
Washashi, FN25
Washensi, FN28
Washington, NR1
Washington Island,
  OV6
WASHO, NT20
Washungwe, FS5
Wasi, FN5
Wasimba, FO41, FO45,
  FR4
Wasira, FQ5
Wasonga, FO27
Wasove, FN9
Wassafwa, FN21
Wassandaui, FN23
Wassania, FL7
Wassiba, FN8
Wassindja, FN8
Wassukuma, FN18
Wataita, FL16
Wataveta, FL16
Watawara, FS5
Watchongoa, FO45
Wateree, NN13
Watindega, FN11
Watling, SW1
Watombwa, FO18
Watonga, FS5
Watshokwe, FP4
WATUBELA, OH17
Watumbuka, FR6
Watutu, FN14
Watyi, FA18
Waunga, FQ5
WAURA, SP18
Waushi, FQ5
Wauyukma, NR18
Wavinza, FO8
Wawa, FH14
Wawamba, FO6
Wawanga, FL4
Wawemba, FQ5
Wawenok, NL4
Wawira, FO11
Wawire, FQ5
Wawiwa, FN21
Waxhaw, NN13
Wayao, FT7
Wayapi, SQ8
Wayoro, SP16
Wayumara, SQ22

Wazezuru, FS5
We, FQ12
Wea, NP9
Webi Shebelle, MO5
WELSH, ES11
Wenachishinga, FQ5
Wenangumbu, FQ5
Wenatchi, NR19
Wends, EL12
Wengana, FO17
Wenrohonron, NG5
Wenya, FO45, FR6
Werni, FJ21
West Africa, French-Speaking,
  FA1
WEST AFRICAN PEOPLES,
  FA2
West Africa, Portuguese,
  FP2
West Africa, Prehistoric,
  FA3
WEST ALASKA ESKIMO,
  NA13
WEST BENGAL, AW20
WEST CENTRAL STATES,
  NQ1
West Central States,
  Historical, NQ2
West Central States,
  Prehistoric, NQ3
WESTERN APACHE, NT21
Western Dakota, NQ11
WESTERN LAO, AO6
WESTERN MONO, NS25
Western New Guinea,
  OJ3
WESTERN POLYNESIA,
  OU1
Western Polynesia,
  Historical, OU2
Western Polynesia,
  Prehistoric, OU3
WESTERN SAMOA, OU11
Western Samoa, OU8
WESTERN SHOSHONE,
  NT22
Western Timbira, SP3
Western Yavapai, NT14
West Fayu, OR21
WEST GERMANY, EL10
WEST GREENLAND ESKIMO,
  NB6
WEST INDIES, S7
WEST IRIAN, OJ3
West Nakanai, OM16
Westo, NN20
West Pakistan, AT1,
  AT3
WEST PANJABI, AT3
WEST SAHARAN ARABS,
  MS29
WEST SIBERIAN TATAR,
  RT2
WEST TIBETANS, AJ4
West Virginia, NM1
WETAR, OF21
Wheelman, OI26
Whilkut, NS11
White Bobo, FA11
White Mountain, NT21
White Russia, RC1
White Thai, AL3
Whonkenti, NN13
Whydah, FA18
WICHITA, NO10
WIDEKUM, FF58
Wiilmen, OI26
WIKMUNKAN, OI22
Wimbee, NN12
Winamwanga, FN21
WIND RIVER, NQ19
WINDWARD ISLANDS,
  ST11
Winikina, SS18

WINNEBAGO, NP12
Wintu, NS26
WINTUN, NS26
Winyaw, NN13
Wira, FJ18
Wisa, FQ5
Wisconsin, NP1
Wishram, NR23
WITOTO, SC19
Wiya, FF51
WIYOT, NS27
Wobe, FA29
Woccon, NN13
Wociare, SS22
Woga, FF12
Wogait, OI23
WOGEO, OJ27
Woko, FH18
Wolamo, MP26
WOLEAI, OR21
WOLLO, MN10
WOLOF, MS30
Wom, FF15
Wongo, FO24
Wonyadiji, FA36
Woolwa, SA15
WORIMI, OI24
WORLD, W1
WORLD HISTORY, W2
Woro, FJ16
Woshijpore, SC10
Wrangel Island, RZ1
Wuba, FF12
Wukchumni, NS29
Wulamba, OI17
Wum, FF39
Wumbu, FI33
Wungu, FN21
Wuri, FH7
WURKUM, FF59
Wu-tai, AF5
WUTE, FH24
WUVULU, OM15
Wyandot, NG5
Wyoming, NQ1

Xagua, SS12
Xam, FX10
Xaraye, SF9
Xayo, FL4
Xevero, SE8
Xhosa, FX17
Xibito, SE14
Xicaque, SA13
Xiriguana, SC10
Xixime, NU6
Xosa, FX17

YABARANA, SS22
YABIM, OJ28
YABUTI, SP24
Yache, FF17
Yachumi, AR13
Yaernungo, OI17
YAEYAMA, AC9
Yafelman, MW5
Yagba, FF62
Yagga, FO49
YAGUA, SE20
Yagui, SS11
YAHGAN, SH6
Yahi, NS28
Yahuna, SQ19
YAKA, FO49
Yaka, FI19
Yakan, OA16
Yakima, NR18
Yakinga, FI22
YAKO, FF60
Yakoma, FI8
Yakori, FF17
Yaku, AB9
YAKUT, RV2

WINNEBAGO, NP12
Yakut A.S.S.R., RV1
YAKUTIA, RV1
Yalcon, SC15
Yale, FF17
Yalna, FI31
Yalonke, FA33
Yalunka, FA33
Yamaci, SC9
Yamalo-Nenets National
  Okrug, RU1
YAMAMADI, SQ33
Yamana, SH6
Yamasee, NN11
Yambassa, FH10
Yambo, FJ4
Yameo, SE20
YAMI, AD17
Yamiaca, SE7
Yamkar, OJ20
Yamna, MP27
YANA, NS28
Yanadi, AW61
Yanaon, AY2
Yandjinung, OI17
YANGARO, MP27
Yangela, FO50
Yangeli, FI6
Yangere, FI6
Yankton, NQ11
Yanktonnai, NQ11
YANOAMA, SQ18
Yanzi, FO17
YAO, AE6
YAO, FT7
Yao, SR12
YAP, OR22
Yapacoye, SR12
Yapel, SC9
Yapua, SQ19
Yaqui, NU8
Yaquina, NR5
Yariqui, SC10
Yaro, SJ5
Yarse, FA15
YARUMA, SP25
YARURO, SS19
YASAWA, OQ11
Yasayama, FO35
Yassing, FI24
Yatenga, FA28
Yauaperi, SQ22
Yauavo, SQ6
Yaulapiti, SP18
Yaunde, FH9
Yavapai, NT14
Yawyin, AE10
YAZIDIS, MH10
Yecoanita, SI14
Yecora, NU29
Yecuana, SS20
Yedina, MS7
Yei, FJ19
Yeke, FO27
Yeke Ju, AH6
Yellowknife, ND14
YEMEN, ML1
Yemeni, ML1, MM3
YEMENITE JEWS, ML4
Yemen, Southern, MM3
Yemma, MP27
YENADI, AW61
Yendang, FF48
Yenesei Samoyeds,
  RU4
Yenisei Ostyak, RU2
Yeniseians, RU2
YERAVA, AW62
YERGUM, FF61
Yeruva, AW62
Yeskwa, FF34
Yeye, FV5
Yezidi, MH10
Yi, AE4
YIRYORONT, OI25